The Faces of Contemporary Russian Nationalism

By John B. Dunlop

Princeton University Press, Princeton, N.J.

Copyright © 1983 by Princeton University Press
Published by Princeton University Press, 41 William Street
Princeton, New Jersey 08540
In the United Kingdom: Princeton University Press,
Guildford, Surrey

Publication of this book has been aided by a grant from the
Henry A. Laughlin Fund of Princeton University Press

This book has been composed in Linotron Caledonia

Clothbound editions of Princeton University Press books
are printed on acid-free paper, and binding materials are
chosen for strength and durability. Paperbacks, although
satisfactory for personal collections, are not usually
suitable for library rebinding.

Printed in the United States of America by
Princeton University Press, Princeton, New Jersey

*The Hoover Institution on War, Revolution and Peace,
founded at Stanford University in 1919 by the
late President Herbert Hoover, is an interdisciplinary
research center for advanced study on domestic and
international affairs in the twentieth century.
The views expressed in its publications are entirely
those of the authors and do not necessarily reflect
the views of the staff, officers, or
Board of Overseers of the Hoover Institution.*

To Maria, John, Olga, *and* Catherine

Contents

Preface

This book was written to acquaint readers with a current of thought and sentiment that has increasingly made its presence felt in the USSR since the mid-sixties and that, in one form or another, could become the ruling ideology of state once the various stages of the Brezhnev succession have come to an end. Despite the critical significance of this phenomenon, Russian nationalism of the post-Stalin period has been little studied and even less understood in the contemporary West. With a few exceptions, American academics began to focus on Russian nationalism only in the mid-seventies, and, at the time of writing, only two books—*Ethnic Russia in the USSR*, a collection of conference papers edited by Edward Allworth, and *The Russian New Right*, a slender study by recent émigré Aleksandr Ianov—had appeared on the subject.

In this book, I have pursued the following aims: to communicate to a Western readership the thought and core feelings of contemporary Russian nationalists; to convey a sense of the range of present-day Russian nationalist positions; to determine, at least roughly, the appeal of Russian nationalists to various elite and mass constituencies in the Soviet Union; and to make some tentative suggestions concerning the direction that Western, and particularly American, policy should take vis-à-vis the nationalists.

The first two chapters provide the historical background to the development of Russian nationalism in the Soviet period. Chapters Three through Eight examine those issues that loom largest in the eyes of contemporary nationalist spokesmen: the preservation of historical monuments and of the environment; demographic and social developments that are seen as harmful to the well-being of the Russian people; cultural expression; the relationship between ethnic Russians and the minority nationalities; the role that should be played by the Russian Orthodox Church; and the significance of nationalist tribunes of the past, such as the early Slavophiles and Dostoevskii. In treating these issues, I attempt to determine why they, in particular, should have attracted the attention of present-day nationalists.

Chapter Nine concentrates on three sharp disputes that broke out between the nationalists and their opponents, both within the regime and in dissident circles, in the late sixties and the seventies; these disputes give some notion of the strengths and vulnerabilities of both "official" and dissenting Russian nationalists. On the basis of the preceding sections of the book, the final two chapters delineate the spectrum of nationalist positions as they exist today and suggest theories about the kind or kinds of nationalism they encompass. Chapter Eleven concludes with some modest policy recommendations.

In seeking to uncover the mind of the contemporary Russian nationalist, I have used the following sources: materials appearing in the Soviet press, particularly in publications of an overtly nationalist orientation; *samizdat* writings circulated by Russian nationalist spokesmen; nationalist writings appearing in the émigré press; interviews with and letters received from recent émigrés, many of them Russian nationalists; and discussions with Western visitors to the USSR. Antinationalist polemics published in the Soviet Union and the antinationalist writings of various representatives of the so-called "third emigration" have also been consulted. As anyone who has attempted to research a controversial movement or phenomenon in the contemporary Soviet Union will attest, it is not possible, due to Soviet censorship restrictions and security concerns, to collect exhaustive data on such a topic. Nevertheless, despite unavoidable problems connected with the collection of information, I believe that a reasonably accurate picture has been given of the strength and political viability of contemporary Russian nationalism.

To conclude, this study represents a necessarily difficult and cross-disciplinary synthesis of a large and disparate body of material. It is my hope that other scholars will correct any faulty analyses or misplaced emphases that they find in the book, and that they will fill in the gaps that must inevitably appear in a project of this scope.

In transliterating, I have consistently followed a variant of the Library of Congress system.

I WOULD like to thank The Hoover Institution for appointing me a National Fellow for the 1978-1979 academic year, thereby affording me an opportunity to write the greater part of this book in the congenial setting of the Stanford University campus. Special thanks are due to Dennis L. Bark, Acting Director of the National Fellows Program, and his able assistant, Janet Dutra, for helping to make my stay at Hoover a productive one. I should also like to convey my gratitude to the National Endowment for the Humanities, which funded my project through a grant to The Hoover Institution.

Warm thanks are due to Constantin Galskoy of Hoover, who read through the entire manuscript and made a number of useful suggestions, and to Hilja Kukk of The Hoover Institution Library, who helped me in ways too numerous to elaborate.

Oberlin College assisted my research by granting me a leave of absence and by awarding me, through the college Research and Development Committee, several modest grants-in-aid to facilitate the collection of materials relevant to my project.

The following specialists generously supplied me, either at my request or at their own initiative, with documents germane to my topic: the late Andrei Amal'rik, Mikhail Agurskii, Frederick C. Barghoorn, Peter Christoff, Stephen F. Cohen, Martin Dewhirst, Milorad Drachkovitch, Bishop Gregory Grabbe, Alexis Klimoff, Serge Kryzytski, Arcadi Nebolsine, Michael Nicholson, Dimitry Pospielovsky, Fr. Victor Potapov, Tatiana Rannit, and Peter Reddaway. My thanks to all of them.

Gail Filion of Princeton University Press and George Marotta of The Hoover Institution Press were most helpful in arranging for the publication of this study; the manuscript was typed in unusually efficient fashion by Pauline B. Tooker.

Finally, it would be churlish not to acknowledge the strong

and unwavering support that this project has enjoyed over the course of many years from my wife, Olga, who prepared excellent draft translations of the materials contained in the appendix, and from my children, to whom this book is dedicated.

The Faces of Contemporary Russian Nationalism

1

The Historical Background (I)
1917-1953

Die Arbeiter haben kein Vaterland.
                    Das kommunistische Manifest[1]

. . . the Revolution means the people's final break with the
Asiatic, with the seventeenth century, with Holy Russia,
with ikons and with roaches.

                                        Lev Trotskii[2]

. . . via Bolshevism, Djugashvili joined the Russian nation.
                                        Robert C. Tucker[3]

When the Bolshevik party seized power in 1917, it appeared
that the days of Russia as a separate cultural and political
entity might be numbered. In the words of historian E. H.
Carr, "Never had the heritage of the past been more sharply,
more sweepingly or more provocatively rejected; never had
the claim to universality been more uncompromisingly asserted; never in any previous revolution had the break in
continuity seemed so absolute."[4] Fervent believers in world
revolution, captives of a vision in which national distinctions
would be submerged in a rising tide of proletarian internationalism, Lenin and his colleagues set about with dedication
and flinty ruthlessness to achieve their utopian aims. Since
Great Russian patriotism had served as one of the legitimizing
props of the old order, the communists were particularly anxious to suppress its manifestations and ensure its eventual

---

[1] Karl Marx and Friedrich Engels, *Das kommunistische Manifest*, Berlin,
1946, p. 48.

[2] Leon Trotsky, *Literature and Revolution*, Ann Arbor, 1960, p. 94.

[3] Robert C. Tucker, *Stalin as Revolutionary, 1879-1929*, New York, 1973,
p. 140.

[4] E. H. Carr, *Socialism in One Country, 1924-1926*, vol. 1, New York,
1958, pp. 3-4.

extinction. In the course of the first years of the Revolution, the sentence from the Communist Manifesto, "the workers have no fatherland," was everywhere repeated, while words such as "patriotism" and "motherland" virtually disappeared from the Russian vocabulary.

In his 1914 essay "On the National Pride of the Great Russians," written to counter the patriotic upsurge that had accompanied Russia's entry into the First World War, Lenin made clear in what narrow and restricted a sense Russian patriotism would be permissible: "We are full of a sense of national pride, and for that reason we *particularly* hate our slavish past . . . and *our* slavish present. . . . The interests of the Great Russians' national pride (understood not in the slavish sense) coincide with the *socialist* interests of the Great Russian (and all other) proletarians. Our model will always be Marx, who, after living in Britain for decades and becoming half-English, demanded freedom and national independence for Ireland in the interests of the socialist movement of the British workers."[5] Only those Great Russians who had devoted themselves to the struggle against the tsarist state— Radishchev, the Decembrists, Chernyshevskii, the revolutionaries of the 1870s, the revolutionary working class of 1905— were singled out by Lenin for praise.

Once established in power, the Bolsheviks proceeded to attack the pillars of the previous order: the family, the Church, the school. Divorce on demand was legalized immediately after the revolution, and abortion on demand followed in 1920. An explosion of sexual license took place, accompanied by a greatly increased use (and abuse) of alcohol and tobacco. Budding theorists speculated that the rearing of children should become a communal responsibility. A campaign was launched to eradicate religious survivals from the Russian land. Traditional school curricula were jettisoned, to be replaced by militant political indoctrination. Not all of this was to the taste

---

[5] V. I. Lenin, *Collected Works*, Moscow, 1964, vol. 21, pp. 104, 106 (Lenin's italics).

of even the Bolshevik leaders; in a sense, the revolution seemed to be hurtling on with a momentum of its own.[6]

A gifted strategist who combined revolutionary fanaticism with a strong streak of pragmatism, Lenin realized during the period of War Communism (1918-1921) that the country had to be slowly and carefully nurtured toward socialism. The countryside in particular, a bulwark of Russian traditionalism, had to be handled delicately. With the successful conclusion of the civil war, therefore, Lenin braked the momentum of the revolution and ushered in the historic "compromise with capitalism" known as the New Economic Policy (NEP). The constituent elements of the NEP were: "the substitution of a tax in kind for the exaction from the peasants of arbitrary quotas of food, so as to increase their incentive to produce; the legalization of a wide measure of freedom of internal trade; and the granting of concessions to private capitalists for the running of industrial enterprises."[7]

Lenin viewed these economic concessions, as well as a certain relaxing of ideological vigilance in cultural matters, as tactical and temporary, something that some Russian nationalists both at home and in the emigration failed to see. Thus in 1921 there appeared in Prague a collection of essays entitled *Smena vekh* (*Change of Landmarks*), written by former participants of the "white movement." Although the authors do not agree on all points, a common thread runs through their contributions: "The revolution is in process of evolution [*Revoliutsiia evoliutsioniruet*]."[8] The NEP and the Kronstadt uprising of 1921 were interpreted by the contributors as signs that Russia was beginning to devour the Bolshevik Revolution, that the revolution was approaching its Thermidor. The most gifted of the collection's authors, N. V. Ustrialov, felt that Lenin, whom he termed a "great opportunist,"[9] had no

[6] Nicholas S. Timasheff, *The Great Retreat: The Growth and Decline of Communism in Russia*, New York, 1946, pp. 192-203.

[7] Leonard Schapiro, *The Origin of the Communist Autocracy*, 2nd ed., Cambridge, Mass., 1977, p. 307.

[8] *Smena vekh*, Smolensk, 1922, p. 59. This volume is a reprint of the 1921 Prague edition.

[9] Ibid., p. 53.

choice other than to be led by the nose toward Thermidor. Ustrialov placed his hopes on this historical process, rather than on any "white movements" that would, if they wished to succeed, inevitably have to ally themselves with foreign powers not having Russia's interests at heart. As émigré scholar Gleb Struve has pointed out, Ustrialov seems to have seen *smenovekhovtsvo* as a "Trojan horse" whose aim was to transform the revolution from within.[10] Ustrialov was a self-proclaimed "National Bolshevik"—the term would reappear in the 1960s—who sharply distinguished Bolshevism from communism.[11] Another contributor to the volume, S. Chakhotin, went so far as to argue provocatively that émigrés should go down on their knees before the Bolsheviks, the servants of history, as Emperor Henry IV had kneeled in penance before the Pope at Canossa.

As might be expected, the *Change of Landmarks* collection caused a stir both among the émigrés, where its arguments were largely rejected, and in intellectual circles in Soviet Russia, where its message was received with interest and some sympathy. In 1922, even Lenin had to admit that the *smenovekhovtsy* expressed "the mood of thousands and tens of thousands of bourgeois of all sorts" in Russia.[12] With the benefit of hindsight, it seems odd that attentive observers of the Soviet scene should have thought that the revolution had spent its energies some three to four years after taking power, but one must remember that the NEP did represent a significant and deceiving step backward from revolutionary *élan* and maximalism. As it turned out, however, it would be almost half a century before the revolution could be said to have expended most of its energy.

Lenin's death in 1924 was, of course, followed by Iosif Djugashvili-Stalin's successful bid for power. Stalin's achievement of autocratic power was eventually to signal an important shift in the fortunes of Russian nationalism. One must remember that Stalin's identification with the Bolsheviks meant

[10] Gleb Struve, *Russkaia literatura v izgnanii*, New York, 1956, p. 32.
[11] Ibid.
[12] Carr, *Socialism in One Country*, p. 58.

that he was parting ways with the majority of Georgian revolutionaries, whose sympathies were with the Mensheviks.
Stalin was quite aware that the Bolsheviks represented the
"Russian party" among the Marxists; in 1907, for example, he
pointedly noted that at the London party congress, "whereas
the majority of the eighty-five Menshevik delegates were Jews,
with Georgians in second place numerically and Russians in
third, the great majority of the ninety-two Bolshevik delegates were Russians, with Jews coming next, then Georgians,
and so on."[13] Disenchanted with his fellow Georgian revolutionaries, Stalin was delighted to join the predominantly Russian Bolshevik party and its forceful leader, Lenin, whom he
seems to have idolized. However, since he was not a Russian,
Stalin apparently felt no inner need to share Lenin's belief
that Russia had to "atone" for past sins against the minority
peoples of the Soviet Union. Nor, it turned out, was he as
intense in a belief that Russia had to immolate herself for the
cause of world revolution.

In the jockeying for power that followed Lenin's death, Stalin, as is common knowledge, used the slogan "socialism in
one country" as a cudgel against his chief rival, Trotskii, and
the latter's doctrine of "permanent revolution." "Socialism in
one country" was not Stalin's invention; he borrowed it from
Bukharin, but, unlike Bukharin, he made it a centerpiece of
his thought. The significance of the victory of Stalin's Russia-
oriented socialism over Trotskii's militant internationalism is
very great. In fact, some scholars would date the rise of Russian nationalism in the Soviet period from the triumph of this
doctrine.[14]

With Stalin's ascent, there ensued a gradual downgrading
of the internationalist thrust of the revolution. Until 1928, a
member of the Soviet Politburo had headed the Comintern
(the Communist International); after 1928, this ceased to be

[13] Tucker, *Stalin as Revolutionary*, p. 139.
[14] This view was expressed by historians Dimitry Pospielovsky and Aleksandr Nekrich at a conference on Russian nationalism held at the Kennan
Institute for Advanced Russian Studies in June 1978.

the case.[15] In spheres other than foreign policy, however, hostility to things Russian and to vestiges of Russian patriotism continued unabated. In fact, the same year of 1928 that marked Stalin's consolidation of power also witnessed the scrapping of the NEP and a new and radical communist "leap forward"—forced industrialization. As E. H. Carr has commented, "the deduction [of a Russian Thermidor] proved unsound. The proclamation of socialism in one country was followed, not by stabilization on the basis of NEP . . . or by further retreat into capitalism, but by a feverish drive for the development of heavy industry—the traditional stronghold of the class-conscious worker . . . In other words, while socialism in one country made its concessions to nationalism, and thus seemed to diverge from the high road of Marxism, the proletarian or socialist element in it was also perfectly real."[16]

And Carr goes on:

> The party continued to carry the political programme of the proletarian revolution. The history of the revolution consisted of the impact of this dynamic force on a society dominated by a backward peasant economy. The coming of NEP had appeared to many to mean that the force of the revolution was spent, and that the party, as the bearer of this force, would be quietly reabsorbed into the traditional society. . . . In reality, the party leadership compromised far enough with the traditional society to ride out the storm; this compromise was the essence not only of NEP, but of socialism in one country. Yet in the sequel it had retained its revolutionary dynamic unimpaired, and imposed on the society the consummation of "revolution from above."[17]

A skilled tactician and pragmatist, Stalin, like Lenin before him, was willing, when necessary, to brake the momentum of the revolution and make concessions to the inchoate traditionalism of the populace. Yet his genuine commitment to what by this time had become known as Marxism-Leninism

[15] Timasheff, *The Great Retreat*, pp. 156-157.
[16] Carr, *Socialism in One Country*, p. 125.
[17] Ibid., pp. 135-136.

required that Stalin accelerate the revolutionary process when this proved feasible. Rapid industrialization and forced collectivization were the results.

During the late twenties and early thirties, persecution of Russian particularism continued apace. The Russian Association of Proletarian Writers (RAPP) kept a sharp lookout for any indications of Russian chauvinism, while in historical studies, Mikhail Pokrovskii, Vice Commissar of Education, and his disciples dominated the scene with their rigidly orthodox Marxist views. For them, prerevolutionary Russia represented a period of virtually unrelieved darkness.[18] A fanatical economic determinist, Pokrovskii had no interest in glorifying human personalities, especially if they happened to be tsars or tsarist generals. During the period of Pokrovskii's reign, distinguished Russian historians, such as Platonov and Tarle, were suspected of sympathy for prerevolutionary Russia and charged with "bourgeois objectivism," which resulted in their arrest and exile.[19] As for the Russian Orthodox Church, waves of persecution rolled across this once powerful body, seeking its annihilation.[20]

Thus, although Stalin tempered the internationalist thrust of the revolution during the 1920s, he permitted—indeed, encouraged—the antinational and antireligious momentum of the revolutionary process to continue into the 1930s. "Socialism in one country" was not matched by any similar retreat on the domestic front. Then, in 1934, Stalin unexpectedly slammed on the brakes. In the words of émigré sociologist Nicholas Timasheff, "the Doctrine [Marxism-Leninism] remained intact up to 1934, when it was entirely rejected and replaced by its very opposite, making flaming patriotism one

[18] See Pokrovskii's *Brief History of Russia*, 2 vols., New York, 1933. The book is prefaced by a congratulatory letter from Lenin: "Comrade Pokrovsky, I congratulate you heartily on your success. I like your new book 'Brief History of Russia' immensely. . . . It reads with tremendous interest. It should, in my opinion, be translated into the European languages" (I, 5).

[19] Gleb Struve, *Soviet Russian Literature, 1917-1950*, Norman, Okla., 1951, p. 261.

[20] On the persecution, see Nikita Struve, *Christians in Contemporary Russia*, New York, 1967, and Fr. Dimitrii Konstantinov, *Gonimaia tserkov'*, New York, 1967.

of the basic virtues."[21] Timasheff's statement is hyperbolic, but the change initiated in 1934 was indeed extraordinary, and Timasheff is justified in referring to a "great retreat," though "great tactical retreat" might be a more apt term for what occurred.

Why the change? There seem to have been two weighty considerations behind Stalin's decision: Marxism-Leninism had resulted in social catastrophe at home; and there was the growth of fascism in Europe and the threat of impending war. Both factors required that Stalin act decisively and expeditiously.

The Communist Manifesto had spoken contemptuously of the "bourgeois family" and Soviet Russia had not been sparing of the hallowed prop of the old order. Divorce on demand, abortion on demand, the de facto legalization of bigamy, and the general weakening of family ties had led to deleterious results. There was a dramatic drop in the birth rate and a marked rise in juvenile delinquency, the latter the result of broken homes. Schools had become "revolutionary clubs for young people," which meant that basic education was spurned and ignored. The upshot of all this was the threat that there would not be enough people to carry out the industrialization of the country, while the wretched state of the schools meant that there would be a lack of trained specialists or even minimally educated persons to direct the Soviet Union's plants and factories.

Stalin decided to act. In 1935, a campaign against abortion was initiated, and in the following year, a stiff law was passed against abortion on demand. Freedom of divorce was curtailed and then virtually abolished. Wedding rings reappeared in the shops. In Timasheff's words: "Destruction, then reconstruction; that was the pattern of the Communist rulers regarding the family."[22] Similarly, the anarchy in the field of education was suppressed; school curricula were drastically overhauled; it was decided to teach history chronologically and to resume the study of geography. And, in a throwback to tsarist times, uniforms were introduced for school pupils.

[21] Timasheff, *The Great Retreat*, p. 190.
[22] Ibid., p. 203.

The prospect of war, and especially of an invasion, required that Stalin seriously ponder how to mobilize the populace against an aggressor. He apparently concluded that the slogans of Marxism-Leninism had little appeal and that patriotic symbols were needed. The terms *rodina* (motherland or homeland) and *otechestvo* (fatherland), which had been out of currency since the revolution, were permitted to make a dramatic reappearance. Soviet citizens heard that they should now love their fatherland.[23] Russia's past was also rediscovered. History, which had been taught only in terms of mass activity, now reappeared as a sequence of great deeds performed by national heroes. Russian historical figures whom Pokrovskii and his school had either ignored or castigated now became objects of a cult, especially Aleksandr Nevskii, Dimitrii Donskoi, and Peter the Great. Even Prince Vladimir, the baptizer of Russia and a canonized saint of the Orthodox Church, was brought back from oblivion. To commemorate the twenty-first anniversary of the revolution, Sergei Eisenstein's patriotic film "Aleksandr Nevskii" was shown on November 6, 1938.

Pokrovskii, now deceased, was attacked as a "vulgarizer" of Marxism, and his disciples fell into disgrace.[24] Platonov and Tarle, on the other hand, were rehabilitated, and Tarle was invited to glorify General Kutuzov, the hero of the "Fatherland War" of 1812. The Popular Army of Minin and Pozharskii, which repelled a foreign invasion and saved Russia at the beginning of the seventeenth century, was shown not to have been a creature of the landed gentry and merchants. A committee headed by Stalin himself rejected a history textbook for schools as being too "sociological" in approach, that is, as putting too much emphasis on mass activity.

A similar process occurred in the cultural sphere. Historical novels on patriotic themes, such as Sergeev-Tsenskii's *The Ordeal of Sevastopol* (1937-1938), began to proliferate, as did plays such as Solov'ev's *Fieldmarshal Kutuzov* (1939).[25] The

[23] Ibid., p. 166.
[24] Struve, *Soviet Russian Literature*, p. 261.
[25] Ibid., p. 262.

Pushkin centennial of 1937 was expanded into a festival and glorification of Russian culture. The Russian language was also lauded, and a campaign was begun against the use of ear-jarring abbreviations and acronyms. "The Russian language," it was boasted, "is more Russian than ever."[26] A revised version of Glinka's highly patriotic opera *A Life for the Tsar* was staged.

Monuments to the past were perceived as effective mobilizational symbols, so a campaign was launched to restore them. First to be refurbished were great battlefields, such as Poltava and Borodino. Monuments to heroes of the Fatherland War, such as General Bagration and General Kutuzov, were restored, as were monuments at Kulikovo field. Tolstoi's estate, Iasnaia Poliana, was opened to tourists, as was the Trinity-Sergius Monastery, a major religious shrine. Pilgrimages were then sponsored to these newly opened sites.

The year 1934 thus initiated a significant break in Soviet historical development. Or, seen another way, it brought Russian domestic politics in line with the implications of Stalin's policy of "socialism in one country," which had first been advanced a decade previously. What is particularly interesting about the "Great Retreat" is that it was sponsored and implemented from above, rather than in reaction to any active demands or demonstrations on the part of the populace. It resulted from Stalin's estimate of what policies would mobilize Russia in a time of crisis and what policies would best enable her to expand her industrial and military might.

Contemporary Russian nationalists, both "official" and dissenting, have recognized the significance of Stalin's dramatic reversal. Vladimir Osipov, editor of the patriotic *samizdat* journal *Veche*, saw the mid-thirties as a watershed in the campaign against "national nihilism," and the beginning of the decline of the views of the "Russophobe and slanderer Pokrovskii."[27] And in an essay appearing in the Komsomol journal *Molodaia gvardiia*, S. N. Semanov wrote,

[26] Timasheff, *The Great Retreat*, p. 178.

[27] Vladimir Osipov, "Beseda redaktora zhurnala 'Veche' s korresponden-tom Assoshieited Press Stivinzom Bronningom i s korrespondentom gazety 'Baltimor san' Dinom Milzom," *Vestnik R.S.Kh.D.*, no. 106 (1972), 299.

A nihilistic raging in respect to the cultural achievement of our past was unfortunately rather fashionable among a segment of our intelligentsia in the twenties. . . . Pokrovskii and his "school" placed a fat minus sign before the entire history of Russia. . . . In his [Pokrovskii's] essays on Russian history (which it would be more correct to term essays in anti-Russian history) the names of Suvorov and Kutuzov are virtually not mentioned, as is the case with the Sevastopol epic of 1854-55 and many other persons and events which became (and have remained!) sacred for every citizen and patriot. . . . Now it is clear that in the task of the struggle with the destroyers and nihilists the break [*perelom*] occurred in the middle of the thirties.[28]

Russian nationalist émigrés at the time of Stalin's "Great Retreat" followed the changes taking place in their homeland with keen interest. In a series of speeches delivered during 1935, for example, Aleksandr Kazem-Bek, leader of the nationalistic Young Russia (*Mladorossy*) organization, declared that Stalin's actions demonstrated that the "Russian element" (*russkaia stikhiia*) was expelling the "communist narcotic" from the life of the country.[29] "The liberation of the Russian revolution from internationalism," Kazem-Bek maintained, "is equivalent to the liquidation of the very essence of Marxism."[30] As for Stalin, his role was that of "gravedigger of the revolution."[31] All that remained to be done once Stalin had completed his historically ordained task was for the Russian military to topple the despot and the revolution would be over.

Kazem-Bek, of course, underestimated Stalin and misunderstood his role. In his controlled tilting toward nationalist symbols, Stalin was emulating his mentor, Lenin, who was quite willing to take a tactical step backward in order to pre-

---

[28] S. N. Semanov, "O tsennostiakh otnositel'nykh i vechnykh," *Molodaia gvardiia*, no. 8 (1970), 318-319.

[29] Aleksandr Kazem-Bek, *Rossiia, Mladorossy i emigratsiia*, Paris, 1936, p. 7. On Kazem-Bek, see Nicholas Hayes, "Kazem-Bek and the Young Russians' Revolution," *Slavic Review*, 39, no. 2 (1980), 255-268.

[30] Kazem-Bek, *Rossiia*, p. 9.

[31] Ibid., p. 16.

serve the revolution. Stalin realized that Pokrovskii's *Brief History* was not going to inspire anyone to defend the motherland and that communist mobilizational slogans, which had worked well during the civil war, were no longer appropriate. But in turning to nationalist symbols—symbols to which he also responded—Stalin did not abandon the Marxist-Leninist world view. As for Kazem-Bek's hopes that the Soviet army would topple the dictator, Stalin had thought of that possibility too, and soon launched a decimating purge of the armed forces.

One mark of the extent to which the revival of Russian nationalism was "controlled" is that the regime's attitude toward religion did not change in 1934. In fact, the following year Emel'ian Iaroslavskii, head of the League of Militant Atheists, declared religion dead in Russia.[32] The regime continued to be aware that Russian Orthodoxy was a potentially dangerous opponent and that Christian teachings were in direct conflict with those of Marxism-Leninism. By 1939, only four bishops remained in office, and only a few hundred parishes were left of the 40,000 that had been active before the revolution.

Serious considerations, however, later prompted Stalin and his associates to reexamine their policy toward religion. A census taken in 1939 astonished the Soviet rulers by establishing that at least half of the adult population of the country had preserved religious faith.[33] This fact the rulers could ignore only at their peril. Then too, the partition of Poland, which also occurred in 1939, resulted in the incorporation into Soviet Russia of several million Orthodox Belorussians and Ukrainians, with 12,000 functioning parishes.[34] This obviously also worried them. The regime acted by gradually toning down the intensity of the antireligious campaign. First Christianity was singled out as a special religion because, so it was said, it performed the praiseworthy task of promoting

[32] Wassilij Alexeev and Theofanis G. Stavrou, *The Great Revival: The Russian Church under German Occupation*, Minneapolis, 1976, p. 24.

[33] Timasheff, *The Great Retreat*, p. 227.

[34] Alexeev and Stavrou, *The Great Revival*, p. xiv.

the cult of abstract man. When, in June 1940, it was decided to restore the seven-day week, Sunday was selected as the day of rest, over the objections of the League of Militant Atheists.[35] Thus, by the time of the German invasion, Stalin was not only fanning the flames of nationalist sentiment but had begun to put a damper on antireligious activities as well.

When the German troops began pouring into Russia in June 1941, Stalin clearly counted on Russian rather than Marxist slogans and symbols. From the beginning, he cast the war in the light of a struggle for national survival.[36] If in some instances he attempted to strike a balance between national and socialist symbols, in other cases he leaned heavily toward the former. On 6 November 1941, in an address to party and state officials, Stalin referred to the Germans as "these people with the morality of animals, who have the effrontery to call for the extermination of the great Russian nation—the nation of Plekhanov and Lenin, of Belinskii and Chernyshevskii, of Pushkin and Tolstoi, of Gor'kii and Chekhov, of Glinka and Chaikovskii, of Sechenov and Pavlov, of Suvorov and Kutuzov!"[37] Here Stalin employed a mixed bag of names that would appeal to doctrinaire Marxists—Plekhanov, Lenin, the "revolutionary democrats" Belinskii and Chernyshevskii, Gor'kii— and those that would appeal to Russian patriots (Kutuzov, Suvorov, Pushkin, Tolstoi, and so on). But the following day, in an address to the troops, Stalin eschewed such a balancing act:

> Comrades, Red Army and Red Navy men, officers and political workers, men and women partisans! . . . The war you are waging is a war of liberation, a just war. May you be inspired in this war by the heroic figures of our great ancestors Aleksandr Nevskii, Dimitrii Donskoi, Minin and Pozharskii, Aleksandr Suvorov, Mikhail Kutuzov! May you be blest by great Lenin's victorious banner! Death to the German invaders![38]

[35] Timasheff, *The Great Retreat*, p. 229.
[36] Alexander Werth, *Russia at War, 1941-1945*, New York, 1965, p. 170.
[37] Ibid., p. 242.
[38] Ibid., pp. 244-245.

This glorification of Russia, according to Alexander Werth, who was present in Russia throughout the war as a correspondent, "had a tremendous effect on the people in general, even though it made perhaps a few Marxist-Leninist purists squirm on the quiet."[39] They continue to squirm to this day, as demonstrated in a letter by a certain I. M. Danishevskii, protesting an article that appeared in the 4 June 1965, issue of *Komsomol'skaia pravda*:[40]

> When, in connection with the attack of Hitlerite Germany on the Soviet Union, people were expecting a statement on the war, what was the whole world expecting from it [the Soviet Union]? They were expecting that the unfurled banner of revolutionary proletarian internationalism, the martial traditions of the revolutionary struggle in our country, as well as in both Germany herself and her satellites, would be opposed to the bestial nationalism of the German fascist robbers. They were awaiting an appeal to all oppressed masses. . . . [Communists] expected that the first victorious socialist state in the world would appeal to the great names of Marx, Engels and Lenin.

Unfortunately, Danishevskii continued, Stalin's appeal " 'to be inspired by the heroic figures' of tsarist satraps demonstrated to the whole world a striving to turn the course of the struggle away from class positions to nationalist grounds. These [Stalin's] appeals might, perhaps, have been appropriate in a 1914 manifesto of Nicholas II concerning the declaration of war against Wilhelm's Germany, but they were certainly inappropriate in a declaration by the General Secretary of the Communist Party, by the most eminent representative of the Communist International, which still existed at that time, by the head of the Soviet state."

And he went on: "There can be no doubt that there were in our country strata [*prosloiki*] for whom this appeal was inspiring. But what kind of strata were they? During the years

---

[39] Ibid., p. 245.

[40] "Pis'mo I. M. Danishevskogo po povodu stat'i V. Peskova 'Otechestvo' " in the "unofficial" neo-Marxist journal *Politicheskii dnevnik*, 1 (1972), 63-71.

of the war we also had strata who sought inspiration in unctuous sermons held in churches. . . . Who can say with certainty what influences other appeals closer to our [that is, Marxist-Leninist] world view, to our traditions and ideology, would have had?" Stalin's invoking of the names of Suvorov and Kutuzov particularly annoyed Danishevskii. Suvorov, he pointed out, was a serf-owner, who led "his soldier-serfs to death, torture, and deprivation" for the sake of oppressor-landowners. He also was responsible for suppressing a mutiny in Poland and for sending the great rebel Pugachev off to Moscow to be executed. As for Kutuzov, he was "a typical serf-owning general."

If Danishevskii felt that Stalin made a woeful error, Solzhenitsyn—hardly an unqualified supporter of the despot—congratulated him for exhibiting common sense during the war: ". . . from the very first days of the war Stalin refused to rely on the putrid decaying prop of ideology. He wisely discarded it, all but ceased to mention it and unfurled instead the old Russian banner—sometimes, indeed, the standard of Orthodoxy—and we conquered!"[41] Solzhenitsyn's sentiments are shared by all Russian nationalists, whether of the "official" or dissenting variety.

The attempts made to cultivate Russian patriotic fervor during the first months of the war were only a token of what was to come. There was, for example, the decision made to set up "Suvorov schools" in areas liberated from the Germans. These were cadet schools closely modeled on the prerevolutionary cadet corps. The nine schools, which enrolled five hundred pupils each, were intended to create an officer caste. Alexander Werth recalls a visit to one such school: "When I visited the Suvorov School in Kalinin, I found that, among the subjects the budding little officers were taught were English, fine manners and old-time ball-room dances. . . . On the walls, there were large pictures of Suvorov, but

---

[41] Aleksandr I. Solzhenitsyn, *Letter to the Soviet Leaders*, New York, 1974, p. 17.

also equally large ones of Stalin and of numerous Red Army generals."[42]

In the cultural sphere, a similar process could be observed. Biographies of Russia's great generals—Suvorov, Kutuzov, Bagration—were rushed into print. Aleksei N. Tolstoi's play in two parts, *Ivan the Terrible*, which glorified a cruel but wise builder of state, appeared in 1942-1943, and Sergei Eisenstein's film of the same title was first shown in 1944. (It is interesting that in the late thirties Stalin seems to have identified with Peter the Great, whereas during the war he felt a kinship with the dread sixteenth-century tsar.) A more dramatic confirmation that the ideological shackles had been loosened was the return of Dostoevskii to the ranks of great Russian writers. Unlike his successors Khrushchev and Brezhnev, Stalin correctly understood that Dostoevskii's writings constituted a powerful ideational challenge to a Marxist state. As he commented to Milovan Djilas during the early stages of the war: "We are not publishing him [Dostoevskii] because he is a bad influence on the youth. But, a great writer!"[43] By the summer of 1942, however, Stalin seems to have changed his mind. Émigré specialist Vladimir Seduro has written:

> In August, 1942, in *Bol'shevik*, theoretical organ of the Party, Emel'ian Mikhailovich Iaroslavskii (1878-1943), member of the Central Committee of the Party and a high functionary of the Agitation and Propaganda Section, director of prewar antireligious campaigns, granted official amnesty to Dostoevskii and summoned him to do battle with the Germans. . . . "With all his faults," Iaroslavskii wrote, "Dostoevskii was and remains a deeply Russian writer who loved his people." . . . When in September, 1942, [Viktor] Ermilov's long article "The Great Russian Writer F. M. Dostoevskii" was published in the newspaper *Literatura i iskusstvo* it was clear that the Bolsheviks had gone as far as

---

[42] Werth, *Russia at War*, p. 676.
[43] Milovan Djilas, *Conversations with Stalin*, New York, 1962, p. 157.

it was possible for them to go in the direction of reconciliation with Dostoevskii.[44]

Beginning in 1941, fitful attempts were also made to reexamine the role and thought of the nineteenth-century Slavophiles.[45]

The regime's most radical concession to the mood of the populace unquestionably related to the Church. As is well known, Metropolitan Sergii (Starogorodskii), locum tenens of the patriarchal throne, came immediately to the aid of the embattled Soviet state at the outbreak of the war, without being asked. The Church's ardent support for the war effort of an atheist government that had previously sought its demise must have impressed Stalin, especially when he saw that the religio-patriotic appeals of Sergii and his fellow bishops were obtaining results. A fortnight after the German attack, Iaroslavskii's weekly *Bezbozhnik* (The Atheist) was shut down.[46] Three months after the outbreak of war, the publication of all antireligious journals was discontinued, and all antireligious museums were closed.[47] In 1943, the "Living Church," a left-wing ecclesiastical organization in schism from the official church, was disbanded.

The Russian faithful responded to Sergii's (and Stalin's) overtures by collecting huge sums of money for the war effort. Sergii provided equipment for a tank batallion named in honor of St. Dimitrii Donskoi; on Red Army Day in 1942, the Moscow churches and clergy contributed a sum of 1,500,000 rubles. The total Church contributions during the war amounted to a staggering 150 million rubles.[48]

In 1943, the state began making major concessions to the Church. It was permitted to convene a council in order to elect Sergii patriarch (the regime had arranged for the pa-

[44] Vladimir Seduro, *Dostoyevski in Russian Literary Criticism, 1846-1956*, New York, 1957, pp. 245-246, 248.

[45] See A. Dement'ev, " 'Kontseptsiia,' 'konstruktsiia' i 'model'," *Voprosy literatury*, no. 7 (1969), 116-117.

[46] Werth, *Russia at War*, p. 402.

[47] Timasheff, *The Great Retreat*, p. 230.

[48] Matthew Spinka, *The Church in Soviet Russia*, New York, 1956, p. 85.

triarchal throne to be vacant since 1925). A Holy Synod was formed to direct the affairs of the Moscow Patriarchate, and the Church was given permission to publish a periodical, *Zhurnal moskovskoi patriarkhii (Journal of the Moscow Patriarchate)*. Orthodox bishops and clergy began to be released from imprisonment and administrative exile.

Despite these concessions, it would be a serious mistake to conclude that Stalin let the patriotic and religious upsurge get out of hand during the war or that he ever lost sight of the Marxist-Leninist legitimization of his regime. The writings of Aleksei N. Tolstoi, who served as one of Stalin's tribunes during the war, show how the dictator's minions attempted to blend nationalist and Marxist motifs. In the essay "*Rodina*" (Homeland), for example, Tolstoi wrote:

> During these bitter months of decisive battles we have all come to realize far more deeply the ties of blood that bind us to our country, the poignant love we have for our native land. . . . My country—it is the advancing march of my people, whose tread resounds over the land from the depths of the ages to the future to which they aspire, a future which they believe in, which they are creating with their own hands for their own common good and for that of generations to come.

Turning to Russian history, he extolled "the red shields of Igor' in the Polovtsi steppes, the cries of the Russians slaughtered near the river Kalka, the army of peasants' spears bristling under Dimitrii's sacred banners on Kulikovo Field, the blood-steeped ice of Lake Peipus, and Ivan the Terrible who advanced the unbroken and now inviolable boundaries of the land from Siberia to the Varangian Sea. . . ."[49] In Tolstoi's essay, one notes an interesting combination of communist and atavistic (the emphasis on blood) motifs. Russia's history is

[49] Alexei Tolstoy, *My Country: Articles and Stories of the Great Patriotic War of the Soviet Union*, London, 1943, pp. 5, 7. The translator of this volume, D. L. Fromberg, takes certain liberties with the text but generally captures the gist of what Tolstoi is saying. For a recent Russian-language collection of Tolstoi's patriotic writings, see Aleksei Tolstoi, *Otechestvo*, Moscow, 1976.

sacred because it has been drenched in the blood of the forefathers, but it is doubly sacred because it is teleological—
leading toward socialism, guided by a stern but wise Ivan the
Terrible reincarnate, Iosif Stalin.

Elsewhere in the same essay, Tolstoi wrote: "A time will
undoubtedly come when the national torrents will merge into
a single tranquil sea, into a single human entity. But for our
age this is a dream beyond our reach."[50] The Russian people
strain forward toward the "bright future" of socialism and the
merging of all peoples into a joyous and unified mass, but
this great hope for the future does not drown out the significance of heroic victories in the past. With similar dexterity,
Tolstoi in his essay "What We Are Defending" interpreted
the victory of the Reds over the Whites in the civil war as a
"patriotic" event,[51] whereas in "Russian Warriors" he artfully,
if illogically, linked Emel'ian Pugachev to the great tsarist
generals:

> Hardly had the reverberations of the mighty Pugachev up-
> rising died away, leaving the people bound hand and foot
> by the government of the tsars and nobles, when Napoleon
> invaded Russia . . . Napoleon circulated the most enticing
> proclamations, in which he promised liberty to the peas-
> ants. But the people decided otherwise—not to surrender
> their country to the foreign enemy but to win liberty with
> their own hands. . . . The Russian soldier followed Suvorov
> across the [A]lps, followed Rumiantsev into Paris, and Sko-
> belev in taking the impregnable Plevna heights.[52]

From a logical standpoint, Tolstoi's potpourri was frequently
nonsense. But his writing was skillfully aimed at the emotions
of his readers and succeeded in harmonizing nationalism and
communism about as well as possible.

Even during the height of the nationalist revival, in 1942-
1943, numerous warnings were carried in the Soviet press to
the effect that the new "patriotic" line should not be inter-

---

[50] Tolstoy, *My Country*, p. 6.
[51] Ibid., p. 15.
[52] Ibid., p. 24.

preted as contradicting Marxist internationalism.[53] In October 1944, a solemn warning was sounded in the official Party journal *Bol'shevik* against "Western" and "bourgeois" tendencies; the article also deplored the tendency of many during the war to show enthusiasm for icons and religious music on the pretext that they represented part of the Russian "national heritage."[54]

In the period following V-E day (May 9, 1945), Stalin permitted himself a few last patriotic flourishes. On May 24, he held a great reception at the Kremlin to honor Soviet marshals, generals, and high-ranking officers, at which he pointedly singled out the Russian nation—"the leading nation, remarkable for its clear mind, its patience and its firm character"—for special praise.[55] A month later, however, Stalin was already engaged in undercutting the power of the "military caste" that the war had created.[56] A systematic debunking of war heroes and an elevation of communist symbols was initiated several months after the conclusion of the war.[57] Clearly Stalin realized that a fusion of militarism and nationalism did not bode well for the communist state and, more particularly, for himself.

Extraordinary changes and concessions had been made during the war, and it is no wonder that even attentive observers felt that a return to oppression was not in the offing. Nicholas Timasheff, whose informative book, *The Great Retreat* (1946), I have been citing frequently, exulted at one point in it: "Concessions! This means victory, though partial victory only, of the nation against a reckless dictatorship."[58] In his final chapter, Timasheff pointed to the fact that faith in the doctrine of Marxism-Leninism had "substantially declined" in Russia and he went on to predict confidently that

[53] Frederick C. Barghoorn, *Soviet Russian Nationalism*, Westport, Conn., 1976, p. 41. This volume is a reprint of the 1956 Oxford University Press edition.

[54] Werth, *Russia at War*, p. 854.

[55] Ibid., p. 902.

[56] Ibid., p. 903.

[57] Ibid., p. 904.

[58] Timasheff, *The Great Retreat*, p. 359.

no new "socialist offensive" would follow the Great Retreat.[59]
He incautiously concluded: "In the course of the Great Retreat, the Russian nation has broken the backbone of the
Communist monster and, having broken it, experienced the
joy of recovery and victory."[60]

Timasheff was, to be sure, mistaken. Stalin would return
to a version of "orthodoxy" after the war, and Khrushchev
would launch a somewhat weak but nevertheless real socialist
offensive whose most salient trait would be a renewed assault
on religion. The "communist monster's" back had most defi-
nitely not been broken. Yet Timasheff's book drew attention
to highly significant phenomena that cannot be ignored. The
period 1934-1945 did markedly alter the course of Russian
history, something that both "official" and dissenting Russian
nationalists stress when they warn of the consequences of ignoring Russia's experiences during the war. As an anonymous
author wrote in *Veche*, in rebuttal to an article that appeared
in *Literaturnaia gazeta* in 1972:

> Why, during the Fatherland War, when mortal danger hung
> over the country and when extraordinary strength of spirit
> was needed, did "Soviet patriotism" prove insufficient, and
> it was necessary urgently to call to remembrance the Church,
> Aleksandr Nevskii, Peter I, and Suvorov, that is, princes,
> tsars, and reactionary generals? Why were not the cult of
> the heroes of the civil war and the cult of the heroes of the
> class struggle enough? And on whom is [the author] placing
> his hopes in the approaching war [with China]?[61]

One encounters this refrain frequently in contemporary nationalist writings. In light of the looming threat of war with
Red China, is it wise, the authors ask, to ignore the lessons
of the Second World War? The *Veche* publicist just cited reminded his *Literaturnaia gazeta* opponent of the process that

---

[59] Ibid., p. 413.
[60] Ibid., p. 415.
[61] "Bor'ba s tak nazyvaemym rusofil'stvom, ili put' gosudarstvennogo samoubiistva," *Vol'noe slovo*, no. 17-18 (1975), 50. This issue contains selections from *Veche*, nos. 7-10.

began in Russia "in the middle of the 1930s" and described his antagonist as an "internationalist" fossil.[62]

By 1946, Stalin's campaign to "freeze" the country and reverse the liberalizations permitted during the war was gathering momentum. First to feel the pressure was literature, which was only to be expected; in Russia, literature has traditionally been at the cutting edge of social criticism and has therefore been monitored closely by the nation's rulers. The collected essays of Stalin's associate, Andrei Zhdanov, capture well the flavor of this dismal period:

> In October, 1917, both the ruling classes and their ideologists and songsters were tossed into the ashcan of history.[63]

> We are no longer the Russians we were before 1917, and Russia is no longer the same, nor is our character. We have changed and grown along with the great transformations that have radically altered the face of our country.[64]

> The brilliant victory of socialism achieved in the Great Patriotic War, which was at the same time a brilliant victory for Marxism, is like a bone in the throats of the imperialists.[65]

Although nationalist motifs continued to make their appearance in these essays, it is clear that Zhdanov consciously subordinated them to the claims of ideology. When Russians were cited as models of behavior, it was the revolutionary democrats (Belinskii, Chernyshevskii, Dobroliubov) and the Russian Marxists (Plekhanov, Lenin) who were selected; gone were the Suvorovs and Kutuzovs.

By 1948 the crackdown of the postwar period was gathering momentum. Viktor Ermilov, one of those who had cautiously attempted to rehabilitate Dostoevskii during the war, had to recant his heresies and do penance by fulminating against the

---

[62] Ibid., p. 33.

[63] Andrei A. Zhdanov, *Essays on Literature, Philosophy, and Music*, New York, 1950, pp. 24-25.

[64] Ibid., p. 42.

[65] Ibid., p. 72.

novelist's "reactionary ideas."[66] The gifted critic Dolinin announced in the same year his intention of "giving up" the study of Dostoevskii in order to concentrate on the revolutionary democrats. The regime also attempted to suppress the historical hero worship that had been encouraged during the war; writers were reminded that they should not seek to escape into historical themes.[67]

Thus there was a revival of Marxist-Leninist orthodoxy during Stalin's last years. The sinister anticosmopolitan campaign and "Doctors' Plot," with their anti-Semitic suspicions and forebodings, added a medieval aura to this supposed resurgence of scientific socialism. One wonders how far this would have gone had Stalin not, in Solzhenitsyn's words, "departed from his rib cage" in 1953.[68]

It is interesting that in only one area did Stalin not seek to choke off the concessions that had been made during the war: religion. Generally speaking, the Church was allowed to continue to enjoy the fruits of wartime détente. Some 22,000 parishes were reported to be functioning in 1946, which was approximately half the number in operation before the revolution. (A disproportionate number of these parishes, incidentally, were in formerly occupied territory.) By 1948, the Church had eighty-nine functioning monasteries, and two theological academies and eight seminaries were preparing new clergy and theologians.[69] In 1950, the Church was reported to have seventy-three bishops. It would be grossly inaccurate to describe the Moscow Patriarchate as "free" during this period, of course. Attacks on religion continued to appear in the press, and religious conviction could be a hindrance to advancement in society; but compared to conditions in the late 1930s, the Church prospered.

How does one explain Stalin's leniency toward religion at a time when he was becoming increasingly repressive and

[66] Struve, *Soviet Russian Literature*, p. 326, note.
[67] Ibid., p. 353.
[68] Aleksandr I. Solzhenitsyn, *The Gulag Archipelago*, 1, New York, 1974, 92.
[69] Spinka, *The Church in Soviet Russia*, p. 119.

paranoid? The answer is not simply the sense of gratitude he felt toward the Church for its ardent and helpful support of the war effort, though this factor should not be discounted. The sycophantic behavior of the Church leadership undoubtedly pleased Stalin, as well. A dissident Russian priest and Russian nationalist, Gleb Iakunin, recently published an essay entitled "The Moscow Patriarchate and the Cult of Stalin," in which he gave numerous examples of the Church's boundless exaltation of the despot in the postwar period.[70] There were also sound political reasons for Stalin to continue his détente with religion. Large swaths of land with a significant Orthodox population had recently been absorbed into the Soviet Union, and it would take time before the population of these areas could be "digested." Moreover, Stalin knew that he could depend on the Patriarchate to be a trusted ally in furthering the foreign policy aims of the Soviet Union, and soon ecclesiastical representatives began a campaign of extensive travel abroad.[71] Fr. Iakunin suggested that the Church leadership may have been motivated by a grandiose vision:

> There are serious grounds for conjecturing that in the post-war period the leadership of the Moscow Patriarchate had a presentiment of even greater approaching changes. Patriarch Aleksii and his closest entourage evidently were expecting the imminent approach of the moment when Stalin, "a new Constantine," would disband or completely reform the Communist Party and would proclaim the country a pan-Slavic Orthodox empire.[72]

Iakunin adduced no evidence to support this thesis, but, in any case, whatever the aspirations of the leaders of the Patriarchate, it is certain that Stalin was far from entertaining

[70] Fr. Gleb Iakunin, "Moskovskaia Patriarkhiia i 'kul't lichnosti' Stalina," *Russkoe vozrozhdenie*, no. 1 (1978), 103-137; and no. 2 (1978), 110-137.

[71] On this, see William C. Fletcher, *Religion and Soviet Foreign Policy, 1945-1970*, London, 1973.

[72] Fr. Iakunin, in *Russkoe vozrozhdenie*, no. 2 (1978), 113. See also Solzhenitsyn's speculations concerning Stalin's attitude toward the postwar Russian Church, in the recently published ninety-six-chapter recension of *The First Circle*, *Sobranie sochinenii*, 1, Vermont and Paris, 1978, 166-168.

such a vision. The Leninist succession and Marxist legitimacy were important to him, and he would never have considered abandoning them for Russian nationalism and the Church. Ever flexible, however, he was more than willing to use the Church as part of his imperialist designs, especially since he seems not to have regarded it as a threat. Outwardly the Church grew in strength during the period 1946-1953, but at the expense of its integrity—which Orthodox dissenters would be at pains to point out during the middle and late 1960s.[73]

SUMMARY

The Bolshevik revolutionaries who seized power in 1917 were essentially "antipatriots" whose aim was world revolution and the disappearance of all national distinctions. Tactical considerations soon required that they mitigate this extremism; thus Lenin initiated the NEP, a concession to economic traditionalism in the country. The first truly major change, however, was Stalin's adoption of the policy of "socialism in one country" in his struggle against Trotskii. This policy served to point Russia away from world revolution— though the aim was never completely abandoned—and in the direction of internal development. Domestic policy was not made to conform to the implications of "socialism in one country" until 1934, when what Timasheff has termed "The Great Retreat" began to occur. The chief reasons behind this turnabout in policy were the failure of an advocacy of Marxist-Leninist ideology to provide the human materiel Stalin needed for rapid industrialization—witness the marked drop in fertility and the dearth of adequately trained industrial technicians—and the looming threat of war. The Second World War accelerated the concessions to nationalism and religion begun in the post-1934 period. By turning to Russian nationalist rather than Marxist-Leninist slogans and symbols, Stalin irritated doctrinaire purists but ensured the eventual victory of the

[73] See, for example, Boris Talantov, "Sergianism, or Adaptation to Atheism," *The Orthodox Word*, November-December 1971, pp. 275-281. Talantov perished in a concentration camp in 1971.

nation against a powerful antagonist. Despite such concessions, however, Stalin never lost sight of the Marxist-Leninist legitimization of his regime. After the war, he clamped down on ideological deviations from Marxist "orthodoxy," although he permitted the Russian Church to continue to enjoy the benefits of wartime détente.

During the postwar crackdown by Stalin, it became evident that the role of Marxist-Leninist ideology in Soviet Russia could never be returned to its pre-1934 status; subsequently, it would have to be adjusted to find room for a positive appreciation of prerevolutionary Russian history and culture. A return to the days of Pokrovskii had become impossible.

In the period 1917-1953, Russian nationalism made its presence felt not as an ideology, and certainly not as a program. Rather, one has largely to do with symbols and slogans that were aimed at mobilizing popular support and that were controlled and carefully manipulated by the regime. Stalin rigorously censored out any attempts to acquaint the Russian people with holistic thinkers, such as Dostoevskii or the philosopher Nikolai Berdiaev, whose polemics opposed the ideational assumptions of the communist state. Religion, in the sense of "serving the cult," was permitted after the war, but the Church was not allowed to question the pronouncements of ideology. Despite the extraordinary degree of control that Stalin exerted over the country, however, the genie of Russian nationalism, or of an admixture of religion and nationalism, could not, once released, be so easily returned to the bottle. In a sense, Stalin's concessions began, slowly and gradually, to take on a life and momentum of their own. Frederick Barghoorn was correct when he wrote, "there are deep tensions between the attitudes derived from the traditional [Russian] culture patterns and the institutions and attitudes created by the Soviet regime."[74] These tensions would prove thorny and problematic for Stalin's successors.

[74] Barghoorn, *Soviet Russian Nationalism*, p. 268.

2

The Historical Background (II)
1953-1981

> Mao was right to remove epaulets from Chinese army uni-
> forms. . . . I think it was a mistake on our part when we
> put epaulets or stripes back onto our own military uni-
> forms. Who the hell needs them? We won the Civil War,
> and I didn't have any epaulets or stripes even though I
> held the rank of commissar. . . . Nowadays our military
> men are all dressed up like canaries.
>
> Nikita Khrushchev[1]

> "Who are you?"
> "Wanderers returning to our native land."
> "Come in with God's blessing."
>
> Vladimir Soloukhin[2]

After Stalin's death, the inevitable power struggle occurred,
and Nikita Khrushchev, a Russian *muzhik* from the Western
Ukraine, seized the helm. Khrushchev contributed to the
growth of Russian nationalism in numerous ways, though this
was clearly not his intention. For if Stalin had manifested a
visceral, though not ideological, attachment to Russian nationalist symbols, the same could not be said of Khrushchev,
a member of the Party since 1918 and a veteran of the Civil
War. While not a fanatic, Khrushchev always evidenced a
strong and unwavering commitment to the doctrines of Marxism-Leninism. Milovan Djilas, who came to know Khrushchev during the war, has condescendingly noted that the
future Party boss's grasp of Marxist theory was "on the level

---

[1] Nikita Khrushchev, *Khrushchev Remembers*, Boston, 1970, p. 475.
[2] Vladimir Soloukhin, "Vladimirskie proselki," in *Izbrannye proizvedeniia*,
vol. 1, Moscow, 1974, 37. English translation: *A Walk in Rural Russia*, New
York, 1967, p. 34. (*Vladimir Back Roads* is a preferable translation of the
title.)

of an intermediate Party school" and that he was a fount of
maxims "learned by rote."[3] But Djilas also confirms that
Khrushchev's Marxism was held "with conviction and frank-
ness."[4]

Khrushchev's antipathy to Russian nationalism, and indeed
to all nationalism, is brought out in his memoirs. It is particularly noticeable in his comments on Mao Tse-Tung, whom
he sees, at times in what appears to be an Aesopian fashion,
as bearing numerous resemblances to Stalin:

> I was put on my guard against Mao's chauvinism as early
> as 1954, when I first went to Peking. Despite his excep-
> tionally cordial manner, I could sense an undercurrent of
> nationalism in his praise of the Chinese nation. His words
> reflected his belief in the superiority of the Chinese race—
> an idea which is completely contrary to the correct Marxist
> notion about nationalities. According to our Communist view
> of the world, all nations are equal; individuals should be
> distinguished not by their nationality but by their class af-
> filiation.[5]

Similar sentiments seem to be behind Khrushchev's dissatisfaction with Solzhenitsyn's 1963 story, "Matrena's Home,"
a work permeated by neo-Slavophile tones: ". . . I didn't particularly care for Solzhenitsyn's second book, *Matrena's Home*.
You can say it's a matter of taste, but I'd say it's more a matter
of mood."[6]

Khrushchev also differed from Stalin, and was closer to
Lenin, in his militant hatred of religion, which prompted him
to launch a wide-ranging persecution against "religious survivals" in the late 1950s. As he put it in a speech to the 22nd
Party Congress in 1961: "Survivals of the past are a dreadful
power, which, like a nightmare, prevail over the minds of
living creatures. . . . Communist education presupposes

---

[3] Milovan Djilas, *Conversations with Stalin*, New York, 1962, pp. 120-121.
[4] Ibid., p. 121.
[5] Nikita Khrushchev, *Khrushchev Remembers: The Last Testament*, Boston, 1974, p. 283.
[6] Ibid., p. 73.

emancipation from religious prejudices and superstitions, which hinder Soviet people from fully developing their creative powers."[7]

An antitraditionalist, Khrushchev was utterly indifferent to the fate of Russian architectural monuments. Vladimir Osipov, editor of the journal *Veche*, writes that the attempts of representatives of the Soviet intelligentsia to get Khrushchev to approve the formation of a voluntary society for the preservation of monuments failed miserably. When the "establishment" figure Sergei Mikhalkov began to read an appeal on this subject in Khrushchev's presence, the latter exploded in wrath and refused to hear the rest of the document.[8]

It would therefore have seemed that the interests of Russian nationalism would have been poorly served by one with Khrushchev's views and prejudices. But what actually occurred was more complex. In 1956, Khrushchev exploded a political bomb at the 20th Party Congress. His "secret speech"—which rapidly became eminently unsecret—revealed a number of Stalin's crimes, particularly those against the Party, and rocked Soviet society with considerable force. "De-stalinization" had several effects: (1) Most importantly— and directly contrary to Khrushchev's wishes—it dealt a blow to the hegemony of Marxism-Leninism in Soviet Russia. If such horrors had been perpetrated in the name of ideology, then what was the ideology worth? (2) A limited and at times convulsive liberalization set in, marked by periods of "thawing" and "freezing" but eventually resulting in greater freedom of expression and a widening of the limits of what was permitted or at least not explicitly forbidden. (3) The gates of the concentration camps were thrown open and some ten to

---

[7] Cited in Donald A. Lowrie and William C. Fletcher, "Khrushchev's Religious Policy, 1959-1964," in Richard H. Marshall, Jr. et al., eds., *Aspects of Religion in the Soviet Union, 1917-1967*, Chicago, 1971, pp. 133-134.

[8] See Vladimir Osipov, "Russkii khudozhnik Il'ia Glazunov," *Veche*, no. 8 (Arkhiv samizdata 1665), 171-172. The Arkhiv samizdata is the collection, maintained by Radio Liberty in Munich, of privately printed materials (*samizdat*) that have circulated clandestinely in the Soviet Union. Henceforth, the numbers that a document bears in this collection will be indicated by the letters "AS."

fifteen million political prisoners were allowed back into society.[9] Many of these individuals, including, of course, future Nobel prize winner Aleksandr Solzhenitsyn, had evolved alternative world views while behind barbed wire. (4) In contrast to these liberalizations, Khrushchev launched a harsh antireligious campaign during the period 1959-1964, which resulted in the forced closing of over half the churches opened by Stalin during and after the war and the physical destruction of many of them, including a number of architectural monuments.

Among these effects was that intellectuals began to desert "orthodox" Marxism-Leninism and to cast about for alternatives. Most affected by Khrushchev's "secret speech" were the university youth; Stalin's crimes seemed to these young people to be so serious as to necessitate a new Nuremberg trial. Neo-Marxism, socialism, and Western-style liberalism were all possibilities, but some chose to move toward variants of Russian nationalism. Those who did began to find a voice—most notably that of Vladimir Soloukhin (b. 1924)—and this time it was not one dictated from above, as had been the case in the 1934-1945 period. The Russian countryside had been rediscovered by a bold writer, Valentin Ovechkin, in his *"Raionnye budni"* (Daily Life in the District), which appeared in 1952, shortly before Stalin's death, and the theme had then been deepened in the first installment of Efim Dorosh's *"Derevenskii dnevnik"* (Countryside Diary) which appeared in 1956.[10] But it was Soloukhin's *Vladimirskie proselki* (Vladimir Back Roads), (1957) which contained in kernel form many of the themes and motifs which Russian nationalists would evolve over the next two decades.

This *ocherk* or "sketch" recounts Soloukhin's rediscovery of the Vladimir countryside, where he had spent his "golden childhood" and whence he and his ancestors had sprung.

[9] Peter Reddaway, ed., *Uncensored Russia*, New York, 1972, p. 18.

[10] On Ovechkin, see the excellent article by Patricia Carden, "Reassessing Ovechkin," in Richard Freeborn et al., eds., *Russian and Slavic Literature*, Columbus, Ohio, 1976, pp. 407-424. On Dorosh, see Gleb Zekulin's contribution to Freeborn et al., eds., *Russian and Slavic Literature*: "Efim Dorosh," pp. 424-441.

Though Soloukhin is careful to pay his dues to the political system—"The attention which the Party has paid to the countryside has warmed and given new life to my native Vladimir"[11]—the sketch reveals a polemical edge which is only partially camouflaged by lyricism. *Vladimir Back Roads* not only points to individual social shortcomings, as Ovechkin's work had done, but in veiled manner challenges a number of Soviet Marxist shibboleths and assumptions. Prime objects of Soloukhin's attack are the prometheanism and historical amnesia fostered by the Soviet period. "Of course," he writes concerning the imminent demise of an ancient church, "this would not cause the death of anyone; but neither would it cause anyone's death if the whole of the Tret'iakov Museum were to disappear."[12] Soloukhin describes how graveyards have been plundered and the bones of the deceased left protruding out of the ground and shows how rivers have been heedlessly polluted.

In Soloukhin, one senses a profound love for Russia's prerevolutionary past, almost a reverence for it. He is appalled at the desecration of the funeral vault of Field Marshal Vorontsov, a prince, and does not attempt to conceal his admiration for Prince Bagration, a hero of the war against Napoleon who was mortally wounded at Borodino. He pays homage to the memory of Prince Pozharskii, leader of the popular army against the Poles in the early 17th century. "Can we visit his grave?" he asks. "After all, he was a hero, a patriot, the saviour of Rus' "[13] And he venerates Ivan Aksakov, the famous Slavophile publicist, showing sympathy for Aksakov's pan-Slav views. A muted religiosity makes itself felt in Soloukhin's description of ancient churches, while a strong love of nature permeates the entire work.

It might be argued that Soloukhin is merely going back to views and sentiments which were permitted, even encouraged, during the war against Hitler, but this would be inaccurate. Soloukhin makes little effort to shape his patriotism

[11] Soloukhin, *A Walk in Rural Russia*, p. 253.
[12] Ibid., p. 116.
[13] Ibid., p. 205.

to fit a Marxist-Leninist mold, and his aim is clearly a radical reform of the social and cultural system. He seeks to rouse indignation in his readers, to gather new troops for the struggle against nihilistic indifference toward Russia and her thousand-year history. One thing is certain: Soloukhin's work struck a chord in his readership. "Several thousand" readers wrote in asking for more writings on the same theme.[14]

With Stalin's death, nationalist sympathizers in other cultural spheres also began to feel less constrained. Soviet folklorists, for example, finally felt free "to criticize the great exaggerations and gross mistakes of folklore research" in the Stalin period,[15] while Dostoevskii studies were once again permitted to emerge from the catacombs.[16]

The general loosening of controls which took place under Khrushchev also resulted in structural and administrative reforms conducive to a rise in Russian nationalist sentiment. As Edward Allworth has pointed out, it was under Khrushchev that a certain parallelism between the RSFSR and other constituent Soviet republics began to be permitted. Stalin, alert to the dangers of granting ethnic Russians their own institutions and publications, had generally prevented this from taking place. In 1956, the Central Committee of the CPSU established, for the first time, a Bureau for the RSFSR, and soon afterward the Bureau, jointly with the RSFSR Council of Ministers, began publication of the newpaper *Sovetskaia Rossiia* (Soviet Russia). Allworth notes that the authorities took some risk in permitting an eponymous press outlet of wide circulation to make an appearance "in the ethnic Russian life of the Soviet Union but outside the direct, strict managerial surveillance of the Union-wide party."[17] (Presumably as a re-

[14] Vladimir Soloukhin, *Rabota*, Moscow, 1966, p. 12.

[15] Felix J. Oinas, "The Political Uses and Themes of Folklore in the Soviet Union," in Felix J. Oinas, ed., *Folklore, Nationalism and Politics*, Columbus, Ohio, 1978, p. 91.

[16] See Vladimir Seduro, *Dostoevski's Image in Russia Today*, Belmont, Mass., 1975, pp. 1-287.

[17] Edward Allworth, "Ambiguities in Russian Group Identity and Leadership of the RSFSR," in Edward Allworth, ed., *Ethnic Russia in the USSR*, New York, 1980, p. 24.

sult of such concern, the Brezhnev regime decided, in 1966, to publish *Sovetskaia Rossiia* under the sole sponsorship of the supraethnic Central Committee of the CPSU itself, but in 1974, a RSFSR connection was reestablished.) Similarly, in 1957, a publishing house devoted specifically to the interests of the life of the RSFSR, and also called "Sovetskaia Rossiia," came into existence. And in December 1959, "after decades of being merged indiscriminately into the USSR Union of Soviet Writers," the writers and poets of the RSFSR were able to hold their first constituent congress.[18] RSFSR organizations and publications are, understandably, more apt to reflect ethnic Russian concerns than are Union-wide organizations and publications. It is not surprising, therefore, that *Sovetskaia Rossiia* should have become a tribune of Russian nationalist sentiment in the 1970s.

Khrushchev's antireligious campaign with its attendent razing of ancient churches was perhaps even more important as a stimulus for the development of Russian nationalism. As has been seen, even before this campaign was launched, Vladimir Soloukhin had been deploring the indifference to the plight of Russian country churches. (A similar concern underlay Solzhenitsyn's "sketches" or prose poems of 1961, which at one point came close to finding a Soviet publisher.) Khrushchev's antireligious assault understandably induced a state of desperation among patriotically inclined Russians, including those relatively indifferent to the religious significance of the churches. The emergence of a multimillion-member voluntary society for the preservation of monuments in the mid-1960s was a direct response to this new socialist offensive. Andrei Tarkovskii's celebrated film, "Andrei Rublev" (1964), about a famous medieval iconographer and saint of the Orthodox Church, was probably also intended to fulfill an educational role. In the film, Rublev and the remarkable beauty he creates are contrasted to the stark barbarism and crudity of the society around him.[19]

---

[18] Ibid., p. 25.

[19] The scenario of the film was published in *Isskustvo kino*, nos. 4 & 5

Thus, one of the results of the Khrushchev campaign was to fuse believers and nationalists in a common struggle against a perceived national nihilism. An eventual fruit of this process was the Christianization of many nationalists and a growing interest in patriotic themes among Orthodox Christians. This did not occur, however, until after Khrushchev had been ousted from power. The fusion was particularly observable among the authors contributing to the *samizdat* journal *Veche*, which appeared from 1971 to 1974.

Another significant Russian nationalist reaction to Khrushchev's rule was the formation in February 1964 of a clandestine military-political organization, the All-Russian Social-Christian Union for the Liberation of the People (known by its Russian acronym, VSKhSON).[20] This organization, which numbered twenty-eight members and had some thirty candidates for membership at the time it was broken up by the KGB in 1967, represented an extremely militant response to Khrushchev and his program. Convinced of the impossibility of reform of the political system, VSKhSON contended that an armed overthrow of the communist dictatorship was the only solution to Russia's dilemma. It is noteworthy that many of the VSKhSON members had been believing Marxist-Leninists in their youth and that Khrushchev's "secret speech" undermined their attachment to the ideology.[21] VSKhSON's "positive" program, heavily influenced by the thought of émigré philosopher Nikolai Berdiaev (1874-1948), was an interesting attempt at a pathbreaking type of liberal Russian nationalism. It sought to envision the kind of society which would replace the Marxist one and anticipated the programmatic efforts of Solzhenitsyn and his friends a decade later.[22]

(1964). The 1972, no. 2, issue of the Belgian film journal *Arec Cinema* was entirely devoted to this film.

[20] On VSKhSON, see the collection of documents which I have compiled: *VSKhSON: Sbornik materialov*, Paris, 1975; and my study *The New Russian Revolutionaries*, Belmont, Mass., 1976.

[21] Dunlop, *VSKhSON: Sbornik materialov*, p. 94.

[22] On VSKhSON's "positive program," see chapter 11 of Dunlop, *The New Russian Revolutionaries*. An appendix in this volume contains a translation of the complete text of the organization's program. Analyzing the ideas of VSKhSON, British historian Geoffrey Hosking writes: "The attempt to com-

In sum, the Khrushchev period had the following results for the development of Russian nationalism: (1) By assaulting the monolithic world view of Stalinism, it tended to erode and undermine the integrity and credibility of Marxism-Leninism in the eyes of much of the populace, particularly the intelligentsia. (2) It galvanized Russian nationalists and Orthodox religious believers into action by virtue of its attack on ancient churches and other national monuments. (3) It began to provide the RSFSR with specifically Russian organizations and publications which were bound to reflect the concerns of ethnic Russians. While these developments affected primarily Russian intellectuals, the most salient effect on the masses was generated by the antireligious campaign, which alienated many of the tens of millions of Orthodox believers from the regime. Some of the reverberations of Khrushchev's rule would, however, be felt only under his successors.

By late 1964, Khrushchev was gone, and the Brezhnev-Kosygin "collective leadership" had assumed power. This dramatic change unleashed new and powerful currents in the country. Brezhnev and his associates set about firmly, though cautiously, to offset and reverse a number of perceived Khrushchevian "excesses." The intelligentsia reacted with agony and alarm. When two writers, Andrei Siniavskii and Iulii Daniel', were brought to trial in 1966 for publishing certain of their works abroad under pseudonyms, an important movement, usually known either as the "Russian Democratic Movement" or the "Russian Human Rights Movement," was triggered. Influential segments of the intelligentsia did battle

---

bine individualism and collectivism, democracy and a concern for inherited values, is extremely interesting. It has never been tried out, and no one can say that it is impracticable. The closest historical parallels are Mussolini's Italy and Tito's Yugoslavia but in those countries the presence of a single governing party would render them repugnant to the theorists of VSKhSON. The weakest aspect of their programme is the absence of any political link other than voting between the population and its rulers" (*Times Literary Supplement*, 3 December 1976, p. 1,509). Recent émigré Aleksandr Ianov (Alexander Yanov) has a lower opinion of VSKhSON's theoretical efforts; see his "The VSKhSON: The Beginning of the Dissident Right," in his study *The Russian New Right*, Berkeley, 1978, pp. 21-38.

to consolidate gains made under Khrushchev and to avert a
return to the Stalin terror.

By 1968 the Democratic Movement was in full swing. It
launched a publication, *Khronika tekushchikh sobytii* (Chronicle of Current Events),[23] and it was involved in the wave of
protest that followed the invasion of Czechoslovakia. The same
year also witnessed the formation of a Jewish "exodus" movement. Most of the participants in the movement were reformist Marxists or Western-style liberals and many of the leaders
were Jewish or part-Jewish, but on the fringes were some
liberal nationalists, such as Solzhenitsyn, as well as Orthodox
religious believers. (The movement's desire to safeguard freedom of conscience led to the formation of a link between it
and various Orthodox dissenters who were seeking to counter
the effects of the Khrushchev persecution.)[24]

The regime had its hands full with the "democrats" and
their supporters abroad, as well as with the increasingly res-
tive minority nationalities of the Soviet Union, and, not wishing to conduct a war on several fronts, moved immediately
after taking power to placate Russian nationalist and religious
elements. It also seems to have been the case that at least
some of the members of the new Politburo—the names of
D. S. Polianskii, deputy chairman of the Council of Ministers, and A. N. Shelepin, secretary of the Central Committee
and deputy chairman of the Council of Ministers, might be
cited here—sympathized with certain aims of the more conservative natonalists. As a result of the regime's retreat from
Khrushchevian socialist militancy, the years 1965-1966 saw a
mushrooming of the influence of Russian nationalism. In July
1965, the All-Russian Society for the Preservation of Historical and Cultural Monuments was founded by a decree of the
Council of Ministers of the RSFSR in order to halt the wanton destruction of Russian historical monuments, particularly
old churches. A year after its official inauguration, this voluntary society had three million members, and by 1972 its

[23] On this important publication, see Reddaway, *Uncensored Russia.*
[24] On these dissenters, see Michael Bourdeaux, ed., *Patriarch and Proph-
ets: Persecution of the Russian Orthodox Church Today*, London, 1969.

ranks had grown to seven million.[25] The journal *Molodaia gvardiia*, an official publication of the Central Committee of the Komsomol was taken over by a group of militant Russian nationalists, who proceeded to publish a series of articles which would give even a nominal communist palpitations. In 1966, for example, it published Souloukhin's bold *Letters from a Russian Museum*, about which a recent émigré has written the following: "In these letters he [Souloukhin] described the ancient Russian icons with unprecedented enthusiasm and artistry. He drew a wave of reader interest to this forbidden theme and doubtlessly influenced the growth of interest in religion in the consciousness of the intelligentsia and the youth."[26] Souloukhin's "Black Boards," another work about Russian icons and the plight of ancient churches, had a similar *succès de scandale* in 1969.

Even more controversial than the writings of Souloukhin during this period were those of such contributors to *Molodaia gvardiia* as S. N. Semanov, M. P. Lobanov, Iurii Ivanov, and Viktor Chalmaev.[27] Chalmaev's writings in particular stunned the Soviet intelligentsia; in Solzhenitsyn's words, he would have been "shoved into the GPU and soon shot" for such articles in the 1920s and 1930s.[28] (The *Molodaia gvardiia* episode will be treated at length in a later chapter.)

Similar changes, though not as dramatic, occurred in the area of state-church relations. As Bohdan Bociurkiw has written:

The hopes for the "normalization" of church-state relations were further strengthened by the evidence of a new "thaw"

[25] Dimitry Pospielovsky, "The Resurgence of Russian Nationalism in *Samizdat*," *Survey*, 19, no. 1 (1973), 52-53; and Thomas E. Bird, "New Interest in Old Russian Things," *Slavic Review*, 32, no. 1 (1973), 22-23, n. 29.

[26] Michael Meerson-Aksenov, "The Debate over the National Renaissance in Russia: Introduction," in Michael Meerson-Aksenov and Boris Shragin, eds., *The Political, Social and Religious Thought of Russian "Samizdat"— An Anthology*, Belmont, Mass., 1977, p. 346.

[27] The Semanov piece appeared in *Molodaia gvardiia*, no. 8 (1970); Lobanov's in no. 4 (1968); Ivanov's two contributions were published in nos. 6 and 12 (1969), and Chalmaev's in nos. 3 and 9 (1968).

[28] Aleksandr Solzhenitsyn, *Bodalsia telenok s dubom*, Paris, 1975, p. 269.

in Soviet ideological and cultural policies, which set in following the October 1964 plenum of the Party Central Committee. . . . The "thawing" of the post-Khrushchev ideological line was paralleled by the loss of momentum of the
anti-religious campaign. . . . In March, 1965, the monthly
Nauka i religiia (Science and Religion) published a sharp
criticism by its editors of the atheist writer Trubnikova for
her slanderous attacks on the clergy and believers and her
use of "undercover" methods to infiltrate the Orthodox circles. Along with *Nauka i religiia*, several Soviet newpapers
and journals opened their pages to the criticism and self-
criticism of the *antireligionzniki* for their vulgarization of
religion and preoccupation with the "frauds" and "immo-
rality" of the clergy, their insults to believers, and, especially, their frequent reliance on intimidation and coercion
in closing the churches and dissolving religious congrega-
tions . . .[29]

Bociurkiw stressed that these concessions "stopped short of
restoring to religious groups their pre-1959 legal and economic rights, or returning to them churches, monasteries and
theological schools which were closed during the Khru-
shchevite anti-religious campaign."[30]

The period of the middle and late sixties also witnessed the
growth of an important literary movement which had made
itself felt during the Khrushchev period—the *derevenshchiki*
or "ruralists," whose interest in the Russian village under the
Soviets dovetailed with a major concern of the nationalists.
Vasilii Belov's *Privychnoe delo* (That's How It Is, 1966), which
has been called "programmatic" by one Soviet critic,[31] was
perhaps the most influential work by a participant in this
movement. By the early 1970s, the *derevenshchiki*—who
boasted among their number such well-known authors as Ev-

[29] Bohdan Bociurkiw, "Religion in the USSR after Khrushchev," in John
W. Strong, ed., *The Soviet Union under Brezhnev and Kosygin*, New York,
1971, pp. 137-138.

[30] Ibid., p. 139.

[31] Iurii Seleznev, *Vechnoe dvizhenie: Iskaniia sovremennoi prozy 60-kh—
nachala 70-kh godov*, Moscow, 1976, p. 111.

genii Nosov, Boris Mozhaev, Vasilii Shukshin, Valentin Rasputin, Fedor Abramov, and Soloukhin—were incontestably the leading school of Soviet letters.

This same period saw a burgeoning of tourism to Russia's historic sites. In 1971, fifty million native tourists did the rounds, double the number for 1964.[32] Intellectuals began to comb the north in quest of rare icons and peasant artifacts. To be sure, much of this was a fad, and those who were snatching up printings of as large as 75,000 on subjects such as Russian architecture and iconography were not all convinced nationalists. But such printings did serve to feed a growing interest in and curiosity about Russia's heritage.

In 1969, with an article in the journal *Voprosy literatury*, Aleksandr Ianov, a journalist and historian who is now in the emigration, provoked an interesting and significant debate on the nineteenth-century Slavophiles.[33] It was the first time this controversial topic had been raised since 1941. The debate will be discussed in chapter 8.

There also emerged during this period certain extreme tendencies at least tangentially related to Russian nationalism. The *Chronicle of Current Events* reported the arrest in 1968 and subsequent confinement in a mental hospital of economist A. Fetisov and architects M. Antonov, V. Bykov, and O. Smirnov, whose views it summarized thus:

> The ideas of Fetisov and his followers are a critique of the Soviet political, economic and social system from an extreme totalitarian and chauvinistic position. Fetisov's work presents the historical development of mankind as having taken the form of a struggle between order and chaos, chaos having been embodied in the Jewish people, who created disorder in Europe for two thousand years, until the German and Slav principles—the totalitarian regimes of Hitler

[32] Georgie Anne Geyer, "A New Quest for the Old Russia," *Saturday Review*, 25 December 1971, p. 16.

[33] Aleksandr Ianov, "Zagadka slavianofil'skoi kritiki," *Voprosy literatury*, no. 5 (1969), 91-135. On the controversy generated by Ianov's article, see Vl. N. Pavlov, "Spory o slavianofil'stve i russkom patriotizme v sovetskoi nauchnoi literature, 1967-1970," *Grani*, no. 82 (1971), 195-209.

and Stalin—put a stop to this chaos. Fetisov and his supporters consider these regimes to have been historically
inevitable and positive phenomena. The economic programme of the group includes, in particular, the de-indus-
trialization of the European section of the U.S.S.R., the
transfer of industry and a mass deportation of workers to
Siberia, and the reestablishment of a system of patriar-
chally run communes on the territory of European Russia.
. . . Incidentally, in 1968, not long before his arrest, Fetisov left the party in protest against the de-Stalinization of
1956 . . .[34]

Since none of Fetisov's writings has reached the West
(though a lengthy study of the Slavophiles by Antonov appeared in *Veche*), the accuracy of the *Chronicle*'s description
cannot be confirmed. *Veche* later reported that Fetisov left
the psychiatric hospital "a hopelessly ill man," while Antonov
was "completely broken" there.[35] The latter journal has also
said that "National Bolshevik" rather than "neo-Fascist" would
be the appropriate term for describing the Fetisovites. (These
terms will be discussed in chapter 10.)

Other extremist phenomena during this period were Va-
lerii Skurlatov's "Code of Morals" and Iurii Ivanov's book
Caution Zionism! (1969). Skurlatov, a leading official of the
Moscow unit of the Komsomol, is reported to have distributed his "code" among activists of the Moscow City Committee and Komsomol Central Committee in 1965. A chilling
document, it calls for the sterilization of women who give
themselves to foreigners, the preservation of racial purity,
and corporal punishment and intensive barrack drill for Russian youth.[36] *Caution Zionism!*, written by a researcher for
the Communist Party Central Committee, puts forward a neo-
Nazi argument in Marxist rhetoric. The author sees the Jews

[34] Reddaway, *Uncensored Russia*, pp. 431-432.
[35] See the collection "Iz zhurnala 'Veche,' " *Vol'noe slovo*, no. 17-18 (1975),
160.
[36] For an English translation of this document, see Yanov, *The New Russian Right*, pp. 170-172.

as an almost cosmic power of evil bent upon Russia's destruction.[37]

By 1970, the regime was beginning to turn back the Democratic Movement and hence felt able to devote its attention to the Russian nationalists. After a struggle between the Central Committee's Bureau of Culture, which reportedly attempted to shield the nationalists, and the Bureau of Agitation and Propaganda, the latter finally managed to have the activities of *Molodaia gvardiia* examined at a session of the Politburo.[38] At this session, held in November 1970, Brezhnev himself came out against the journal's "line" and a decision was taken to remove the editor, Anatolii Nikonov, from his post. This crackdown was the first step in a cautious campaign against "russophilism." Brezhnev warned that "patriotism was good but that extremes of patriotism represented the danger of a departure from class consciousness."[39] Nationalists were advised that an interest in old churches could be dangerous and that the nineteenth-century Slavophiles had been reactionaries.

The year 1970 thus marked a watershed in the regime's tolerance for Russian nationalism. From then on it began to persecute manifestations of Russian patriotism which were not melded with Marxism-Leninism or at least combined with the so-called "Lenin theme."

At the same time, there was also an important turning point within the Russian dissident movement. Up until this time, "democrats" and liberal Russian nationalists had worked together fairly amicably within the Democratic Movement. Beginning in 1969-1970, however, the nineteenth-century controversy between Slavophiles and Westernizers was revived in *samizdat* writings. Though preceded by isolated polemical efforts in the sixties,[40] it was two neo-Westernizer docu-

[37] On this work, see Mikhail Agursky, "Selling Anti-Semitism in Moscow," *New York Review of Books*, 16 November 1972, pp. 19-23.
[38] "Osuzhdenie linii zhurnala 'Molodaia gvardiia,' " *Politicheskii dnevnik*, 2 (1975), 702.
[39] Geyer, "A New Quest," p. 16.
[40] For example, G. Pomerants, "Chelovek niotkuda," in the collection of his essays, *Neopublikovannoe*, Frankfurt/Main, 1972, pp. 123-175.

ments—the "Program of the Democratic Movement of the Soviet Union," published in Amsterdam in 1970, and a collection of articles appearing in the Paris publication *Vestnik russkogo studencheskogo khristianskogo dvizheniia* (Messenger of the Russian Student Christian Movement) in the same year—which served as the major catalysts for the debate.[41] The effect of the *Vestnik* essays, in fact, could be compared to that of Chaadaev's famous "philosophical letter" of 1836 which ignited the original Slavophile-Westernizer dispute. The "Program of the Democratic Movement" generated one important conservative nationalist statement, "The Nation Speaks" (1971), while the *Vestnik* contributions produced a flurry of rebuttals from many leading Russian nationalist spokesmen: Solzhenitsyn, Osipov, Leonid Borodin, Gennadii Shimanov, and others.[42] Two proto-programmatic works by Solzhenitsyn and his friends—*Letter to the Soviet Leaders* (1974) and *From under the Rubble* (1974)—can also in part be seen as a reply to the *Vestnik* authors. The appearance of Solzhenitsyn's *August 1914* in 1971, incidentally, served to place him squarely in the ranks of the nationalists, though some of them felt at the time that the novel was insufficiently patriotic.

The demise of *Molodaia gvardiia* as a militant nationalist tribune did not, it turned out, long deprive Russian nationalists of a forum for their views. Two months after Anatolii Nikonov's dismissal, there appeared an important *samizdat* journal, *Veche*, named after the medieval Russian popular assembly. The journal's editor, Vladimir Osipov (b. 1938), had earlier been arrested for *samizdat* activities and sentenced to seven years in the strict-regime camps. At the time he en-

---

[41] *Programma demokraticheskogo dvizheniia Sovetskogo Soiuza*, Amsterdam, 1970; and *Vestnik*, no. 97 (1970). The original title of this latter journal was *Vestnik russkogo studencheskogo khristianskogo dvizheniia*; in 1974, however, the word *studencheskogo* [student] was dropped. Henceforth, the journal will be cited simply as *Vestnik*.

[42] For statements by Osipov, "Ibragimov," and "Radugin," see *Vestnik*, no. 106 (1972), 294-296, 309-319. For Shimanov, see *Vestnik*, no. 104/105 (1972), 319-322, and AS 1132. For Borodin, see *Veche*, no. 8 (AS 1665), 131-160. Solzhenitsyn's comments on the *Vestnik* authors and their views can be found in the collection *From under the Rubble*, Boston, 1975, pp. 121-128, and in *Vestnik*, no. 111 (1974), 7.

tered the camps in 1961, Osipov had been an adherent of Yugoslav socialism; when he emerged in 1968, his views had altered. In his words: "Not without reason is a concentration camp officially called a corrective labor colony. They come in atheists and go out Christians. They have been *corrected*." And he continues: "The camp made me a man believing in God, in Russia, and in the legacy of my forefathers."[43] Before *Veche* was suppressed by the KGB in 1974, it succeeded in attracting a considerable audience. Correspondents fed in news, articles, translations, and letters to the editor from such diverse locations as Moscow, Leningrad, Kiev, Vladimir Province, Kalinin, Irkutsk, and Barnaul. In an interview given to two American correspondents in 1972, Osipov outlined the aims of his journal:

1. to protect monuments of material and spiritual culture from destruction;
2. to foster a respect for national shrines and for one's own national dignity;
3. to recover Russia's cultural greatness;
4. to support a love for one's homeland and the Orthodox Church;
5. to elucidate and discuss pressing problems related to contemporary national life;
6. to elucidate and discuss problems of contemporary Russian culture.[44]

The significance of *Veche* for the study of contemporary Russian nationalism can scarcely be exaggerated. The ten bulky issues of the journal, which are available at the Radio Liberty Samizdat Archive, represent a unique window on the thought and core sentiments of contemporary Russian nationalists. *Veche* successfully realized its goal of serving as a forum for Russian nationalists of all persuasions; virtually all strands of the tendency, though to varying degrees, make an appearance in its pages.

[43] Vladimir Osipov, "Ploshchad' Maiakovskogo, stat'ia 70-aia," *Grani*, no. 80 (1971), 131, 135 (Osipov's italics).
[44] See *Vestnik*, no. 106 (1972), 300-301.

Although *Veche* was at pains to underline its nonpolitical character and complete loyalty to the regime, the KGB continually harassed its editors and contributors. Sometime in late 1973 or early 1974 the regime seems to have attempted to co-opt at least some of *Veche*'s participants. According to Jewish activist Mikhail Agurskii, who had close links to the nationalists, this failed because the *Veche* contributors found the neo-pagan national socialism being proposed by representatives of the regime out of keeping with their Christian convictions.[45] The authorities then put intense pressure on the journal's network; homes were searched, typewriters and other materials were seized, and a score of persons were summoned to the KGB for interrogations. In March 1974, Osipov announced that he was suspending publication; in July, another *Veche* faction, after publishing a tenth number of the journal, was forced to make a similar announcement.[46] Undaunted by these events, Osipov and a deputy editor, Viacheslav Rodionov, launched a new nationalist journal, *Zemlia* (The Land), in August 1974. On November 28, after the appearance of the second issue of *Zemlia*, Osipov was arrested, and no new numbers of the journal have come out since that time. A former member of VSKhSON, Leonid Borodin, started up another *samizdat* nationalist journal, *Moskovskii sbornik* (Moscow Miscellany, named after a nineteenth-century Slavophile publication), in 1974, but it too was quickly suppressed.

The period 1971-1974 thus marked an important stage in the evolution of contemporary Russian nationalism—what might be called its *samizdat* stage. Compared with the middle and late sixties, when nationalists were free to an astonishing de-

[45] Mikhail Agurskii, "Neonatsistskaia opasnost' v Sovetskom Soiuze," *Novyi zhurnal*, no. 118 (1975), 199-204. An English translation of this essay, entitled "The Intensification of Neo-Nazi Dangers in the Soviet Union," appears in Meerson-Aksenov and Shragin, *Political Social and Religious Thought*, pp. 414-419. A slightly revised version can be found in *Midstream*, February 1976, pp. 35-42.

[46] Vladimir Osipov, "Ekstrennoe zaiavlenie dlia pechati" (AS 1705); Anonimnoe soobshchenie, "O vykhode 10-go nomera zhurnala 'Veche' " (AS 1706); and "Po povodu vystupleniia V. Osipova protiv zhurnala 'Veche' " (AS 1787).

gree to air their views in the official press, the early seventies saw a crackdown by the regime against perceived excesses of "russophilism"; this campaign, in turn, served to radicalize dissenting nationalists and to alienate them further from the social and political system. During this period, the ideology of the Soviet state and Russian patriotism were increasingly seen as incompatible by nationalists, while a communality of interests with the Russian Church was more and more recognized. In their *samizdat* polemics against neo-Westernizer dissidents, the nationalists began to think in increasingly programmatic terms, as for example in Solzhenitsyn's *Letter to the Soviet Leaders* and the collection *From under the Rubble*.

During the early 1970s, the Democratic Movement was evidently in a growing state of disarray. By 1972, the regime appeared to be in command of the situation and winning the battle against the movement. It achieved this result through an astute use of coercive tools: some "democrats" were encouraged to emigrate, some were arrested and placed in prisons and camps, some were confined to prison mental hospitals, some were subjected to administrative exile. The 1973 show trial of human-rights activists Petr Iakir and Viktor Krasin, in which the two principals betrayed many of their former friends, demoralized many. Forced emigration, however, was undoubtedly the most successful weapon employed by the regime; by the mid-seventies most of the leaders of the Democratic Movement were in the West, though some, such as Academician Andrei Sakharov, remained to carry on the fight.

In early 1973, a moderate Russian nationalist, writing under the pseudonym "K. Zhitnikov," penned an important essay on the decline of the Democratic Movement.[47] The movement, he concluded, had been only

> the last splash of the wave whose crown was the 22nd [Party] Congress. The idea of this period of our history [was] to

---

[47] K. Zhitnikov, "Zakat demokraticheskogo dvizheniia," *Vestnik*, no. 106 (1972), 275-293. For an English translation, see Meerson-Aksenov and Shragin, *Political, Social and Religious Thought*, pp. 233-255.

reform communism, to pour new vital forces into it. . . . The end of the "Democratic Movement" is not the end of attempts to free the nation from communism, but is, evidently, the end of the last serious attempt to re-vitalize communism in our country. . . . It is quite possible that Khrushchev's reformation, and the "Democratic Movement" which continued it, attempted to coordinate fundamentally incompatible tendencies, i.e., they were destined to lose. The example of our country and that of Czechoslovakia are indications of this. . . . The "Democratic Movement" in general has asked few questions. Its literature consisted primarily of appeals; its activity of protests. For this reason, it may not be so surprising that in this literature the following simple and fundamental question has not been asked even once: *What has been the meaning of our history in the last half century?*[48]

While "Zhitnikov's" essay neglected some points—for example, the evolution of members of the Democratic Movement from reformist Marxists and socialists to Western-style liberals[49]—he was essentially correct in maintaining that the movement carried on the momentum of the Khrushchev reforms. Had that momentum been permitted to continue, the end result would have been a dismantling of the communist totalitarian apparatus. By the early 1970s, however, the era of the "democrat" had passed and that of the nationalist had arrived.

"Zhitnikov" emphasized in his essay that the Democratic Movement had performed valuable services for the country:

. . . we should remember that which was a great discovery for our nation: the "Democratic Movement" provided the first opportunity for each person to realize that the fate of the country could depend on the actions of an individual. The feeling of the freedom of the will was resurrected, the

[48] Meerson-Aksenov and Shragin, *Political, Social and Religious Thought*, pp. 250-251, 253 (Zhitnikov's italics).

[49] See, Andrei Sakharov's interview with Swedish radio correspondent Olle Stenholm, in *Sakharov Speaks*, New York, 1974, pp. 166-178.

freedom of choice was created, the path of sacrifice was opened. This is, of course, the moral example of such martyrs of the "Movement" as Galanskov and Bukovskii. They will have an influence on all our future history while the inaccuracies of their own world-view or the apostasy in the disorderly ranks of the "Movement" will soon be forgotten.[50]

Some Russian nationalist activists agree with "Zhitnikov's" charitable view of the services of the "democrats," while others do not. An interesting *samizdat* debate on this topic took place in 1973-1974 between Vladimir Osipov, who defended the "democrats," and Gennadii Shimanov, who attacked them.[51] Osipov's views were essentially those of "Zhitnikov," though he agreed with Shimanov in deploring the fact that so many "democrats" had "run off" to the West. Shimanov, on the other hand, while admitting that only God can serve as the judge of man, nevertheless criticized Andrei Sakharov as "only a nominally Russian man," promoting an antinational, Westernizing, and bourgeois-democratic program. General Petr Grigorenko was castigated for not being able to go any further in his thinking than "liberal communism," while Andrei Amal'rik was accused of "blindly and haughtily" passing judgment on his own people.

FATHER DUDKO

The year 1974, as we have seen, witnessed a serious crackdown against the dissenting variant of Russian nationalism; the years 1979-1980 saw another. In the interval, center stage for the dissenting nationalists was occupied by two Russian Orthodox priests, Fr. Dimitrii Dudko and Fr. Gleb Iakunin, and by their associates and followers and two important reli-

[50] Meerson-Aksenov and Shragin, *Political, Social and Religious Thought*, p. 255.
[51] See AS 1846, which contains Shimanov's "Pis'mo Natal'e Sergeevne," Osipov's "Otkrytoe pis'mo Gennadiiu Shimanovu," and Shimanov's "Kak otnosit'sia k Sovetskoi vlasti (otvet V. N. Osipovu)."

gio-philosophical seminars which were held in Moscow and Leningrad.

In the period preceding his arrest in January 1980, Fr. Dimitrii Dudko achieved a moral stature among Russian nationalists which rivaled that of Solzhenitsyn. He became, in a certain sense, a "shadow patriarch" of the Russian Church. Fr. Dudko first attracted national attention in late 1973, when he began to give the sermons which he preached every Saturday night the character of a dialogue with the faithful. In the words of one commentator:

> [Fr. Dudko] suggested that questions might be submitted to him in writing, so that answers might be given in the following sermon. Soon, however, he also began to answer direct questions presented by members of the congregation. Inevitably the questions touched upon antireligious propaganda, upon repression of religion, upon government control of the church. Fr. Dudko did not ask for such provocative questions, but he did not avoid them either. . . . The character and content of the sermons was so unusual that the small church of St. Nicholas [in Moscow] was soon full beyond capacity on Saturday night. Young people, intellectuals, believers and non-believers—and also foreign journalists—flocked to hear Fr. Dimitrii.[52]

Fr. Dudko did not attempt to conceal his strong Russian nationalist views. He was a contributor to Osipov's short-lived journal *Zemlia* and signed his Easter sermon for 1977, in which he advocated a spiritual war for Russia's liberation from cap-

[52] Fr. John Meyendorff, "Foreword" to Fr. Dmitrii Dudko, *Our Hope*, Crestwood, N.Y., 1977, p. 9. This volume is a translation of *O nashem upovanii: Besedy*, Paris, 1975. Two other volumes of Fr. Dudko's writings and conversations with believers have been published in the West: *Veriu, Gospodi!*, London, Ont., 1976, and *Voskresnye sobesedovaniia*, Montreal, 1977. See also the collection of Fr. Dudko's writings in *Vol'noe slovo*, no. 33 (1979). Those interested in the reasons for the current religious revival in Russia should consult two recent writings of Fr. Dudko: "Kreshchenie na Rusi (Iz dnevnika sviashchennika)," *Vestnik*, no. 117 (1976), 188-208, and "Pokaianie na Rusi: Iz dnevnika sviashchennika," *Vestnik*, no. 119 (1976), 254-280. On Fr. Dimitrii, see Anatolii Levitin-Krasnov, "Otets Dimitrii Dudko," *Posev*, no. 1 (1975), 26-36.

tivity, "Fr. Dimitrii Dudko, Soldier of the Russian Army."[53]
The authorities, of course, came to regard Fr. Dimitrii's activities, particularly his successful overtures to Russian youth, with displeasure. The docile Moscow Patriarchate was required several times to transfer him to parishes outside Moscow, an attempt seems to have been made on his life, and he was savagely attacked in *Literaturnaia gazeta* in early 1977.[54]
He was arrested in early 1980 and apparently broken in captivity. On 20 June 1980, he abjectly confessed his "errors" on Soviet television, and his statement was printed in *Izvestiia* the following day.[55]

THE CHRISTIAN COMMITTEE

On 27 December, 1976, the Christian Committee for the Defense of the Rights of Believers in the USSR was founded in Moscow by Orthodox priest Gleb Iakunin, Deacon Varsonofii Khaibulin, and layman Viktor Kapitanchuk. Fr. Iakunin's name had been known to readers of *samizdat* since 1965, when he cosigned a lengthy appeal to Patriarch Aleksii of the Moscow Patriarchate protesting the ravages wrought by the Khrushchev persecution of 1959-1964. Khaibulin and Kapitanchuk had been active in nationalist affairs and had links to the journal *Veche*. In a declaration explaining the reasons for the establishment of their committee, Fr. Iakunin and his colleagues wrote: "At the present time, the episcopate of the Russian Orthodox Church and the leaders of other religious organizations [in the Soviet Union] do not, for various reasons, engage in the defense of the rights of believers. Under such conditions, the legal defense of believers must become

[53] "Paskhal'noe privetsvie o. Dimitriia Dudko," *Russkaia mysl'*, 5 May 1977, p. 2.

[54] The apparent attempt on Fr. Dudko's life occurred on 9 April 1975. See the account in *Russkaia mysl'*, 29 January 1976, p. 6. For the newspaper attack, see Boris Roshchin, "Svoboda religii i klevetniki," *Literaturnaia gazeta*, 13 April 1977, p. 14, and 20 April 1977, p. 14.

[55] On the television statement, see *New York Times*, 21 June 1980, p. 2. Subsequently, Fr. Dudko came to regret this statement. See his private letters published in *Novaia gazeta* (New York), 8-14 September 1980, p. 10.

the task of Christian social opinion [*obshchestvennost'*]."[56] The
aims of the committee, they said, were:

1. to collect, study, and disseminate information on the
   position of believers in the USSR;
2. to offer consultative assistance to believers in case of the
   infringement of their civil rights;
3. to address state agencies on questions concerning the
   rights of believers;
4. to carry out research to determine the legal and *de facto*
   position of religion in the USSR;
5. to assist the improvement of Soviet legislation on religion.[57]

The committee set about with zeal and dedication to pub-
licize abuses of the rights of believers in the USSR; by late
1979 it had issued hundreds of documents. In a sense, the
committee and its activities could be seen as continuing the
work of the Democratic Movement. But the presence on it
of two obvious Russian nationalists, Khaibulin and Kapitanchuk, and its championing of such popular causes as the re-
opening of the Kiev-Pechersk Lavra (Monastery), a national
shrine which had been closed down by the authorities in 1961,
permit one to consider it as to some degree a nationalist organization.

The Christian Committee was the last of the Helsinki Accord monitoring groups to be subjected to arrests. The committee's turn seemed to have come in April 1977, when *Literaturnaia gazeta* attacked Fr. Iakunin and other religious
activists in unambiguous terms. However, nothing happened

[56] "Declaration" of 27 December 1976 in "Khristianskii komitet zashchity
prav veruiushchikh v SSSR: Dokumenty," *Vol'noe slovo*, no. 28 (1977), 3.
Ten volumes of committee documents, entitled *Documents of the Christian
Committee for the Defense of Believers Rights in the USSR: Russian Texts
with English Summary Translations*, have been issued by the Washington
Street Research Center in San Francisco. A fourth member, Vadim Shche-
glov, was added to the committee in December 1977. Fr. Khaibulin resigned
from the committee in December 1978. Two other Orthodox priests, Fr.
Vasilii Fonchenkov and Fr. Nikolai Gainov, subsequently joined the committee.

[57] "Declaration," *Vol'noe slovo*, no. 28 (1977), 4.

at that time. Fr. Iakunin attempted to explain the regime's hesitancy at a press conference held in Moscow in late April 1977. "Christianity," he said, "has a powerful social base in our country and abroad—we have tens of millions of believers [in the USSR]. The authorities, naturally, are afraid of drawing the broad strata of believers into a movement of protest against religious oppression." And he continued: "If the influx of people into the Baptists, Adventists and Pentecostalists can be measured in the hundreds and the thousands, the influx into the Orthodox Church may be measured in the hundreds of thousands, i.e., the process may be a mass one. And the authorities fear this."[58]

Between November 1979 and March 1980, however, three leaders of the committee—Fr. Iakunin, Kapitanchuk, and Lev Regel'son—were arrested. In August 1980, Fr. Iakunin was sentenced to five years in the camps, to be followed by five years of exile. But Kapitanchuk and Regel'son expressed "sincere contrition" over their activities and received five-year suspended sentences.[59] The Christian Committee had been decimated, if not permanently destroyed.

THE RELIGIO-PHILOSOPHICAL SEMINARS

Meanwhile, a number of religio-philosophical *kruzhki* (circles) and seminars sprang up in the middle and late 1970s. If there was a single impetus for the formation of these circles, it was probably the overtures made toward Russian youth by Fr. Dudko in Moscow in 1973. In October 1974, a religio-philosophical seminar was initiated in Moscow by Aleksandr Ogorodnikov (b. 1950).[60] The seminar combined religious and national themes, and it is significant that *Literaturnaia gazeta*, in an attack on Ogorodnikov in April 1977 accused him of being a monarchist.

[58] *Vol'noe slovo*, no. 28 (1977), 80, 85.
[59] On the trials, see *Russkaia mysl'*, 4 September 1980, p. 3; 2 October 1980, p. 4; and 16 October 1980, p.3.
[60] On the Moscow seminar, see the materials in *Vestnik*, no. 119 (1976), 281-334; and in *Vol'noe slovo*, no. 29 (1978) and 39 (1980).

From 1976 on, the authorities subjected the Moscow seminar to unremitting persecution. Members were sent to mental hospitals, homes were searched, and, beginning in 1979, prison sentences were meted out to the leaders and the most active rank-and-file members. Ogorodnikov was given a one-year sentence in 1979, and then a six-year sentence (plus five years of exile) in 1980. Another leader, Vladimir Poresh (b. 1949), was sentenced in 1980 to five years in the camps, to be followed by three years of exile. Other seminar members sentenced were: Sergei Ermolaev, four years; Igor' Poliakov, three-and-a-half years; Tat'iana Shchipkova, three years; and Vladimir Burtsev and Viktor Popkov, eighteen months each.[61] The seminar was seriously stricken by this wave of arrests.

Like the Christian Committee, the Moscow seminar adopted the opening of the Kiev-Pechersk Lavra as a short-term goal. Before his arrest, Ogorodnikov and two friends, Poresh from Leningrad and Nikolai Khovanskii from Vitebsk, formed a committee to achieve that end. In a letter to Brezhnev, dated 10 November 1977, they wrote:

We the Orthodox youth of Russia, who from childhood on have been isolated from truth and from history, have found Truth in the Church of Christ the Saviour and address the Supreme Soviet with these words: return to the Russian Church the hearth [ochag] of Russian sanctity—the Kiev-Pechersk Lavra. . . . Destroyed several times by the Tatars in 1240, 1299 and 1316 and lovingly restored by the people, it was turned into an antireligious museum in 1961. The closing of the Lavra is a coarse insult to the religious feelings of believers and a trampling under foot of the national dignity of every Russian.[62]

It will be noted that religious and national motifs are combined in this letter, which is militant in tone. The Moscow

[61] Concerning the trials, see *Russkaia mysl'*, 17 April 1980, p. 1; 12 June 1980, p. 4; 10 July 1980, p. 4; 4 September 1980, p. 6; and 25 September 1980, p. 2; and *New York Times*, 9 September 1980.

[62] *Documents of the Christian Committee*, vol. 1, p. 46.

seminar also published a *samizdat* journal, *Obshchina* (Commune), which the KGB sought to suppress.[63]

Some useful background information is available on the participants in the Moscow seminar.[64] Most of them were raised in atheist families and, after rejecting the official ideology at an early age, moved through various currents, such as left radicalism, nihilism, hippyism, youth counterculture and "existential anguish," to an affiliation with the Russian Church. The journey, Ogorodnikov has written, was seldom an easy one and was in no way assisted by the official Church, which he described as "a captive church hierarchy, frightened to death, by whose hands the atheists administer the Church."[65]

In the fall of 1975, a religio-philosophical seminar was founded in Leningrad, when several members of the "creative intelligentsia" decided to join together to study the Church Fathers.[66] By the second year of the seminar's existence, its active membership had grown to 2,000, and there were a number of sympathizers as well. In early 1977, due to shifting interests among its burgeoning membership, the seminar changed its focus from the Church Fathers to more socially oriented themes, such as "Religion and Culture," "Religion and Ethics," "Christianity and Humanism," and "Christianity and the National Question." The attitude that a participant should have toward the authorities and politics was apparently also an item of lively discussion at sessions of the seminar. As of early 1981, the Leningrad seminar was reported to be flourishing, untouched by the authorities.[67]

[63] For selections from *Obshchina*, see *Vol'noe slovo*, no. 39 (1980).

[64] See A. Ogorodnikov, "Khristianskii kruzhok v Moskve," *Vestnik*, no. 119 (1976), 296-308, and "SSSR: Khristianstvo molodeet?," *Vol'noe slovo*, no. 29 (1978), 53-55.

[65] Ogorodnikov, "Khristianskii kruzhok," p. 299.

[66] See E. Giriaev, "Religiozno-filosofskii seminar v Leningrade," *Vestnik*, no. 123 (1977), 169-174; N. Giriaev, "Obzor materialov publikovannykh v samizdatovskom zhurnale '37,'" *Vestnik*, no. 121 (1977), 294-300; "Kul'turno-dukhovnoe dvizhenie v Leningrade," *Posev*, no. 3 (1977), 9-18; and Tat'iana Goricheva, "Khristianstvo i kul'tura. Zdes' i teper': Doklad prochitannyi na religiozno-filosofskom seminare 17 fervralia 1978 goda," *Russkaia mysl'*, 21 September 1978, p. 5; and "Vstrecha dvukh zhurnalov," *Posev*, no.4 (1979), 6-7.

[67] T. Goricheva, "O nashem religioznom opyte," *Veche: Nezavisimyi rus-*

Recently, there has also emerged a remarkable Russian Orthodox "women's movement" in the Soviet Union, centered around the so-called Maria Club. Although the original leaders of the club—Tat'iana Goricheva, Natal'ia Malakhovskaia, and Iuliia Voznesenskaia—have been deported or forced to emigrate, the organization continues to exist. As its documents show, the Maria Club is unquestionably Russian nationalist in orientation.[68]

The problem which Christian *kruzhki*, seminars, and clubs present for the regime is self-evident. Students of Russian history are aware of the role which *kruzhki* have played in the past in crystallizing ideas and paving the way for political change. According to Evgenii Vagin, a former leader of VSKhSON who was permitted to emigrate to the West, some of the participants in the *kruzhki* eventually decided to devote themselves full-time to the service of the Church but others began "to interest themselves more deeply in social and political problems." He concluded: "On the basis of the experience acquired in such circles, there could appear the seeds of future political organizations." Vagin also believes that the outreach of the *kruzhki* to the provinces is politically significant: ". . . unquestionably, the future of Russia depends a great deal on the extent to which the provinces will awaken, the extent to which all the processes of democratization and spiritual rebirth will touch their depths."[69]

A comment made by Solzhenitsyn in 1976 provides a concise conclusion to this discussion of the dissenting nationalists. Religion, he said, is the "organizing pivot" of intellectual ferment in today's USSR.[70]

---

skii al'manakh, 1 (1981), 31-33. This new *Veche*, published in West Germany and edited by Oleg Krasovskii and Evgenii Vagin, seeks to provide a forum for Russian nationalist views both in the USSR and in the emigration.

[68] See the informative articles by Vadim Nechaev in *Russkaia mysl'*, 17 July 1980, p. 4, and 14 August 1980, p. 6; and the pieces by Iu. Voznesenskaia and N. Malakhovskaia in *Posev*, no. 4 (1981).

[69] E. A. Vagin, "Litsom k Rossii: Interv'iu E. A. Vagina 'Posevu,' " *Posev*, no. 10 (1976), 53-54.

[70] Aleksandr Solzhenitsyn, "O rabote russkoi sektsii 'Bi-Bi-Si,' " *Kontinent*, no. 9 (1976), 218.

The "Official" Nationalists

As far as nationalists who seek to work within the Soviet system to achieve their aims are concerned, the evidence suggests that they are as strong as, if not stronger than, they were during the *Molodaia gvardiia* period in the middle and late sixties. (It is noteworthy that most of *Molodaia gvardiia*'s controversial authors during that period—Semanov, Lobanov, and Chalmaev—have been permitted to continue publishing.[71]) To be sure, "official" nationalists must now express themselves more circumspectly in print than they did earlier, but they have nevertheless succeeded in making their views clear to friend and foe alike. The nationalists appear to be a controlling faction on the newspaper *Sovetskaia Rossiia*, which had a circulation of 2.7 million in 1975,[72] and are at times granted access to the pages of other newspapers, including *Pravda* and *Literaturnaia gazeta*. They play a major role on the editorial boards of such journals as *Molodaia gvardiia* (1981 circulation, 870,000), *Moskva* (500,000), and *Nash sovremennik* (336,000). Other publications influenced by the nationalists are *Literaturnaia Rossiia*, *Volga*, *Don*, *Avrora*, *Neva*, *Sever*, and *Sibirskie ogni*. Still other journals and magazines, for instance *Ogonek*, frequently open their pages to the nationalists.[73] A number of Soviet publishing houses—for example, "Sovetskaia Rossiia," "Molodaia gvardiia," and "Sovremennik"—regularly bring out nationalist writings, often in editions in the hundreds of thousands.

The journal *Roman-gazeta* deserves separate discussion, since it publishes longer prose works in mass editions (the average printing for the 1980 issues was 2,540,000). In 1980, the editorial board of *Roman-gazeta* contained six identifiable Rus-

[71] See, for example, M. Lobanov, *Nadezhda iskanii: Literaturno-kriticheskie stat'i*, Moscow, 1978; V. Chalmaev, "Vozvrashchenie k muzyke," *Sever*, no. 8 (1976), 111-125; and S. Semanov, *Serdtse rodiny*, Moscow, 1977.

[72] Edward Allworth, "Ambiguities in Russian Group Identity," p. 24.

[73] Lev Z. Kopelev, "A Lie Is Conquered Only in Truth," in Roy A. Medvedev, ed., *The Samizdat Register*, New York, 1977, p. 225; and Mikhail Agursky, "The New Russian Literature," Research Paper no. 40 (1980), Soviet and East European Research Centre, Hebrew University of Jerusalem, pp. 20-21.

sian nationalists: Iurii Bondarev, Leonid Leonov, Evgenii Nosov, Petr Proskurin, Valentin Rasputin, and Sergei Zalygin. Works published during the period from 1978 to 1980 included writings by Bondarev, Proskurin, and Rasputin as well as by such other nationalists as Viktor Likhonosov, Fedor Abramov, Iurii Nagibin, and Viktor Astaf'ev. The last-mentioned, a Siberian writer, received a state prize in 1978 for his nationalist polemic *Tsar'-ryba* (Kingfish), which had appeared in *Roman-gazeta* the preceding year.

One does not have to explain to specialists the unique role of belles-lettres in the contemporary Soviet Union. As in nineteenth-century Russia, censorship conditions are such that literature and "literary criticism" are the easiest and safest ways to get one's ideas into print. It is largely in contemporary belles-lettres and in criticism that the battle between the nationalists and their opponents is taking place.

THE SHUKSHIN AFFAIR

What degree of mass support do nationalist writers and artists enjoy? Since the Soviet authorities do not encourage public polls, and since they do not publish any evidence they may have on the subject, this question is not easily answered. Occasionally, however, a dramatic incident augments our knowledge. The Vasilii Shukshin episode of 1974 was such an incident.

When the gifted writer, actor, and film producer Vasilii Shukshin died in 1974 at the age of forty-five, an extraordinary outpouring of tribute took place. A two-volume *Selected Works* was issued in a printing of 200,000, a one-volume compendium of his writings appeared in an edition of 300,000, and two numbers of *Roman-gazeta* were devoted to his stories.[74] The Shukshin family and the State Cinema Committee

---

[74] See Michel Heller, "Vasily Shukshin: In Search of Freedom," in Donald M. Fiene, ed., *Vasily Shukshin: Snowball Berry Red and Other Stories*, Ann Arbor, 1979, p. 213. The Russian original of this article appeared in *Vestnik*, no. 120 (1977), 159-182. See also my review article "The Search for Peace," *Times Literary Supplement*, 30 June 1978, pp. 739-740.

received a total of 160,000 letters of condolence, and people lined up at Shukshin's grave for weeks after his death. A Moscow street was named for the writer, and a cinema scholarship was established in his honor.[75] For his film *Kalina krasnaia* (Snowball Berry Red), which had created a sensation when released in 1974, Shukshin was posthumously awarded the Lenin Prize. Such hommage for a Russian nationalist and "ruralist" writer with a keen interest in ancient churches and a strong curiosity about Orthodox Christianity was unusual, to say the least. (This episode will be examined in greater detail in chapter five.)

THE GLAZUNOV AFFAIR

The Moscow and Leningrad exhibits of paintings by Il'ia Glazunov (b. 1930), a fervent nationalist who does not conceal his sympathy for Russian Orthodoxy, were also noteworthy events of this period. A driving force among "official" nationalists, Glazunov was more responsible than anyone else for bringing about the founding of the All-Russian Society for the Preservation of Historical and Cultural Monuments in 1965. In June 1978, he was permitted to show 400 of his canvases at the Manezh Exhibition Hall in Moscow. The exhibit, which drew as many as 20,000 visitors a day, was the major Russian cultural event of 1978.[76] The greatest attraction of the show was a ten-by-six-foot oil titled "The Return of the Prodigal Son," which an American correspondent described thus:

It depicts a young man in blue jeans kneeling before a Christlike figure. Behind and below the young man are symbols of his (Russia's?) ill-starred past—three huge pigs around a modern skyscraper; a banquet table stained with blood and wine and bearing the head of a man on a platter; a harlot and a run-down church; a monument to a young boy [Pav-

[75] Information conveyed by former Moscow correspondent Nils Morten Udgaard at a conference on Russian Nationalism held at the Kennan Institute in June 1978.

[76] Craig Whitney, "Unbridled Artist Proves Popular at Soviet Show," *New York Times*, 18 June 1978, p. 12.

lik Morozov] who betrayed his father as a "kulak." Behind
the Christ figure are ghostly faces from Russia's religious
and cultural past.[77]

The month-long Moscow exhibit attracted some 500,000 to
600,000 viewers.[78] The following year the exhibit moved to
Leningrad, where it was reported that 1,000,000—a quarter
of the city's population—queued up to see the paintings of
their native son.[79] The comment books from the two exhibits
have reached the West and have been published, and they
strongly suggest that Glazunov's religio-patriotic message has
wide appeal. The comment books will be discussed in detail
in chapter 5.

Obviously the nationalists could not survive, let alone
flourish, without powerful support. The Leningrad Party authorities are reported to have strenuously objected to the
Glazunov exhibit, and it was derided in *Leningradskaia pravda*,
yet the exhibit nevertheless took place; some individual or
individuals must have intervened to overrule the Leningrad
authorities.[80] The degree and nature of support for the nationalists at the top of the Party and State apparatus, and the
relevance of this support to the Brezhnev succession, will be
considered in chapter 10.

The development of Russian nationalism during the Brezhnev period may be summarized as follows: (1) From 1964 to
1970, the regime generally maintained a "hands off" policy in
order to concentrate on its opponents within the Democratic
Movement and in order to separate itself clearly from the
policies of the Khrushchev era. This led to the *Molodaia
gvardiia* affair and to a strikingly open discussion of nationalist themes in the official press. The Khrushchev war on re-

[77] Dan Fisher, "Russian Masses Jam Ilya Glazunov Exhibit," *San Francisco Chronicle*, Sunday *This World* magazine, 10 September 1978, p. 56.

[78] Fisher gives the figure as "some 500,000 visitors," whereas West German specialist O. Krasovskii sets it as "almost 600,000" (*Publitsisticheskaia
tetrad'* no. 5 [1978], published by the Rossiiskoe Natsional'noe Ob"edinenie
v Federativnoi Respublike Germanii).

[79] *Khudozhnik i Rossiia*, Düsseldorf, 1980, p. 154. This volume contains
the comment books to both the Moscow and Leningrad exhibits.

[80] Ibid., pp. 153-154.

ligion was toned down, though no attempt was made to permit the Church to recoup its losses. Toward the end of this period, a split between neo-Slavophiles and neo-Westernizers appeared in the ranks of Soviet dissidents. (2) In 1970, the regime purged *Molodaia gvardiia* and began to persecute what it considered to be extreme versions of Russian nationalism, i.e., those which sought in too obvious fashion to downplay the import of Marxist-Leninist ideology or of military-industrial expansion. This period was marked by a campaign, albeit a relatively cautious one, against "russophilism." (3) The years 1970-1974 witnessed the *samizdat* response of Russian nationalists to the regime's new stance and to the attacks by its neo-Westernizer opponents. The journal *Veche* was founded and Solzhenitsyn and his friends issued several important liberal nationalist texts. With the weakening of the Democratic Movement in the early seventies, the role of the nationalist revival increased in strength and influence. (4) In the period from 1974 until 1979-1980, i.e., following the suppression of *Veche* and the expulsion of Solzhenitsyn, the most active role among the dissenting nationalists was assumed by Russian Orthodox clergymen and their associates and by the Orthodox youth meeting in religio-philosophical seminars. In 1979-1980, after several years of hesitating, the authorities clamped down on these organizations and individuals, and a wave of arrests and trials decimated their ranks. "Official" nationalists, on the other hand, continued and still continue to air their views in mass editions of their works—for which they receive honors and state prizes—though they must do this a bit more cautiously than they did in the late 1960s.

The year 1982, which witnessed the deaths of Brezhnev and Suslov and the removal of Kirilenko from the Politburo, left the Soviet Union poised on the brink of potentially major changes. As Brezhnev and his fellow rulers—the "last generation of Russian communists," as Andrei Amal'rik has called them[81]—inevitably pass from the scene, it becomes appropri-

[81] In a discussion between Amal'rik and the author in 1979.

3

The Voluntary Societies

". . . When the church was closed they took all the icons
away."
"Where to, do you remember . . . ?"
"They turned them into horse-troughs. There might be times
when you'd be feeding a horse and you'd bend over the
trough and get the fright of your life to see the face of
Christ or the Virgin looking up at you. Such stern faces
and big eyes—it made your heart stop beating."
Vladimir Soloukhin[1]

Our homeland comprises a sixth part of the dying planet.
The gloom of industry hangs suspended over the vast spaces
of [St.] Sergii of Radonezh. And we ask: *Is there still time
to save Russia?*
Veche, no. 3[2]

We have dirtied and disfigured the heart of Russia, our
beloved Moscow. . . . We have squandered our resources
foolishly without so much as a backward glance, sapped our
soil, mutilated our vast expanses with idiotic "inland seas"
and contaminated belts of wasteland around our industrial
centers . . .
Aleksandr Solzhenitsyn[3]

The preservation of historical and cultural monuments and
of the Russian environment stands high on any list of present-
day Russian nationalist concerns. It is significant, for example, that, as was noted in the preceding chapter, the editor
of *Veche*, Vladimir Osipov, chose to name the saving of "our

[1] Vladimir Soloukhin, "Chernye doski," in *Slavianskaia tetrad'*, Moscow,
1972, pp. 350-351. English translation: *Searching for Icons in Russia*, New
York, 1971, p. 155.
[2] "Skol'ko nam ostalos' zhit'?" *Veche*, no. 3 (AS 1108), 4 (italics in original
text).
[3] Aleksandr Solzhenitsyn, *Letter to the Soviet Leaders*, New York, 1974,
pp. 25-26.

material and spiritual monuments from destruction" first in outlining his journal's aims to two American correspondents in 1972.[4] When addressing audiences on the subject of Russian nationalism, one often encounters a perplexity as to why specifically *preservation* should be a Russian nationalist issue. After all, one is frequently asked, are Americans who seek to safeguard historical monuments or to protect the environment necessarily fervent American patriots? The "mirror image" inherent in such a question is of course unwarranted when one is comparing such dissimilar societies as the United States and the Soviet Union. But the question nevertheless retains a certain validity: Why should there be so close a connection between preservation and Russian nationalism?

Much of the answer, one suspects, is to be found in the well-known phenomenon of nationalism as a reaction to modernization. When, as has occurred in the USSR, modernization is carried out rapidly and harshly, the nationalist reaction is likely to be quite strong. In addition, the ruling ideology, Marxism-Leninism, has been interpreted as encouraging prometheanism; the past is to be swept aside and the Russian land is to be exploited to the fullest by the champions of "progress" and "the scientific and technical revolution." Ecological and preservationist concerns are seen as insignificant in the face of military and technological interests.

Furthermore in Soviet society where overt expressions of Russian nationalist sentiment are discouraged, preservation can become an immensely symbolic act. It is a relatively "safe" way of contesting the direction being taken by the regime and encouraged by the ruling ideology. Were preservation the concern of merely a few elites, the regime would have no problem. But, as shall be seen, membership statistics for the voluntary societies with preservationist aims indicate that the issue has a mass appeal, particularly, it seems, for Russian youth. Preservation appears to have considerable mobilizational significance as well. If historical and cultural monu-

---

[4] See *Vestnik*, no. 106 (1972), 300-301.

ments and the Russian land itself are desecrated and defiled, Russia's sons may be less inclined to defend the homeland in, say, a conflict with China. According to the Russian nationalists, preservation equals patriotism; anti-preservation equals national nihilism. Such considerations seem to have prompted the Brezhnev regime to attempt to co-opt rather than suppress the preservationist organizations. Since, however, Marxist prometheanism and preservation are natural opponents, they can only with great dexterity be yoked together, and only for a time.

The preceding chapter recounted how Nikita Khrushchev's neo-socialist offensive against religion resulted in the destruction of numerous ancient Russian churches and historical monuments. A believer in Soviet prometheanism, Khrushchev supported a radical modernization of Moscow and showed himself indifferent to the historic face of the capital city. The assault conducted on Russian antiquity during his rule produced a state of near-desperation among a considerable segment of the Soviet intelligentsia, but all efforts to ameliorate or reverse the situation were rebuffed by the first secretary and his associates. When Khrushchev had been removed from power, conditions became more favorable for the preservationists. Faced with myriad problems in other spheres, the new Politburo—whose ranks may have included individuals sympathetic, or at least not hostile, to the aims of the preservationists—moved quickly to placate an aroused Russian patriotic sentiment which, moreover, appeared to enjoy mass support.

In 1964, permission was given for the founding of the *Rodina* (Homeland) Club, an organization whose purpose was to promote the study of historical monuments and to sponsor exhibitions and lectures in rural areas and at workers' clubs. The idea for the club arose after a group of students was inspired by a visit to the ancient Russian towns of Zagorsk, Suzdal', and Vladimir. By the end of 1965, the new organization had about 500 members and enjoyed support from such influential figures as the painter Pavel Korin, the sculptor

Konenkov, the airplane designer Antonov, and the cosmo-
naut Aleksei Leonov.[5]

The following year, a more important organization, the All-
Russian Society for the Preservation of Historical and Cultural Monuments—known by its Russian acronym, VOO-
PIK—was established by a decree of the Council of Ministers
of the RSFSR. The new society held its first conference in
June 1966, and the following month its charter was approved
by the RSFSR Council of Ministers. The ranks of this voluntary society have grown steadily and impressively. By January
1972, it numbered more than seven million members, and by
January, 1977, more than twelve million—9.3% of the population of the Russian Republic.[6]

It is important to note that similar societies already existed
in certain of the minority republics, and they seem to have
served as a model and stimulus for the formation of VOOPIK.
This is suggested, for example, in an essay by Soloukhin published in 1965:

> Not long ago I was in Georgia. This is practically the only
> republic in the USSR where there exists a society for the
> preservation of cultural monuments. More than 300,000
> volunteer members have enrolled in the society. They pay
> small dues, as a result of which a decent sum is collected,
> which can be used either to preserve monuments or to
> restore those which cannot do without it. . . . The society
> organizes lectures which explain the meaning of cultural
> monuments in general and the historic and artistic value of
> individual monuments (about a thousand lectures have been
> given so far). . . . I do not see any reason why such socie-
> ties should not exist in other republics of our country, in-
> cluding the Russian Federation. This society could have its

[5] Dimitry Pospielovsky, "The Resurgence of Russian Nationalism in Samizdat," *Survey*, 19, no. 1 (1973), 52. Pospielovsky drew his information
from a TASS dispatch of 2 December 1965.

[6] *Materialy k III s"ezdu Vserossiiskogo Obshchestva Okhrany Pamiatnikov
Istorii i Kul'tury: Obzornaia spravka o deiatel'nosti Vserossiiskogo Obshchestva Okhrany Pamiatnikov Istorii i Kul'tury za iiul' 1972—iiul' 1977 gg*.
(1977). This document was issued in a printing of 750 copies for the use of
participants in *VOOPIK's* Third All-Russian Conference.

own museum, its own journal, substantial financial means and, most importantly, social initiative. The atmosphere concerning the preservation of monuments would change for the better.[7]

The evidence is clear that VOOPIK was founded principally by initiative from below. This is brought out, for instance, in a piece appearing in the no. 9 issue of *Veche*, which sought, among other aims, to sketch in the background for the formation of the society:

One should make clear that the decisive factor in the creation of the *Rodina* Club and of the All-Russian Society for the Preservation of Historical and Cultural Monuments was not at all an understanding of these problems by government circles but . . . an elemental pressure, a change in the mood of Russian society. People saw in Khrushchev's destructive campaign a *final blow*. Churches were not only being closed, they were being *blown up*. This was perhaps the most symptomatic but not the only cause for alarm. Russian culture was being wiped from the face of the Russian earth, while it was found possible to take the national feelings of other peoples into consideration. Thus, for example, societies for the preservation of monuments were created in Georgia, Armenia and the Baltic many years earlier than in the RSFSR. Such asymmetry looked sinister.[8]

The charged atmosphere of the mid-1960s concerning this question was reflected in a collection of letters published in a 1967 issue of *Molodaia gvardiia*. The letters were elicited by the publication in that journal of Soloukhin's *Letters from a Russian Museum* (1966), a work which sought to dramatize the neglect of ancient Russian architecture and to cultivate an appreciation for Russian icons. A broad spectrum of Soviet society was represented in the *Molodaia gvardiia* letters: construction workers, soldiers, engineers, writers, sailors in the

[7] Vladimir Soloukhin, *S liricheskikh pozitsii*, Moscow, 1965, p. 185.

[8] O. M., " 'Survey' o russkom natsionalizme," *Veche*, no. 9 (AS 2040), 169 (O. M.'s italics).

merchant marine, artists, schoolteachers, professors, and students. "Readers write in," the editors of the journal reported, "that people are standing in lines for *Molodaia gvardiia*. They discuss Soloukhin's *Letters*; many copy out whole pages by hand . . ."[9] A major interest of the correspondents was the newly formed VOOPIK: "Readers place great hopes in the newly organized society. It is very important, they write, that the society should stand on its own feet, that the period of holding meetings should pass over into that of productive work . . ."[10] Readers pressed for the enlisting of "millions of volunteers" to help with the preservation work and suggested that the Komsomol and schools be activated to assist with this task.

The fervor reported by the *Molodaia gvardiia* editors was borne out by the selection of letters published in the journal. Two women from Moscow wrote to Soloukhin: "Thank you for your story about icons. We have begun to look at them in a new way . . . One would like very much to know what the Society for the Preservation of Monuments is doing and whether those monuments that still remain will be preserved . . ."[11] And a professor from Moscow State University wrote:

> . . . one cannot compensate for that which we have destroyed in the Kremlin itself—the Krasnoe Kryl'tso of the Granovitaia Palace, the Chudov and Voznesenskii Monasteries. We destroyed the ancient walls and towers of Kitai-gorod, the Sukharev Tower, the Palitsyn palaces in Okhotnyi Row, the Triumphal and Red Gates, a dozen ancient monasteries, the famous churches of Potapov (on Pokrovka) and Kazakov (on Zemlianyi Bank), and 400 other valuable architectural monuments . . . And we have uprooted the gardens in Sadovoe Ring![12]

[9] "Po povodu 'Pisem iz russkogo muzeia,' " *Molodaia gvardiia*, no. 4 (1967), 282.
[10] Ibid., p. 293.
[11] Ibid., p. 282.
[12] Ibid., p. 285.

Another letter came from two Old Bolsheviks, who wrote to counter an attack on Soloukhin in the newspaper *Vecherniaia Moskva*:

> Does the veteran of the "Dynamo" plant, G. Morgunov, consider the erection of a compressor plant in an ancient church of the 15th century (the Nativity Church in Staryi Simonov), literally on the bones of the buried heroes of the Battle of Kulikovo, Peresvet and Osliabia, to be a model of patriotism? . . . After all, the Battle of Kulikovo served as the beginning of our liberation from the Tatar yoke . . .[13]

In view of the intense preservationist sentiment of what Russians call *obshchestvennost'* (social or public opinion), the regime approved the establishment of VOOPIK, while, at the same time, attempting to co-opt the organization to its purposes. This did not escape the attention of preservationist leaders. An open letter which appeared in the 30 October, 1965 issue of *Literaturnaia gazeta*, and which was signed by such figures as Soloukhin, the writer Efim Dorosh, the pianist Sviatoslav Rikhter, and Academician Nesmianov, protested that the Moscow section of the committee which was to organize the founding congress of VOOPIK was top-heavy with bureaucrats who had previously distinguished themselves by destroying churches rather than saving them.[14] The same issue of *Literaturnaia gazeta* also contained a passionate letter by the well-known writer Leonid Leonov, deploring the "uprooting" of monuments and the "liquidation" of Russian antiquity.

A similar complaint against excessive bureaucratic control was voiced by the writer and environmentalist Petr Dudochkin at the second conference of VOOPIK's Kalinin chapter, held in March 1968:

> The All-Russian Society for the Preservation of Monuments—I repeat, the *All-Russian* Society—has neither its

[13] Ibid., p. 288.
[14] Pospielovsky, "Resurgence of Russian Nationalism," p. 52.

own newspaper, nor its own journal, nor its own printing house. . . .

Our printing workshop in Kalinin prints the journal *Cuba*, a journal which is not at all progressive, to say the least. Like Fidel Castro, it leans toward adventurism. For this semi-official publication, first-class paper, the best colors, and credits are found. But for our All-Russian Society and its noble aims the workshop does not even offer the scraps and leavings from *Cuba*! . . .

I would like to address the following question to the member of the Central Council of the All-Russian Society for the Preservation of Historical and Cultural Monuments who is present with us today: Georgii Gerasimovich, dear Comrade Ansimov, can it be that even you, the Central Council, are unable to become the possessors of a newspaper, journal, and printing house? Do it! It's a sacred task! Perhaps our [Kalinin] printing workshop will give you the scraps from the journal *Cuba* so that you can print a journal entitled *Fatherland*, which all of us need, which Russia needs.[15]

This gibe at the deficient patriotism of the regime and its follies overseas is characteristic of the freedom which nationalists enjoyed in the middle and late 1960s. (Dudochkin continued to speak his mind even later, as a review by him in a 1976 issue of *Sever* indicates.)[16]

The regime seems to have tactically retreated under pressure from *obshchestvennost'*, but only to a point. The number of authentic preservationists on the central bodies of VOOPIK was increased, but the regime made sure that its interests were represented as well. VOOPIK was not given a newspaper, journal, or printing house—that was apparently too risky—but it has been permitted occasional publications in conjunction with established printing houses such as "Sovremennik" and "Molodaia gvardiia," as well a series of brochures and booklets.

[15] *Veche*, no. 6 (AS 1599), 96-97 (Dudochkin's italics).
[16] Petr Dudochkin, "Volshebnoe v obychnom," *Sever*, no. 5 (1976), 124.

The society makes its concerns known to the Russian public through these limited publication efforts and through public lectures. Public lectures are given in such locations as factories, schools, technical institutes, and military bases. During these lectures, listeners are told "about historical and cultural monuments, about the history of their particular area, and about the activity of VOOPIK."[17] The volume of such activity

[17] *Materialy*, p. 41. These *Materials* and a draft of the *Statute* adopted at the third conference give us a fair picture of how far the society has come since its founding. (I would also like to acknowledge information generously supplied by Professor Arcadi Nebolsine, formerly of the University of Pittsburgh, the foremost American authority on the activities of VOOPIK and the founder of an American society for the preservation of Russian monuments.)

Any Soviet citizen fourteen years or over can become a member of VOOPIK, as long as he accepts the organization's charter and joins a local chapter. The highest legislative organ of the society is the All-Russian Conference, which must be convened at least once every five years. In the period between conferences, the ruling organ of the society is the Central Council, whose members are elected at the All-Russian Conference; this body meets at least twice annually. Members of the Central Council elect a Presidium from among their number, and it is this body that serves as the executive organ of the society. The Presidium, in turn, "creates" a Bureau to run the day-to-day affairs of the organization; the Bureau consists of a chairman (who in 1977 was Viacheslav Kochemasov, also at the time deputy chairman of the Council of Ministers of the RSFSR), a deputy chairman (in 1977, Vladimir N. Ivanov, de facto director of the society's activities), and a secretary. There is also a Central Revision Committee, elected by the All-Russian Conference, which oversees the finances of the organization. "Democratic centralism" is said to be the philosophy behind the society's structure.

Local chapters of VOOPIK hold conferences once every two or three years, at which they elect councils and revision committees, which serve for a commensurate period. The councils, in their turn, elect presidiums that handle the everyday affairs of the chapter. All voting in VOOPIK is conducted by open ballot.

Membership statistics provided by the *Materials of the Third Conference* indicate (as of January 1, 1977) the regions of the RSFSR in which the society is strong and those in which it is weak. The highest percentages of population are in Severo-Osetinsk (22.3%—123,372 members) and Kabardino-Balkarsk (22%—130,002 members), two areas adjacent to Georgia where interest in historical monuments has long been active. As of 1977, the following chapters enjoyed enrollments of more than 12% of their populations: Kursk (20.4%—300,800 members), Briansk (17.7%—280,756), Orel (17.1%—159,115), Belgorod (16.6%—209,102), Stavropol (14.7%—340,093), Smolensk (14.2%—157,486), Krasnodar (13.3%—600,520), Saratov (13.3%—326,635), Kaluga (13.2%—131,151), Rostov (12.8%—489,230), Volgograd (12.5%—290,918), Kuibyshev (12.2%—337,381), and Moscow Province (12.2%—702,276). The

is impressive; during the period from 1973 to 1976, for example, 44,000 lectures and speeches were given in Belgorod province (*oblast'*) alone. For the same period, the figure for Vladimir province was 15,000 lectures, and for Leningrad province, 13,000.

The publishing house "Sovremennik" has published two collections of articles, both of them entitled *Monuments of the Fatherland* (1972), which reflect the society's concerns, and the "Molodaia gvardiia" publishing house was reported in 1977 to be preparing a similar volume, entitled *Father's House*. Since 1972, the society has been engaged in publishing a series of brochures and booklets which deal with monuments and historical events in various areas of the RSFSR. A number of Soviet newspapers and journals have also actively promoted the society's causes, e.g., *Sovetskaia Rossiia, Izvestiia, Literaturnaia gazeta, Molodaia gvardiia, Smena, Krokodil,* and, at the regional level, *Belgorodskaia pravda* and *Sovetskii Sakhalin.*

Television and radio have also been used to further the knowledge of historical and cultural monuments, though the society's leadership has said that more could be done in this area. In Vologda, a "Fatherland" cinema club has been founded which regularly shows films on monuments of the RSFSR and the other union republics.

---

figures for the capital cities are: Moscow, 617,059 members (8.7% of population); Leningrad, 303,101 members (7.7% of population).

As can be seen, membership in European Russia is quite high. Membership in Siberia and the Far East, on the other hand, is relatively low; for example, Tiumen' (5% of population—70,745 members), Chita (4.8%—55,174), Krasnoiarsk (4.6%—134,870), Altai (4.6%—122,377), Magadan (4.4%—15,505), Primorsk (2.7%—46,730), Irkutsk (1.8%—42,134). The Amur chapter, which enrolls 17.4% of the local population (137,943 members), is an obvious anomaly. One wonders whether the proximity of the Chinese border might not, at least in part, be behind this high figure.

The low percentages of population in Siberia and the Far East are to be expected. The area does not have nearly as many historical monuments as does European Russia, and, in addition, the inhabitants of this region tend to be less cultured and more rough-hewn, as well as more transient, than their compatriots to the west. In view of the possibility of a conflict with China, it might be to the regime's advantage to encourage VOOPIK's activities in Siberia and the Far East in order to provide an additional patriotic prop for the armed forces and for the populace at large.

The promotion of indigenous tourism within the Russian Republic appears to be another of the society's principal aims. Routes such as the "Golden Ring," which covers monuments in Moscow, Zagorsk, Pereiaslavl'-Zalesskii, and adjacent areas, and the "Northern Ring"—Vologda and Arkhangel provinces and Karelia—are actively promoted. In Orel, Tambov, and Tula provinces, the society has published brochures and guidebooks with such titles as *Literary Places of the Orel Region* and *From the Oka to Kulikovo Field*.

One of the society's more ambitious projects in recent years was elicited by the government's plan to carry out a mass transformation of the so-called "non-Black Earth" area in the vicinity of Smolensk. The plan called for a reduction to one-quarter of the original number of rural villages in the region. VOOPIK conducted extensive photography work so that future generations of Russians would not lose their link to these villages. During the period from 1971 to 1976, almost all of the villages were photographed and questionnaires were distributed to their inhabitants; some 50,000 documents were collected in all.

The society has actively been collecting material relating to Russian folk music and folk dances, and has sponsored concerts—which have been well received by the public—at which this material has been performed. Recently, attention has also been devoted to preserving and restoring "garden and park art." Another activity of the society has been to ensure that the jubilees of Russian cities—e.g., the 950th anniversary of Suzdal', the 600th anniversary of Kaluga, the 400th anniversary of Ufa—have been properly marked. The 600th anniversary of the Battle of Kulikovo Field was commemorated in 1980. It should be emphasized, however, that VOOPIK's principal concern remains the preservation and restoration of historical monuments. Between 1972 and 1976, the annual income of the society averaged ten million rubles, of which six or seven million went toward preservation and restoration work or toward the study of historical and cultural monuments. Another 400,000-500,000 rubles were earmarked each year for the distribution of information about monuments and for educational work among the masses.

The published proceedings of VOOPIK's Third Conference, held in 1977, relate a number of incidents in which the society and its supporters had come into conflict with organizations or individuals indifferent or actively hostile to the fate of historical monuments. In 1974, as one example, a firm was fined and ejected from the premises of the Vladimir Church in Vologda for flagrant misuse of the property. The punishment was administered by the Vologda Municipal Executive Council in response to "the demand of public opinion." In a similar case, it is reported that "public opinion" in Smolensk had for many years been demanding the removal of a macaroni factory from the property of the Trinity Monastery, a seventeenth-century monument, and that this was eventually accomplished. In the city of Kalinin, two houses under state protection as architectural monuments had been torn down to make room for the expansion of a bank. The Kalinin province Executive Committee punished the leaders of the Kalinin municipal Executive Committee and the local branch of the State Bank for ignoring established procedures and ordered them to restore the destroyed monuments. (The proceedings also mention, incidentally, that the Kalinin province chapter of VOOPIK took a "strange position" on this incident; the reference seems to be to the presence on this body of persons indifferent to the aims of the society.)

The *Materials* report a number of other struggles whose outcome, as of 1977, was still unclear. The Epiphany Church in the city of Kasimov, Riazan' Province, for example, was still being used for the soaking of sheep hides, with the salt solution employed in the process being kept right on the floor of the church. Similarly, in a case also criticized by *Krokodil*, the Balakhninsk Executive Committee was criticized for turning the Trinity Church, an eighteenth-century monument, into a funeral bureau. The 2 February 1977 issue of *Literaturnaia gazeta* was cited approvingly for its expression of alarm that a number of wooden churches have not been provided with lightning rods and other appropriate protective devices.

In the village of Tipinitsy, the wooden Church of the Ascension, a historical monument, had recently burned down.

Several provincial executive committees had, according to the *Materials*, been lax in sending prospective plans for the reconstruction of historical cities to VOOPIK. Other problems concerned delays in the carrying out of needed repairs and "voluntarism" on the part of those engaged in restoration work. The head architect in charge of restoration work on the Resurrection Monastery in the city of Istra, for example, decided on his own to change the shape of the historic cathedral's dome. There had also been instances in which architectural monuments had not been brought into proper order and in which the question of their ultimate use had not been decided—e.g., the home of the artist Levitan, the Vladichnyi, Staro-Golutvinsk, and Bobrenev monasteries in Moscow Province, and the cathedrals of the cities of Volokolamsk and Kolomna. The Presidium of VOOPIK expressed alarm at the condition of such important museum-monuments as the twelfth-century Transfiguration Cathedral in Pereiaslavl'-Zalesskii, the Church of John the Forerunner in Iaroslavl' with its seventeenth-century frescoes, and the Divna Church in Uglich, all of which had inexplicably remained closed to visitors. Harsh words were exchanged with the administration of the International Youth Center in Rostov for not observing the museum character of the complex it occupies—the Rostov Kremlin and the Boris and Gleb Monastery.

In carrying out its work, VOOPIK has sought to mobilize Russian student youth, something which the *Materials* say leads to "the esthetic, moral and patriotic education" of young people.[18] A detachment of students from the Moscow Institute of Engineering and Physics worked for nine years on the restoration of the St. Kirill of Belozersk Monastery, while a brigade from the physics department of Moscow State University had been working since 1967 at Solovki, site of a former monastic complex and fortress and, under the Bolsheviks, of a dread concentration camp. Students from the Moscow

Institute of Architecture had helped to restore the New Jerusalem Monastery in Istra, while students at the Moscow Polygraphic Institute had done service in Kolomna. Other student groups were said to be active in Amur, Kostroma, Leningrad, and Smolensk provinces, and in Karelia.

The *Materials of the Third Conference* stress that dedicated individuals played an important role in the society's work. Assisted by students and by the members of neighboring collective farms, a high-school principal in Riazan' province had organized the restoration of the Staro-Cherneev Monastery, and the deputy chairman of the Alpaev district chapter of VOOPIK had formed a brigade of retired persons to repair and partially restore an eighteenth-century monument, the Transfiguration Church in the village of Nizhniaia Siniachikha.

In a recent collection of essays, *Vremia sobirat' kamni* (A Time to Collect Stones), Vladimir Soloukhin chronicled in minute detail—citing the complete texts of numerous official documents—the attempts of preservationists to rescue the estate of the noted nineteenth-century writer, Sergei Aksakov, from destruction.[19] The collection also contains an important essay on the (so far unsuccessful) efforts to restore the famous Optina Pustyn' monastery.[20]

Following the Second All-Russian Conference of the society, held in 1972, VOOPIK began to pay increased attention to historical monuments of the Soviet period, as well as to monuments of the revolutionary-democratic movement in tsarist times—e.g., "Lenin places" in the Volga region, the first communes, kolkhozes, and sovkhozes, and memorials to the Pugachev uprising, the Decembrists, and the 1905 Revolution. It seems that the regime's campaign against russophilism in the early seventies at least partially necessitated this new emphasis. On the other hand, one gains the impression that it has been a largely cosmetic change; VOOPIK's funds continue to be devoted primarily to the preservation and restoration of monuments of antiquity, and instances of

[19] Vladimir Soloukhin, *Vremia sobirat' kamni*, Moscow, 1980, pp. 24-81.
[20] Ibid., pp. 169-234.

neglect which draw criticism from the society invariably concern ancient churches and monuments, not "revolutionary-
democratic" or Soviet-period monuments. Moreover, evidence suggests that local authorities are often no more
interested in safeguarding Soviet era monuments than those
of the past. Osipov, for example, reports that "many buildings" connected with Lenin and the revolutions of 1905 and
1917 have been torn down in Moscow—e.g., the building
where the first session of the Moscow Soviet of Workers'
Deputies was held in 1905 and the Ul'ianov (Lenin) home on
Kompozitorskaia Street.[21]

Though the leadership of VOOPIK has always included high-
ranking Soviet officials—in 1977 V. M. Striganov, deputy
minister of culture of the RSFSR, and A. G. Anikin, first
deputy chairman of the Vladimir province Executive Committee, were members of its Presidium[22]—and though the
organization has regularly stressed its intention to foster "Soviet" patriotism, the society has not been immune to attack
by Marxist-Leninist purists. For instance, in 1973, the antireligious monthly *Nauka i religiia* published a critical review
of the collection *Monuments of the Fatherland.* (Among the
contributors to this collection were Leonid Leonov, Academician B. A. Rybakov, Vice-Admiral and Hero of the Soviet
Union G. N. Kholostiakov, and People's Artist E. V. Vuche-
tich.) The reviewer, Aleksandr Shamaro, centered his complaint on the volume's failure to mention various negative
traits associated with Russian historical monuments. He reminded his readers that churches, as well as mosques and
synagogues, have always served as "ideological centers" supporting the ruling classes. It is possible, he admitted, to view
the Cathedral of St. Basil the Blessed on Red Square as a
masterpiece of Russian architecture, but, he went on, one
cannot ignore the fact that during the First World War this
building, the scene of sermons by the reactionary monarchist
Archpriest Vostorgov, was a nest of "chauvinistic and po-

---

[21] Vladimir Osipov, "Poslednii den' Moskvy," *Vestnik*, no. 111 (1974), 228.
[22] "Spisok redaktsionnoi komissii III s"ezda Vserossiiskogo Obshchestva
Okhrany Pamiatnikov Istorii i Kul'tury" (unpublished).

gromistic agitation." A plot was even hatched within the cathedral's walls against the newly established Soviet regime.[23]

Historian Sergei Semanov, one of those singled out for criticism by Shamaro, replied in an article in *Moskva*. To lend weight to his argument, Semanov referred to a speech delivered in 1972 by V. I. Kochemasov, chairman of the Presidium of VOOPIK's Central Council and deputy chairman of the Council of Ministers of the RSFSR. In this speech, Kochemasov had spoken of the "incorrect attitude toward the preservation of monuments" which had manifested itself in certain places in the early 1960s. Citing the "battles" and "many arguments" which characterized the society's formative period, Semanov concluded: "Now the Society for the Preservation of Monuments has entered firmly into the structure of our civic life." The words of his *Nauka i religiia* opponent reminded him of the "times gone forever" of Leopold Averbakh and the Russian Association of Proletarian Writers and of the anti-Russian "nihilists" of the 1920s and 1930s.[24]

Shamaro stuck to his guns in a reply appearing in a later issue of *Nauka i religiia*. One must remember, he stressed, the social function served by ancient Russian monasteries, palaces, and country estates, built as they were on the "bitter tears" of the Russian working people. The Trinity-Sergius Lavra, for example, which his opponent had cited with esteem, served as "a center for religious influence on the surrounding populace." Ancient Russian architecture is one thing, but "hegumens, archimandrites, and bishops—those boyars in cassocks" are another. One must, Shamaro concluded, adopt a Leninist "dialectical" approach to the problem of historical monuments.[25]

The reader will have noted that Semanov's arguments were largely patriotic and mobilizational, while Shamaro's were more doctrinal, focusing in particular on the religious dimension of

[23] Aleksandr Shamaro, "Razdum'ia nad knigoi," *Nauka i religiia*, no. 6 (1973), 17-22.

[24] S. Semanov, "Moskva stroilas' ne srazu," *Moskva*, no. 7 (1974), 172-178.

[25] Aleksandr Shamaro, "Pis'mo v redaktsiiu," *Nauka i religiia*, no. 7 (1975), 46-50.

ancient monuments. Neither author appears to have "defeated" the other, and both remained at their posts to do battle if another occasion should present itself.

The struggle to gain government approval for the formation of VOOPIK in the mid-sixties was followed by an equally heated effort in the early 1970s to halt the ongoing destruction of Moscow's historic architecture. Russian nationalists had, of course, been emphasizing this issue during the middle and late sixties. Soloukhin, for example, had dramatized the fate of the capital's architecture in his *Letters from a Russian Museum*. Here is what he wrote concerning the razing of the Cathedral of Christ the Saviour in the 1930s:

> Forty years were spent building a grandiose architectural monument, the Church of Christ the Saviour, on the money of the people [i.e., on donations which were collected]. It was built as a memorial to the famous Moscow fire, as a monument to the defiance of Moscow before a powerful enemy, as a memorial to the victory over Napoleon. The great Russian artist Vasilii Surikov painted its walls and arches. It was the tallest and most majestic building in Moscow. One could see it from any corner of the city. The building was not an ancient one, but, together with the Kremlin, it served to organize the architectural center of our capital. They tore it down . . . and built a swimming pool in its place.[26]

The chief sources on the subsequent battle to save Moscow's architecture are an anonymous article entitled "The Fate of the Russian Capital," which appeared in the first issue of *Veche*, and Vladimir Osipov's essay, "Moscow's Last Day," which was published in the Paris-based *Vestnik*. The former piece, apparently written by an individual who has had professional training in architecture and city planning, was a bitter exposé of the activities of the Main Architecture and Planning Administration of the City of Moscow (known by its Russian

[26] Vladimir Soloukhin, "Pis'ma iz russkogo muzeia," in *Slavianskaia tetrad'*, pp. 129-130.

acronym: GlavAPU) and of its head, Chief Architect of Moscow Mikhail Vasil'evich Posokhin.

The records of the Nuremberg trial, the *Veche* author pointed out, show that Hitler intended to construct a vast sea on the spot where Moscow stood, so that the Russian capital would disappear forever. A similar plan, he contended, had been followed by Moscow architects and city planners since the adoption of the infamous *Genplan* (General Plan) of 1935, the brainchild of Lazar' Moiseevich Kaganovich, the de facto master of historic Moscow's fate during the middle and late thirties, even though he had no specialized training in architecture. The drafters of the *Genplan*, the author asserted, sought "maximal destruction of the architectural monuments in Moscow."[27]

The conceptual core of the plan was a "radial-ring" structure, in which numerous radii-avenues would feed into the city like the spokes of a wheel and would be connected one to another by highway-rings. As one result of this plan, the convergence of the radii-avenues at the center of the city would necessitate the large-scale destruction of existing buildings. The author found it interesting that the distinguished Western architect Le Corbusier had sharply criticized the "radial-ring" theory of city planning in a book which appeared in Russian translation in 1933, i.e., two years before the adoption of the *Genplan*. Another effect of the adoption of the plan was to be the extensive razing of monuments of antiquity: ". . . since the period of the end of the twenties, more than 400 monuments known to scholarship have been torn down."[28] Among them were:

> the Cathedral of the Kazan' Mother of God on Red Square, built by Prince Pozharskii in honor of his victory over the Poles, the Resurrection Monastery in the Kremlin, built by Princess Evdokiia in honor of the victory at Kulikovo Field . . . the Cathedral of Christ the Saviour—the main monument of Russia and the world to commemorate the

[27] "Sud'ba russkoi stolitsy," *Veche*, no. 1 (AS 1013), 83.
[28] Ibid., p. 85.

victorious conclusion of the greatest war of the 18th and 19th centuries—the war against Napoleon . . .[29]

That the author was speaking in mobilizational terms became clear at the conclusion of his essay when he asked: "On the basis of what patriotic feelings will it be possible to win the approaching war?"[30] A blow at Moscow's historic architecture was seen as a blow at patriotism and an unconscionable undermining of military morale.

After the war, the *Veche* author continued, the work of Kaganovich and his associates was continued by the deputy chief architect of Moscow, Abram Moiseevich Zaslavskii, who is reported to have told two protesting Russian architects: "*We* will leave nothing of *your* monuments."[31] By stressing the Jewish origins of Kaganovich, Zaslavskii, and certain of their colleagues, the author seemed to be placing the responsibility for the destruction of Moscow's architecture on the Jews, a crude simplification and distortion of the facts.

The most recent wave of destruction, the author wrote, had been headed by Mikhail Posokhin, who rose to power under Khrushchev. One of Posokhin's first actions was to tear down the Palace of the Russian Tsaritsas, dating from the fifteenth and sixteenth century, and to construct a conference center in its place. This act elicited a "storm of protest"—letters poured into the press from cultural and scientific luminaries and from historians and architects, criticizing Posokhin's policies, and numerous protests were sent to government offices and to Khrushchev himself, but all to no avail.

The construction of the huge Rossiia (Russia) Hotel in Moscow, a building familiar to most foreign tourists who visit the capital, particularly aroused the ire of the author of the *Veche* article. Describing the hotel as "a dull trunk, gray and monotonous," he said it defaced and defamed the Moscow skyline. "In large letters," he wrote, "without any quotation marks, is written the word Russia [i.e., at the top of the hotel], and

[29] Ibid., pp. 85-86.
[30] Ibid., pp. 112-113.
[31] Ibid., p. 88 (italics in the original).

underneath it is explained what Russia is: a hotel, bar, res-
taurant, cafe, and dance floor."[32] Moreover, if one took all
factors into consideration, the cost of this monstrosity had
been staggering. The hotel cost 180 million rubles to construct, but that was only part of the story: the foundations of
the building turned out to be so heavy that they seriously
damaged those of a number of surrounding edifices, which
required repair work totalling 700 million rubles. The final
cost of the Rossiia Hotel thus amounted to 880 million rubles,
a sum which would have been more than sufficient to restore
all of the ancient architectural monuments in Moscow.

The *Veche* author charged that Posokhin and his associates
had succeeded in neutralizing the preservationist efforts of
VOOPIK, i.e., that the regime had co-opted the organization. The "inspection" of Moscow's monuments had been
subordinated to GlavAPU, while Posokhin had had himself
made a member of the society's Central Council. At meetings
of VOOPIK, he was seated in the ranks of the society's Presidium and was permitted to give speeches. Thus the success
of his policy seemed to be assured, and "for Posokhin and his
ilk, as previously for Kaganovich, the policy of anti-Russian
chauvinism is the general line of their lives and activity."[33]

The tone of "The Fate of the Russian Capital" was darkly
pessimistic. To be sure, there had been some minor victories—the architect Antropov, the architect-restorer Baranov-
skii, and People's Artist P. D. Korin managed, for example,
to save the Church of St. Simeon the Stylite on Kalinin Avenue from the wrecker's ball.[34] But more typical was the fate
of the Church of Sts. Joachim and Anna on Dimitrov Street,
a seventeenth-century monument, which was blown up on
Posokhin's orders on the night of 3-4 November 1969. The
author even suggested that the logic of the converging radii-
avenues in the center of Moscow would eventually require
the razing of the Kremlin itself. One is scarcely surprised to
learn that the KGB has been conducting an intensive search

[32] Ibid., p. 90.
[33] Ibid., p. 91.
[34] Ibid., p. 95.

for the author of this article, and probably not "in order to present him with an award."[35]

Osipov's essay, "Moscow's Last Day," is in an emotional vein similar to that of the *Veche* piece. His picture of the destructive campaign of the 1930s mirrored that given by his anonymous compatriot:

> Kaganovich personally pushed the button which blew up the monument to the victory of 1812, the Church of Christ the Saviour, in November, 1933. He is reported to have gloated at the time: "We will raise the hem of the skirts of Mother Russia!" . . . In the thirties of the 20th century monuments of Russian national culture were torn down throughout the country. . . . All former provincial centers were ordered to destroy their cathedrals, which they subsequently did (except for Astrakhan and Tula—out of negligence). In Nizhni Novgorod, the Transfiguration Cathedral containing the tomb of Koz'ma *Minin* was solemnly blown up.[36]

During the 1935-1941 period, Osipov reported, 426 monuments were torn down in Moscow alone. "At the time of Hitler's attack on the Soviet Union, all that remained for the domestic barbarians to do was to blow up the Kremlin, the Church of Basil the Blessed, and the house of Pashkov—in a word, the remaining crumbs from the gold-domed capital. But they did not succeed in doing this . . . Stalin at last came to understand that for simple soldiers the fatherland is immeasurably dearer than the theories of Marx and Engels."[37]

After the war, a brief respite ensued; laws were passed to protect historical monuments in 1947 and 1948, and in 1954 the Soviet Union signed an international convention entitled "On the Defense of Cultural Objects of Value in the Event of Armed Conflict."[38] In 1958, however, the new "standard-bearer of Marxism," Nikita Khrushchev, resumed the anni-

---

[35] Osipov, "Poslednii den' Moskvy," p. 221.
[36] Ibid., p. 220 (Osipov's italics).
[37] Ibid., pp. 222-223.
[38] Ibid., p. 223.

hilation of Russian antiquity. A blatant example of this policy was the newly constructed Kalinin Avenue, which Osipov claimed was a copy of a plan for Havana drawn up by American architects in 1954. The Soviet "cosmopolitans" (Osipov presumably used this term to refer to de-nationalized Russians and anti-Russian Jews) who designed Kalinin Avenue did not realize that a tropical model might not be appropriate for a northern city. In Havana, it might be an excellent idea, for example, to funnel cooler air into the center of the city; in wintry Moscow, the idea had its drawbacks.

Since 1958, a "new bacchanalia of destruction" had reigned in Moscow, with the process particularly intensifying since 1971. Osipov warned: "The vandals of GlavAPU, headed by Posokhin, are successfully advancing toward their cherished goal—to wipe historic 'nationalistic' Moscow from the face of the earth and to erect in its place a new Babylon after the measure of Detroit or Chicago."[39] The eventual result of this process, he predicted, would be that the Kremlin would become a souvenir toy, as had already happened in the case of the Church of St. Simeon the Stylite on Kalinin Avenue. House by house, street by street, historic Moscow was being destroyed: between April 1971 and June 1972 alone, 100 valuable monuments were torn down. As for the "bureaucratized organization" of VOOPIK, Osipov said that it had done more to curb the efforts of preservationists than to save monuments.

Osipov's article and the "chronicle" section of several issues of *Veche* recorded the effort waged by Moscow *obshchestvennost'* in the early 1970s to halt the campaign of destruction. Letters of protest arrived at government offices from such eminent scholars and cultural leaders as Academician Rybakov, Cinema Director Bondarchuk, Choirmaster Sveshnikov, and academicians Artsimovich, Kapitsa, and Tupolev. A request to halt the razing of historic Moscow was sent to General Secretary Brezhnev by seventeen corresponding members of the Academy of Science and forty-two

[39] Ibid., p. 220.

doctors of science. The Union of Artists mobilized its forces to conduct a struggle against GlavAPU and was joined in its efforts by the indefatigable Il'ia Glazunov.

The efforts of "social opinion" seemed initially to have borne some fruit. Acting on behalf of the Party Central Committee, P. N. Demichev requested the Moscow City Committee to study the question of monuments and to take into account the opinions of specialists and of *obshchestvennost'*.[40] On 25 June 1972, a resolution was passed by the City Committee stressing the need to deal carefully with cultural monuments.

On July 13 of the same year, at the initiative of the Party Central Committee, a meeting was held at the Manezh Exhibition Hall between Posokhin and representatives of the Union of Artists. At the meeting, Posokhin acquainted the artists with GlavAPU's general plan for the reconstruction of Moscow and showed them models of various projects. The artists reportedly reacted with acute displeasure to the chief architect's disclosures. Under considerable pressure, Posokhin was forced to admit that not he but Party and government organs were responsible for deciding Moscow's architectural fate.[41]

Also at this meeting, the artist Artem'ev asked Posokhin to name one example of successful modern architecture in the center of Moscow, a request which Posokhin declined. The artists present underlined their opinion that the planned reconstruction of the capital would lead to the "complete destruction of Moscow as a unique Russian city . . ."[42] Veterans of the Second World War recalled the significance which Moscow had had for the Russian people during the war and warned that the destruction of historic cities "undermines the foundations of Russian and Soviet patriotism."[43]

A similar meeting was arranged by the Moscow City Committee on 15 September 1972, between certain of its mem-

[40] I. Petrov, "Eshche raz o drevnei Moskve," *Veche*, no. 5 (AS 1230), 138.
[41] "Khronika," *Veche*, no. 6 (AS 1599), 135-136.
[42] Ibid., p. 136.
[43] Ibid.

bers, representatives of the Moscow intelligentsia, and Posokhin.[44]

None of the efforts of Muscovite "social opinion" proved capable of thwarting the plans of Posokhin and his associates, who clearly enjoyed protection where it counted. In the spring of 1973, GlavAPU launched a new attack on historic Moscow, marshaling the media to aid in its campaign. The Union of Artists reacted by compiling voluminous photo albums on the reconstruction of Moscow, which were then circulated among members of the Establishment and soon succeeded in reaching Brezhnev, Suslov, and other members of the Politburo. This resulted in the formation by the Party Central Committee of a special commission to look into the matter; this body, in turn, requested the State Construction Bureau to create a commission of experts to examine the question. The commission, consisting of about forty persons, split into eleven subcommittees and conducted a thorough investigation into the planned reconstruction of the capital. In their reports, all eleven subcommittees took issue with the policies of GlavAPU, but to no avail. As Osipov put it, Posokhin and his colleagues seemed to be "wizards" over whom no one has any power. And this led him to the pessimistic conclusion: "Russia's social opinion turned out to be powerless."[45]

Veche was suppressed in 1974, and Osipov was arrested later the same year, but the war over historic Moscow continued. In a booklet published by the "Pravda" Publishing House in 1978, for example, Iurii Seleznev wrote:

Do many know that Peresvet and Osliabia [heroes of the Battle of Kulikovo Field] are buried in Moscow in the Church of the Nativity? The church is presently located on the property of the "Dynamo" plant. A 180-kilowatt motor has been set up next to the old church and has been put a meter deep into the earth . . . The ancient ground has been shamelessly and coarsely torn up. The building shakes from the din. . . . The motors roar over the ashes of heroes.

---

[44] Ibid., p. 137.
[45] Osipov, "Poslednii den' Moskvy," p. 232.

Such is their monument and glory. And yet how filled with noble indignation we would be, would we not, if (to admit something completely fantastic) Frenchmen, Englishmen, or Germans were to permit themselves such an action![46]

Seleznev (b. 1939) won the "Ogonek" Prize in 1976 and the Lenin Komsomol Prize in 1977. His brochure indicates continued support for preservation among Soviet elites.

One must be careful not to give the impression that Russian nationalists in the Soviet Union have been interested only in the fate of ancient churches. The fate of icons and ancient church books has, for instance, been of equal concern, as a reading of Soloukhin's *Black Boards* (1969) will confirm.

The preservation of the Russian environment has been another cause championed by Russian nationalists. This has been reflected in *Veche* and in official publications of a nationalist bent, such as the journal *Nash sovremennik*. Writer Petr Dudochkin, whose interest in the activities of VOOPIK has already been noted, reported in 1971 that a voluntary society called The All-Russian Society for the Preservation of Nature had nineteen million members, "an army of nature-lovers."[47] The society's Upper Volga chapter alone, he said, boasted 150,000 members. The principal aim of this society has been the care of so-called "living monuments": large forest tracts, parks, oak-groves, lakes, islands, burial mounds, centuries-old trees. Examples of important living monuments in the Upper Volga region are the botanical garden of the Pedagogical Institute of the city of Kalinin, which contains over 300 species of trees; a park in Karacharovo, downriver from Kalinin, which features sixty-four different garden alleys; and a combination burial-mound and fortress near the village of Sepotino, dating back to the twelfth century. The region as a whole contains over 200 ancient parks planted by serfs on the

---

[46] Iurii Seleznev, *Sozidaiushchaia pamiat'*, Moscow, 1978, p. 17.
[47] Petr Dudochkin, "Kak chelovek sdaet ekzamen prirode?," *Veche*, no. 4 (AS 1140), 115.

estates of landowners and now preserved as "people's treasures."

The Soviet Union's "army of nature lovers" has frequently encountered opposition from those who regard nature merely as a tool. Doctor of Biological Sciences N. Reimers protested against this shortsighted view in an article in *Nash sovremennik*. "From our school days," he wrote, "we remember Turgenev's phrase, 'Nature is not a temple but a workshop, and man is a worker in it.' But nature is nonetheless both a temple and a workshop. It is humanity's eternal workshop and eternal temple, a place which man is obliged to preserve as the apple of his eye, not to destroy."[48] In another issue of the same journal, a doctoral candidate in biological sciences, F. Shtil'mark, wrote concerning the endangered state of the Siberian cedars, the victim of heedless practices by Siberian loggers.[49] Several articles have appeared in the journal *Don* arguing for the formation of nature preserves in the steppe. "The wild inheritance of the steppe," the author of one of these pieces declared "has a right to life."[50]

The struggle against pollution has, understandably, become an obsession among Russian environmentalists. Dudochkin has referred to "nature-lovers who broke not a few lances in battle" with industry leaders who sought to discharge untreated wastes into the Volga and contemptuously referred to their opponents as *klikushi* (hysterical women).[51] What, he asked, has been the result of the activities of Russia's captains of industry? The Upper Volga basin, which formerly provided drinking water for the city of Moscow, has

[48] N. Reimers, "I khram i masterskaia," *Nash sovremennik*, no. 9 (1973), 145.

[49] F. Shtil'mark, "Nashi kedrovye lesa," *Nash sovremennik*, no. 9 (1975), 160-172.

[50] E. Kandaurov, "Stepnym zapovednikam—Byt'!," *Don*, no. 2 (1976), 159. See also G. Zozulin, "Neobkhodimy etalony prirody," in the same issue, pp. 159-161; and B. Bogdanov, "Zasluzhivaet podderzhki . . . ," *Don*, no. 8 (1976), 157-158.

[51] Dudochkin, "Kak chelovek sdaet," p. 115. On the growing environmental crisis in the Soviet Union, see Boris Komarov, *Unichtozhenie prirody: Obostrenie ekologicheskogo krizisa v SSSR*, Frankfurt/Main, 1978; and Fred Singleton, ed., *Environmental Misuse in the Soviet Union*, New York, 1976.

become unusable, and another river has had to be diverted, at enormous expense, to serve the capital's needs. Thus the attempt to save a few million rubles by not cleaning up the Volga resulted in the state's eventually having to pay hundreds of millions. The popular adage was confirmed: "They searched for a kopeck and lost ten rubles."

The most ambitious article on ecological questions appearing in *Veche* was published under the title "The House We Are Building." The author, who is anonymous but seemed to be well acquainted with Western and particularly American ecological literature, wrote about pollution problems in the West but also discussed serious threats to the Russian environment, e.g., dangers to the Caspian and Aral seas and to Lake Baikal, which contains 10% of the world's fresh water.[52] In the case of Baikal, the author charged that Soviet industrialists had resorted to "de facto sabotage" to thwart the efforts of environmentalists. The extermination of wildlife in Moscow Province is said to have gone so far that one finds more hunters there than hares. Turning philosophical, the *Veche* author suggested that the root of the problem lay in man's attitude toward nature. Man must cease having a "consumer's" view of nature, must stop seeing nature as something "lifeless." The cult of the body and of material things, and the foolish desire to "overtake and pass" the United States, would spell ruin for Russia. Like Soloukhin and Solzhenitsyn, the *Veche* contributor came out sharply against an obsession with material "progress."

A strong commitment to ecology was recently voiced also by Siberian writer Valentin Rasputin. He listed Lake Baikal, the Angara River (which flows out of Baikal), and the Siberian forest as his primary environmental concerns. Our descendants will not forgive us, he asserted, if, for example, the purity of Lake Baikal was not safeguarded. The preservation of the environment, he wrote, was a matter of the most urgent state and national interest.[53]

[52] "Dom kotoryi my stroim," *Veche*, no. 3 (AS 1108), 112.
[53] Valentin Rasputin, "Byt' samim soboi" (an interview), *Voprosy literatury*, no. 9 (1976), 149.

In 1980, *Moskva*, another official journal generally sympathetic to Russian nationalist concerns, published an account of a recent "round-table" discussion sponsored by the journal's editorial board. Among the participants were Academician V. N. Vinogradov, chairman of the Presidium of the Central Council of the All-Russian Society for the Preservation of Nature, and V. B. Elistratov, an instructor of the Komsomol Central Committee. The focal point of the discussion was the fate of the Volga basin. In one of his statements, Vinogradov referred to the critical role played by writer Vladimir Chivilikhin's sketch *Zemlia v bede* (The Land in Trouble), which had appeared more than a decade previously and had served as a spark for Russian ecological concern. "The article," Vinogradov recalled, "produced a colossal impression on the readers of our country . . ."[54] And indeed, Vinogradov added, "the land which nourishes us (*zemlia-kormilitsa*) is in need of our defense . . ."[55]

Elistratov, in his remarks, stressed that the Central Committee of the Komsomol saw the preservation of the environment as directly related to the question of "the ethical upbringing of youth." And he added: "For ten years now there has existed in the Central Committee of the Komsomol a Council for the Preservation of Nature, headed by B. N. Pastukhov, first secretary of the Komsomol Central Committee . . ."[56] According to Elistratov, the Komsomol's "fixed attention" was being directed to the fate of the Volga basin.

At this round-table discussion, both Vinogradov and Elistratov came across as anxious and alarmed. The efforts of the Society for the Preservation of Nature were perceived as being thwarted. Elistratov, for example, noted that the whole of Moscow Province seemed to exist "in isolation" from the society's preservationist efforts. The evident disappointment of the Komsomol leadership with this state of affairs seems particularly noteworthy.

[54] "Glavnaia ulitsa Rossii: Zasedanie 'kruglogo stola' redaktsii zhurnala 'Moskva'," *Moskva*, no. 11 (1980), 177.

[55] Ibid.

[56] Ibid., p. 181.

The voluntary societies, to conclude, represent a serious and at times frenetic attempt to mobilize Russian public opinion to save Russia's past and the Russian environment from extinction. Their opponents appear to consist of heedless devotees of industrial "progress" and modernization, whose views are often perceived as related to the teachings of Marxism-Leninism, a doctrine which can encourage a disregard and even contempt for the past and a crudely exploitative attitude toward nature. One senses, therefore, an important political undercurrent to the struggle between the preservationists and their opponents.

The existence of the voluntary societies and the broad-based support they enjoy in Soviet society present the regime with a dilemma. Marxism-Leninism prompts the leadership to brush aside vestiges of the past—particularly those with religious associations, such as ancient churches and monasteries—and to press ahead with rapid industrialization and modernization. The official ideology encourages a leveling of the historic face of Moscow and the construction of a model "socialist" city in its place. The recent delay in the passing of a law in the RSFSR on the protection and use of historical monuments—the law was finally enacted in December 1978, more than a year after similar laws were passed in the other union republics[57]—testifies to the Soviet leaders' unease over the efforts of Russian preservationists.

Two factors require that the regime proceed with caution toward its ideological goals: (1) The dissatisfaction of Russian public opinion with the destruction of monuments and abuse of the environment could spell political trouble if permitted to get out of hand. (2) Such disaffection could adversely affect mobilizational considerations in particular—for example, those connected with the possibility of a conflict with China. The regime appears to be sensitive and vulnerable to the charge that a destruction of the nation's traditional art and architecture leads to an undermining of patriotism. In addition, even

---

[57] Sergei Voronitsyn, "The RSFSR Belatedly Enacts a Law on the Protection and Use of Historical and Cultural Monuments," Radio Free Europe-Radio Liberty Bulletin of 26 February 1979.

in the top positions of government, there seem to be individuals in sympathy with the aims of the voluntary societies—e.g., Sergei Mikhalkov, head of the RSFSR Union of Writers, and Iurii Melent'ev, minister of culture for the RSFSR. Such support may even extend to the ranks of the Politburo, where it would, however, be a minority position. Faced with such a complex web of considerations, the regime has chosen to be alternately inflexible and willing to make concessions. In dealing with the societies, it has been forced to offer the members of these very large organizations a real possibility of achieving at least some of their aims—hence the restoration of numerous ancient churches and monasteries and the incongruous preservation of the Church of St. Simeon the Stylite on the socialist showpiece, Kalinin Avenue—while not permitting their patriotic fervor and militancy to get out of bounds—hence the refusal to permit VOOPIK to have its own newspaper, journal, or printing house. How long the regime will be able to walk this tightrope is a matter for conjecture.

4

Demographic and Social Dislocations

The Soviet government has been able to control mortality
and international migration to a great degree, but has been
unable to control fertility and internal migration.

Robert A. Lewis et al.[1]

Urban life has corroded the old values and the traditional,
stabilizing relationship of the village. Divorce rates are high,
family control is weak.

David K. Shipler[2]

In 1965, there were 11.9 births and 11.3 deaths for every
thousand inhabitants of Pskov province, which results in a
natural population growth of 0.6.

One-half a man per thousand inhabitants! . . .

In a demographic sense, Pskov province can be seen as
a small model of Russia . . . Yesterday's demographic situation for the Pskov region is being repeated today in many
provinces of the RSFSR.

K. Voronov, in *Veche*[3]

Per capita consumption of hard liquor in the Soviet Union
is the highest of any country in the world.

Robert G. Kaiser[4]

The previous chapter showed how a concern over the fate of
Russian historical monuments and of the Russian land itself
had become a major nationalist issue. It is understandable

[1] Robert A. Lewis, Richard H. Rowland, and Ralph S. Clem, *Nationality
and Population Change in Russia and the USSR: An Evaluation of Census
Data, 1897-1970*, New York, 1976, p. xxv.

[2] David K. Shipler, "Soviet Crime Problem Tied to City Life and Social
Ills," *New York Times*, 6 March 1978, p. A10.

[3] K. Voronov, "Demograficheskie problemy Rossii," *Veche*, no. 9 (AS 2040),
116-117. The name Voronov is apparently a pseudonym.

[4] Robert G. Kaiser, *Russia: The People and the Power*, New York, 1976,
p. 86.

that a fixation with the present and future prospects of the ethnic Russians themselves should have become a second Russian nationalist cause. In the eyes of nationalist spokesmen, the Russian nation is being subjected to unprecedented demographic and socio-moral attrition, the result of governmental policies which are de facto and in essence "anti-Russian." One finds a consistent awareness of this, for example, in the nationalist *samizdat* journal *Veche*. The Soviet Union's immense demographic and social difficulties are viewed, moreover, as closely linked, with the nexus of the problem being the decaying and rapidly disappearing Russian village. As Solzhenitsyn put it in his *Letter to the Soviet Leaders*: "The village, for centuries the mainstay of Russia, has become its chief weakness."[5]

THE MIGRATION PROBLEM

As is well known, beginning with the five-year plans the Soviet Union actively encouraged the migration of labor from the village to urban industrial centers. Modernization was to be achieved at any cost, and working hands were urgently needed in the city. The result was an almost unparalleled rate of urbanization. In the words of three Western students of Soviet demographic processes:

> The rate of urbanization since the turn of the century and particularly since the inception of the five-year plans very probably has been surpassed by few, if any, populations in human history. The Russian urbanization process has been so spectacular that the number of [Great] Russians residing in cities today is roughly 50 million more than would be the case if the Russian level of urbanization in the mid-1920s still persisted. . . . Russians are now about as urbanized as such advanced regions as Western Europe and Japan . . .[6]

[5] Aleksandr I. Solzhenitsyn, *Letter to the Soviet Leaders*, New York, 1974, p. 33.
[6] Lewis et al., *Nationality and Population Change*, pp. 141-142.

Although this vast migration was originally promoted by the authorities, the results of the 1959 census must have given them pause, for it revealed that the rural population of the Soviet Union had decreased by almost 25% in the preceding years. Subsequent attempts by the regime to halt the out-flow—including the much-publicized withholding of internal passports from *kolkhozniki*—seem to have failed. In the period between the censuses of 1959 and 1970, there was a net migration of 16.4 million from the villages to the cities of the Soviet Union. The figure was 15.6 million for the period between the censuses of 1970 and 1979.[7] In 1970 alone, the figure was 1.9 million.[8]

In addition to migration from village to town, another important migratory pattern has been discerned, toward what might be called the Soviet "sunbelt." Migrants have been leaving North and Central Russia for the warmer climes of the Kuban' and the Ukraine, and city dwellers in Western Siberia have been moving to urban centers in the Ukraine, Moldavia, the North Caucasus, and Central Asia, their places being taken by migrants from the Siberian countryside, leaving the West Siberian village the biggest loser.[9] Between 1959 and 1970, net out-migration from Western Siberia was 768,000, and the figure for Siberia as a whole was 924,000.[10] In light of the military threat from China, this represents a serious and unsettling problem to the regime. As the demographer "K. Voronov" has written, the outflow of population from Siberia gradually creates an empty population "reservoir" which the Chinese, according to the "laws of nature," will attempt to fill.[11]

Soviet demographer Viktor Perevedentsev (b. 1931), whose

[7] *Naselenie SSSR po dannym vsesoiuznoi perepisi naseleniia 1979 goda,* Moscow, 1980, p. 3. This figure of 15.6 million resulted both from migration and from the transformation of rural locations into urban ones.

[8] Viktor Perevedentsev, "Iz derevni v gorod," *Nash sovremennik,* no. 11 (1972), 100.

[9] Voronov, "Demograficheskie problemy," p. 131, and Perevedentsev, "Iz derevni," p. 108.

[10] Voronov, "Demograficheskie problemy," p. 121, and Perevedentsev, "Iz derevni," p. 107.

[11] Voronov, "Demograficheskie problemy," p. 121.

views have attracted attention in the Western press, published several pathbreaking studies of Soviet demographic and social issues in the nationalist-oriented journal *Nash sovremennik* in the early and middle 1970s. Migration in the Soviet Union, he emphasized, is primarily a youth phenomenon. Girls leave the villages at age fifteen in order to be residents of urban centers at the time that passports are issued, at age 16, so that they will not thereafter be limited to village residence. Young Soviet males, on the other hand, tend to remain in the village until the conclusion of their military service, when they choose to seek employment in the city rather than returning to the farm. The internal passport system, according to Perevedentsev, has been ineffective in slowing down the outflow of youth and may in fact have encouraged migration. It was perhaps a realization of the correctness of Perevedentsev's contention which prompted the Soviet government recently to begin reexamining its passport policy vis-à-vis the collective farms.

Why do Russian youth feel compelled to leave the countryside? Two factors seem to be at work. First, conditions of employment on the collective and state farms are perceived as so bleak and hopeless that many young people are willing to take their chances in the city. Second, since educational institutions in the countryside are generally viewed as inferior to those in the city, persons seeking career advancement through education feel prompted to migrate for that reason as well. The result of this youth flight has been detrimental to the Russian village. The most energetic, intelligent, and motivated youths are drawn to the city and its opportunities, while parents seeking good careers for their children discourage them from remaining in the countryside. As Perevedentsev sadly concluded: "The city selects the best people."[12] Voronov put it more starkly: "The Russian village is dying out."[13] Many rural areas in the RSFSR are already experiencing serious labor shortages; if massive out-migration contin-

---

[12] Viktor Perevedentsev, "Dlia vsekh i dlia kazhdogo: Zametki sotsiologa," *Nash sovremennik*, no. 1 (1974), 148.
[13] Voronov, "Demograficheskie problemy," p. 129.

ues, Soviet agriculture and the economy as a whole will suffer.

If the flow of population from village to town and from North and Central Russia and Siberia to the south were the Soviet Union's only demographic problem, it would be serious enough. It is, however, only one of numerous ripple effects set in motion by the decline of the Russian village.

THE DECLINE IN FERTILITY

What has happened to the millions of migrants who over the years have poured into Russia's urban centers? Perhaps most dramatically, they have stopped reproducing. The decline in Russian fertility during the Soviet period has been extraordinary. One Western specialist has written: "The decline in the Soviet birth rate has been drastic, one of the most rapid in history, dropping from 44.3 per thousand in 1928 to 24.9 in 1960."[14] Since 1960, the decline has accelerated. "In our country," Perevedentsev wrote in 1975, "a million fewer children are now born each year than in 1960."[15] And a *New York Times* correspondent reported in 1977 that the birthrate had been hovering "near 18 per 1,000 of population" for a decade.[16] Moreover, aggregate statistics for the Soviet Union as a whole do not tell the full story, since the birth rates of certain Central Asian and other minority nationalities have been soaring while those of Russians and Eastern Slavs have been dwindling. Citing the calculations of demographer B. Ts. Urlanis, Perevedentsev has said that Soviet couples capable of bearing children will have to produce an average of 2.65 offspring simply to replenish the population.[17] But a poll of 34,000 Soviet citizens taken in 1969 ascertained that they desired an average of 2.4 children per family, i.e., not enough

[14] H. Kent Geiger, *The Family in Soviet Russia*, Cambridge, Mass., 1968, p. 187.
[15] Viktor Perevedentsev, "Sem'ia: Vchera, segodnia, zavtra . . . ," *Nash sovremennik*, no. 6 (1975), 118.
[16] Christopher S. Wren, "Sexual Revolution in Soviet Straining Strict Morality," *New York Times*, 25 September 1977, p. 1.
[17] Perevedentsev, "Sem'ia," p. 123.

for replenishment. Furthermore, this figure of 2.4 reflects
the high fertility expectations of "certain national and autonomous [i.e., non-Slavic] republics" included in the survey.[18]
A recent poll of Moscow women showed that 54.5% of those
contacted wanted two children, while 43% wanted only one.[19]
According to the 1979 census, the average family in the RSFSR
(and in the Ukraine and Belorussia as well) consisted of only
3.3 persons.[20]

Among the reasons why ethnic Russians are alarmed over
their low fertility rate are the enormous population losses and
birth deficits which they have suffered as a people during the
Soviet period. K. Voronov has estimated that the Eastern Slavs
lost three million during the Civil War, six million during the
famine of 1921-1922, and seven million during the famine of
1930-1933, as well as untold victims during Stalin's "waves of
repression." (Neo-Marxist dissenter Roy Medvedev has con-
servatively calculated this loss at 25-26 million[21]). Voronov
has figured the Soviet birth deficit due to the First World
War as 30 million and due to World War II as 70 million with
most of this deficit, of course, being borne by the Eastern
Slavs.[22] The USSR, as is common knowledge, also lost approximately 20 million citizens in the war against Hitler's
Germany. These appalling figures have led Solzhenitsyn to
exclaim: ". . . with and without wars we have lost *one-third*
of the population we could have had and almost *half* of the
one we in fact have!"[23] The calculations of Voronov and other
Russian nationalists may be too high—writing in the late 1950s,
David J. Dallin estimated Soviet population losses, including
birth deficits from the two world wars, at 100 million[24]—but

[18] Ibid.
[19] Ibid.
[20] *Naselenie SSSR*, p. 17.
[21] See Medvedev's response to Solzhenitsyn's *Letter to the Soviet Leaders*,
in AS 1874, p. 13. English translation in Roy A. Medvedev, *Political Essays*,
Nottingham, 1976, pp. 93-109.
[22] Voronov, "Demografischeskie problemy," pp. 123-124.
[23] Solzhenitsyn, *Letter*, p. 30 (Solzhenitsyn's italics).
[24] Cited in Geiger, *Family in Soviet Russia*, p. 120.

by anyone's figures, Russian population losses during the Soviet period have been staggering.

Coupled with the rapid growth of the Muslim and Turkic birth rates, the decline in Russian and Eastern Slav fertility threatens eventually to alter the ethnic "balance of power" of the state. The 1979 census reported the following average family sizes: Tadzhikistan, 5.7; Uzbekistan, 5.5; Turkmenia, 5.5; and Azerbaidzhan, 5.1.[25] These compare to the figure already noted of 3.3 for the RSFSR, the Ukraine, and Belorussia. According to demographer Murray Feshbach, if the trends confirmed by the 1979 census continue until the year 2000, ". . . the Great Russians may be expected to continue their decline as a share of the Soviet population. In 1959, they were 54.6 percent of the total; in 1970, 53.4 percent; and in 1979, 52.4 percent. By the year 2000, the figure may be 46-48 percent."[26] Moreover, Chinese pressure on Siberia will surely grow more acute if Eastern Slav fertility continues to plummet.

WORKING WOMEN

Soviet demographers, Perevedentsev among them, have attempted to elucidate the reasons behind the dramatic falling-off of Russian fertility. Their research has yielded the explanation that the most significant factor has been the economic necessity for urban Russian women to be employed full-time. A recent questionnaire distributed to women living in Leningrad showed that 53.5% of those contacted cited "the necessity of extra salary for the family" as the chief reason for their going to work.[27] Life for the average Russian working woman can be described as a heavy burden. After putting in a full day's work at the plant or office, urban Russian women then have to put in four to five hours (or more) doing the shopping, cooking, and housework (few Russian men seem

[25] *Naselenie SSSR*, p. 17.
[26] Murray Feshbach, "Between the Lines of the 1979 Soviet Census," *Problems of Communism*, 31, no. 1 (January-February 1982), 35.
[27] Perevedentsev, "Sem'ia," p. 130.

willing to pitch in and help). Readers of Solzhenitsyn's *Cancer Ward* may recall the scene in which the eminent specialist Doctor Dontsova has to begin her "second" day shopping for bargains after an enervating day at work. Of the women polled by the Leningrad questionnaire, 82% reported that they had to do the housework alone (i.e., without a maid), and only one-fourth received any assistance from relatives.[28]

With the above in mind, it can cause little wonder that one out of three women contacted in the Leningrad survey complained of an excessive physical load, while one out of five admitted to general exhaustion.[29] Overworked and fatigued women are, for obvious reasons, disinclined to bear large families. Most of those who become pregnant—birth control devices are only sporadically and irregularly available—opt for an abortion, which is free for working women. In the mid-1970s, the chief gynecologist of Moscow told Hedrick Smith, "For each birth, we figure two abortions," and he added there were 170,000 abortions performed in Moscow during 1973. If this percentage were extended nationwide, it would mean roughly five million abortions annually.[30] Many Russian women undergo four, five, or six abortions in a lifetime; even ten abortions are not unheard of.

Evidently, neither Russian women nor their spouses are happy that women are forced to work, especially when a child of preschool age is at home. Among Leningrad husbands questioned in the survey reported by Perevedentsev, 73% accepted their wife's working only as a necessity, and 74% of the parents polled were displeased that young children had to be left at the Soviet equivalent of day-care centers. Thus, approximately three-quarters of those reponding to the Leningrad questionnaire were opposed to the status quo.

The fact that wives are economically compelled to work is only one reason behind the marked drop in fertility. A serious housing shortage often makes hopes for finding an apartment unrealistic. Migrants to the city are usually forced to live for

[28] Ibid.
[29] Ibid.
[30] Hedrick Smith, *The Russians*, New York, 1976, p. 142.

years with relatives, in workers' dormitories, or in squalid rented rooms. Young people tend to put off marriage in order to complete their education, and an increase in the incidence of divorce has also adversely affected fertility.

THE EROSION OF TRADITIONAL MORALS AND MORES

The crush of migrants into the city has created a socially combustible situation. Many sources underline the deleterious effects of the erosion of traditional village morals and mores. The young people who swarm into the cities become intoxicated with "freedom," and the results include upsurges in premarital sex, births out of wedlock, divorce, alcoholism, and juvenile delinquency.

A recent survey of Leningrad students revealed that 52.5% of males and 14.5% of females had had sexual intercourse before the age of eighteen. By age twenty-one, the figure rose to 85.3% for men and 64.9% for women. Though morals in Leningrad may be laxer than elsewhere in the country (for example, in Central Asia), they appear to be indicative of a trend. The same survey showed that 53% of student males and 38% of student women approved of premarital sex, while only 16% of men and 27% of women condemned it (the rest were "indifferent").[31] Another survey, conducted by Professor A. Kharchev in sixteen cities of the RSFSR, the Ukraine, and the Baltic, revealed that 42% of the young married women questioned had engaged in premarital sex, 38% of them with several men. In addition, of the young marrieds questioned, 62% of the men and 42% of the women admitted to engaging in extramarital sex.[32]

The frequency of premarital and extramarital sex, in a country where birth control is only erratically practiced, has further implications. In 1966, one out of three newborns in the city of Perm' was illegitimate.[33] An article entitled "He Promised

[31] Perevedentsev, "Sem'ia," p. 127.
[32] Il'ia Zemtsov, "Sovetskaia molodezh': Poteria perspektivy," *Russkaia mysl'*, 2 March 1978, p. 4.
[33] Perevedentsev, "Sem'ia," p. 127.

to Marry Me," written by Larisa Kuznetsova, which appeared in *Nash sovremennik* in 1975, dealt with the fate of young female migrants living in workers' dormitories, where some three and a half million Soviet youths are housed.[34] Many of these girls become pregnant and ultimately have to return to their native village with a child and without an education. In light of Russia's acute fertility problems, it could be argued that any child, even an illegitimate one, is to be welcomed, and, in fact, an article pointing in that direction did appear in *Literaturnaia gazeta* in the spring of 1977.[35] Other commentators, e.g., Perevedentsev, will have nothing to do with such "solutions." After all, what kind of children will be raised by embittered and demoralized migrant girls forced to return to the village against their will?

Divorce is a related problem. The number of divorces in the Soviet Union increased tenfold between 1950 and 1973, from 67,000 to 679,000. In 1950, there were thirty-two divorces for every thousand marriages; in 1973, 270 for every thousand.[36] This rate may not seem particularly high when compared with that of contemporary Western societies, but the crux of the issue is that two-thirds of the divorces strike marriages of less than five years' duration, and one-third, those of less than one year. Moreover, while second marriages do take place, they occur only half as frequently as first marriages, and the gap between them is widening.[37] According to Dr. N. Iurkevich, the major causes of divorce in the Soviet Union are alcoholism and adultery.[38] Historian Igor' Bestuzhev-Lada, writing in the journal *Nedelia*, complained that one-third of marriages were ending in divorce and lamented the disappearance of large families. In addition to alcoholism as a cause of divorce, Bestuzhev-Lada cited the difficulty of finding an adequate apartment, which results in many cou-

[34] Larisa Kuznetsova, "Obeshchal zhenit'sia . . . ," *Nash sovremennik*, no. 9 (1974), 124-136.
[35] Wren, "Sexual Revolution," p. 1.
[36] Perevedentsev, "Sem'ia," p. 128.
[37] Ibid., p. 129.
[38] Cited in ibid., p. 128.

ples' having to live together with parents in cramped quarters.[39]

ALCOHOLISM AND CRIME

Alcoholism, the Soviet citizen's tranquilizer, contributes to considerably more than the rapidly rising divorce rate. Hedrick Smith has reported: "High officials have disclosed that intoxication is the major factor in the majority of all crimes (90 percent of murders), accounts for more than half of all traffic accidents, is a major cause in 40 percent of all divorce cases, figures in 63 percent of all accidental drownings, one-third of all ambulance calls in Moscow. It is the prime cause of the absenteeism that plays havoc with the Soviet economy."[40] Though chiefly affecting men, this disease also extends to women, and it is not unusual to see intoxicated women on Russian streets. According to K. Voronov, more than 95% of the Russian populace regularly indulge in vodka, and far too few do so in moderation.[41] The pervasiveness of this social plague finds reflection in both official and *samizdat* Soviet literature. In fact, according to recent émigré Iurii Mal'tsev, "alcoholic prose" is becoming an identifiable genre in Russian underground literature.[42]

Rising crime, particularly juvenile crime, is another offshoot of the processes being examined. The *New York Times* reported in early 1978:

Not long ago, a law journal published findings that newcomers in cities were more vulnerable than longtime residents to the anonymity and disorientation of city life.

"Deformed or totally disintegrated family and kinship ties are much more common among migrants than among people who have always lived in the city," said the law institute journal *Gosudarstvo i pravo*. "A distinctive kind of

[39] "High Divorce Rate Worries Russians," *New York Times*, 8 September 1977, p. A24.

[40] Smith, *The Russians*, p. 121.

[41] Voronov, "Demograficheskie problemy," p. 138.

[42] Iu. Mal'tsev, *Vol'naia russkaia literatura, 1955-1975*, Frankfurt/Main, 1976, p. 103.

vacuum forms around such individuals and is often filled by people whose influence is very harmful."

A sample of lawbreakers showed that twice as many new arrivals as longtime residents spent their free time with former convicts, and the percentage of offenders was higher among newcomers. . . .

"Only 15 percent of urban couples with children live with any of their parents," the magazine reported. "Since in nuclear families the parents both work, as a rule, and there are no other adult relatives in the family, teen-agers and young people often spend a good part of the day on their own. This is a contributing factor in the higher level of juvenile crime in cities compared to rural localities."[43]

The *Times* correspondent, David Shipler, had also reported an interesting case in which the police, Komsomol and "others of influence" overcame the objections of Party officials and schoolteachers to the showing of a play which boldly investigates the causes of juvenile delinquency.[44]

To sum up, in the eyes of Russian nationalists, the contemporary Soviet Union's demographic and social problems are links in a chain extending back to the decaying and ever less viable Russian village. The flight of migrant youth from the farms spells agricultural and economic woe and gives rise to serious demographic difficulties. Russia's urban centers, as well as a number of cities outside the RSFSR where Russians are wont to cluster, can no longer absorb the outflow from the countryside. Squalid, crowded living conditions greet the migrants and help effect the breakdown of village morals and mores. Sexual license, alcoholism, and juvenile delinquency are the result. The nuclear family crumbles and corrodes in the uncongenial milieu of the modern city. Urban life is particularly hard on women, both migrants and longtime residents. Forced to put in long days at the factory or office and then to add four or five hours of fatiguing shopping and

---

[43] Shipler, "Soviet Crime Problem," p. A10. See Also Walter D. Connor, *Deviance in Soviet Society: Crime, Delinquency, and Alcoholism*, New York, 1972.

[44] David K. Shipler, "Rising Youth Crime in Soviet Troubles Regime and Public," *New York Times*, 5 March 1978, p. 16.

housework, Russian women go about exhausted and irritable. Divorce spirals upward, while the Russian birthrate continues to decline to the point where it is insufficient to ensure replenishment of the population. This, in turn, raises two specters: (1) a fear that the rising birth rates of the Turkic and Muslim peoples will alter the ethnic mix of the country and eventually affect the balance of power among the different Soviet nationalities; and (2) an anxiety that dwindling Russian and Eastern Slavic fertility will encourage China to increase its pressure on the borders of Siberia.

The regime, to be sure, is cognizant of these problems, but it is hampered in coping with them by Marxist-Leninist ideology. Serious reforms in the agricultural sector are virtually ruled out by the commitment to collectivism. The traditional support of the defense-heavy industry complex, a support justified by ideology, and the effort to meet the rising consumer expectations of the urban populace make a reordering of priorities in favor of the countryside unlikely. As for urban social problems, the regime is constrained in dealing with them by the ideological myth that such phenomena as crime and alcoholism represent disappearing "survivals" of the past. As Lenin once wrote: "We know that the fundamental social cause of violations of the rules of society is the exploitation of the masses, their want and poverty. With the removal of the chief cause, excesses will inevitably begin to 'wither away.' "[45] The tendency for the present regime is to limit itself to minor reforms and to avoid grappling with root problems. An improvement of conditions in Siberia's villages and urban centers would seem to be compatible with ideology, but one wonders whether the regime is willing to invest the necessary funds and human resources to achieve this goal.

PROPOSED REFORMS

Russian nationalists advocate decisive reforms in a number of areas where the regime has been unable or unwilling to act. Perevedentsev, for example, has suggested these re-

---

[45] Cited in Valery Chalidze, *Criminal Russia: A Study of Crime in the Soviet Union*, New York, 1977, p. 204.

forms: (1) Improve the organization of agricultural labor, the "main link in the chain of the migration problems of the village" and the chief reason for the labor shortage in the Russian countryside. (2) Ameliorate the overall quality of life in the villages. (3) Improve the village schools and the level of their teaching staffs. (4) Make provincial urban centers more attractive for skilled workers from other regions in order to slow down the migration to them of local rural inhabitants. (5) Seek an end to the widespread denigration of the village; stress those areas in which the village enjoys advantages over the city, e.g., housing, the existence of good neighbors, traditional customs. (6) Devote increased attention to the adjustment difficulties of newly arrived migrants to the city.

K. Voronov, writing in *Veche*, offered these suggestions for remedying Russia's birth deficit problem: (1) Award tangible grants to mothers on the birth of a second and third child. (2) Give parents a pay raise upon the birth of a child. (3) Improve housing. (4) Provide working mothers with the option of part-time employment. (5) Raise the salaries of textile workers. The problem leading to this last proposal is that salaries for textile workers are frequently so low that men refuse to accept them, and so textile centers have come to be largely inhabited by women.

In his *Letter to the Soviet Leaders*, Solzhenitsyn proposes the following reforms, predicated upon the regime's jettisoning of Marxist-Leninist ideology: (1) Give up the collective farms. "Our 'ideological agriculture' has already become the laughingstock of the entire world. . . . For centuries Russia *exported* grain, ten to twelve million tons a year just before the First World War . . . It's shameful—it really is time we came to our senses!"[46] (2) Develop and cultivate Russia's provincial capitals and cities, and put an end to Soviet centralization practices. "Without these sixty or eighty towns Russia does not exist as a country . . ."[47] (3) Develop the Northeast; in addition to economic and developmental reasons, "a well-

[46] Solzhenitsyn, *Letter*, p. 33 (Solzhenitsyn's italics).
[47] Ibid., pp. 38-39.

established Northeast is also our best defense against China."[48]
(4) Alleviate the lot of Russian working women. "In practice,
a man's wage level ought to be such that whether he has a
family of two or even four children, the woman *does not need*
to earn a separate paycheck and *does not need* to support her
family financially on top of all her other toils and troubles.
. . . The undermining and destruction of the family is part of
the terrible price we have paid for those Five-Year Plans."[49]

Other Russian nationalist programmatic writings of the 1960s
and 1970s have advocated similar reforms. Thus, "The Nation
Speaks," a right-wing manifesto, fulminates against "Trotskii's
view, inimical to the peasantry," that the village represents
an internal colony whose purpose is to provide the means for
the industrialization of the country. Trotskii's view, the authors asserted, was in effect adopted by Stalin, despite his
official denunciation of it, and it underlay the forced collectivization of agriculture. "A flourishing agriculture," the manifesto declared, "is a general popular necessity, and if in order
to achieve it we are required to allow strong individual econ-
omies to exist, then we must do so, unimpeded by any dog-
mas. We buy bread from Canada—we should rather cultivate
a Canada of our own."[50]

Similarly, the program of the All-Russian Social-Christian
Union for the Liberation of the People excoriates the USSR's
backward economy: ". . . a free, small-scale economy most
effectively assures food for the populace and raw material for
industry. Collectivization . . . has over the course of decades
produced economically harmful results which cannot be rec-
tified within the present system."[51] The program also focuses
upon the plight of Russian working women: "Because of their
irreplaceable role, women must be given special rights to make
the performance of their duties less onerous. Social Christianity would lead to a system in which women would not eco-

[48] Ibid., p. 35.
[49] Ibid., p. 40 (Solzhenitsyn's italics).
[50] See *Survey*, 17, no. 3 (1971), 194-195.
[51] "The VSKhSON Program," in John B. Dunlop, *The New Russian Revolutionaries*, Belmont, Mass., 1976, p. 259.

nomically be forced to participate directly in social production."[52]

In view of the acuteness of Russia's demographic and social problems, one might expect a Russian nationalist government to take decisive action to alleviate the difficulties we have been examining. The following steps would seem likely to be taken: (1) an abolition of the collective and state farms, and a marked upgrading of the importance ascribed to the agricultural sector; (2) a raising of the stature and quality of Russia's provincial capitals and cities through administrative decentralization and other measures; (3) an energetic attempt to improve living conditions—both urban and rural—in areas of mass outmigration, such as the Russian Northwest and Western Siberia; and (4) encouragement of Russian and Eastern Slavic fertility through cash or salary bonuses, improved housing, and a real concern for the problems of working women. (If the non-Slavic republics were given a degree of real autonomy to run their own affairs—and to regulate their own fertility—this would not necessarily smack of "racism.") Authoritarian nationalists might feel tempted to revive a version of Stalin's harsh laws against divorce and abortion, and in both these areas they could find support in the teachings of the Russian Orthodox Church. (5) Maximum support for the nuclear family and for revival of traditional morality (here again the Russian Church could offer useful support). (6) A diverting of funds presently employed in the support of foreign "liberation movements" to urgently needed domestic tasks.

Such a series of steps seems so "logical" in light of Russia's demographic and social difficulties that the next leadership will surely be tempted to implement them, especially since they coincide with the solution to the problem of how to mobilize the populace for a conflict against China. Whether "logic" will in fact prevail should become evident in the fairly near future.

[52] Ibid., p. 279.

5

Cultural Manifestations of Russian Nationalism

> I paint the truth. The proof is the half-million Russians who
> came to see my show.
>
> Il'ia Glazunov[1]

> . . . without a deep insight into modern Soviet literature
> and art, which have become a political battlefield, no rel-
> evant Soviet studies are possible.
>
> Mikhail Agurskii[2]

> The time of Aksenov, Evtushenko, and Voznesenskii has
> passed. They offered us a surrogate and not the bread of
> art.
>
> Mikhail Morozov, in *Veche*[3]

As in the case of the nationalists' concern with preservation
and with the social-demographic well-being of the Russian
people, it is not difficult to understand why cultural expression should have become a nationalist issue. Due to censorship restrictions, literature and the arts have traditionally served
as the cutting edge of social and political inquiry in Russia.
Speaking elliptically and, if necessary, in Aesopian terms, the
artist is better able to evade the censorship than is, say, the
political essayist or historian. This fact is, of course, appreci-
ated in Soviet society, with the result that cultural events can
at times take on a mass character. In addition, from the nineteenth century on, the Russian nationalist tendency has been

---

[1] Quoted in Joseph Kraft, "Letter from Moscow," *New Yorker*, 16 October
1978, p. 139.

[2] Mikhail Agursky, "The New Russian Literature," Research Paper no. 40
(1980), Soviet and East European Research Centre, Hebrew University of
Jerusalem, p. 64.

[3] Mikhail Morozov, "Neskol'ko zamechanii o sovremennom literaturnom
protsesse," *Veche*, no. 2 (AS 1020), 70.

keenly interested in art as an expression of Russian "original-ity" (*samobytnost'*), i.e., that which distinguishes Russia from the contemporary West. Finally, the close attention paid to the traditional Russian village in present-day nationalist art seems logical, since the village is seen as a repository of val-ues perceived as under attack by Soviet prometheans.

In 1969, the critic Anatolii Lanshchikov pointed out to a seminar of literary specialists that the writings of the so-called *derevenshchik* or "ruralist," school represented "not at all vil-lage literature (no one reads it in the village), but literature for the intelligentsia."[4] And he added: "We want to return to our sources, not in order to remain there, but, proceeding from their morality and ideals, to move further along, to build something new."[5] I would underline Lanshchikov's words "to build something new."

Similar views were advanced by *derevenshchik* writer Fe-dor Abramov (b. 1920) in a speech to the Sixth Congress of Soviet Writers.[6] In his address, Abramov offered some tongue-in-cheek comments about the state of contemporary Russian letters:

Around us a scientific and technical revolution is taking place, it is the era of *sputniks*, but our writers (including some who are well-known) have gotten hopelessly bogged down in village back-roads. What has happened to the *avant-garde* role of literature? . . . Viktor Astaf'ev genuflects be-fore his long-deceased grandmother . . . Valentin Rasputin hovers and bustles about a dying old woman. And Vasilii Belov's famous Ivan Afrikanovich—can one really call him progressive? . . . So what is this? Perhaps our literature is, to put it mildly, not exactly marching in step with the times? Perhaps it is lagging behind, suffering from provincialism?

[4] "Na seminare literaturnykh kritikov," *Politicheskii dnevnik*, 1, (1972), 505-506.

[5] Ibid., p. 506.

[6] Fedor Abramov, "O khlebe nasushchnom i o khlebe dukhovnom," *Nash sovremennik*, no. 9 (1976), 170-172. Much of the account which follows rep-resents a condensed version of my article, "The Ruralist Prose Writers in the Russian Ethnic Movement," in Edward Allworth, ed., *Ethnic Russia in the USSR*, New York, 1980, pp. 80-87.

Or, to borrow an expression from contemporary intellectuals, perhaps it is not sufficiently intellectual?

Abramov then went on to explain why it was appropriate, indeed necessary, for Russian writers to concern themselves with the fate of the disappearing Russian village. "What does it mean," he asked, "that the old village is departing forever? It means that the age-old pillars are giving way, that the soil [pochva] of many centuries in which our entire national culture has been rooted—its ethics and esthetics, its folklore and literature, its miraculous language—is disappearing. Because, to paraphrase Dostoevskii, all of us have come out of the village. The village represents our primal source [istok] and our roots [korni]." Moreover, Abramov continued, when one contemplates Russia's future, her youth, one all too frequently observes "overweening egocentrism and individualism, parasitical and acquisitive inclinations, the loss of a careful and loving attitude toward the land and toward nature, and a cold rationalism." These failings contribute to the vast youth out-migration from the farm which Abramov, like all "ruralists," deplores. It may be, he suggested, that today's Russian youth has something to learn from the traditional Russian village.

Over the past two decades, the *derevenshchiki*, as well as other nationalist cultural activists, have been attempting, consciously or unconsciously, to carry out a quiet revolution aimed at changing the attitudes of their countrymen. In muted fashion—not so muted in the cases of Solzhenitsyn and another recent émigré, Vladimir Maksimov—they have contested Soviet "titanism": the USSR's traditional commitment, based on its ideology, to unrestricted industrial growth and an accompanying lack of concern for the effect of such growth on the environment and on the Russian people themselves. The cult of the "NTR" (scientific and technical revolution) is challenged at every step. As nationalist critic Iurii Seleznev has pointed out, ". . . our era is not only the epoch of the NTR but, above all, a great period of self-determination—

ideological, social, and moral-spiritual self-determination."[7] And he asked, "What about those who do not poeticize the NTR but reveal, for example, the poetry of the Russian soul, the feeling of love for one's homeland, for its nature and people?"[8] The NTR, such authors suggest, has nothing to offer with which to fill the spiritual vacuum in the souls of modern man; in fact, it may even contribute to creating that vacuum.

The positive mission of the "quiet revolution" has been to resurrect from near-extinction values and moral reflexes which have been out of fashion—indeed, subjected to persecution and derision—during the Soviet period. "Ethics and esthetics" is how many nationalists choose to sum up this cluster of desired qualities.[9] The writer Sh. Galimov has written that the yearning of Russian nationalists is "not simply for the village, but for lofty moral achievements, for humaneness, and for spiritual perfection. And this is not at all elicited by a striving to preserve the past but by a thirst to find the true path and by anxiety for the future."[10] Abramov offered this list of virtues which, he contended, flow to contemporary man from the Russian village: "Boundless self-sacrifice, an alert Russian conscience and sense of duty, the capacity to practice self-limitation and compassion, love of labor, love of the earth and everything living . . ."[11] The nationalists insist that they are doing battle for the allegiance of Russia's youth, upon whom the fate of the country depends. In their writings, Soviet youth is depicted as rootless and confused but not de-

---

[7] Iurii Seleznev, *Vechnoe dvizhenie: Iskaniia sovremennoi prozy 60-kh—nachala 70-kh godov*, Moscow, 1976, p. 7.

[8] Ibid., p. 13. See also Solzhenitsyn's highly favorable comments on the *derevenshchiki*, contained in a February 1979 interview with Janis Sapiets of the BBC: Aleksandr I. Solzhenitsyn, *East and West*, New York, 1980, pp. 157-160. On the "village prose" movement, see Geoffrey Hosking, *Beyond Socialist Realism*, London, 1980; N. N. Shneidman, *Soviet Literature in the 1970s*, Toronto, 1979; John B. Dunlop, "Reclaiming the Russian Past," *Times Literary Supplement*, 19 November 1976, p. 1,447; and Agursky, "New Russian Literature."

[9] For example, M. Lobanov, *Vnutrennee i vneshnee: Literaturnye zametki*, Moscow, 1975, p. 156.

[10] From a collection of articles devoted to "the sociological aspect of contemporary 'village prose,' " *Voprosy literatury*, no. 3 (1973), 55.

[11] Abramov, "O khlebe nasushchnom," p. 172.

praved, capable of being educated and returned to the path
of their fathers, a path brightly illumined by the "sun" of
nineteenth-century classical Russian literature.[12]

One should also not ignore the historical and religious dimensions of this cultural phenomenon. A strong sense of
"thousand-year-Russia" and a feeling of sharing in the glories
and degradations of this history make themselves felt. Likewise, one observes an awareness that from 988 until 1917
Russia was an Orthodox Christian land and that Russia in
partnership with Orthodoxy achieved great things. Such historical and religious dimensions, of course, come into conflict
with Marxist-Leninist ideology, which tends to reject the significance of both.

In order better to understand the strength and socio-polit-
ical resonance of Russian nationalist cultural expression in the
Soviet Union, the rest of this chapter will examine four episodes which attracted, not to say riveted, national attention
during the Brezhnev period. Two of these episodes, as shall
be seen, took on an unmistakably mass character, a development which was not lost on the regime.

THE BELOV AFFAIR

Vasilii Belov's novel *Privychnoe delo* (That's How It Is,
1966)[13] was, in the words of Slavicist Deming Brown, "the
single agrarian novel most talked about in the sixties . . ."[14]
In this work, Belov, who was born in 1933 in a village in
Vologda Province, tells the tale of a peasant, Ivan Afrikanovich Drynov, living in a northern Russian village in the period following the Second World War, of which he is a veteran. The hero is married to an exemplary peasant woman,
Katerina, who has borne him nine children. Drynov's idyll of
"organic" peasant domesticity and hard but rewarding physi-

---

[12] Seleznev, *Vechnoe dvizhenie*, p. 235.
[13] Vasilii Belov, "Privychnoe delo," *Sever*, no. 1 (1966), 7-92.
[14] Deming Brown, *Soviet Russian Literature since Stalin*, Cambridge, 1978,
p. 245. See also the comments on the novel in Geoffrey A. Hosking, "The
Russian Peasant Rediscovered: 'Village Prose' of the 1960s," *Slavic Review*,
32, no. 4 (1973), 717-720.

cal labor suffers two blows in the course of the novel. First, Ivan's seemingly innocent indulgence in drink and revelry leads him to miss the birth of his ninth child and to cause grief to his wife, whom he adores. And second, his foolish and irresponsible brother-in-law, Mit'ka, convinces him to leave the village temporarily in search of more remunerative employment in the city of Murmansk. While Ivan and Mit'ka knock about on their travels, Katerina dies, leaving Drynov a widower with nine children. He contemplates suicide but is revived by the Russian woods and countryside (and perhaps by his mother-in-law's prayers as well). Friends soon provide him with a new peasant wife, and a chastened and wiser Ivan will presumably find the strength to carry on.

That's How It Is, a novel of considerable power, raises a number of issues of concern to Russian nationalists. Drinking and migration to the city are, of course, perceived as two of the greatest dangers to the health of the Russian people and to the continued viability of the Russian village. The village is depicted as a repository of authentic existence and vivifying mores; Belov delights in the richness of spoken, peasant Russian, in the bracing rhythm of life in the countryside (Ivan and his family rise at dawn), in good neighbors, and in peasant customs, songs, and dances. Katerina's nine children, each of whom has an engaging personality, obviously represent a solution to the Russian birth deficit problem. Yet Ivan Afrikanovich and the Russian village are shown to be in danger of extinction. As one character puts it in the novel: ". . . in five years, no one will remain in the village, they will all have gone off."[15] Belov does not pull any punches in criticizing the state for ruinous agricultural policies. Ivan and Katerina are required to circumvent the law and cut hay by stealth at night in order to feed their cow, while it is the family's poverty which leads Ivan to succumb to Mit'ka's blandishments and contemplate migration.

Ivan Afrikanovich is obviously far from the "positive hero" of vintage socialist realism. Though morally decent and phys-

---

[15] Belov, "Privychnoe delo," p. 50.

ically resilient, he is weak and indecisive and relies heavily on women. Moreover, it is not Marxist-Leninist ideology but nature and religion which are portrayed as the two securest refuges for the fast-disappearing Russian peasant.

The reasons for the work's popularity are not difficult to divine. The decline of the village has been of immense significance for contemporary Russia, and Belov's novel is a spirited attempt to help arrest this trend, to show the strengths and advantages which the countryside enjoys over the formlessness and atomization of modern urban life.

THE *Kalina krasnaia* EPISODE

The year of Vasilii Shukshin's death, 1974, also witnessed his greatest triumph—the film *Kalina krasnaia* (Snowball Berry Red), which he directed and in which, as an actor, he played the leading role.[16] The film enjoyed almost unprecedented success; the "overwhelming majority" of the readers of a popular film magazine, *Sovetskii ekran*, chose it as the year's best picture, while another film journal, *Iskusstvo kino*, reported: "Viewers of *Kalina krasnaia* not only 'watched' the film, it really stirred them. For that reason letters arrive at newspapers and journals requesting that they speak at greater length about the picture, explain something in it, write about how it was made."[17] A scrutiny of this film and its reception by the Soviet public can tell us something noteworthy about contemporary Soviet society.

Briefly, *Kalina krasnaia* is the story of a deracinated peasant, Egor Prokudin, who has moved to the city, adopted urban ways, fallen into bad company, and ended up in prison. The film opens with Egor's release from jail and his return to the company of his former criminal associates. His "soul," however, begins insistently to draw him to the countryside

[16] For the Russian original of the tale upon which the film is based, see *Nash sovremennik*, no. 4 (1973), 86-133. An English translation by Donald M. Fiene appears in Donald M. Fiene, ed., *Vasily Shukshin: Snowball Berry Red and Other Stories*, Ann Arbor, 1979, pp. 125-199.

[17] *Iskusstvo kino*, no. 10 (1974), 113. The information about the readers of *Sovetskii ekran* comes from Fiene, *Vasily Shukshin*, p. 203.

and to the peasant girl Liubov' Baikalova, whom he has never met but with whom he has corresponded while in prison. In the company of Liuba, her patriarchal parents, and her convivial *muzhik* brother, Petro, Egor searches for his roots, plowing the soil and, incognito, visiting his mother in a nearby village. Distressed at Egor's apostasy, his former criminal companions demand that he return to them. When he refuses, they kill him and are then, in turn, dispatched by an enraged Petro, who rams their getaway car with his truck and sends it flying into the Volga.

Despite the ravages of censorship—the London *Times* reported that the censors cut some twenty-five minutes from the film[18]—*Kalina krasnaia* contains both unmistakable political thrusts (e.g., the humorous scene in which bored Soviet citizens are shown walking about beneath exultant communist banners) and religious gropings (e.g., the abandoned church, half-submerged in the springtime floods depicted at the beginning of the film, or the church which appears in the background as Egor accuses himself after his visit to his mother). While good directing and fine acting obviously contributed to the film's success, it was the picture's theme—that of the uprooted peasant—which seems to have been the principal factor behind *Kalina krasnaia*'s extraordinary reception by the Soviet public.

An interesting round-table discussion devoted to the film has been published in *Voprosy literatury*. The assembled writers and critics testified unanimously to the almost unprecedented impact of the film. "Very few events," B. Runin remarked, "have taken place in recent times in our art which have so stirred the social and esthetic self-consciousness of the viewer."[19] G. Baklanov recalled that he had spent "ten days under the influence of this astonishing film,"[20] and S. Zalygin declared, ". . . it is a very profound, human, noble

[18] *Times* (London), 4 October 1974, p. 18.
[19] "Obsuzhdaem 'Kalinu krasnuiu': Kinopovest' i fil'm V. Shukshina," *Voprosy literatury*, no. 7 (1974), 31.
[20] Ibid., p. 46.

film, a genuine work of art."[21] L. Anninskii seems to have summed up the sentiments of many when he asserted, "Vasilii Shukshin is at present the most interesting figure in our cinema."[22]

The participants in the colloquy were in general agreement as to the reason for the film's success—its portrayal of an urbanized peasant who yearns for his roots. According to B. Runin, the film's protagonist is a "fractured man, one of those tens of millions of people who, by the will of history, have at various times left their native village and ceased to be peasants."[23] Egor, L. Anninskii added, "has only just lost contact with his native soil. This is not Belov's Ivan Afrikanovich, who is organically and lastingly fused with nature's 'bosom.' But it is also not [Vasilii] Aksenov's student-intellectual, who feels at home in airless spaces 'halfway to the moon.' Shukshin's hero is between two supports. He has left his roots but has not yet grafted onto other roots. He has abandoned the village but is a stranger to everyone in the city. But—and here is the crux of the matter—he is unable to get accustomed to this alienation. He grows insulted, irritated, enraged."[24] And V. Kisun'ko commented: "As an artist, Shukshin has always been stirred by processes which are of huge historic importance—the turning of millions of peasants into urban dwellers. He reflects on how these processes have not been and are not easy on people."[25]

Such interpretations gained credence from Shukshin's own, made some five years before his death: ". . . it turns out that I'm not yet really a citizen of the town, but I don't belong to the country any more either . . . That's worse than falling between two stools: it's like having one leg on the shore and the other in a boat. You can't stay where you are, but you're afraid to jump into the boat."[26] Shukshin's and Egor Proku-

---

[21] Ibid., p. 53.
[22] Ibid., p. 62.
[23] Ibid., p. 36.
[24] Ibid., p. 65.
[25] Ibid., p. 81.
[26] Cited by Geoffrey A. Hosking in his introduction to Fiene, *Vasily Shukshin*, p. 3.

din's dilemma is that of millions of Russian migrants who feel themselves like fish out of water in the city, who yearn for the countryside, good neighbors, nature, religion, but who find themselves tainted and dragged down by the city, unable to free themselves from its pervasive and debilitating influence.

THE RASPUTIN AFFAIR

With the recent death of Iurii Trifonov and the emigration abroad of satirist Vladimir Voinovich, Siberian author Valentin Rasputin stands as perhaps the most gifted prose writer in the contemporary USSR. Rasputin won the prestigious State Prize for his novel *Live and Remember* (1974), which was published as part of the mass-edition *Roman-gazeta* series, but he earned the authorities' strong disapproval for his next work, *Farewell to Matera* (1976), a powerful, quasi-allegorical novel which seems to call the whole phenomenon of breakneck Soviet modernization into question.[27]

An ambitious, resonant work, *Farewell* recounts the fate of the inhabitants of an island, Matera, located in the middle of a Siberian river, the Angara, in the last few summer months preceding their evacuation to the mainland.[28] The island's evacuation is required by the construction downriver of a huge hydroelectric plant, which will cause the level of the river to rise, inundating Matera and other nearby islands. The majority of the island dwellers whom we get to know are elderly peasants who have spent their entire lives on Matera. Their imminent removal to an urban-type sovkhoz settlement or to similar semi-industrial settings fills them with apprehension,

[27] For the Russian originals of these two works, see Valentin Rasputin, *Povesti*, Moscow, 1976. English translations were published by Macmillan in 1978 and 1979. For an example of the authorities' attitude toward Rasputin, see the discussion between Party Central Committee member Boris Stukalin and Liudmila Gvishiani (Kosygin's daughter), director of the All-Union State Library of Foreign Literature, in *Moskva*, 1 (1980), 14.

[28] The following represents a condensed version of my essay, "Valentin Rasputin's *Proshchanie s Materoi*," which appeared in Evelyn Bristol, ed., *Russian Literature and Criticism*, Berkeley, 1982, pp. 63-68.

while their plight offers Rasputin an opportunity to examine the fast-disappearing life of the traditional village and to compare it with the urban settlements sprouting up on the banks of the Angara.

In a reading of *Farewell*, it soon becomes apparent that Rasputin, though a relatively young author (b. 1937), has little sympathy for modern industrialized Soviet Russia, at least in its present form, a sentiment which serves to link him with the "ruralist" school of letters. The elderly grandmother Dar'ia, who speaks for Rasputin, believes that modern man has grown proud, has sought to clamber out of his "human skin," has uprooted himself from the earth, from nature, and from God; he is a "muddle-head" (*putanik*), who has forgotten that he has a soul and a conscience. As for modern cities, they remind her of the frenetic scurrying of ants and the swarming of midges.

Rasputin scrutinizes the slow passage of Matera's waning summer days with keen attention. The threat of fire, like that of the approaching great flood, has been present from the novel's beginning when Dar'ia and her friends succeed in driving off an "unclean power," workers ordered to burn down the village cemetery. But the "unclean power" cannot be held at bay for long. Soon a semi-demented village lad, Petrukha, burns down his hut, and its apocalyptic glow warns of conflagrations to come. Then shock workers, who are brought in to help with the harvest and who have no respect for the island's uniqueness, burn down the village mill and office. Fire, the ever swifter rush of time, and the specter of a final flood accompany the island's last days. At the novel's end, the sovkhoz director, Vorontsov, and others are attempting to make their way through unusually dense, perhaps unprecedented fog to take Dar'ia and a few remaining dwellers off the island. The mood is one of acute apprehension and alarm.[29]

The flooding of Matera—a place name derived from the

---

[29] The bleak pessimism at the book's conclusion is somewhat mitigated on the symbolic level. The burners, whom the island dwellers call "arsonists," succeed in scorching everything on Matera with their terrible power, except one huge larch tree, which defies all their efforts.

word *mat'* (mother)—will culminate a process of national matricide. The very Russian earth, family cemeteries, venerable churches (Matera's church has been converted into a storehouse and its crosses knocked off)—all are being sacrificed for "electricity" and the specious cult of progress touted by Soviet prometheans. It is not that Rasputin scorns the fruits of modern civilization, nor that he is obsessed with *byt* (mores). But modern Russia, he believes, must be rooted in the mind and wisdom of centuries-old traditional Russia. If not, then fire and flood will inevitably ensue.

Underlining the political significance of *Farewell to Matera*, recent émigré Mikhail Agurskii has written:

> The old people of Matera do not understand what a power station is; such things are beyond their comprehension. But the reader is assumed to know that the Angara River was in reality dammed by several power stations, the most famous of which was the Bratsk power station completed in 1967. . . . In his inaugural address [Politburo member Andrei] Kirilenko called the Bratsk station "a beautiful fruit of the really great cultural and technical revolution accomplished during half an age of the Soviet system." And yet to Rasputin it is far from beautiful. He contradicts one of the most powerful Soviet leaders and claims it to be a disaster.
>
> As a writer Rasputin did not need to call the river of his novel by its real name. He could have invented any name for it without diminishing the artistic quality of his story. But if he designated the river by its real name—the Angara—he knew very well what he was doing. He was consciously and defiantly indicating to his readers that the roots of the crime against Matera (Russia) are the actions of those whose foremost objective is to develop at any price Soviet military-industrial potential—a pillar of Soviet international influence and expansion.[30]

[30] Agursky, "New Russian Literature," pp. 3-4.

On May 3, 1981, the *New York Times* reported that Rasputin had been savagely beaten in Irkutsk a year previously and—suffering since from severe headaches and an "unceasing flow of tears"—was unable to resume writing.[31] The newspaper also reported that Rasputin had been badly beaten in 1977, a year after the appearance of *Farewell to Matera.* Whether these attacks were the work of hooligans—Irkutsk is a notoriously violent city—or of KGB "hit squads" is something one cannot know. In any case, Rasputin has been silenced for the time being.

THE GLAZUNOV EXHIBITS

The June 1978 and October 1979 exhibits in Moscow and Leningrad of 400 paintings, many of them on nationalist themes, by artist Il'ia Glazunov (b. 1930) were a cultural event perhaps surpassing the *Kalina krasnaia* episode in significance. At previous showings of his paintings, the authorities had forbidden Glazunov to display controversial or "programmatic" works, but at the Moscow and Leningrad exhibits, only the canvas "The Mystery of the Twentieth Century" was not permitted to be shown.[32] Moreover, while at earlier Glazunov exhibits the authorities had carefully controlled access to the visitors' comment book, no such restrictions were in effect in Moscow, with the result that a unique collection of

---

[31] *New York Times*, 3 May 1981, p. 13.

[32] Concerning this ten-by-twenty-foot painting, see S. Frederick Starr, "Soviet Painter Poses a Question," *Smithsonian*, December 1977, pp. 101-106. Starr's generally excellent piece is marred by a controversial contention that "Glazunov leaves us no doubt as to his positive view of Stalin" (p. 104). I would interpret Glazunov's depiction of the despot differently. On Glazunov, see the painter's autobiographical essay, "Doroga k tebe, iz zapisok khudozhnika," *Molodaia gvardiia*, no. 10 (1965), 91-142, and no. 12 (1965), 191-242. See also the 82 page collection, *Russkaia ideia ili K.G.B.? Kto Glazunov?*, issued by the émigré journal *Chasovoi* in 1977. Attacks on Glazunov, signed by A. Esenin-Volpin, S. Kudirka, V. Maksimov, V. Nekrasov, and others, appeared in the émigré daily *Novoe russkoe slovo*, 1 July 1976 and 9 January 1977. An unpublished defense of the painter, written by nationalist activist Anatolii Ivanov (Skuratov), has been circulating in the United States, along with statements by recent émigrés Nikolai Tetenov, Iosif Gurvich, and others.

viewers' reactions, was compiled.[33] (In Leningrad, on the other hand, a militiaman prevented viewers from seeing the remarks of previous visitors, a factor depriving the Leningrad comment book of a certain spontaneity.[34])

We do not at present know the details of any bureaucratic struggles which may have preceded the permission given to Glazunov to stage the Moscow exhibit. That the exhibit was a tremendous success seems incontestable; 600,000 visitors waited in long lines to see the paintings. (A three-month-long exhibit which had been held in Moscow to commemorate the sixtieth anniversary of the founding of the USSR, by contrast, drew only 50,000 visitors.[35]) A great deal more is known about the infighting that preceded and accompanied the Leningrad exhibit, which was attended by 746,000 persons (when the number of those who arrived at the showing on excursions from their places of employment is added, the total figure rises to approximately one million, i.e., a quarter of the city of Leningrad).[36]

According to one well-informed émigré source, the Department of Culture of the Leningrad provincial Party committee, headed by G. Pakhomova, did all that it could to block the exhibit.[37] When this failed, an attempt was made to obtain the removal of Glazunov's most "dangerous" canvases. At that point, Glazunov threatened to cancel the exhibit. Next, the Department of Culture sought to hold down the number of potential viewers by decreeing that only persons who signed up for excursions to the exhibit at their places of employment or at certain organizations could attend. This ploy backfired when some 500,000 individuals indicated that they wished to go on the excursions. The restriction on attendance was then lifted, and entrance to the exhibit was permitted, as in Moscow, through tickets purchased at the gate.

On the average, about 5,000 persons a month attend a typ-

---

[33] See *Khudozhnik i Rossiia*, Düsseldorf, 1980, pp. 15-16.
[34] Ibid., p. 153.
[35] Ibid., p. 15.
[36] Ibid., p. 154.
[37] Ibid., pp. 153-154.

ical exhibit held in Leningrad. But 10,000 viewers showed up on the opening day of the Glazunov exhibit, and in the closing days of the showing, 45,000 persons a day were assembling outside the Konnogvardeiskii Manezh in an attempt to see the paintings.[38] None of this was to the liking of the Leningrad Party committee, which, shortly before the exhibit closed, organized a discussion of Glazunov's paintings attended by 200 carefully chosen persons: art critics, representatives of Leningrad *obshchestvennost'*, and members of the departments of culture of the Leningrad Party committee and municipal soviet. (Earlier, Glazunov had also been attacked in *Leningradskaia pravda*.[39]) At this meeting, Glazunov was severely taken to task by the head of the Leningrad branch of Novosti Press Agency, the head of the Department of Culture of the Leningrad municipal soviet, and many others. In response, Glazunov stated defiantly that he did not work for the "assembled auditorium" but "for those who stand for hours in the rain and piercing cold wind" to see his paintings.[40] As can be seen, in this fairly heated conflict Glazunov was able to hold the Leningrad Party establishment at bay; to do so, he needed powerful protection.

The clearly attested hits of the two showings were the programmatic "Return of the Prodigal Son," based, of course, on a parable from the Gospel of St. Luke, and the polemical "To Your Health," which assails the scourge of Soviet alcoholism. The former canvas depicts a shirtless young man in blue jeans on his knees and being comforted by a Christ-like figure, behind whom stand holy men and cultural figures from Russia's past (St. Sergii of Radonezh, Dostoevskii, Gogol', etc.). In the painting's foreground, from which the young man has turned away, are scenes associated with wild debauch, Soviet prometheanism, and political terror (e.g., a banquet table, a harlot, two exceedingly plump and smug swine, barbed wire, a skyscraper).

Such an unorthodox exhibit obviously needed mediation to

[38] Ibid., p. 153.
[39] Ibid., p. 154.
[40] Ibid.

the Soviet public, a task *Pravda* reporter Dmitrii Zhukov undertook to perform in a review appearing in the paper's issue
of 15 June 1978. Lengthy excerpts follow:

> Internationalism is impossible without a love for one's
> Fatherland and for its history. And it is not at all accidental
> that attention is being attracted to those paintings [of Gla-
> zunov] which are connected with the history of Russia. The
> artist's interest in the art of ancient Russia and in the sources
> of [Russia's] culture of many centuries is well-known, while
> he has fruitfully given new meaning to the canons of an-
> cient Russian painting in his own manner and with his own
> palette. The unfading beauty of Russia—her cities and
> churches, fields and forests—is imprinted in the historical
> canvases. "A Russian Song," "Legend of the Tsarevich
> Dimitrii," the cycle "Kulikovo Field," "Lord Great Nov-
> gorod," "Boris Godunov"—the titles alone force one to re-
> call heroic and dramatic pages from the past of our people.
> Unfortunately, the people itself does not receive sufficient
> reflection in the works of the artist.
>
> In discussing the originality of Il'ia Glazunov and his con-
> tinuation of the traditions of remarkable Russian painting,
> one would like to underline that this artist is a man who
> thinks, who seeks answers to the complex questions of con-
> temporaneity. In his canvases there is always depth, at times
> one of alarm, but always one which gives hope . . .
>
> The work of Il'ia Glazunov is far from uncontroversial. A
> certain one-sidedness in the selection of themes, a predi-
> lection for religious motifs, an accenting of the tragic as-
> pects of Russian history all draw attention to themselves.
> There is insufficient reflection in the artist's works of those
> moments and moving forces of history which led to the
> birth of the mighty Soviet state and of an authentically
> democratic culture. Incontestably, one should not forget
> one's roots. But does one have to affirm this so deliber-
> ately? Sometimes the artist loses a sense of measure, is
> carried away by conceptual rhetoric, unthinkingly opposes
> the spiritual life of the past to contemporary social and sci-

entific-technical progress, thereby contradicting his own effort to reveal the indestructible links between times.

One could include "The Return of the Prodigal Son" in
the ranks of such controversial paintings. Having inserted
a new meaning into a traditional subject, the artist evidently wanted to express a hope that those who are still
painfully wallowing in the filthy mire of piggish mores, of
a nihilistic attitude toward culture, of a narrow practicality,
and of spiritual poverty should return to their great primal
sources. But if the painting's general meaning does not give
grounds for doubts, the symbols which the artist had chosen in order to convict evil offer food for various fabrica-
tions and false rumors. . .

One would like to wish the artist a deeper understanding
of our Soviet reality and, of course, of history. And an overcoming of the failings which were mentioned above.

I already see a movement in that direction in many of
his portraits of our contemporaries . . . I see such an artist
in "Prince Igor'," whose clear gaze speaks of elevated de-
votion to the Homeland and of the calm courage of a man
of conviction.

In sum, Zhukov, though far from hostile toward the exhibit, criticizes Glazunov for these failings: (1) his paintings
present a non-Marxist-Leninist view of history and of the role
of the masses in particular; (2) they tend to overemphasize
the spiritual and even the religious; (3) they bespeak a lack
of socialist optimism; (4) they show insufficient enthusiasm for
the scientific and technical revolution and for modernization
in general. There was, of course, a time when such lapses
would have led to more than the cancellation of Glazunov's
exhibit, but it seems that patriotism is now accorded an extremely high priority by the regime, though, as Zhukov makes
clear, the authorities would prefer a non-Christian version of
nationalism, celebrating steely, Spartan-like Russian warriors. In any case, *Pravda*'s strictures are surprisingly mild.
Compare Zhukov's views, for example, to those which one

doctrinaire Marxist-Leninist indignantly penned in the exhibit's comment book:

> Where, in what world, in what country, in what epoch does
> the artist Glazunov work? What ideas does he preach, what
> does he want to say to his viewers? . . . He "does not no-
> tice" that for more than sixty years the teaching of Marx
> and Lenin has triumphed in our country . . . And the gen-
> eral mood of his work is mystical, with troubled, gray clouds
> . . .[41]

Fr. Dimitrii Dudko, before his 1980 arrest the spiritual
leader of the contemporary Orthodox renaissance in Russia,
was one of the half-million visitors to the exhibit, and afterward he offered this ringing endorsement of Glazunov's
achievement: "A true Russian artist has appeared who is not
carried away by the whims of fashion. A bold, daring man
who loves Russia as she is . . ."[42] In response to the *Pravda*
article, he wrote: ". . . the contemporary 'truth' is atheistic,
while we are believers. A Russian cannot be an unbeliever!
. . . Glazunov sees farther than the *Pravda* reporter."
Concerning the canvas "Return of the Prodigal Son," Fr.
Dudko commented that the father welcoming the returning
son is, of course, Christ, but also the traditional "all-forgiving
and loving" Russian father, while the kneeling son represents
"contemporary man." The debauchery and desolation depicted in the painting's foreground, asserted Fr. Dudko, can
delay but not stop the prodigal son's return to the Father's
House, where

> the beloved faces of St. Sergii, who represents militant
> Russia, and St. Seraphim [of Sarov], who represents loving
> Russia, look upon you. Easter. Christ is risen. Let us em-
> brace one another. [Refrains from the Orthodox Easter
> service.] And over there is Dostoevskii, who makes sense
> of everything, and there is Rakhmaninov. A vigil service is

---

[41] *Publitsisticheskaia tetrad'*, no. 6 (1978), 6. Issues nos. 5 & 6 (1978) of
this journal, contain excerpts from the Moscow comment book.

[42] Sviashchennik Dimitrii Dudko, "O vystavke khudozhnika Il'i Glazunova," *Russkaia mysl'*, 24 August 1978, p. 5.

taking place . . . A liturgy is being served in holy Russia at the destroyed, defiled walls of churches . . . Immerse yourself in Russian history, return to it! It is time!

Fr. Dudko concludes by asking prayers for "the servant of God" Il'ia and his wife and two children.

That Fr. Dudko's response may have been more in tune with that of the half-million viewers who attended the exhibit than that of the *Pravda* reporter would seem to be confirmed by the entries in the comment book, the overwhelming majority of which are appreciative of Glazunov's accomplishments. In the words of one *samizdat* author: ". . . the endless crowds moving about the perimeter of the [Moscow] Manezh are people going to a healing, and the hundreds of thankful responses in the comment book testify to the effect of this healing."[43]

The following are representative samples of entries expressing approval of Glazunov's endeavor:

. . . I spent a whole week under the impression of these works. I was particularly moved by the painting "Return [of the Prodigal Son]." A very necessary painting!

Dear Il'ia Sergeevich! Many thanks for the exhibit and for the joy of communing with Rus', with the Homeland. (a group of students)

. . . Long live the great Russian idea, risen up like a Phoenix!!! (a group of Russian youth)

We, the inhabitants of Russia, will not give you over to insult! (an engineer)

Who is concealing Glazunov from the people? And why?

. . . an unusually powerful artist, bold with the pathos of civic struggle for the Russian national renaissance . . .

The artist has immortalized himself with the paintings "To Your Health" and "Return."

[43] Leonid Borodin, "Po povudu vystavki I. Glazunova," *Russkoe vozrozh-denie*, no. 5 (1979), 71.

. . . Thank you for the festival of Russian culture. (a professor, with a doctorate in physical and mathematical sciences)

Bravo!   —Students at Moscow State University

. . . Who are you—a great artist of the past who has raised up the palette of [Andrei] Rublev or the prophet of a new renaissance? With deep respect. (member of a polytechnical institute in Sverdlovsk)

God is with us. Understand ye nations. [Liturgical refrain from the Orthodox Christmas and Epiphany services]

. . . The whole *people* has highly evaluated this great artist
. . . (many signatures)

. . . Thank you for the truth. Thank you for "Return."

. . . That which I have seen will remain with me my whole life.

Thank you for Rus'! For that which lives in us always and everywhere, which is impossible to kill in us, to which we shall return . . .

. . . One senses a deep faith in Christ, the saviour of our poor fatherland, and one senses the passionate, grieving soul of Il'ia Glazunov. (a doctor)

I have no strength left for a comment: five hours in line and three hours in the halls. . . . Wonderful! (a candidate in chemical sciences)

. . . One appraisal of your work is provided by the fact that people wait many hours in lines which extend around the Manezh. I am sure that your critics entered by a side door. (a doctor of physical and mathematical sciences)

One wants to believe in the national renaissance of the Russian people . . . (an engineer)

. . . Thank you for your fiery love for much-suffering Russia
. . .

. . . Thank you not only for the esthetic enjoyment but for forcing us to *think*. (a teacher from the city of Noginsk)

. . . One is struck by his philosophic works: "Return," "To Your Health," "The Peasant." This is payment for sixty years of Soviet power, during which demagogues mouth off from elevated rostrums while the lower classes, as before, remain without any rights . . . (a Moscow artist and teacher)

The much-suffering but not broken people, having experienced fire and misfortunes, as well as the "swine," will find the strength to return to the original Russian sources.

I am thirty-five years old . . . for the first time I have come to understand the meaning of the phrase "national self-awareness." Thank you . . . (a female employee of a scientific institute in Moscow)

. . . I spent six hours in front of your pictures, and, if I could, I would have stayed longer. . . . *The country needs heroes [bogatyri], and they have come. Their names are unknown, but now we know the name of one of them: Il'ia Glazunov.*[44]

As these comments indicate, Glazunov succeeded in tapping wellsprings of Russian patriotic and religious sentiment on the part of his viewers. The fact that the regime felt it necessary to sanction this exhibit and to permit the inclusion of such—to put it euphemistically—"revisionist" paintings as "Return of the Prodigal Son" demonstrates its increasing need to accommodate to a rising tide of Russian nationalism. The exhibit also shows that nationalistically inclined Russians are more and more often distinguishing between "us" and "them." Glazunov's detractors will undoubtedly argue that he is permitting himself to be "used" by the regime. But who, one wonders, is using whom?

Conclusions

The essential preoccupation of present-day Russian nationalist cultural expression is, as Mikhail Agurskii has noted, "re-

---

[44] *Publitsisticheskaia tetrad'*, nos. 5 and 6 (1978), passim (emphases in the original).

sistance to modernization imposed by force . . ."[45] The inevitable focal point of conflict is the NTR. Again in Agurskii's words: "A major manifestation of industrial society is the so-called scientific-technical revolution, which is part and parcel of the official Party programme. So criticism of this scientific-technical revolution amounts to an almost open challenge to the existing system."[46] Modernization is seen as a fundamentally un-Russian and anti-Russian phenomenon, as is its perceived sponsoring ideology, Marxism-Leninism. Thus, while not overtly advocating political change, nationalist art is deeply and necessarily political.

In their art, contemporary Russian nationalists concentrate upon those issues which are seen as most injurious to the well-being of the Russian people: the decline of the village; the razing of historical and cultural monuments; the rape of the environment; the socio-demographic and moral aftershocks of headlong modernization and urbanization. The positive "program" of nationalist cultural expression is less clearly articulated but nonetheless easily distinguishable. Basically, the nationalists want to throw the onrushing Soviet juggernaut into reverse and to promote a concern for the physical and spiritual health of a people threatened with decline and even extinction (in the sense of ceasing to play a meaningful role in history). Viewed in this light, the Russian village derives its importance chiefly from serving as a repository for age-old values and reflexes which are seen as being eroded and destroyed by the aftereffects of breakneck modernization. It is these values, the nationalists believe, which must be grafted onto the contemporary Soviet way of life.

An indication of the strength and influence of Russian nationalist cultural activists was provided by the recently held Seventh Congress of Soviet Writers (1981), which followed closely upon the heels of the 26th Party Congress.[47] In his keynote address, Georgii Markov, first secretary of the Writ-

[45] Agursky, "The New Russian Literature," p. 19.
[46] Ibid., p. 23.
[47] The proceedings of the Congress were covered in the 3 July 1981 and 10 July 1981 issues of *Literaturnaia Rossiia*.

ers' Union, implicitly confirmed that the nationalists were raising and defining the issues of most concern to present-day Soviet literature. "Over the past five years," he reported, "we have had a fair number of discussions. Let us recall the most significant: the [nineteenth-century] Russian classics and the appropriate evaluation of that heritage; the traditions of the revolutionary democrats; the literature devoted to the contemporary village; the civic character of poetry; the problem of the contemporary short story, and others."[48] The first three issues cited by Markov are unmistakably nationalist ones. It is the nationalists who stress the bonds linking nineteenth-century Russian literature with the concerns of the present; it is they who call into question the received wisdom of the revolutionary democrats; and it is the nationalists, of course, who focus attention upon the fast-disappearing traditional Russian village. Markov's list thus shows that, in cultural matters at least, the nationalists are taking the battle to their opponents.

Throughout the congress, the speakers were generally deferential toward the Russian nationalists and their "causes." Markov, for example, paid fairly lavish tribute to the preservationist and ecological concerns of the nationalists, as did Feliks Kuznetsov, first secretary of the Board of the Moscow Writers' Organization, who is not a nationalist. Kuznetsov even chose to speak approvingly of the concern of nationalist writers for "the human soul."[49] In his speech, on the other hand, Fedor Abramov, a leading nationalist spokesman, was less irenic; he wondered angrily why such works as Vasilii Belov's *That's How It Is* had been denied publication in the mass-edition *Roman-gazeta* series.[50]

Nationalists did quite well in the elections to the secretariat of the Writers' Union: clear-cut nationalists selected were Abramov, Iurii Bondarev, Egor Isaev, Leonid Leonov, and Petr Proskurin; also chosen were such nationalist sympathizers as Mikhail Alekseev, the editor of *Moskva*, and Sergei

---

[48] *Literaturnaia Rossiia*, 3 July 1981, p. 8.
[49] Ibid., 10 July 1981, p. 5.
[50] Ibid., pp. 7-8.

Mikhalkov and Mikhail Sholokhov. Of course, non-nationalists and even anti-nationalists—for example, Kuznetsov, Anatolii Anan'ev, the editor of *Oktiabr'*, and A. Chakovskii, the editor of *Literaturnaia gazeta*—were also selected, as were various representatives of the minority republics.

While the Seventh Congress testified to the growing influence of the Russian nationalists, it likewise demonstrated the limitations of that influence. At one point, for example, Markov felt compelled to issue a stern warning to the nationalists:

> I should like, comrades, to underline that Belinskii, Dobroliubov, Chernyshevskii, Herzen, all the revolutionary democrats . . . are connected by blood ties to us, the builders of a communist society which is being created on the land of the former tsarist empire. We, communists, are their direct descendants and heirs. I repeat: their sole and direct inheritors. To forget this fact is nothing less than to forget one's genealogy, to repudiate one's forefathers.[51]

Communists, Markov emphasized, are constructing a *new* society. There is no unbroken continuum, no "single stream" linking tsarist and Soviet Russia. To call into question the views and direction taken by the revolutionary democrats is, by inference, to question the wisdom of Marx, Engels, and Lenin, the ideological pillars of the Soviet state. It should be noted, however, that Markov's warning tended to be overshadowed by the general tolerance shown toward the nationalists by him and by other spokesmen at the congress.

Not yet dominant but increasingly influential, Russian nationalists promise to make their presence strongly felt in cultural matters in the 1980s. In fact, their concerns may well provide the framework for the cultural debate of the coming decade. Through the transitional art of the nationalists, one may observe a larger social and political transition in process of being effected.

[51] Ibid., 3 July 1981, p. 8.

6

The Nationalities Problem

... the nations [of the USSR] will draw still closer together, and their complete unity will be achieved.
"Party Program," 22nd Congress of the CPSU[1]

... long live Galiia Izmailova, who dances in the Uzbek fashion, Goar Gasparian, who sings in Armenian, and Rasul Gamzatov, who writes in Avar. Long live Tadzhik decorative patterns, the Kazakh opera, Estonian drawings, and Chukot carvings on walrus ivory. Long live the great Russian language, but long live, too, the sweet-singing, incomparable Ukrainian *mova*.
Vladimir Soloukhin[2]

... the disappearance of nations would impoverish us not less than if all men should become alike, with one personality and one face. Nations are the wealth of mankind, its generalized personalities; the least among them has its own coloration and harbors within itself a unique facet of God's design.
Aleksandr Solzhenitsyn[3]

As with every man, so every nation possesses unique features and inimitable qualities which have to be manifested and cultivated.
Anonymous, in *Veche*[4]

According to the 1979 census, there were 137.4 million Great Russians, 42.3 million Ukrainians, and 9.5 million Belorus-

[1] Cited from Teresa Rakowska-Harmstone, "The Dialectics of Nationalism in the USSR," *Problems of Communism*, May-June 1974, p. 18.
[2] Vladimir Soloukhin, " Chto nas rodnit: Zametki pisatelia," *Literaturnaia gazeta*, 6 February 1962, p. 3.
[3] Aleksandr Solzhenitsyn, "Nobel Lecture," in John B. Dunlop, Richard Haugh, and Alexis Klimoff, eds., *Aleksandr Solzhenitsyn: Critical Essays and Documentary Materials*, 2d ed., New York, 1975, p. 566.
[4] Anonymous, "Mysli-prozhektory," *Veche*, no. 2 (AS 1020), 31.

sians dwelling in the Soviet Union. Central Asian, Transcaucasian, and other non-Slavic peoples amounted to 72.9 million—including 12.5 million Uzbeks, 6.6 million Kazakhs, 6.3 million Tatars, 5.5 million Azerbaidzhani, and 4.2 million Armenians—and, as noted previously, fertility trends promise to increase their proportion of the population significantly in the years to come. Russian nationalists are keenly aware of the relevance of what is commonly called the "nationalities problem" to the future well-being of their country. Academician Igor' Shafarevich, a contributor to the collection *From under the Rubble*, has called it the "most painful" of all the problems currently facing the Soviet Union,[5] and a conservative nationalist statement, "The Nation Speaks," circulated in about 1970, referred to it as a "fundamental problem."[6] Before examining the views of contemporary Russian nationalists on this issue, however, it would be well to consider some pertinent historical and demographic factors.

Nationalities specialist Teresa Rakowska-Harmstone has written that two fateful decisions by the early Bolshevik leadership shaped the development of the nationalities problem in the USSR: the decision to establish a federal state, and the decision to accelerate industrialization and modernization from above.[7] The federal structure offered major Soviet ethnic groups the forms of statehood and the trappings of a national culture, while rapid industrialization, contrary to what used to be the received view among scholars, served to stimulate national self-awareness and to exacerbate relations among the peoples of the multinational Soviet state.

Under its various leaders, the Soviet regime has pursued erratic and at times contradictory policies vis-à-vis the minor-

[5] Igor' Shafarevich, "Separation or Reconciliation? The Nationalities Question in the USSR," in *From under the Rubble*, Boston, 1975, p. 88.

[6] *Survey*, 17, no. 3 (1971), 195. In translating the Russian title of this document (*Slovo natsii*) as "The Nation Speaks," I am following the advice of Professor Dimitry Pospielovsky of the University of Western Ontario. For an important, if controversial, recent study on the Soviet nationalities problem, see Hélène Carrère D'Encausse, *L'Empire Éclaté*, Paris, 1978.

[7] Teresa Rakowska-Harmstone, "The Study of Ethnic Politics in the U.S.S.R.," in George W. Simmonds, ed., *Nationalism in the USSR and Eastern Europe*, Detroit, 1977, p. 22.

ity nationalities. Immediately after the revolution, these peoples were exalted above Great Russians, who had, it was felt, the guilt of tsarist imperialism to atone for. Under Stalin, the situation gradually changed, as the despot, particularly during and after the Second World War, increasingly identified with the Great Russian people. This process culminated at the nineteenth Party Congress in 1952, when the theory of the "lesser evil"—which had sought to justify the conquest of border peoples by the tsarist state on the grounds that it was better for them to have come under the Russians than, say, the British—was discarded in favor of a theory of the "greater good."[8] Heroes such as Shamil'—an Avar from Daghestan and the leader of Muslim resistance to Russian penetration of the North Caucasus in the nineteenth century—who had previously been lionized were now denounced as insidious reactionaries. The first edition of the *Large Soviet Encyclopedia* (1934) had had this to say about Shamil's campaign:

The movement was aroused by the colonial policy of Russia, which robbed the basic population of their forests, tore away the best parts of their land for Cossack colonization, and in every way supported and sustained the despotism of the local feudalists. The popular rising carried out against Russia and against the local ruling strata was basically antifeudal.[9]

By 1947, the authorized view of Russian expansion into the Caucasus had changed to this:

Despite the arbitrary acts and cruelty of the Tsarist colonizers, the annexation of the Caucasus to Russia played a positive and progressive role for the peoples of the Caucasus. . . . The striving of advanced people in the Caucasus

[8] S. Enders Wimbush, "Contemporary Russian Nationalist Responses to Non-Russians in the USSR," Rand Paper Series, P-5941 (1978), Rand Corporation, Santa Monica, Cal., p. 2.

[9] Quoted in Robert Conquest, *The Nation Killers: The Soviet Deportation of Nationalities*, London, 1970, p. 85.

for union with Russia reflected the mood of the broad masses of the people.[10]

Stalin's harsh and militant Great Russian chauvinism understandably aroused the resentment of the minority nationalities, particularly their intelligentsias. Even more radical was his deportation, during the period from 1941 to 1944, of eight nations consisting of approximately a million and a half persons from their historic homelands—Volga Germans, Crimean Tatars, Meskhetian Turks, Chechens, Ingushi, Karachai, Balkars, and Kalmyks.[11]

As in other spheres, Khrushchev boldly reversed Stalin's policies on the nationalities question. After 1956, national leaders such as Shamil' were once again allowed to be viewed in a positive light, though Khrushchev, in characteristic fashion, at times retreated from such liberalism. At the 22nd Party Congress in 1961, a formulation was adopted to the effect that the peoples of the Soviet Union would "draw together" (*sblizhat'sia*) and eventually "merge" (*slit'sia*).[12] "Merging" here betokened the ideological and cultural unity of all Soviet peoples but also was intended to suggest a biological homogenization of the national components of the USSR. The concept of *sliianie* gave rise to apprehension both in the ranks of minority nationalists—who feared that it would result in Russification and assimilation—and in those of Russian nationalists, who foresaw a loss of their cultural and biological identity.

Once in power, the Brezhnev-Kosygin collective leadership moved to put a halt to Khrushchevian excesses in this area, as in others. The inflammatory term *sliianie* was dropped and replaced by a bland *polnoe edinstvo*, or "full unity," intended to suggest the clustering of Soviet peoples about commonly held ideals without any implication of biological oneness.[13] No return to Stalin's aggressive Great Russian chauvinism was sanctioned, although objectively, as shall be seen, a policy of Russification was continued.

[10] Ibid., pp. 90-91.
[11] Ibid., passim.
[12] Rakowska-Harmstone, "Dialectics of Nationalism," p. 18.
[13] Wimbush, "Contemporary Russian Nationalist Responses," p. 13.

Throughout the Soviet period, the regime, in accordance with the Bolshevik doctrine of "internationalization," has encouraged the migration of certain mobile nationalities—most notably Great Russians, but also Ukrainians, Belorussians, Armenians, and Jews—into less developed republics in order to carry out rapid industrialization in those areas. Possessing the necessary educational background and technical skills, these migrants were able to accomplish their assigned tasks, but at the cost of stimulating resentment on the part of indigenous peoples envious of their higher salaries and superior living conditions and suspicious or contemptuous of their life styles and customs.

The "minority republics" of Kazakhstan, Kirgizia, the Ukraine, Estonia, and Latvia have already experienced such significant Russian in-migration that the ethnic dominance of the native populace has either disappeared or been seriously eroded. In Kazakhstan, the 1979 census showed Russians outnumbering native Kazakhs by 40.8% of the population to 36.0%.[14] In Kirgizia, the percentages were 25.9% for Russians and 47.9% for native Kirgiz.[15] The Baltic republics, to which Russians have been migrating to satisfy growing labor requirements due to a very slow rate of indigenous population growth, offered these percentages: Russians 32.8% and Latvians 53.7% of the population of Latvia; Russians 27.9% and Estonians 64.7% of the population of Estonia.[16]

The Ukraine represents a special case. As of 1979, Russians were only 21.1% of the republic's total population, but in the eastern part of the republic the situation was markedly different. The Crimea had in effect become a Russian enclave, with Russians comprising 67.3% of the province's population as early as 1970.[17] Similarly, in 1970, Russians constituted approximately half of the population of such major cities of the

[14] *Naselenie SSSR po dannym vsesoiuznoi perepisi naseleniia 1979 goda*, Moscow, 1980, p. 28.

[15] Ibid., p. 30.

[16] Ibid., pp. 29, 30.

[17] Robert A. Lewis, Richard H. Howland, and Ralph S. Clem, *Nationality and Population Change in Russia and the USSR: An Evaluation of Census Data, 1897-1970*, New York, 1976, p. 147.

Donbas region as Makeevka, Donetsk, Gorlovka, and Voroshilovgrad. In Voroshilovgrad and Donetsk provinces, Russians amounted to more than 40% of the urban population.[18] This trend promises to continue: in the period between the 1959 and 1970 censuses, the ethnic Ukrainian population of the Ukraine increased by 9.7% (from 32 million to 35.1 million), whereas the Russian population of the republic increased by 28% (from 7.1 million to 9.1 million). In the latter year, 84.6% of the Russian population of the Ukraine resided in cities.[19] By 1979, there were 10.5 million Russians living in the Ukraine.

Assimilation—e.g., the adoption by Ukrainians of Russian as their native tongue—is a related phenomenon. During the period from 1959 to 1970, East and West Siberia and the Far East were the principal areas where such assimilation occurred,[20] but the process was also taking place in the eastern Ukraine. As one specialist has written: "In 1970, 3,017,000 or 8.5% of all Ukrainians living in the Ukraine reported Russian as their native language. This represents a 2.6% increase since 1959 . . . In the cities this percentage is much higher. According to the census of 1970, 24.27% of all Ukrainians living in the Kharkov region (*oblast'*) regarded Russian as their native language and 44.62% said they knew Russian."[21]

The other republics of the Soviet Union have experienced considerably less penetration by Russians. In 1979, Russians represented these percentages of population: Armenia, 2.3%; Georgia, 7.4%; Azerbaidzhan, 7.9%; Lithuania, 8.9%; Tadzhikistan, 10.4%; Uzbekistan, 10.8%; Belorussia, 11.9%; Turkmenia, 12.6%; and Moldavia, 12.8%.[22] However, since Russians tend to migrate to the cities and particularly the capital cities of minority republics, their presence has a heightened visibility. As of 1970, Russians comprised an absolute majority of the capitals of Kazakhstan (70.3%) and Kir-

[18] Ibid., p. 148.
[19] Wsevolod W. Isajiw, "Social Bases of Change in Ukraine since 1964," in Simmonds, *Nationalism in the USSR*, p. 59.
[20] Lewis et al., *Nationality and Population Change*, p. 286.
[21] Isajiw, "Social Bases," p. 61.
[22] *Naselenie SSSR*, pp. 28-30.

gizia (66.1%), and they were the largest nationality, though not a majority of the population, in the capitals of Uzbekistan (40.8%), Latvia (42.7%), Tadzhikistan (42%), and Turkmenia (42.7%). Indeed, in 1970, they represented more than 20% of the population of all republican capitals except two: Georgia (14%) and Armenia (2.8%).[23]

In discussing the ramifications of Russian migration into non-Russian areas, one should not ignore the situation of the thirty-one non-Russian nationality units within the RSFSR (autonomous republics, autonomous provinces, and national *okrugs*). In 1970, Russians were the largest nationality among the urban population of thirty of these thirty-one units and an absolute majority of the urban population in twenty-seven.[24]

Assimilation has been a fact of life for Soviet peoples other than the Ukrainians. Belorussians (particularly in West Siberia), Jews, Poles, Germans, Karelians, Mordvinians, and others have shown a tendency to assimilate to the Russian nationality. Traditional religious adherence is one of the factors relevant to assimilation. In a recent article on ethnic reidentification in the Russian Republic, one American demographer wrote: ". . . the correlation between traditional Orthodoxy and the proportion of a group that declares Russian as the mother tongue is quite strong and statistically significant, indicating that members of traditionally Orthodox groups are more likely to declare Russian as the mother tongue than are members of traditionally non-Orthodox groups."[25]

The evidence thus shows that Russian migration, encouraged by the Bolshevik policy of "internationalization," has been a critical factor affecting the evolution of the "nationalities

---

[23] Ibid.

[24] Ibid., p. 144.

[25] Barbara A. Anderson, "Some Factors Related to Ethnic Reidentification in the Russian Republic," in Jeremy R. Azrael, ed., *Soviet Nationality Policies and Practices*, New York, 1978, p. 320. In his contribution to the same collection, "Language Policy and the Linguistic Russification of Soviet Nationalities," Brian D. Silver wrote: "Ethnic groups that traditionally adhered to Islam are much less susceptible to language shifts than are non-Muslim groups. . . . In contrast, groups that belonged to the Orthodox Church prior to the Revolution tend to acquire the Russian language much more readily" (p. 278).

problem" in the Soviet Union. Differences in rates of fertility may, it should be noted, eventually blunt the effects of Russian migration into Central Asia and the Transcaucasus and even dramatically alter the present ethnic mix in such highly "internationalized" areas as Kazakhstan and Kirgizia. (The 1979 census showed that this had already begun to happen.) Some Soviet and Western demographers believe that another important migration may be forthcoming. Central Asians have up until now been extremely reluctant to leave the farm for the cities (the opposite of the problem in the RSFSR!), with the result that in 1970 only 21% of the Turkic-Muslim population lived in urban centers of over 15,000.[26] Rural overpopulation and labor surplus are already realities in Central Asia, while critical labor shortages exist in the Russian Republic. Consequently, the regime may be tempted to import large numbers of Central Asian "guest workers" into the RSFSR, a policy whose social and demographic effects are not difficult to envision. It also seems clear that the Soviet army is increasingly going to have to be staffed by non-Russians, a situation fraught with political uncertainties.

RUSSIAN NATIONALIST VIEWS

What do contemporary Russian nationalists have to say about the "nationalities problem," and what solutions, if any, do they offer to it? With the possible exception of certain extremist neo-Stalinist and National Bolshevik elements, contemporary nationalist spokesmen tend to be *polycentric* rather than ethnocentric nationalists—i.e., they regard other peoples and their cultures and institutions as being of intrinsic worth.[27] This view is usually justified theologically or "scientifically" or both. One instance of a theological defense of polycentric nationalism is Vadim Borisov's "Personality and National Awareness."[28] "The nation," Borisov writes, "is a level

[26] Lewis et al., *Nationality and Population Change*, p. 354.
[27] For a discussion of this distinction, see Anthony D. Smith, *Theories of Nationalism*, London, 1971, pp. 158-159.
[28] *From under the Rubble*, pp. 194-228.

in the hierarchy of the Christian cosmos, a part of God's immutable purpose."[29]

Probably the most influential case of a "scientific" defense of nationalism is found in the writings of Lev Gumilev, the son of two famous poets, Anna Akhmatova and Nikolai Gumilev, and himself a concentration camp "graduate." *Veche* has carried two articles inspired by Gumilev's theories,[30] and they have also been aired in the official Soviet press. According to one of the *Veche* commentators, A. Vaniagin, Gumilev is attempting to found a science of "ethnology" which would be as superior to present-day ethnography as modern biology is to the descriptive botany and zoology of the past.[31] While ostensibly polycentric, Gumilev's nationalism could lead undiscriminating followers into national and racial exclusivism.

Contemporary Russian nationalists generally believe that the Soviet regime has mishandled the nationalities issue. An essay in *Veche* has referred to the "thoughtless policy" of attempting to create a "Soviet nation" and excoriated the "elemental Russification" resulting from the development of industry in the borderlands and the migration to those areas of Russian workers and professional cadres.[32] The author found it ironical that the very regime which opposes "Russophilism" is seeking to Russify the borderlands. A later contribution to *Veche* sharply criticized the regime for seeking to stifle the growth of national self-awareness in the minority republics and warned that this could give rise to "zoological nationalism," a truly centrifugal force as far as the Soviet federation was concerned. "Let the Uzbeks, Tatars and Georgians," he declared, "concern themselves with their antiquity, their history, let them pride themselves on their individual cultures . . ."[33] Academician Shafarevich has suggested that "contra-

---

[29] Ibid., p. 210.

[30] Mikhail Ruzhenkov, "Passionarnaia teoriia L. N. Gumileva," and A. Vaniagin, "Rozhdenie nauki," *Veche*, no. 8 (AS 1665), 108-130. See also Iurii Mekler, "Nasha zhivuchest'," *Dvadtsat' dva*, no. 10 (1979), 137-144.

[31] Vaniagin, "Rozhdenie nauki," p. 113.

[32] Anonymous, "Russkoe reshenie natsional'nogo voprosa," *Veche*, no. 6 (AS 1559), 9-10.

[33] Anonymous, "Bor'ba s tak nazyvaemym 'rusofil'stvom' ili put' gosudarstvennogo samoubiistva," *Veche*, no. 7 (AS 1775), 7.

dictory historical processes" have been at work in the Soviet period. The separating out of the different nations and their drive for maximum independence coincided with the regime's attempt to subordinate all of life to socialist ideology. Non-Russian separatist tendencies were first "deliberately encouraged as a counterweight to Russian nationalism" and then treated "as the greatest menace."[34]

Russian nationalist spokesmen ask that the minority nationalities not make the mistake of identifying Russia with the often foolish and destructive policies of the Soviet regime. Russians, they insist, have been as victimized as any other peoples; in fact, their culture and religion were the first to be attacked by the communists. Undue significance should not, they stress, be ascribed to the fact that the Russian language is the language of state; it represents a kind of emasculated Esperanto and nothing more. As for the Bolshevik Revolution, it was the work of many nations, all of whom bear responsibility for its aftermath. "Did not," Solzhenitsyn has asked, "the revolution throughout its early years have some of the characteristics of a foreign invasion? When in a foraging party, or the punitive detachment which came to destroy a rural district, there would be Finns and there would be Austrians, but hardly anyone who spoke Russian? When the organs of the Cheka teemed with Latvians, Poles, Jews, Hungarians, Chinese? When in the early phases of the civil war it was foreign and especially Latvian bayonets that turned the scales and kept the Bolsheviks in power?"[35] And Academician Shafarevich has said: "Since the blame for the present situation cannot be laid at one people's door, it follows that to a certain extent *all the peoples are to blame*. . . . We have all had a hand in creating the problems that now confront us: the Russian Nihilists, the Ukrainian 'Borotbists,' the Latvian riflemen and many others have each done their bit."[36]

[34] Shafarevich, "Separation or Reconciliation," pp. 92-93.
[35] Alexander Solzhenitsyn, "Repentance and Self-Limitation in the Life of Nations," in *From under the Rubble*, p. 126.
[36] Shafarevich, "Separation or Reconciliation," pp. 97-98 (italics in the original).

In his recently published study, *Lenin in Zurich*, Solzhenitsyn stressed that the founder of the Soviet state was only
one-quarter Russian by blood.[37] Such a preoccupation with
Lenin's ethnic make-up may strike the Western reader as eccentric, morbid, or outright racist, but it should be remembered that Lenin's "Russianness" is one of the elements employed by the regime to link Russian patriotism and Marxist
ideology together.

Veche has featured a number of fairly emotional discussions
on the controversial issue of whether or not Great Russians
should intermarry with other nationalities. In order to place
such discussions in perspective, one should keep in mind the
present low rate of Russian fertility, as well as Khrushchev's
radical policy concerning the "merging" of the national components of the USSR. A further factual clarification: Up until
now Great Russians have largely intermarried with Eastern
Slavs and Jews, though it is possible that a large-scale migration of Central Asians into the RSFSR and their subsequent
Russification could eventually change that picture.

One contributor to *Veche*, M. A. Sergeev, asserted that not
all mixed marriages were to be welcomed.[38] If Russians marry
Ukrainians, it was not a problem, but what if they marry peoples ethnically remote from them? (It might be pointed out
here that Russia's greatest poet, Pushkin, was part Ethiopian
by blood and prided himself on the fact.) Russians, he continued, are not the only ones concerned with the dilution of
their race: in Germany, there have been protests against "half-
breeds" fathered by black American G.I.s; some Englishmen
have objected to the immigration of peoples of different races
into their country; and some Israeli Jews seek "racial purity."
Mixtures of races, Sergeev emphasized, is not only an esthetic question; it is a psychological and social one as well.

A letter to *Veche* by a certain "N.S." took issue with the
journal's stand against mixed marriages. Such marriages, he
argued, "always have been, are, and always will be . . . It is

[37] Alexander Solzhenitsyn, *Lenin in Zurich*, New York, 1977, p. 95.
[38] M. A. Sergeev, "V publitsisticheskom zadore," *Veche*, no. 4 (AS 1140),
133-135.

God's will . . ."[39] As a powerful river absorbs smaller tribu-
taries, so Russia has received many national structures into
herself, and from this she has grown both richer and more
prepossessing. Moreover, the true Church, Orthodox Christianity, teaches that other nations must be respected as one's
own. Christianity is a path open to all nations, peoples, and
individuals.

The editors of *Veche* responded to the letter from "N.S."
with a nuanced reply.[40] Nations, they contended, like all living organisms, undergo different stages of development. In
the formative stages, they are so "plastic" that they easily
absorb other peoples, but with time they lose this ability, and
it is at this point that the introduction of a "foreign ethnos
[*etnos*]" can lead to a nation's collapse. Furthermore, the in-
fusion of some ethne can be especially deleterious (the reference is presumably to Jews, who are regarded as a particularly powerful nation). Does one, the editors asked, mix
herring and ice cream? (Were Russians, one wonders, supposed to be the herring or the ice cream?) As for Orthodox
Christianity, it, unlike Roman Catholicism, does not push
peoples into intermixing but sanctions the existence of autocephalous national churches, which serve the liturgy in their
native tongue.

The next issue of *Veche* carried a letter from the well-known
Orthodox dissenter Anatolii Levitin-Krasnov (whose father was
Jewish—though a Russian monarchist in his politics—and his
mother, a Russian noblewoman), protesting the journal's position.[41] "In Christ," Levitin asserted, "there is neither Jew
nor Greek," and he warned that nonsensical talk about half-
breeds could lead to the policies of Hitler and Rosenberg.

Levitin's letter elicited replies from Osipov and several *Veche*
correspondents.[42] Osipov disputed Levitin's implication that
patriotism and Christianity were incompatible. What about
Sergii of Radonezh (who blessed Russian troops to do battle

---

[39] *Veche*, no. 8 (AS 1665), 221.
[40] Ibid., pp. 223-227.
[41] *Veche*, no. 9 (AS 2040), 180-190.
[42] Ibid., pp. 190-205.

against the Tatars), he asked, or Patriarch Germogen (a leader of the seventeenth-century resistance against the Polish invasion), or Gogol', Khomiakov, Dostoevskii, John of Kronstadt,[43] or Patriarch Tikhon?[44] As for mixed marriages, the marked rise of such unions over the past fifty years was legitimate cause for concern and alarm.

A contributor to the same issue of *Veche* joined Osipov in attacking Levitin's position that Christianity and patriotism were incompatible.[45] By permitting the liturgy to be translated into different languages, the Orthodox Church had sanctioned the existence of different ethne. Those who deny the category of nation merely seek a standardized void. Citing the theories of Lev Gumilev, the writer argued that to recognize the existence of nations is at the same time to recognize their originality.

Another *Veche* correspondent, B. Zaitsev, wrote that nations have the right to forbid intermarriages. Nothing is wrong, he contended, with such legislation; after all (and here a peculiar logic makes its appearance), the Church forbids adultery—i.e., actively prevents people claiming to be in love from living together.

In his essay "Personality and National Awareness," to which reference has already been made, Borisov attacked the racial approach to national questions. "Insofar as nationalism," he wrote, "believes a people to be endowed with its particular characteristics by its very nature, it insists on biological purity for the preservation of the national type. If a nation declines, nationalism tends to blame the decline on an adulteration of this 'purity'; conversely, if a national renaissance is to be achieved, purity must be reestablished."[46] Such a racialist nationalism, which Borisov called "atheistic," does not, he said, differ qualitatively from socialist universalism. And he quotes the nineteenth-century thinker Konstantin Leont'ev: "To love

[43] On this important figure, see G. P. Fedotov, ed., *A Treasury of Russian Spirituality*, New York, 1948, pp. 346-416.
[44] On this first head of the Russian Church during the Soviet period, see Matthew Spinka, *The Church in Soviet Russia*, New York, 1956, pp. 3-50.
[45] *Veche*, no. 9 (AS 2040), 194-199.
[46] *From under the Rubble*, p. 227.

a tribe as a tribe is to exaggerate and deceive. . . . The purely tribal concept contains nothing germinal, nothing creative; it is nothing but a *private perversion* of the cosmopolitanist idea of universal equality and sterile universal happiness. . . . The national principle without religion . . . is a principle of slow but sure destruction."[47] Only an authentic Orthodox Christian nationalism—equally foreign to Marxist universalism and to ethnocentric nationalism—can, Borisov argued, serve as a pledge of Russia's rebirth and renewal.

The reader will have noted that the nationalist debate over intermarriage essentially boils down to two visions—one religious and the other purportedly "scientific" but de facto racialist, though it seeks at times to give a religious gloss to its arguments. The religious view does not deny the importance of the category of nation—indeed, as has been seen, Borisov attempted to provide a theological underpinning for it—but its adherents feel that Russians have little to fear from intermarriage and that a spiritual renaissance, not biological exclusivism, is what is called for. The other view, though admitting the obvious fact that present-day Russians are a racial mixture, holds that the Russian nation has aged to such a degree that it can no longer absorb new ethnic bodies into it, particularly such alien and powerful bodies as Jews. The citing of Russian Orthodoxy by proponents of this position makes little actual sense. The fact that Orthodoxy sanctions the existence of autocephalous churches in no way forecloses intermarriage, at least not with representatives of other Orthodox peoples. In Russian history, one thinks of Prince Vladimir's marriage in the ninth century to the sister of a Byzantine emperor, or of Ivan III's marriage in 1492 to the Byzantine princess Sophia Paleologue.

SOVIET JEWS

As should be apparent from the preceding section, dislike of and hostility toward Soviet Jews runs like a red thread

[47] Ibid., p. 228 (Borisov's italics).

through nationalist writings. Russian nationalists are almost obsessed with this small group of people, who were reported by the 1979 census to number 1.8 million, or considerably less than one percent of the Soviet population. In his *Soviet Russian Nationalism*, which first appeared in 1956, Frederick C. Barghoorn reported that "the ethnic group most disliked by Soviet people with whom I discussed such matters in the USSR, and also by refugees whom I interviewed, was the Jews."[48] Twenty-three years after the appearance of Barghoorn's book, I can only confirm, on the basis of my research and of conversations with non-Jewish members of the "third emigration," that the Yale political scientist's words remain in effect today. In fact, animosity toward Jews in the Soviet Union may well be growing.

Dimitry Pospielovsky of the University of Western Ontario has written two excellent essays on the views held by contemporary Russian nationalists concerning the Jews, and there is no need to repeat his information.[49] Essentially, it seems to me, the sources of Russian nationalist resentment against the Jews can be summed up in three perceptions: (1) Jews played a major role in establishing and strengthening the Bolshevik Revolution but now refuse to take moral responsibility for it. (2) Jews—particularly Jewish intellectuals—are instinctively Russophobic, automatically hostile to all manifestations of Russian national consciousness. (3) Jews live better than the other peoples of the Soviet Union.[50] As one moves toward the extreme right of the Russian nationalist spectrum, and then passes out of it into the sphere of neo-national socialism, these resentments expand into phobias and mysticisms which

[48] Frederick C. Barghoorn, *Soviet Russian Nationalism*, 2d ed., Westport, Conn., 1976, p. 118.
[49] Dimitry V. Pospielovsky, "Russian Nationalist Thought and the Jewish Question," *Soviet Jewish Affairs*, 6, no. 1 (1976), 3-17, and "The Jewish Question in Russian Samizdat," *Soviet Jewish Affairs*, 8, no. 2 (1978), 3-23.
[50] See the candid discussion of these resentments by Vladimir Maksimov, one of the more philo-Semitic of contemporary Russian writers, in his novel, *Seven Days of Creation*, London, 1975, pp. 303-304, 318-319, 331. See also the comments by Leonid Borodin in his essay, "Vestnik R.S.Kh.D. i russkaia intelligentsiia," *Veche*, no. 8 (AS 1665), 156-157.

elevate the Jews to an almost cosmic force of evil.[51] There is abundant evidence that elements in the regime are presently utilizing rabid anti-Semitism as a substitute for Marxism-Leninism, whose mobilizational appeal has dwindled to the point of ineffectiveness in recent years.[52]

One other factor should be kept in mind: Soviet Jews are not a monolithic group. Soviet Jewish intellectuals may be roughly divided into three groups: (1) Zionists, who seek to emigrate to Israel; (2) Western-style liberals, who seek to remake the Soviet Union after the model of Western societies or, failing that, to emigrate to North America or Western Europe; and (3) converts to Christianity. The last-named group may be further subdivided as follows: (a) those who converted to Russian Orthodoxy and willingly identify with the history and traditions of the Russian Church; (b) those who converted to Orthodoxy but seek to retain a sense of Jewish identity and, where deemed necessary, a critical attitude toward Russian history and the Russian Church; (c) those who converted to Roman Catholicism, not infrequently because this church is not viewed as tainted with Russian chauvinism; and (d) "Hebrew Christians," who seek a church with services conducted in Hebrew and the introduction of traditional Jewish rites and observances. Representatives of (b) and (c) frequently find common cause with Western-oriented liberals in the Soviet Union, while representatives of (d) often ally themselves with Zionists desiring to emigrate to Israel. The relations of Russian nationalists with Zionists or "Hebrew Christians" are generally better than their relations with liberals, while relations with assimilationist Jewish converts to Orthodoxy can be genuinely warm and friendly.[53]

[51] See Ivan Samolvin, "A Letter to Solzhenitsyn," and the anonymous "Critical Comments of a Russian Regarding the Patriotic Journal Veche," in Michael Meerson-Aksenov and Boris Shragin, eds., The Political and Religious Thought of Russian "Samizdat"—An Anthology, Belmont, Mass., 1977, pp. 420-448.

[52] See "Noveishaia politicheskaia kampaniia: Sovetskaia pechat' atakuet masonstvo i iudaizm," Russkaia mysl', 21 December 1978, p. 3.

[53] On Jewish Christianity in Russia, see Archpriest Aleksandr Men', "Evrei i khristianstvo," Vestnik, no. 117 (1976), 112-117, and D. Samoilov, "Po povudu interv'iu prot. Aleksandra Menia 'Evrei i khristianstvo,' " Vestnik, no.

The most important discussion in recent years between a Soviet Jew and Russian nationalist representatives was undoubtedly that between the Zionist and "Hebrew Christian" activist Mikhail Agurskii (before his emigration to Israel) and the editors of *Veche*.[54] In an open letter published in *Veche*, Agurskii sought fully and as objectively as possible to discuss and elucidate the "Jewish question" in Soviet Russia. Historically, he began, this question arose out of the territorial expansion of the Russian state begun under Peter I. No Jews lived in Russia until the reign of Catherine II and the partition of Poland. Moreover, until the middle of the nineteenth century, Russian Jews actually resisted attempts by the tsarist government to get them to leave the pale. In the latter part of the century, however, Jews in quest of an education began to leave their settlements, a migration which led to a breakdown of Jewish traditions and to a sense of alienation from the time-honored life of the pale. The influx of large numbers of this new element into Russian life evoked dissatisfaction on the part of broad layers of the Russian populace, while Jewish migrants resented the limitations on their rights as distinct from those of the rest of the population. A marked decline of Jewish religious belief occurred during this period; Russian Jews were affected by the atheism which had begun among the Russian nobility in the eighteenth century and had been spread by Russian nihilists, many of whom were the sons of clergy. In 1881, anti-Jewish pogroms began to take place, the result of the decline of religious influence on the populace at large, and national conflicts were exacerbated.

Farsighted Jews saw at the time that conflicts between Russians and Jews would inevitably grow and intensify; this mood or sentiment evolved into Zionism, which developed into a real force in 1896 with the growth of anti-semitism in Europe. At first, Zionism found some sympathy among Orthodox Christian theological circles in Russia, but, as the movement

---

120 (1977), 95-99. See also the novel *Otverzi mi dveri* (Paris, 1978), written by Feliks Svetov, a Jewish convert to Orthodoxy. This novel contains an extremely frank discussion of Jewish-Russian relations in the Soviet Union.
[54] *Veche*, no. 9 (AS 2040), 205-222, and no. 10 (AS 2452), 147-150.

became more secular, such elements lost interest in it. Zionism, it should be remembered, elicited hostility on the part of all left-wing parties, including the Jewish Bund, while the Russian government generally did not hinder its activities. In 1906, there appeared the well-known *Protocols of the Elders of Zion*, a work which Agurskii claimed was fabricated by the foreign department of the tsarist police. In this document, Jews, or more precisely participants in the Zionist movement, were portrayed as a cosmic power of evil opposed to the interests of all humanity.

After the October Revolution, the influence of Zionism among Russian Jews declined because "the Jewish population of the country was in captivity to illusions" and thought it could easily assimilate. The Jewish youth directed all their "supplanted messianic ardor into the creation of a new earthly paradise, which, however, turned into the exact opposite for them."[55] Since all national restrictions were removed after the revolution, and since the Russian intelligentsia almost disappeared, Jews and other "aliens" (*inorodtsy*) took over many key positions in the government and in the cultural and scientific life of the country. Hundreds of thousands of Jews rushed into the center of Russia and soon formed the second largest national group in the capital cities of Moscow and Leningrad.

An important negative effect on the mutual relations of Russians and Jews resulted from the antireligious persecutions which, from 1928 on, were directed against all religions in the Soviet Union. Russians saw this persecution as anti-Christian and inspired by Jews. And indeed Jews did participate in the closing of many Orthodox churches and in the persecution of Orthodox clergy and believers, while the closing of synagogues and the persecution of believing Jews was left primarily to Jewish communists. For this reason, many Russians saw the new regime as "alien" or even a "foreign invasion." By 1936-1938, however, this "alien" element in the communist leadership had been largely destroyed.

[55] M. S. Agurskii, "Otkrytoe pis'mo v zhurnal 'Veche,' " *Veche*, no. 9 (AS 2040), 218.

During the war, the Germans exterminated the patriarchal, religious Jewish population of the country. It was a blow comparable to the effect which "the eradication of almost the entire Russian peasantry" would have had on Russia. The Jewish population which survived the war was generally rootless and non-traditional in orientation.

After the war, hostility toward Jews increased from above and below, and it was only the death of Stalin which prevented a new catastrophe from occurring. Despite these developments, Jews did not on the whole change their assimilationist thinking, and it was only beginning in 1956, due to the successful Sinai campaign, and in particular following the successful "Six-Day War" of 1967, that they began to abandon their rootlessness and to contemplate emigration.

Zionism, Agurskii concluded, is not directed against the interests of the Russian people and makes no claims to any Russian territories. On the contrary, its only desire is for future good relations, perhaps even a political alliance, between the states of Russia and Israel.

In Agurskii's approach, there were no emotional accusations of anti-Semitism and "Black Hundredism" (which, Agurskii knew, would only elicit countercharges of "Russophobia"). Rather, he offered a calm, lucid, historical exposition of the "Jewish question" in Russia, a sensitive, fair-minded unraveling of the many threads of mutual hostility between Russians and Jews, an explanation and defense of the Jewish position, but also an understanding of the historical and emotional roots of Russian anti-Semitism. Though a Jewish patriot and religious believer, he is yet able to sympathize with the concerns of Russian nationalists, while his solution to the problem of Jewish-Russian relations—the exodus of all Jews to their historic homeland—has a clear-cut finality about it.

The response of the editors of *Veche* to Agurskii's statement was decidedly warm. They thanked him for his "on the whole favorable and even solicitous attitude toward the Russian national movement" and expressed gratitude for his "sincere desire to achieve agreement and mutual understanding between the Russian and Jewish national movements."[56] And the editors continued: "We want to say to our Jewish readers that 'Russian' does not at all signify 'anti-Semite.' To the contrary, the Jewish national movement, where it does not pretend to a privileged position for Jews in Russia, where it is not infused with racism, and where it does not hope for the world rule of the 'chosen people,' elicits the warmest sympathy on our part, just as would be the case with any other national movement."[57] In the various factual corrections and addenda offered to Agurskii's letter, the editors took issue with Agurskii's claim that Jews created a hell for themselves in Russia: "Don't the Jews live in the very best material conditions? If you call that a hell, what about the conditions of the rest [of the peoples of the USSR]? "[58]

In his reply, Agurskii in turn thanked the editors for publishing his letter without abridgment and continued: "I had hoped that I could at least in some measure assist the mutual understanding of Russians and Jews, and my intentions were understood precisely thus by the editors. The achievement of such mutual understanding between the Russian and Jewish national movements can only be the result of extensive efforts and good will on the part of each side. Indeed, Jews often perceive the Russian national movement as aggressive, whereas in essence it is a defensive one." And he went on:

The responsibility for the situation which has been created cannot be placed exclusively at the feet of Russians. In the course of at least the first 20-25 years of Soviet power, years which were decisive, the direction of state affairs in the country was conducted not only by Russians. An enormous responsibility for the situation which was created is also borne by Jews, Latvians, Poles, Georgians, Armenians and other nationalities, whose role was incomparably greater than their numerical share of the populace.[59]

[56] "Nash kommentarii," *Veche*, no. 9 (AS 2040), 221, 222.
[57] Ibid., p. 222.
[58] Ibid.
[59] M. S. Agurskii, "Otvet zhurnalu 'Veche,' " *Veche*, no. 10 (AS 2452), 147.

On the issue of mixed marriages, Agurskii wrote: "It is well known that Israeli laws, while not forbidding mixed marriages, nevertheless place children born in such marriages in a less privileged position than those born from pure-blooded Jewish marriages. For that reason, Jews hardly have a moral right to condemn Russian nationalists for a hostile attitude toward mixed marriages, since the danger of assimilation and degeneration is no less real for Russians than for Jews."[60]

On two matters, Agurskii took exception to the views of contemporary Russian nationalist spokesmen. The Russian nationalist movement, he wrote, "clearly exaggerates the role of Jews in arousing distrust" of the movement, and the *Veche* editors "clearly exaggerate the material well-being of Jews as a people" in Russia.[61] Jews are no longer admitted into the upper Party-state elite; they are not rich, but they are not impoverished either—they should be regarded simply as middle-class.

In their short reply, the editors once again underlined their respect for Agurskii and stressed their agreement with him "about the undesirability of the assimilation of ethne standing as far from one another as Russians and Jews."[62] And they concluded: "The only thing that Russian people would like to see from representatives of the Jews living within the boundaries of the Soviet Union is more tact and a sense of proportion . . ."[63]

Agurskii's approach to the thorny issue of Russian-Jewish relations strikes this observer as a hopeful and productive one (though I am unable to agree with his views, or those of the *Veche* editors, on the undesirability of intermarriage). In light of the very real danger of a growth of elemental anti-Semitism in Soviet Russia—a growth which was deliberately fostered by circles in the Brezhnev regime—Agurskii's insistence that Jews emigrate (Zionists to Israel, Western-oriented liberals presumably to North America or Western Europe) seems both

[60] Ibid.
[61] Ibid., p. 148.
[62] Ibid., p. 149.
[63] Ibid.

justified and sensible. Writing in *Soviet Jewish Affairs*, recent émigré Simon Markish expressed agreement with such a position:

> Liberalization, democratization, humanization of the regime in the spirit of Sakharov or Medvedev would most likely bring some benefit to the Jews; but the likelihood of the "Democrats" succeeding is negligible. . . . Another scenario for the future—the nationalistic—is more feasible. Such a policy commands considerably greater sympathy among the oppressed population, even among the oppressing New Class. At worst, it would be a form of Russian Hitlerism, and at best, the incarnation of Solzhenitsyn's ideals. Of the former case, nothing is to be said, it is quite clear; as for the latter case, the Jews would at least acquire the right of unobstructed emigration and religious freedom. But no more. . . . Solzhenitsyn does not wish us evil, he genuinely wishes us good—in our own house, in our own affairs, in our own land. For nationally-conscious Jews this is all that is necessary; for the assimilationists, it is a warning not to fall into the trap yet again.[64]

Ukrainians and Belorussians

Next to Soviet Jews, it is Ukrainians and Belorussians and the vexed question of their future relations with Great Russians that most absorb contemporary Russian nationalist thinkers. Academician Shafarevich, himself reportedly of Belorussian ancestry and therefore particularly sensitive to the issue, has pointed out that Russians often betray an "inability

[64] Simon Markish, "Jewish Images in Solzhenitsyn," *Soviet Jewish Affairs*, 7, no. 1 (1977), 78-80. Agurskii earlier had come to similar conclusions: "religious nationalism is the chief opponent of racism among the Russian people because the liberal democratic movement does not have much of a future. . . . Russian religious nationalism, the natural counter-balance to neo-Nazism, must have broad international support; everything that can be accomplished toward that end will be compatible with the basic interests of the Jewish people and of Israel . . ." "Russian Neo-Nazism—A Growing Threat," *Midstream*, February 1976, pp. 41, 42.

to see the line" which divides them from the other Eastern Slavs,[65] and the sources tend to substantiate his viewpoint.

A leading nationalist spokesman recently stated in an interview for the émigré journal *Sintaksis* that, whereas he could look with equanimity on the secession of certain non-Slavic nations from the Russian federation, the continued union of Russians, Ukrainians, and Belorussians was essential if Russia were to remain "a mighty nation." Ukrainian separatist tendencies, he warned, are "very dangerous, very harmful for the future of our people and our culture, which stem from a common source."[66]

"We consider Ukrainians and Belorussians to be our own kind . . . ," declared a contributor to *Veche*, I. Starozhubaev. And he then apostrophized his fellow Eastern Slavs:

Ukrainians and Belorussians, a fraternal voice addresses you! You should not kindle hatred toward your brothers . . . Let us create a common Homeland—Russia. Only in Russia can our originality [*samobytnost'*] and yours be preserved. Let us remember how a part of Rus' was once trampled under the hooves of Tatar horses as a result of internecine conflict and how another part was trodden under the boot of Lithuanians and Poles. We share a common history. Once Kiev was the center, now it is Moscow. But it is not on the center that everything depends; everything depends on ourselves. We can all unite in what is most sacred—in Christianity, in Orthodoxy.[67]

"From of old," S. Seryi wrote in a letter appearing in a subsequent issue of *Veche*, "it has been known that Ukrainians, Belorussians and Russians are brothers, both according to faith and in blood, and it would be a great mistake to chop

---

[65] Shafarevich, "Separation or Reconciliation," p. 102. For an important statement by Solzhenitsyn on Russian-Ukrainian relations, see his article, "Ne opyt razdora, no opyt edinstva," *Novoe russkoe slovo*, 21 June 1981, p. 2.

[66] "Ne nazyvaia imen" (interview), *Sintaksis*, no. 2 (1978), 47.

[67] I. Starozhubaev, "Neskol'ko slov po povodu," *Veche*, no. 7 (AS 1775), 82.

off the fingers of one's own hand. . ."[68] The editors of *Veche* added: "Whether one likes it or not, 'Ukrainians' and 'Belorussians' are one of the historical misunderstandings which emerged from the *political* partition of formerly united Rus' into Lithuanian Rus' (which later fell under the control of Poland) and Muscovite Rus'."[69]

Even such liberal nationalists as Solzhenitsyn and Shafarevich seem convinced that Eastern Slavs should remain together, though they would not resort to force to preserve this union. As a footnote, it should be mentioned that separatist tendencies in Belorussia are reported to be quite weak, and those in the Ukraine—particularly among the predominant Orthodox populace—are not as strong as is often believed in the West. With the exception of a few individuals, Peter Reddaway of the London School of Economics told a U. S. Congressional commission in 1977, "Ukrainian nationalism . . . is not separatist."[70]

One suspects that the potential for dialogue between Russian and Ukrainian nationalists is significant. When the authorities recently put former *Veche* editor Vladimir Osipov and imprisoned Ukrainian nationalist spokesman Viacheslav Chornovil together in the same prison camp, they seem to have expected that the two would soon be at each other's throats. Instead, they became close friends. In a letter to Osipov's wife written shortly after his release, Chornovil praised Osipov as a "marvelous comrade upon whom one can always rely." As for Russian-Ukrainian relations in the years to come, Chornovil added: "How everything will take shape in the future, life will show . . ."[71] Without being fatuous, one may hope that the friendship which developed between Chornovil and Osipov bodes well for the future.

---

[68] *Veche*, no. 8 (AS 1665), 208.
[69] Ibid., p. 219 (italics in the original).
[70] *Hearings before the Commission on Security and Cooperation in Europe, Ninety-Fifth Congress, First Session, on Implementation of the Helsinki Accords*, vol. 2, Washington, 1977, p. 9.
[71] *Russkoe vozrozhdenie*, no. 4 (1978), 60-61.

Proposed Russian Nationalist Solutions

Let us now turn to the solutions which Russian nationalists offer to the aggravated and increasingly combustible nationalities problem. Basically, nationalist spokesmen may be divided into two groups—one advocating, or at least consenting to, the secession of minority nationalities from the present Soviet federation, and the other seeking to preserve it, albeit with perhaps altered and adjusted borders. The first group has generally taken its cue from the collection *From under the Rubble* and that compendium's lofty and moralistic approach to the nationalities issue. In his contribution to the collection, Solzhenitsyn readily admitted that Russians have committed grievous sins against other nations of the federation, e.g., against the mountain peoples of the Caucasus, just as other peoples, e.g., the Tatars or Latvians, have at various times victimized the Russians. "Who has no guilt?" he asks. "We are all guilty. But at some point the endless account must be closed . . ."[72] Elsewhere, he has insisted that all peoples who wish to secede from the federation should be free to do so, though he seems to hope that the Eastern Slavs will choose to remain together.[73] He is firm in the contention that all peoples who wish to emigrate to their "historic homelands"—Jews, Volga Germans, Poles—should be permitted to do so. Solzhenitsyn, in general, seems to feel that the RSFSR is large enough, that it is time Russians ceased hankering after empires and brazenly involving themselves in the concerns of other peoples, especially since their own affairs are in a state of ruination and chaos.

In his contribution to *From under the Rubble*, Academician Shafarevich develops arguments along a line similar to Solzhenitsyn's, except that he evidently hopes that all the minority nationalities will, of their own free will, decide to remain in federation with the Russians. Secession, he warns, does not automatically mean bliss; even the smallest states

[72] Solzhenitsyn, "Repentance," p. 134.
[73] Press conference of 12 December 1974, *Russkaia mysl'*, 16 January 1975, p. 6, and *Kontinent*, no. 2 (1975), 351.

can be rent by conflict or absorbed by powerful (non-Russian) neighbors. The "rapprochement of peoples" is the real and only solution to the nationalities problem.[74]

Recently, two new émigrés from Leningrad, Petr Boldyrev and Igor' Siniavin, both Russian nationalists, caused a stir when they decided to take this approach a few steps further.[75] Russia's central problem, they argued, is to achieve liberation from a communist yoke which has brought the nation to the brink of extinction. But liberation cannot be attained if the minority nationalities remain hostile to the Great Russians; the slogan of the White Army, "a single and indivisible Russia," was a failure and contributed to the loss of the civil war. The specter of China suggests, moreover, that Russia can ill afford to have the minority nationalities as unfriendly neighbors. In addition to such pragmatic considerations, there are more important spiritual ones: Holy Russia must be based on spiritual values, and there must be no coercion of other peoples. Historically, the Russian people were forced to participate in tsarist expansion, but the "Asianized Russian autocracy" was no closer to them than "Europeanized proletarian internationalism." The slogan advanced by Boldyrev and Siniavin is "Russians for the liquidation of their empire." All minority nationalities comprising the present Soviet federation must, they insisted, be set free, and this should be done without plebiscites, since such referenda can be easily manipulated in countries without stable traditions of democracy. Even if a minority nation should *ask* to be accepted back into the Russian federation, the request should be denied. Once independent, each nation must decide what form of government is most appropriate and desirable for itself. For obvious reasons, Boldyrev's and Siniavin's proposal has proven popular with Ukrainian separatists in the emigration.

A considerable majority of contemporary Russian nationalists would, one suspects, like to retain some vestiges of an

---

[74] Shafarevich, "Separation or Reconciliation," passim.

[75] Igor Sinjavin and Peter Boldyrev, "Re: Nationalities' Problems in the U.S.S.R.," press release dated February 1978, distributed in English and Russian by Americans to Free Captive Nations, Inc.

empire. In the journal *Veche*, for example, which represents a cross-section of nationalist views, a preponderance of the contributors seems to advocate the retention of a "Greater Russia." One issue contained a letter from self-proclaimed "democrat" Roal'd Mukhamed'iarov (probably a Tatar), which asks the editors to dissociate themselves from Stalin's ethnic policies and then proceeds, in fairly tactless fashion, to pose a series of provocative questions: (1) What is the attitude of the editors to the aggressive, expansionist wars conducted by the tsarist empire? (2) What, in general, is their stance on the nationalities policies of the tsarist state? (3) What are their views on minority nationality wars of liberation, such as Shamil's rebellion or the Polish uprising of 1863? (4) What is their ethical—not political—position on such issues as the status of the Uniate Catholic Church, Roman Catholics, and Baptists, the struggle of Crimean Tatars and Volga Germans to reestablish their autonomies, the desire of Meskhetian Turks to return to their homeland, and the existence of unofficial anti-Semitism?[76]

In their response, the editors admitted that Russian excesses, such as the indefensible partitioning of Poland, had indeed taken place in the past, but then they counterattacked by asking: "Why take only those moments when other peoples and not Russians played the role of sufferer?"[77] What, for example, about the Tatar-Mongol invasion, or the seventeenth-century Polish intervention? Mukhamed'iarov also, they said, ignores the contributions which non-Russians made to the greatness of the Russian empire—the contribution, for instance, of the Georgian Bagration, the Armenian Loris-Melikov, or the Jew Shafirov. Turning to theoretical matters, the editors underlined their belief that, whether one likes it or not, in affairs between states the "law of strength" (*zakon sily*) has always ruled and always will. As for wars of liberation, they are, of course, always justified by their participants and condemned by those against whom they are directed. In re-

[76] Roal'd Mukhamed'iarov, "Pis'mo v redaktsiiu zhurnala 'Veche,' " *Veche*, no. 4 (AS 1140), pp. 151-153.
[77] "Otvet R. Mukhamed'iarovu," *Veche*, no. 4 (AS 1140), 154.

lations between states, ethics must inevitably be subordinated to politics. The best that one can do is to have a "chiv-
alrous attitude" toward one's opponents.

An article in a later issue of *Veche* took a similar tack.[78]
Russification of some borderlands, the anonymous author
conceded, did occur in the nineteenth century, though it was
usually a reaction to the activities of extremist nationalists in
those areas. As a rule, however, Russian colonizers did not
interfere in the internal affairs of the peoples they subjected.
(Russian nationalists generally like to compare the behavior
of their countrymen toward conquered peoples with that displayed by the Americans toward the Indians as the United
States expanded westward.) The author ascribed importance
to the fact that some nations—the Ukraine, Armenia, Kazakhstan—chose willingly to join the Russian federation, thereby
deeming the Russians less of a threat than other more hostile
neighbors. The often castigated Russian bayonets served objectively to protect these peoples from the encroachments of
others. Be that as it may, what must be accomplished now,
the author wrote, is to undo the mistakes of the Soviet era.
Minority nationalities must be given the full right to flourish
culturally, while Great Russians should eschew the errors of
the Stalin period—there must be "no tactless praising of oneself" as the first nation among equals.

Similar arguments were developed by the author of yet
another article on the problem in *Veche*. "For many small
peoples," he wrote, "annexation to Russia was unquestionably the least of all evils. In this regard, the example of the
Kalmyks is instructive: a part of them, not wishing to remain
under Russian rule, set off for China, but soon the refugees
recovered their sight: 'We have exchanged shackles of rope
for shackles of iron.' "[79] The example of India, he contended,
demonstrates that peoples ethnically remote from one another can live together in harmony.

When it first appeared, the *samizdat* statement "The Nation Speaks" (ca. 1970) struck a number of Western readers

[78] "Bor'ba s tak nazyvaemym rusofil'stvom," pp. 7-9.
[79] S. A., "O 'kolonial'noi' politike Rossii," *Veche*, no. 10 (AS 2452), 42.

by the testiness and even surliness of its treatment of the nationalities issue. *Veche* has offered an explanation for the document's combative mood, reporting that the statement, which was the result of a compromise agreed upon by "legal Slavophiles" and nationalist dissenters, was intended as a rebuttal to the *Program of the Democratic Movement of the Soviet Union*, a *samizdat* manifesto signed by "Democrats of Russia, the Ukraine and the Baltic" and published in the West in 1970.[80] "The *Program*," *Veche* fumed, "demanded in particular that all union and autonomous republics be made separate states and that even the Don, Kuban', Siberia, etc., be made separate; in a word, it demanded the destruction of Russia as such. Naturally, such proposals could not evoke a positive reaction on the part of any healthy Russian."[81]

The *Program* held that the USSR—which it defines as "a forced union of peoples around a Great Russian national nucleus"[82]—must, like the European colonial powers before it, grant independence or cultural autonomy to all peoples who desire it. The document exhibited an unfortunate tendency to identify the Soviet regime with Great Russians—"After the October Revolution of 1917 . . . Russia constantly continued to strive for the seizure and submission of new territories . . ."[83]—though it at times attempted to distinguish between the Russian people and the "Russian chauvinists and Black Hundreds" it saw as ruling the Soviet Union.[84] Assailing the slogan of "one, indivisible Russia," the *Program* advocated that the United Nations be placed in charge of supervising plebiscites to determine the fates of the various peoples of the Soviet Union and to settle disputed issues (such as, presumably, national boundaries). However, the authors proclaimed their view that even before the U. N. was asked to give its opinion, the Kuban', Stavropol, and Don regions should

[80] O. M., " 'Survey' o russkom natsionalizme," *Veche*, no. 9 (AS 2040), 171-172.
[81] Ibid., p. 172.
[82] *Programma demokraticheskogo dvizheniia Sovetskogo Soiuza*, Amsterdam, 1970, p. 45.
[83] Ibid., p. 47.
[84] Ibid., p. 53.

be transferred from the RSFSR to the Ukraine. The document could also be interpreted as recommending the removal from the RSFSR of all autonomous republics (ASSRs), the Urals, East and West Siberia, and the Far East.[85] It likewise seemed to assume that the Ukraine, Belorussia, the Baltic states, Moldavia, the Transcaucasus, and Central Asia would all seek liberation from the federation, leaving a diminutive, shrunken Russia as the heir of a once mighty empire.

"The Nation Speaks" answered truculence with truculence. For a slogan, it adopted the very words denounced by the "democrats"—"a single and indivisible Russia." The Russian empire, it argued, is historically justified, but if it came to secession, then let the minority nationalities be advised that Russia intended to keep the following: (1) Belorussia, whose separate existence was "artificially maintained"; (2) those eastern provinces of the Ukraine with a predominantly Russian population—Kharkov, Donetsk, Lugansk, Zaparozh'e, and the Crimea—as well as those provinces "whose population has become Russified to a considerable extent and which were opened up by the efforts of the Russian state"—the provinces of Odessa, Nikolaevsk, Kherson, Dnepropetrovsk, and Sumy (the resulting Ukraine would be landlocked and deprived of its major industrial centers); (3) Moldavia, which would not be surrendered to Rumania; (4) Kazakhstan, only one-third of whose population is indigenous; (5) Kirgizia, which has become "half Russified"; and (6) certain areas of Georgia, e.g., Abkhazia, which has expressed a desire to unite with Russia and to escape Georgian "great-power mentality." The statement also advocated that certain "purely fictitious ASSRs" within the Russian Republic, such as Mordovia, Bashkiria, and Karelia, be abolished.[86]

By the process of elimination, it appears that "The Nation Speaks" would reluctantly agree to the secession of the western Ukraine, a shrunken Georgia, Armenia, Azerbaidzhan, Turkmenia, Uzbekistan, Tadzhikistan, Estonia, Latvia, and

[85] Ibid., pp. 46-47.
[86] The entire document has been reprinted in *Survey*, 17, no. 3 (1971), 196-197.

Lithuania from the present Soviet federation. The authors, however, counseled these nations to consider the matter of secession carefully and to ponder what their relations with non-Russian neighbors would be—the inference being that Armenia might have something to fear from Turkey, Azerbaidzhan, and Georgia, or that Central Asians might consider the fate of ethnic minorities under the People's Republic of China, etc.

Before emigrating from the Soviet Union—in fact, while still imprisoned in a concentration camp—Evgenii Vagin discussed the question of Russia's future borders with the dissident lawyer, Iurii Handler. "If Russia is divided up into pieces," he declared, "it will mean the end of Russian civilization." To say that, for example, the Kalmyks should comprise a separate state is, he said, ridiculous. The only secession which Vagin might countenance would be that of various non-Orthodox peoples—Muslim Central Asians, Catholic and Protestant Balts, Uniate Catholics in the Western Ukraine. Georgia, on the other hand, would have to remain in the federation, since she is an Orthodox nation. Vagin also stated that historical considerations were relevant—for instance, the fact that both Georgia and the Ukraine had asked to be admitted to the Russian federation.[87] (The reference—one also made by the author of "On Russia's 'Colonial' Policies" in *Veche*—is to a decision by the Ukrainian Rada in 1654 to swear allegiance to the tsar rather than accept subjugation to Poland or swear allegiance to Turkey, and to Georgia's decision during the first decade of the nineteenth century to join Russia rather than risk domination by Moslem Persians and Turks.)

Conclusions

The "nationalities problem" has become a major Russian nationalist issue. The minority nationalities cannot be wished away; they unmistakably exist. Moreover, present fertility trends threaten seriously to erode the traditional ethnic dom-

[87] From an interview which I conducted with Handler following his emigration to the United States.

inance of Russians and Eastern Slavs in the Soviet Union. Some arrangement or accommodation will have to be reached with the minority nationalities, particularly the Turkic Muslims, and soon. Russian nationalist spokesmen are well aware of the situation and appear willing to contemplate such drastic steps as permitting the secession of certain republics from the Russian federation or initiating a rollback of "internationalization" policies which, in the past, have encouraged Slav cadres to migrate to the borderlands.

Many Western analysts believe that the nationalities issue, more than any other, will prevent the post-Brezhnev leadership from discarding or even downgrading Marxist-Leninist ideology, since, it is asserted, a Russian nationalist government would inevitably alienate the minority nationalities more than one which is ostensibly Marxist. One wonders if this is in fact the case. Most contemporary Russian nationalists appear to be in agreement that all nations presently in the Soviet federation should be given at least the right to develop culturally and to enjoy freedom of religion. Many, as has been said, would support a withdrawal of Russian migrants from the borderlands. On the controversial question of Russia's future boundaries, it seems that a majority of Russian nationalists would tend to agree with the views of "The Nation Speaks" and of Evgenii Vagin, which would imply that at least Latvia, Estonia, Lithuania, the western Ukraine, Armenia, Azerbaidzhan, Tadzhikistan, Turkmenia, and Uzbekistan might be offered the choice of secession. Minority nationalities remaining in the federation would presumably be granted greater autonomy in running their own affairs than they presently enjoy. In addition, Russian nationalists would be less likely than putative Marxist-Leninists to hinder the emigration abroad of ethnic Germans, Jews, and Poles,[88] while Crimean Tatars

---

[88] On the emigration of ethnic Germans, see I. Ratmirov, "Re Patria," *Zemlia*, no. 2 (AS 2060), 63-65. Some conservative Russian nationalist spokesmen think that Soviet Jews should be offered a chance to live in an autonomous republic somewhere in the present USSR. National Bolshevik ideologue A. Fetisov has said that such a unit should be located in the Crimea (" 'Survey' o russkom natsionalizme," p. 172), while Gennadii Shimanov did not specify the area he had in mind ("Gennadii Shimanov: Iz inter'viu

and Meskhetian Turks would probably be permitted to return to their homelands. In short, it is quite possible that Russian nationalists might be perceived by some minority nationalities as the "lesser of two evils."

The nationalities question will represent a morass for whoever rules the USSR. The Brezhnev system, with its uneven fertility rates, Russification of the borderlands, and suppression of the culture and religions of all Soviet nationalities, appeared to be charting a direct course toward catastrophe. The new leaders of Soviet Russia may realize this and resolve to change direction.

sotrudniku samizdatskogo zhurnala 'Evrei v SSSR,' " *Vestnik*, 121 [1977], p. 123). Shimanov would also not oppose the emigration of Jews abroad. According to the 1979 census, there were 1.9 million Germans, 1.8 million Jews, and 1.2 million Poles living in the Soviet Union. (*Naselenie SSSR*, pp. 23-24.)

7

The Church

They shot all the priests in the twenties and closed the
churches, so where have you slime come from?
> Words of a major in the militia to participants in
> the Moscow Religio-Philosophical Seminar[1]

. . . we are yesterday's Young Communists, who through
searchings and spiritual struggles, having beaten a path from
Marxism to idealism and barely crossed the threshold of
the Church . . . have placed ourselves under the blows of
the machinery of state security.
> From an appeal to Philip Potter, Secretary
> General of the World Council of
> Churches, signed by ten members of the
> Moscow Religio-Philosophical Seminar[2]

A Church ruled dictatorially by atheists—this is a spectacle
unseen in two thousand years.
> Aleksandr Solzhenitsyn, "Lenten Letter"[3]

No, I will not cast a stone at Russia!
I will go and be crucified with her.
> Fr. Dimitrii Dudko, "Verses about Russia"[4]

Most contemporary Russian nationalist spokesmen believe
that in order to be Russian one must be Orthodox. "I believe
in the power of Orthodoxy, and I believe in Russia!" ex-
claimed one contributor to *Veche*. "Russia is saved by Orthodoxy. Orthodoxy is indestructible. It is God's work, and a

---

[1] *Vestnik*, no. 119 (1976), 302.
[2] Jane Ellis, ed., *Letters from Moscow: Religion and Human Rights in the
USSR*, London and San Francisco, 1978, p. 107.
[3] Quoted from John B. Dunlop, Richard Haugh, and Alexis Klimoff, eds.,
Aleksandr Solzhenitsyn: Critical Essays and Documentary Materials, 2d ed.,
New York, 1975, p. 554.
[4] *Russkoe vozrozhdenie*, no. 1 (1978), 100.

Russian can only be Orthodox . . ."[5] In its statement of purpose, the journal *Zemlia* states categorically: "Any form of pagan or atheistic nationalism is demonic. . . . People without mercy, magnanimity, and love for God and man are not Russian."[6] Like preservation, cultural expression, and the nationalities question, the fate of the Russian Church has become an important Russian nationalist issue.

It is the issue, moreover, which serves to put the most strain on relations with the regime. First, and most obviously, there is the sphere of ideology: the regime's legitimizing ideology, Marxism-Leninism, requires the eradication of all religious survivals from the Russian land, a factor which naturally inflames relations with religious nationalists. Second, the Church, though not doctrinally opposed to modernization, inevitably prompts its adherents to question the value of a phenomenon that is accompanied by such social and moral ills as the breakup of the family, an upsurge in crime, and widespread alcoholism. Finally, the Church is pro-preservationist, seeking to safeguard from destruction ancient monuments, most of them churches or monasteries, and it tends to be pro-ecological as well, viewing the natural environment as God's handiwork.

All the major dissenting nationalist spokesmen—Solzhenitsyn, Shafarevich, Osipov, Ogurtsov, Vagin, Borodin, Ogorodnikov, Shimanov—are professed Orthodox believers; indeed, religion occupies a, if not the, central place in their world views. These comments by Shafarevich may be taken as representative:

I consider that the beginning of our national history (or, to put it more precisely, of the people which over the course of several centuries called itself Russian and then branched off into three kindred peoples: the Belorussian, Ukranian and Russian) is inseparably connected with the acceptance of Orthodoxy. It was then [i.e., late in the tenth century]

---

[5] Russkii khristianin, "Zametki russkogo khristianina," *Veche*, no. 1 (AS 1013), 51.
[6] *Vol'noe slovo*, no. 20, (1975), 5.

that there emerged an awareness of national unity and of certain common national goals. Orthodoxy was the spiritual pivot which helped us to bear the Tatar yoke and to preserve our national goals. It gave us the strength to overcome the disintegration of the Russian state in the seventeenth-century. . . It seems to me completely unlikely that any people can repudiate the source which has nourished its spiritual life for a thousand years and remain a spiritually alive organism. For that reason, I am convinced that if the life of our country is not over, then it is possible on the path of Orthodoxy and of Russian national tradition.

I do not belong to any group . . . But I think that many [in Soviet Russia] hold views close to mine. It is of course impossible to estimate their number, but I think that there are a great many of them. The reaching out of the youth for religion speaks of this—formerly, one could see only elderly women in church (and it was precisely they who defended the Church in the most terrible time), but now on major feasts it is basically the youth who squeeze into the churches. Or there is the interest in ancient icons, buildings, and churches, the movement in defense of monuments of antiquity. And especially there is the remarkable literature concerning the Russian village which has arisen in recent decades, one of the most significant phenomena in the culture of our country.[7]

This view of an inextricable link between Orthodoxy and Russia ran like a red thread through *Veche*, that most important of nationalist forums, while the two *samizdat* journals which briefly succeeded *Veche*—Osipov's *Zemlia* and Borodin's *Moskovskii sbornik*—devoted even more attention to religious themes and to the persecution of the Russian Church.

Russian nationalists who choose to promulgate their views through the Soviet media must often resort to Aesopian hints and cautious circumlocutions when touching upon religious questions. Nevertheless, despite the constraints of Soviet

---

[7] "Interv'iu korrespondentu gazety *Frankfurter Allgemeine Zeitung*," *Vestnik*, no. 126 (1978), 224-225.

censorship, important cultural figures such as Soloukhin and Glazunov, as well as many representatives of the "ruralist" school of prose, manage to make known their sympathy for Russian Orthodoxy. In his novel *Imia tvoe* (Thy Name), which was carried as part of the mass-edition *Roman-gazeta* series in 1978, nationalist author Petr Proskurin, presently a member of the Secretariat of the Soviet Writers' Union, virtually insisted upon the necessity of adherence to Orthodoxy as a prerequisite for a healthy and powerful Soviet state.[8] A number of contributors to Soviet journals which have at various times served as vehicles for nationalist thought—*Molodaia gvardiia, Nash sovremennik*—or to publications which are at least willing to let the nationalists have their say—*Moskva, Literaturnaia Rossiia, Sever*—exhibit a marked lack of hostility toward the religious traditions informing a thousand years of Russian history.

A central question for analysts of the Soviet Union is whether this connection between Orthodoxy and Russian nationalism concerns only a few elites or takes on a mass dimension. The evidence strongly suggests the latter. It has been estimated that some fifty million Soviet citizens adhere to the Russian Orthodox Church, and, if one were to add to this number those merely attracted to or interested in Orthodoxy, the figure could well be doubled.[9] Any link between this huge and

[8] Petr Proskurin, *Imia tvoe*, Moscow, 1978. The novel also appeared in *Roman-gazeta*, nos. 13-16 (1978).

[9] According to recent émigré Anatolii Levitin-Krasnov, who is well informed about church life in the USSR, Furov, deputy chairman of the Council for Religious Affairs, reported to the government in 1971-1972 that "more than forty million" Soviet citizens belong to the Russian Orthodox Church. Citing such factors as unregistered baptisms, Levitin considers this figure to be too conservative and suggests that fifty million would be more appropriate (*Russkaia mysl'*, 5 December 1974, p. 5). Prominent Orthodox churchmen gave Anglican activist Dr. Paul Anderson the same figure of fifty million when he recently visited the USSR (see Barbara Wolfe Jancar, "Religious Dissent in the Soviet Union," in Rudolf L. Tökes, ed., *Dissent in the USSR*, Baltimore, 1975, p. 197). Christel Lane maintains that "between 20 and 25 percent" of the Soviet populace "regard themselves as Orthodox believers" (*Christian Religion in the Soviet Union: A Sociological Study*, Albany, 1978, p. 46). William C. Fletcher estimates that "25% to 35%" of the population in the Russian areas of the USSR continue to be religious (*Soviet Believers: The Religious Sector of the Population*, Lawrence, Kansas, 1981, p. 208). On

amorphous body and Russian nationalism would obviously be of immense political significance. That there is such a link is shown by many of the *samizdat* letters and petitions, coming from numerous locations in the Soviet Union, which were collected by the Christian Committee for the Defense of Believers' Rights in the USSR before its decimation by the authorities in 1979-1980. The link was also, of course, demonstrated by the Soviet Union's experience during the Second World War.

The voluntary societies—the All-Russian Society for the Preservation of Historical and Cultural Monuments and the All-Russian Society for the Preservation of Nature—clearly exhibit the connection as well. Both organizations, which, as we have seen, are nationalist in orientation, are said to enjoy broad-based support among Orthodox believers. A contributor to *Zemlia*, for example, described the Society for the Preservation of Monuments as "existing completely on church money," i.e., on donations from believers.[10] Religious conviction thus motivates many of the 12 million Soviet citizens committed to rescuing Russia's ancient churches and monasteries from destruction.

With this background in mind, let us proceed to examine the issues which are of most concern to contemporary Russian

the basis of a careful analysis of Soviet sources, Academician Igor' Shafarevich concludes that "more than seventy million" believers adhere to the Orthodox Church (*Zakonodatel'stvo o religii v SSSR*, Paris, 1973, pp. 42-43). Utilizing fragmentary data, such as officially published burial and baptismal statistics, one émigré specialist, Gleb Rar, recently calculated that at least 115 million Soviet citizens remain at least passively attached to Orthodoxy ("Skol'ko pravoslavnykh v Rossii?," *Posev*, 3 [1973], 39-42). It should be noted that, due to historical circumstances, a large percentage of Orthodox parishes are in the Ukraine. Bohdan Bociurkiw has written that in 1959 the Ukraine, with about 19% of the USSR's population, accounted for more than half of all the Orthodox parishes in the country ("The Religious Situation in the Soviet Ukraine," in Walter Dushnyck, ed., *Ukraine in a Changing World*, New York, 1977, p. 174). Christel Lane says of the Ukraine that it "must have one of the highest levels of religiosity among the Union republics, with around 40 per cent of the population being religiously committed. This percentage is higher in the Western, more recently (1945) incorporated and more rural parts and lower in the eastern industrial parts" (*Christian Religion*, p. 223).

[10] *Vol'noe slovo*, no. 20 (1975), 16.

nationalists who believe that "in order to be Russian one must
be Orthodox."

THE NEW MARTYRS

A major concern of contemporary believers is the memory
of the large number of Orthodox believers who either were
killed outright by the Bolsheviks—often following mockery
and physical torture—or suffered drawn-out deaths in Stalin's
Gulag Archipelago. Shafarevich has referred to one list of
Russian "new martyrs" containing more than 8,000 names.[11]
A moving contribution to *Veche*, entitled "Unadorned Stories," related a series of purportedly true tales concerning the
tribulations of Orthodox martyrs and confessors, mostly in
concentration camps, during the Stalin era.[12] In these sketches,
believer-convicts are shown serving a hushed liturgy in a
mineshaft at four in the morning, a priest sacrifices his life
for his fellow-prisoners, etc. V. Nikiforov-Volgin's "Wayfar-
er's Staff," which appeared in the first issue of the religious
samizdat journal *Nadezhda*, offered an only partly fictional-
ized account of the trials endured by a Russian priest during
the bleak years of the great persecution. The story told how
Russians were forced to carry their icons into the forest for
safekeeping, just as they had done during the Tatar invasion
of the thirteenth-century. Militant atheists were depicted
looting icons from a cathedral and hurling them down on the
pavement outside, an action resulting in fisticuffs with believers.[13]

The account also related an incident in which a Red Army
soldier conducts a blasphemous "red mass" in a church, during which he communicates those present with home brew.
In his "sermon," he begins to "shower mother curses on the
Lord, on His Mother, and on all the saints."[14] Enraged, the

---

[11] Igor' Shafarevich, "Tele-interv'iu radiokompanii Bi Bi Si," *Vestnik*, no.
125 (1978), 212.

[12] "Prostye rasskazy," *Veche*, no. 6 (AS 1599), 45-56.

[13] V. Nikiforov-Volgin, "Dorozhnyi posokh," *Nadezhda: Khristianskoe
chtenie*, no. 1 (1978), 228-270.

[14] Ibid., p. 262.

villagers throw themselves on him and trample him under foot, so that "all the icons were splattered with his brains and blood." In retaliation, the soldiers open up with machine guns and kill some fifty townspeople.

Looking back over his years of wandering through the Russian land, the priest reminisces: "I have passed by defiled temples, burned-down chapels, monasteries turned into barracks and warehouses. I have been a witness of the violation of relics and of miracle-working icons. I have come into contact with the beastly face of man . . ."[15] The prevailing sentiment in the work, nonetheless, is one of optimism and hope.

ORTHODOX SHRINES

Together with a veneration for the memory of the new martyrs and a growing sentiment in favor of their official canonization, one often encounters in religious *samizdat* a concern for Christian shrines which have been closed and frequently desecrated by the communists. As noted earlier, Orthodox believers are active in the ranks of the Society for the Preservation of Monuments. Certain religious shrines, however, have not been placed under the society's protection, probably because of their great emotional resonance among the Russian faithful. One example is the Kiev-Pechersk Lavra, Russia's oldest shrine, which both the Christian Committee for the Defense of Believers' Rights in the USSR and members of the Moscow Religio-Philosophical Seminar attempted to have opened.[16] Another would be Optina Pustyn', site of numerous pilgrimages by noted Russian writers and intellectuals during the nineteenth and early twentieth centuries. An issue of *Veche* carried a report by Viktor Kapitanchuk, until his arrest a member of the Christian Committee, concerning a visit he made to this monastery. "In its last decades," he wrote,

[15] Ibid., p. 269.
[16] *Documents of the Christian Committee for the Defense of Believers' Rights in the USSR*, vol. 1, San Francisco, 1978, pp. 36, 46.

Optina shone brightly for all Russia with the living fire of Christian holiness, and the best minds and hearts of Russia turned toward its light. To this spot came the Slavophiles, the poet A. Tolstoi, the brothers Kireevskii, N. Gogol'. L. Tolstoi came here several times, without, however, finding in himself the strength to return to the bosom of the Church. Solov'ev and Dostoevskii came here. For the latter, Optina served as the prototype of the monastery in *The Brothers Karamazov*. The poet Apukhtin, who visited here, wrote the narrative poem "A Year in a Monastery." One of the most brilliant Russian thinkers, K. Leont'ev, was tonsured a monk here and was in obedience to the Elder Amvrosii. . . . Already during times of external and internal shocks, Akhmatova and Blok used to come here . . . The monastery was closed in the twenties.[17]

Upon entering the monastery, Kapitanchuk discovered that "the destruction caused to it by time and by men has been very great."[18] The two churches which had not been razed were being used as workshops for the repair of agricultural machinery. "Instead of the ringing of bells over Optina, one hears the screech of a saw and the roar of iron."[19] The graves of the monastery's famous elders—Leonid, Makarii, Amvrosii—are unmarked but not difficult to locate, since the Kireevskii brothers, whose graves *are* marked, had themselves buried at the elders' feet. "If you travel to Optina," Kapitanchuk wrote, "Kireevskii will lead you to the elders."[20] Commenting on the USSR's neglect of this shrine, he fulminated: "Even now, when the state has taken what remains of the material embodiment of our religious Russian culture under its protection, even now Optina is not under the state's protection."[21]

[17] Viktor Kapitanchuk, "V Optine," *Grani*, no. 102 (1976), 108. The text is also available in *Veche*, no. 10 (AS 2452), 23-29. On recent attempts to restore the monastery, see Vladimir Soloukhin, *Vremia sobirat' kamni*, Moscow, 1980, pp. 169-234.
[18] Kapitanchuk, "V Optine," p. 109.
[19] Ibid.
[20] Ibid., p. 110.
[21] Ibid., p. 109.

The *samizdat* journal *Nadezhda*, to which reference has already been made, contains an absorbing account by a Russian priest of a pilgrimage which he and some companions made to Sarov to visit sites associated with the life of St. Seraphim of Sarov.[22] This remarkable document—which could have been written in the seventeenth-century—contrasts "all the destruction, all the defilement" encountered at Sarov with the "height of humility" of St. Seraphim, whose presence the priest senses everywhere about him.

THE RUSSIAN CHURCH AND THE BOLSHEVIK REGIME

Moving from the martyrdom of the past to the present situation, it appears to be the common conviction of Russian nationalist writers on religious themes that the aim of the regime today remains what it was at the time of the Revolution: to extirpate all religious survivals from the Russian land. There also seems to be a consensus that the leadership of the Moscow Patriarchate is bound hand and foot by the regime and cannot or will not do anything to ameliorate the Church's position. Nationalist authors are not, however, in agreement as to the extent to which the Patriarchate leadership itself shares the blame for the results of the persecution. In order to put the differing views on the Patriarchate leadership in perspective, a digression on the history of the Russian Church under the Soviets is necessary.

The Russian Patriarchate, which had been abolished under Peter the Great, was restored during the tumultuous All-Russian Church Council of 1917-1918, just after the seizure of power by the Bolsheviks. The new patriarch, Tikhon, formerly Metropolitan of Moscow, immediately found himself confronted by the new regime's all-out assault on the traditional prerogatives of the Church. In January 1918, he sharply condemned a number of measures passed by the state, such as the secularization of marriage, the nationalization of schools, the confiscation of Church property, and various acts of des-

[22] "Iz perepiski dvukh sviashchennikov," *Nadezhda*, no. 1, pp. 124-152.

ecration at churches and monasteries. He termed this assault "a satanic act, for which you shall suffer the fire of Gehenna in the life to come, beyond the grave, and terrible curses of posterity in this present, earthly life."[23] He forbade those guilty of such deeds to come to the sacraments and anathematized them, and he counseled the faithful "not to commune with such outcasts of the human race in any manner whatever."[24] The All-Russian Church Council, which was still in session, resolutely supported the patriarch. As shall be seen later, Tikhon's stance at the time of the Bolshevik coup is admired by many contemporary religious activists, who on occasion refer to themselves as "Tikhonians."

Undaunted by the Church's firm and even defiant opposition, the Bolsheviks proceeded to publish a law on the separation of church and state, which bore little resemblance, however, to similar-sounding laws in the West. All properties of the Church were annexed as "national wealth," and religious communities were deprived of the right of judicial representation. Believers were limited to serving the "cult" and nothing more.

Despite the obviousness of the regime's intentions, Tikhon, who had boldly celebrated a requiem for the murdered Tsar Nicholas and his family in July 1918, was soon forced to revise his uncompromising stand toward the Bolsheviks. First, the outbreak of the civil war required that he assume an "apolitical" stance if he were to remain on the patriarchal throne; his new tack was to attempt to hold the state to the noninvolvement in Church affairs proclaimed by Soviet law. An even more threatening circumstance was the emergence of the so-called "Living Church" schism within the ranks of the Church itself. A revolt of certain elements in the "white" (i.e., married) clergy, the "Living Church" represented a pro-Soviet, modernizing movement, seeking the abolishment of the patriarchate, rule of the Church by the lower clergy and laity, and the active participation of the faithful in "socialist upbuilding." Faced with this specter, Tikhon seems to have

---

[23] Matthew Spinka, *The Church in Soviet Russia*, New York, 1956, p. 15.
[24] Ibid.

felt that he could not afford a war on two fronts, and in June 1923, after an extended period of imprisonment, he published a "Confession" stressing that he was "no longer an enemy of the Soviet government" and repenting his earlier anathematization of it. (The text of the "Confession" was probably drafted for him.) Since the Orthodox laity steadfastly refused to support the schismatics, Tikhon eventually won out, and the regime withdrew its support from the "Living Church" movement. Tikhon died in 1925, perhaps not of natural causes, and shortly before his death is supposed to have authored a "Will" advocating that the faithful be "sincere in our attitude toward the Soviet government . . ."[25] The authenticity of this will—or at least of its having been written by Tikhon of his own free volition—is disputed by some church historians.

Thus, from a position of defiance, Tikhon had moved by the end of his short but trying term as patriarch toward some kind of *modus vivendi* with the authorities. Fr. Gleb Iakunin, a dissident priest who has been under suspension by the Moscow Patriarchate since 1966 for coauthoring an open letter to the late Patriarch Aleksii and who was arrested by the authorities in 1979, recently criticized Tikhon for his act of "repentance." "The just courageous word which up to that time had sounded from the lips of the patriarch convicting the moral and spiritual fall of the people, the terrible bloody excesses and murders of innocent people, the raging of satanic spite and hatred, the defilement of religious and national shrines . . . ," he wrote, "all this the patriarch now declares to have been 'anti-Soviet politics.' Notwithstanding the greatness of the person and of the ascetic exploit of Patriarch Tikhon, one must with great regret recognize that precisely he first applied the principle of employing the lie, of false witness for the sake of 'saving the Church,' in the Moscow Patriarchate."[26] Fr. Iakunin appears to be almost alone in seeking to cast a shadow on the activity of Patriarch Tikh-

[25] Ibid., p. 43.
[26] Fr. Gleb Iakunin, "Moskovskaia Patriarkhiia i 'kul't lichnosti' Stalina," *Russkoe vozrozhdenie*, no. 1 (1978), 114.

on, whom most believers consider to have been a confessor and martyr. Solzhenitsyn, for example, has stated that in composing his letter to Patriarch Pimen in 1972, he "continually tested it mentally with the eyes of Patriarch Tikhon."[27] There is also the following episode, reported by Aleksandr Ogorodnikov, until his arrest leader of the Moscow Religio-Philosophical Seminar, in his description of a six-hour search carried out by the authorities in May 1978 at the Smolensk apartment of Tat'iana Shchipkova, a teacher at the Smolensk Pedagogical Institute and a member of the seminar:

> Closing the bookcase, he [one of the officials conducting the search] looked at the photographs attached to the glass on the door. He was interested. "And who's that?" The photograph shows Patriarch Tikhon (it is one of his best photographs). Hearing that it was Tikhon, the assistant procurator threw down his work and also went to look.
> "Well, even Tikhon, even he recognized the Soviet government, and he was a patriarch," he said.
> "And when did he die?" asked the first man.
> "In 1925."
> "Yes, yes," continued the assistant procurator. "After all he was also against the Soviet government at first, but then, right before he died, he made peace with it and wrote a work of penance."
> "Well, [Ogorodnikov, who was present, interjected] that's not known yet, who wrote the penance. Yes, and did he die by himself?"
> The first man silently examined photographs of Solzhenitsyn and Dostoevskii. He did not say anything.[28]

Following Tikhon's death, Metropolitan Sergii eventually became locum tenens of the patriarchal throne, a position he was to hold until permitted by Stalin to be elected patriarch in 1943. In 1927, after spending three-and-a-half months in

---

[27] *Novoe russkoe slovo*, 9 August 1972.
[28] *Documents of the Christian Committee*, vol. 4, p. 489. I have utilized the translation appearing in *Documents*, vol. 3, p. 306, but have made some minor stylistic alterations.

prison, Sergii issued a fateful "Declaration" which was to alter the course of the Russian Church. "We need to show not in words, but in deeds," Sergii affirmed in this document, "that not only people indifferent to Orthodoxy, or those who reject it, may be faithful citizens of the Soviet Union, loyal to the Soviet Union, but likewise the most fervent adherents of Orthodoxy, to whom it is as precious with all its canonical and liturgical treasures as truth and life. We wish to remain Orthodox and at the same time to recognize the Soviet Union as our civil fatherland whose joys and successes are our joys and successes, and whose misfortunes are our misfortunes."[29] As should be clear, in this document the Russian Church made some important concessions beyond those previously extracted from Patriarch Tikhon; in fact, the Church virtually identified itself in it with a regime which in effect was seeking its destruction. Sergii's "Declaration" caused great consternation among the Orthodox faithful and prompted a significant exodus of bishops, clergy, and laity from the Moscow Patriarchate into the "catacombs"; remnants of this exodus remain today, as members of the so-called "True Orthodox Church," a proscribed body sharply persecuted by the authorities.[30]

Even Sergii's act of obeisance accomplished little for the Church, however, and by 1939 only four bishops and a few hundred parishes remained active. It was, as already seen, the war which revived a moribund Church, once Stalin became convinced of the necessity of its use for mobilizational purposes and to offset German attempts to exploit religious sentiment among the population in occupied Soviet territory.[31] In 1943, Metropolitan Sergii was allowed to be elected

[29] Spinka, *Church in Soviet Russia*, p. 163.

[30] On the "catacomb" church, see William C. Fletcher, *The Russian Orthodox Church Underground, 1917-1970*, London, 1971, and Evgenii Vagin, "Izgnanii pravdy radi . . . ," *Russkoe vozrozhdenie*, no. 4 (1978), 33-57.

[31] On the Russian Church under the occupation, see Wassilij Alexeev and Theofanis G. Stavrou, *The Great Revival: The Russian Church Under the German Occupation*, Minneapolis, 1976, and Harvey Fireside, *Icon and Swastika: The Russian Orthodox Church Under Nazi and Soviet Control*, Cambridge, Mass., 1971. For an important study of the Russian Church under the communists during the period 1917-1945, written by an Orthodox

the second patriarch of the Soviet period, and following his death, the like-minded Metropolitan Aleksii was made patriarch in 1945. Sergii's historic "compromise with atheism" has generally been viewed unfavorably by *samizdat* publicists, although, as shall be seen, the policy still has its supporters, particularly in circles close to the center of power of the Moscow Patriarchate.

The next major change in the life of the Russian Church occurred in 1960, during the early stages of Khrushchev's war on religion. At that time, G. G. Karpov, who had overseen the Church in the period following the war and whose attitude toward it had been fairly benign, was replaced as head of the Council for Religious Affairs by Vladimir Kuroedov, formerly chairman of the Novosibirsk *obkom* and a militant atheist. As of 1979, Kuroedov was still head of this important body; his deputy, Furov, was said by an article in *Veche* to hold the rank of general in the KGB.[32]

It was also in 1960 that Metropolitan Nikolai of Krutitsk, the Church's second highest official, who briefly but bitterly contested the regime's unilateral termination of Stalin's postwar policy of détente with the Church, was ousted from his position as head of the Patriarchate's Department of External Affairs and, three months later, was removed from the episcopate. He died in 1961 under ambiguous circumstances. "At Nikolai's funeral," William C. Fletcher has written, "attended by exceedingly large crowds at the monastery of Zagorsk, near Moscow, members of a group of Western churchmen were told by people that no funeral would have been held at all except for the insistence of the large crowds that appeared at Zagorsk and would not be put off. Nikolai was buried in utter disgrace so far as the state was concerned."[33]

As Nikolai's replacement, the regime chose the young and

dissenter still in his thirties, see Lev Regel'son, *Tragediia russkoi tserkvi*, Paris, 1977.

[32] *Veche*, no. 9 (AS 2040), 7. For important excerpts from two annual reports by Furov to the Party Central Committee, see *Vestnik*, no. 130 (1979), 275-344, and no. 131 (1980), 362-372.

[33] William C. Fletcher, *Nikolai: Portrait of a Dilemma*, New York, 1968, p. 201.

more tractable Bishop Nikodim (b. 1929), who, together with several other young hierarchs—Metropolitan Aleksii (b. 1929), Metropolitan Philaret (b. 1929), and Metropolitan Iuvenalii (b. 1935)—soon took over the direction of church affairs. (Neither Patriarch Aleksii nor his successor, Patriarch Pimen, who was elected first hierarch at a National Church Council in 1971, seems to have been able to exert much control over events.) Nikodim and his colleagues did nothing to contest the regime's harsh persecution of religion and closure of some 10,000 churches during the period from 1959 to 1964, and, by imposing ecclesiastical sanctions on clergy who did protest, they assisted the authorities in their task. Nikodim unexpectedly died of a heart attack in 1978 while conversing with the newly-elected Pope John Paul I in Rome, but the period of his tenure as metropolitan might well be termed the "Nikodim period" of the Russian Church. While the philosophy of this period was essentially that of Metropolitan Sergii's "Declaration," the Nikodim orientation seems to have offered even less opposition to the state than had been evident in the previous generation of hierarchs. A gifted but shadowy individual, Nikodim seems almost to have relished the double role required of him by the regime.[34]

In 1961, a Bishops' Council, convoked in an unusual and anti-canonical manner, effected important changes in the parish life of the Russian Church. It altered the 1945 Church regulations in such a way that the priest (and even the bishop) was deprived of any real control over the life of the local parish, which was, instead, to be run by twenty founding members approved by the local authorities. Under such a system, it became relatively easy for the regime to include unbelievers and even immoral individuals among the parish "twenty" (dvadtsatka) and to name enemies of the Church as parish warden (starosta), a situation which of course served to demoralize the Orthodox faithful.

In November 1965, two young priests, Frs. Nikolai Eshliman and Gleb Iakunin, circulated an open letter to Patriarch

[34] On Nikodim, see Dimitry Pospielovsky, "Mitropolit Nikodim i ego vremia," Posev, no. 2 (1979), 21-26.

Aleksii protesting Khrushchev's antireligious campaign and the complicity in it of the Moscow Patriarchate hierarchy.[35] This detailed and tightly reasoned document caused a major stir in the Russian Church; in fact, its effects continue to be felt today. (Fr. Eshliman dropped out of active church affairs soon after being suspended by the patriarchate, but Fr. Iakunin, a founding member of the Christian Committee for the Defense of Believers' Rights in the USSR, became a major spokesman for the persecuted Church.) The letter of the two priests coincided with or spawned similar efforts in the decade to come—open letters by Archbishop Ermogen of Kaluga, Boris Talantov, Anatolii Levitin-Krasnov, and Solzhenitsyn, among others. Nationalist *semizdat* journals, such as *Veche* and *Zemlia*, gave extensive coverage to abuses of believers' rights, while the Christian Committee sent to the West hundreds of pages of documentation concerning the infringement of religious and human rights in the USSR. From September 1978 until January 1980 a weekly newsletter edited by Fr. Dimitrii Dudko provided similar documentation.

Next to the letter of the two priests, it was probably Solzhenitsyn's open letter to Patriarch Pimen, written during Lent of 1972, which evoked the greatest response among believers. The letter, as well as several reactions to it, was published in *Veche*.[36] "Why," Solzhenitsyn began, "on coming to church to christen my son did I have to present my [internal] passport? For what canonical purposes does the Moscow Patriarchate require the [civil] registration of the newly baptized?" Here Solzhenitsyn was pointing to a violation of Soviet legality frequently stressed by Orthodox dissenters: it is not Soviet law but unwritten instructions which require the registration of baptism, a practice which can then result in the firing or demotion of a believer at his place of work.

Assailing the Moscow Patriarchate leadership, Solzhenitsyn explicity aligned himself with the "two priests" and their work:

[35] A complete translation appeared in *St. Vladimir's Seminary Quarterly*, 10, nos. 1-2 (1966).
[36] *Veche*, no. 5 (AS 1230), pp. 33-36; translation in Dunlop et al., *Aleksandr Solzhenitsyn*, p. 551.

"It will soon be seven years since the two righteous priests Iakunin and Eshliman wrote their celebrated letter to your predecessor, confirming by their sacrifice and example that the pure flame of Christian faith had not been extinguished in our land . . . they were punished for the truth—and prohibited from serving in church."[37] He also cited the fates of Boris Talantov, who died in a concentration camp in 1971, and of Archbishop Ermogen of Kaluga, who died in 1978 while under virtual house arrest in Zhirovitskii Monastery.

Referring to the acute shortage of churches resulting from the mass closings under Khrushchev, Solzhenitsyn wrote:

> For every functioning church there are twenty which have been levelled or irreparably wrecked and twenty more abandoned and desecrated; is there a sight more soul wrenching than a church-skeleton left to the birds and to warehouse keepers? How many population centers are there in the country, to which no church is closer than 100 or even 200 kilometers? . . . But every attempt by concerned individuals, by donors, and by testators to *restore* even the smallest church is blocked by our one-sided laws of the so-called *separation* of Church and State.[38]

After citing the near impossibility of obtaining religious literature, including the Gospels, Solzhenitsyn proceeded to describe how the Church is administered in practice: "The entire governance of the Church, the appointment of priests and bishops (even of disreputable ones, so that the Church might more easily be mocked and destroyed) is conducted as secretly as before by the Council for Religious Affairs. . . . Given over to the atheists' control is also the entirety of the operational management of the Church and the allocation of Church funds."[39] Apropos of the decisions of the Bishops' Council of 1961, he wrote: "Priests have no authority in their own parishes, only the service is still entrusted to them, and that only within the confines of the church; to venture be-

---

[37] Dunlop et al., *Aleksandr Solzhenitsyn*, p. 553.
[38] Ibid., pp. 553-554 (Solzhenitsyn's italics).
[39] Ibid., p. 554.

yond the door to a sick parishioner or to a cemetery requires permission from the town council."[40]

Solzhenitsyn concluded that the Moscow Patriarchate was following a false and perverse path which could lead only to the eventual extinction of the Church. "By what reasoning," he asked, "could one convince oneself that the calculated *destruction*—one directed by atheists—of the body and spirit of the Church is the best method of preserving it?"[41] And he ended by calling upon the patriarch to sacrifice himself for the Church: "He who is deprived of all material strength always achieves victory in sacrifice."

Solzhenitsyn's indignant and skillfully written letter, which cut through the deceit and subterfuges of both the Council for Religious Affairs and the Moscow Patriarchate leadership, had a considerable impact. Later, in his literary memoirs, he recalled that the letter "elicited choking rage on the part of state security—more than many of my previous and subsequent steps (and small wonder: atheism is the heart of the whole communist system)."[42]

Veche carried a reply to Solzhenitsyn's letter from Fr. Sergii Zheludkov, a dissident Orthodox priest with modernist leanings whose writings are well known to Western students of *samizdat*.[43] Zheludkov accused Solzhenitsyn of repeating the "moral error" of the two priests, i.e., criticizing a patriarch who was "deprived of any possibility of answering." Moreover, he charged, Solzhenitsyn showed himself to be completely unrealistic in his approach; a legal organization in the Soviet Union cannot be an "island of freedom" in an unfree society. The Church was "not permitted" to undertake the religious education of children or of adults and should reconcile itself to this. In effect, Fr. Zheludkov argued, the Russian Church had only two choices before it: to go underground, which was impossible; or to use those possibilities, such as the right to perform church services, which the Soviet

---

[40] Ibid.
[41] Ibid., pp. 554-555 (Solzhenitsyn's italics).
[42] Aleksandr Solzhenitsyn, *Bodalsia telenok s dubom*, Paris, 1975, p. 355.
[43] *Veche*, no. 5 (AS 1230), 37-39.

system afforded it. There was no other choice. Solzhenitsyn was profoundly wrong in seeking to coerce others into sacrifice and martyrdom. Nevertheless, despite his advocacy of quiescence, Fr. Zheludkov underlined his firm belief that there would be a "renaissance of Russian Christianity."[44]

Another response, in the same issue of *Veche*, sought to report various reactions to Solzhenitsyn's letter. Patriarch Pimen is supposed to have "bitterly smiled" when asked his opinion of the letter and stated: "He [Solzhenitsyn] should spend even two days in my position."[45] Russian priests are said to have reacted negatively to the letter because Solzhenitsyn struck at someone (i.e., Pimen) perceived as defenseless and because the letter represented a repetition of the efforts of the two priests, and the results of their endeavors were well known. Only certain "intellectuals" (*intelligenty*) were reported to have welcomed the letter.

In spite of Solzhenitsyn's exertions, the author of the reply concluded, nothing was going to change. Antireligious propaganda would continue, the education of Soviet youth would remain in the hands of atheists, the authorities would continue to control the life of the Church and to demand documents from parents upon the baptism of a child, the patriarch would remain in his place "as in a hot frying pan," and there would even be Orthodox hierarchs who would work hand in hand with the enemies of the Church. "All will be as it has been; that is the kind of time we live in."[46] Still, the author said, "it is good that Solzhenitsyn wrote the letter."

The next issue of *Veche* contained an article entitled "Mnenie bogoslova" (Opinion of a Theologian) which continued the discussion.[47] The author made no attempt to deny that the atheist authorities sought to uproot the Church, but he stressed that the question should concern what the reaction of the Church, which has had all of its rights taken away, should be.

[44] Ibid., p. 39. For Solzhenitsyn's *samizdat* reply to Fr. Zheludkov, see Dunlop et al., *Aleksandr Solzhenitsyn*, p. 556.
[45] Ochevidets (Eyewitness), "Po povodu pis'ma Solzhenitsyna Patriarkhu," *Veche*, no. 5 (AS 1230), 40.
[46] Ibid., p. 41.
[47] Kandidat bogoslovskikh nauk (candidate in theological sciences), "Mnenie bogoslova," *Veche*, no. 6 (AS 1599), 43-44.

His categorical answer was: "Patience, of course." Even Patriarch Tikhon, he pointed out, had come to the conclusion that loyalty to the Soviet state was necessary, and he went on to single out Solzhenitsyn and the two priests for criticism, charging them with calling for a schism in the Church. Their demand that the regime observe its own laws relating to the Church, he said, reflected either naivete or pride. The Church was not a "political organization," and any adoption by it of political methods would prove futile. The principal task of contemporary believers was to preserve the traditions of the Church.

The astonishing passivity pervading such documents—something difficult for many Western readers even to understand—shows how deeply *Sergianstvo* (i.e., the policies stemming from Metropolitan Sergii's 1927 "Declaration") has taken root in the contemporary Russian religious consciousness. As Igor' Shafarevich recently said sardonically, the Russian believer is not likely to encounter difficulties if he "attends atheistic lectures and gives his children an atheistic upbringing; if he does not protest when they sack a priest whose services have attracted a great many people; if he keeps quiet when they decide to close the church which he has grown used to attending; if he does not seek to obtain the opening of a new church in its place, etc., etc. That type of believer is in accord with the spirit and letter of [Soviet] legislation on religion."[48]

As scores of documents issued by the Christian Committee for the Defense of Believers' Rights in the USSR demonstrate, many Orthodox believers have opted for a middle path between the maximalism urged by Solzhenitsyn and the two priests and the passivity recommended by the above-quoted "theologian." Each year petitions flood the offices of the Council for Religious Affairs and the Moscow Patriarchate seeking to obtain the opening of a church which has been "temporarily" closed for repairs for a decade, the reinstatement of a priest suspended for excessive zeal, the removal of professed atheists from the ruling "twenty" of a parish council, etc. At best, an obdurate letter declining the believers' request is re-

---

[48] Shafarevich, "Tele-interv'iu," p. 213.

ceived. Petitioners who become too involved in seeking to achieve their aims can suffer demotion or dismissal at their place of work and even court arrest or detention in a mental hospital. Shafarevich has suggested that these petitions have been undervalued by Western observers of the Soviet Union:

> Eight years ago believers in the city of Gor'kii began to petition for the opening of a church. They wrote that in a city with a population of over one million there were de facto no churches—three small churches located far away on the outskirts of the city did not count. They collected more than 1,500 signatures on a petition and achieved nothing, except threats and unpleasantness at work. Now they have begun everything anew, have collected almost 3,000 signatures and are presently attempting to get an answer from the authorities (so far without result). Perhaps in your country [Great Britain] these are small numbers, but in our country they are enormous. Under no petition devoted to the rights of man did any one succeed in collecting more than one-tenth that number of signatures. And so it always is: when the question concerns the Church, thousands and thousands of people offer support.[49]

During the early and middle 1970s, several of the more conservative elements among the Russian nationalists attempted to interest the regime in a détente with the Church. There was, for example, a letter to participants in the 1971 Church Council, authored by Deacon Varsonofii Khaibulin and others which urged a *sblizhenie* (drawing together) of state and church "on the basis of good will, common interests and sincerity, patriotic duty and the complete absence of interference [by the state] in the internal life of the Church."[50] For its part, the Church was to promote "unhypocritical patriotism and faithfulness to the homeland," while the state would make a number of concessions, such as permitting the ordination of more clergy, opening new monasteries and con-

---

[49] Ibid., pp. 209-210.
[50] "Proshenie Pomestnomu Soboru Russkoi Pravoslavnoi Tserkvi 1971 g.," *Veche*, no. 3 (AS 1108), 62-67. This document has become notorious for its reference to the dangers of "Zionism and satanism" (p. 63).

vents, permitting the expanded publication of religious literature, and sanctioning the religious instruction of youth. A similar aim was pursued by Gennadii Shimanov, a frequent contributor to *Veche* on religious topics, in a 1975 essay "Ideal'noe gosudarstvo" (The Ideal State), whose central thesis was that "the Soviet regime is pregnant with theocracy."[51] A spiritual transfiguration of Soviet power, Shimanov maintained, must be effected, and the ideocratic Communist Party of the Soviet Union must gradually become "the Orthodox Party of the Soviet Union." (Shimanov's early immersion in Marxist theory—about which he spoke in his autobiography[52]— makes itself felt in his fixation on "dialectics" and his unconscious historical determinism.)

The regime, predictably, has shown little interest in the olive branch extended by Fr. Khaibulin, Shimanov, and others, and religious advocates of détente often grow disappointed and abandon the attempt. By 1978, Khaibulin, head of the "All-Russian Brotherhood of the Most Holy Mother of God," had come full circle and was counseling religious disobedience to Soviet regulations which seek to thwart "the active evangelization of all peoples."[53] As for Shimanov, he has of late begun to speak in less strident terms about "theocracy." A recent interview published in the émigré journal *Sintaksis* suggested, however, that some believers continue to hope for a reconciliation between church and state.[54]

THREE DISPUTED ISSUES

There are three issues disputed among contemporary Orthodox believers which, if the Church were granted limited autonomy to run its own affairs, could result in serious divisions in the ranks of the faithful. The first of these issues is

---

[51] Gennadii Shimanov, "Ideal'noe gosudarstvo," 8 pp. Available from Keston College, Centre for the Study of Religion and Communism, Heathfield Road, Keston, Kent BR2 6BA, England.

[52] Genadii Shimanov, *Pered smert'iu*. Available from Keston College (see note 51).

[53] "Vserossiiskoe Bratstvo Presviatoi Bogoroditsy (Spravka)," *Russkoe vozrozhdenie*, 4 (1978), 23.

[54] "Ne nazyvaia imen" (interview), *Sintaksis*, no. 2 (1978), pp. 47-48.

modernism. *Veche* has published a letter to the 1971 Council written by Fr. Nikolai Gainov and three laymen requesting that that body examine possible heresies being preached by Nikodim of Leningrad, two archbishops, and two professors at the Leningrad Theological Academy.[55] Nikodim and his associates were charged with seeing technical progress as the "greatest good" and with viewing socialist society as "a realization of the ideal of the Gospel." The authors of the letter also disputed the view, attributed to the modernists, that Christians are forbidden ever to resort to arms against enemies. They make reference to St. Sergii of Radonezh, who blessed Russian troops to do battle with the Tatars. The clergy indicted by the letter were said to have followed the path of the schismatic "Living Church," and the faithful were reminded of a prophecy of St. Seraphim of Sarov, foretelling the day when Russian hierarchs would "depart from preserving Orthodoxy in all its purity . . ."

If modernism represents one issue dividing contemporary Orthodox, ecumenism—particularly the question of Orthodox-Catholic relations—is an even more controversial topic. The election of John Paul II ("a brother Slav") as pope and his stated desire to achieve union with the Orthodox Church promise to exacerbate the situation further. A letter in *Veche* by "V.N." drew attention to the "Catholic danger"; Catholic strategists, the author warned, see that the atheists have "methodically destroyed the Orthodox Church" in Russia, thereby clearing a path for "subsequent expansion." The books which Catholic activists send into Russia are aimed at introducing a "Catholic injection" and preparing the way for the "Catholicization of Russia." The author foresaw a transformation to "Catholic-Orthodoxy" (*Katoliko-pravoslavie*) which would evolve into a "modernized form of Uniatism."[56]

A letter by "N.V.," published in a subsequent issue of *Veche* supported this view, asserting that Catholicism was a significantly greater danger for Russia than atheism, since the latter

[55] Nikolai Gainov and others, "Ser'eznye i svoevremennye voprosy," *Veche*, no. 2 (AS 1020), 34-47.

[56] *Veche*, no. 4 (AS 1140), 166-167.

had lost its hold on the populace, while Catholicism remained "a power."[57] The time may have arrived, the author wrote, for a winnowing out of " 'Catholicizing' Orthodox" from the fold. Also, whereas contemporary atheists may in the future become Orthodox and Russian patriots, the same cannot be said, he asserted, about Catholics, who almost instinctively detest Russia.

The editors of *Veche* have stressed their disagreement with this position on several occasions, and the Christian Committee went so far as to address a lengthy open letter to the successor of Pope John Paul I (John Paul II had not yet been elected) in which its members scored the "age-old suspicion toward Catholicism" in Russia and offered advice on how a new pontiff could allay such endemic mistrust.[58] In 1973-1974, Fr. Dimitrii Dudko was wont to refer to the Catholic Church as the "Western half" of the one Church and to advertise his ecumenical convictions, but by 1978-1979, as evidenced by his weekly newsletter, he had become more cautious in such declarations and might in fact have changed his mind.[59]

The third disputed issue concerns the seventeenth-century Old Believer schism—not so much the question of whether the schismatics should be welcomed back into the fold (all discussants agree that they should) but rather the legitimacy of the schism itself. Solzhenitsyn has more than once championed the justness of the cause of the Old Belief, while, on the other hand, an article in *Veche* took issue with what it regarded as the prevalent excessive sympathy for the schismatics and the historically unjustified harsh criticism of Patriarch Nikon and the original opponents of the Old Believers.[60]

---

[57] *Veche*, no. 6 (AS 1599), 129-130.

[58] *Documents of the Christian Committee*, vol. 5, pp. 700-716.

[59] See, for example, Fr. Dimitrii Dudko, *Our Hope*, Crestwood, New York, 1977, pp. 46-47, and his weekly newsletter, *V svete Preobrazheniia*, no. 4, 24 September 1978.

[60] A. Solzhenitsyn, "Tret'emu Soboru Zarubezhnoi Russkoi Tserkvi," *Vestnik*, no. 112/113 (1974), 107-108, and A.D., "Patriarkh Nikon i nachalo raskola v Russkoi Pravoslavnoi Tserkvi," *Veche*, no. 8 (AS 1665), 69-87.

FATHER DUDKO

Before concluding this chapter, I should like to focus first upon an individual and then upon an organization whose activities demonstrate the potential significance of a fusion of Russian nationalist and Russian Orthodox concerns: Fr. Dimitrii Dudko (b. 1922) and the Moscow-based Religio-Philosophical Seminar. Until he was broken in captivity during 1980, Fr. Dudko might have been termed a "shadow patriarch" of the Russian Church, a moral counterweight to the supine and passive Patriarch Pimen of Moscow. Of peasant background, from Briansk Province in southern Russia, he was conscripted into the Soviet army during the Second World War. At the war's conclusion, he was admitted to the Moscow Theological Seminary and later was permitted to transfer to the Moscow Theological Academy. In his second year of studies, however, he was arrested after a fellow student stole some of his poems and brought them to the attention of the authorities. For these verses, which Anatolii Levitin-Krasnov, the author of a useful short biography of the priest,[61] has termed "typical poems of a religious youth," Fr. Dudko received seven years in a concentration camp. While in the camps, he was given a second seven-year sentence for "conversations" with inmates, but in 1956, during the period of de-Stalinization, he was fully rehabilitated and released, having served eight-and-a-half years in all.

Eventually, Fr. Dudko succeeded in regaining admittance to the theological academy, whence, despite harassment by the authorities, he managed to graduate in 1958. In November 1960, he was ordained to the priesthood and given a Moscow parish. In 1963, the authorities, seeking to reduce the influence of the zealous priest's activities, transferred him to the St. Nicholas Church at the Transfiguration Cemetery, located on the outskirts of Moscow. Soon, in Levitin-Krasnov's words, "all believing Moscow" was beating a path to the church to hear the preacher's increasingly renowned sermons.

In November 1973, Fr. Dudko decided to add a new di-

---

[61] A. Levitin-Krasnov, "Otets Dimitrii Dudko," *Posev*, no. 1 (1975), 26-36.

mension to his priestly service. He had grown accustomed to receiving letters from believers soliciting his advice on a variety of spiritual matters and concluded that it might prove useful to provide oral responses to such letters following the vigil service on Saturday evenings. These "discussions with believers," which commenced on 19 November 1973, immediately created a sensation in Moscow, and large crowds of believers, nonbelievers, foreign correspondents, and representatives of state security flocked to the small church to hear the celebrated preacher. The text of these "discussions" was published in Russian by YMCA Press in Paris and became a *tamizdat* best-seller in the Soviet Union; an English translation has appeared in the United States.[62]

In May 1974, Fr. Dudko was ordered by the Patriarchate to cease holding such "discussions," and when he bridled at an attempt to assign him to a new parish beyond the Moscow city limits, he was suspended from the priesthood. The harassment of the now famous priest attracted wide attention in Moscow and—through the foreign radio—in the Soviet Union as a whole. In September 1974, in a compromise with the episcopate, Fr. Dudko agreed to accept assignment to a parish in Kabanovo, fifty miles from Moscow, and the suspension was lifted. His removal from the capital did not, however, end his influence; soon followers were making the journey to Kabanovo to communicate with their former pastor. On 9 April 1975, the authorities apparently attempted to kill Fr. Dudko in an automobile crash, an effort which narrowly missed succeeding.[63]

In December 1975, Fr. Dudko was removed from the Kabanovo parish on orders of governmental authorities, but by Easter of 1976, he had gained appointment as pastor of the church in Grebnevo, twenty miles from Moscow. In April 1977, he was sharply attacked in *Literaturnaia gazeta*; the main burden of the accusation was that he was "educating

[62] Dimitrii Dudko, *O nashem upovanii: Besedy*, Paris, 1975. (English translation, Dudko, *Our Hope*.)

[63] *Russkaia mysl'*, 29 January 1976, p. 6. For Fr. Dudko's comments on the episode, see *Church Times*, 5 August 1977.

youth," a crime for a Soviet cleric.[64] Though he had previously been criticized in the book *Diversion without Dynamite*, this new diatribe seemed to be aimed at preparing the ground for a trial of the defiant priest. In September 1978, he initiated a new form of priestly outreach with the publication of a *samizdat* weekly "newspaper-sermon," called *V svete Preobrazheniia* (In the Light of the Transfiguration).[65] The newsletter contained advice on spiritual matters and information on religious events in various parts of the USSR (e.g., Volgograd, Voronezh, Novosibirsk, the Altai region, Tashkent, the Ukraine) and on the treatment of believers in Soviet society, particularly in the armed forces. The newsletter appeared until January 1980, when Fr. Dudko was arrested again.

To a superficial observer, it might seem that Fr. Dudko's activities were purely religious. An examination of his writings and of published transcripts of his sermons shows, however, that it was a fusion of Russian Orthodox and Russian nationalist concerns which inspired his "mission" to Soviet society. Consider, for example, this *samizdat* response to the attack in *Literaturnaia gazeta*:

> . . . They want to try me because I cannot forget how they executed the Russian Tsar with all his family and servants. . . . They wish to try me because I cannot forget how they slaughtered the Russian peasantry . . . And now the villages are homeless, the wind of godlessness howls, and Russian women are groaning in all the villages. The youth has run off to the cities; there is no one left to work in the fields.
>
> They wish to try me because I am unable to forget the Russian nobility, which was destroyed in the most ruthless way. . . . And with them they executed Russian literature, which only now is beginning little by little to return to life.
> . . .

[64] For the text and for Fr. Dudko's reply, see Jane Ellis, ed., *Letters from Moscow*, pp. 80-83, 89-93.

[65] This valuable source has not yet been published in its entirety. For selections, see *Vol'noe slovo*, 33 (1979).

They wish to try me because I cannot forget how they annihilated our priests, how they placed them before the firing squads, or left them to rot in prison, or crucified them over the altars, or covered them with tar in barrels; and now there is nobody to minister to the needs of a morally degenerate population. . . .

They wish to try me because I cannot forget the millions of those who were shot, the millions who were buried in the northern snows, who died from hunger, cold, and illness.

They wish to try me because of my concern for souls devastated by atheism, because of my concern over the universal drunkenness in our country, for the debauchery and disintegration of family life, for our destroyed churches, and for all the ruins scattered over our Russian land.[66]

As can be seen, Fr. Dudko touches upon the whole gamut of Russian nationalist issues: the decline of the village and (by inference) the precipitous drop in Russian fertility; the social aftershocks of headlong modernization, such as the breakup of the family and the rise of alcoholism; the destruction of historical monuments; the "execution" of Russian literature and culture. Monarchist sentiments are also discernible in his response.

During his Saturday evening dialogues with believers, Fr. Dudko stressed the deep connection between Orthodoxy and patriotism, as in this exchange:

Question: Say something about the patriotism of the Orthodox Church. I came to Orthodoxy having felt precisely its deep interest in the unity and strength of Russia, its ennobling influence on the morals of our fellow citizens, its teaching of a love for one's neighbors which is also obviously a love for one's Fatherland. Do you understand this to be one of the goals of contemporary Orthodoxy?

Answer: As we know, our Orthodox Church in all periods has been afflicted with the afflictions of her people, and

[66] *Church Times*, 5 August 1977.

her suffering has been profound at having been numbered among the enemies of our people and our Fatherland. You are correct in writing that it is precisely the Church that has a deep interest in the unity of Russia, that precisely the Church has an ennobling effect on the morals of our fellow citizens, that she fosters love within them. And that is precisely love for the Fatherland. . . . I think that only the Church can teach us how to love people and our Fatherland and help us to do so. . . . That's why I've taken up arms against atheism, which sows enmity between people and in particular sets the masses against the faithful. To the honorable atheist I reach out my hand: "Look, our country is in danger. Drinking, the disintegration of the family, debauchery—aren't these a danger?" But atheism doesn't deliver you from them.[67]

The Orthodox Church, Fr. Dudko emphasized, is a bulwark of Russian patriotism and sound morals. The Church's enemies de facto seek the physical and spiritual destruction of the Fatherland.

In his weekly newsletter, *In the Light of the Transfiguration*, Fr. Dudko frequently invited the authorities to a dialogue:

> To whose profit is it to set unbelievers and believers against one another? To whose profit is it that we, citizens of one country, should not understand one another? To whose profit is it that, faced with the Chinese danger, we should be at enmity one with another?
>
> We remind the atheists. During the Fatherland war, believers did not spare their lives defending the homeland . . . but now all that is forgotten? . . . We believers call the atheists to peace. Think it over, what are you doing? Can it be that there are not enough destroyed churches and defiled shrines in our land? Can it be that there are not enough devastated souls without faith in God—drunkards, hooligans, thieves?[68]

[67] Dudko, *Our Hope*, pp. 105-106.
[68] *V svete Preobrazheniia*, no. 2, 10 September 1978.

Here again, Fr. Dudko was assuring his opponents that the Russian Church could serve as a bastion of patriotic sentiment in the event of war and could greatly assist in halting the socio-moral disintegration of the Russian people. In another issue of the newsletter, he referred to the "demographic pit" which the regime had dug for the Russian family and for itself, the result of the "general Russian family catastrophe" stemming from Russian women being forced to enter the labor market, whether they wanted to or not.[69] He also assailed the ecological blight resulting from heedless industrial policies.[70]

The regime responded to Fr. Dudko's offer of dialogue by arresting him. With the active assistance of the Moscow Patriarchate leadership, the authorities eventually succeeded in breaking the intrepid priest's resistance, and in June 1980, he abjectly confessed his errors on Soviet television.[71]

THE MOSCOW RELIGIO-PHILOSOPHICAL SEMINAR

The same *Literaturnaia gazeta* article in which Fr. Dudko was attacked in 1977 also took to task young Aleksandr Ogorodnikov (b. 1950), the founder of the Moscow-based Religio-Philosophical Seminar. Ogorodnikov was raised in Chistopol, Tatar ASSR, son of a Party member and convinced atheist. "For ideological reasons," he was not permitted to complete a degree in philosophy at either Moscow State University or the Ural District University. He then enrolled in the Drama and Film Department of the State Institute of Film in Moscow, where, at the age of 23, he converted to Orthodox Christianity. This led to his being expelled in 1973, when he

---

[69] Ibid., no. 7, 15 October 1978.
[70] Ibid., no. 20, 14 January 1979.
[71] On the role of the Moscow Patriarchate in attaining Fr. Dudko's confession, see Anatolii Levitin-Krasnov, "O tekh kogo nedavno sudili," *Posev*, no. 11 (1980), and *The Orthodox Monitor*, January-June 1980, pp. 26-27. For statements of regret over his behavior, issued after his release from prison, see Fr. Dudko's letters in *Nasha gazeta*, 8-14 November 1980, p. 10, and in *Vestnik*, no. 133 (1981), 293.

was a third-year student, for attempting to make a film "on the religious quest of Soviet youth."[72]

The following year Ogorodnikov founded the Religio-Philosophical Seminar, presumably named after the several religio-philosophical societies which sprang up in Moscow and Petersburg in the first decade of the twentieth century.[73] It caused a stir among the youth of the capital, many of them from Party families, and soon the seminar had spread its influence to Leningrad and the provinces (Ufa, Kazan', Smolensk, Grodno, L'vov, Odessa, Kalinin province). Over forty papers were read at meetings of the seminar on such topics as "Orthodoxy," "The Russian Idea," "The Type of Russian Sanctity: Saints and the State," and "The Discussions of Fr. Dimitrii Dudko."[74]

Mark Popovskii, a journalist and religious believer who was permitted to emigrate in late 1977, has described one session of the seminar, held in June 1977.[75] In a Moscow apartment, under conditions of "strict conspiracy," some forty young people have gathered. A majority of those present live in the provinces; by profession, they are students, teachers, and "the extremely widespread type of the *intelligent-rabochii* [worker-intellectual]." Papers delivered at the session touch upon the relations between the neophytes (i.e., the newly baptized) and the Church and upon contemporary leftist thought in the West, but the greatest interest is aroused by a talk entitled "The Culture of the Catacombs or Quests for Relatively Free Forms of Life in Soviet Totalitarian Society." Projects discussed at the meeting include the opening of a summer camp where believers could spend their vacations in the company of like-minded friends, and the opening of a kindergarten to

[72] On Ogorodnikov and the organization he founded, see the materials in *Vestnik*, no. 119 (1976), 281-308; *Vol'noe slovo*, no. 39 (1980); *Documents of the Christian Committee*, vol. 4, pp. 482-508. For the *Literaturnaia gazeta* attack on Ogorodnikov and the response of seminar members to it, see Ellis, *Letters*, pp. 74-77, 105-115.

[73] On these societies, see George F. Putnam, *Russian Alternatives to Marxism*, Knoxville, 1977, pp. 56-92.

[74] "O seminarakh A. Ogorodnikova," *Posev*, no. 2 (1979), 5-7.

[75] Mark Popovskii, "SSSR: Khristianstvo molodeet," *Vol'noe slovo*, no. 29 (1978), 53-55.

foster the Christian upbringing of the participants' children. Popovskii also reported that Ogorodnikov and his fellow seminar members had made "missionary journeys" to a number of areas of the Soviet Union.

As for the seminar's attitude toward Russian nationalism, the following selection from its "Declaration of Principles" provides a useful window on the members' thinking:

V. About Russia

At the center of the seminar's interest stands the question of the history and subsequent fate of Russia and the Russian Orthodox Church. This question cannot be resolved without taking into consideration the multinational composition of our country.

Russia has been revealed to us by the incorruptible beauty of the Church. To understand Russia one must love her. To love the real Russia means to take her cross upon oneself. We hope that the extended Russian crisis represents the torturous discovery of a new historic path. . . .

The time has come for Russian youth to take upon itself the "sweet burden of freedom and responsibility." (Russia, having undergone the terrible experience of violence, is preparing its last and great Word.)

We are aware of and bear the common Russian fate. Presently, we are experiencing the terrible torment of Gethsemane before the Russian Golgotha.

Our principles can be formulated thus: *We are united by*
1. Love for Russia as our Mother;
2. A fraternal love for Christians of all nationalities;
3. A respect for the national dignity of people of diverse ethnic groups.

VI. About Politics

The political convictions of the members of the seminar cannot serve as a hindrance to their work in the seminar. This is in accordance with a resolution of the National Council of the Russian Orthodox Church of February 15, 1919. . . An exception would be membership in the Communist Party of the Soviet Union, due to its extreme, shameless atheistic policies and to many other moral reasons.[76]

In 1977, the seminar undertook to publish a *samizdat* journal entitled *Obshchina* (The Commune), but the authorities succeeded in seizing the mock-up of the first issue while Ogorodnikov was in the hospital.[77] In May of the following year, they broke into the home of a teacher at the Smolensk Pedagogical Institute and confiscated the second issue of the journal.[78] However, the table of contents of this second issue had been sent abroad, and from it we can learn something of the seminar's interests. In this document, one notes, for example, a section headed "The Religious Movement," which contains a piece on the Kiev-Pechersk Lavra; a copy of a letter written from prison by Igor' Ogurtsov, formerly head of the underground Social-Christian Union; an article on "The Seminar and the KGB"; and a contribution on the trials of an Orthodox parish in the Ukrainian city of Nikolaev. There is also an account of the murder of the imperial family in 1918, written by a former Red Army man.

The authorities were understandably piqued at the appearance of this militant and highly energetic youth organization with a threatening outreach to the provinces. An initial wave of persecution struck the seminar in 1976, when a number of members were expelled from institutes of higher learning; one participant, Valentin Serov, had his arm broken by "thugs" using professional methods of attack; and two members, Aleksandr Argentov (b. 1951) and Georgii Fedotov (b. 1950), were forcibly interned in mental hospitals. Argentov and Fedotov were released at least in part because of *samizdat* activity on their behalf by Orthodox believers of all political persuasions, including such nationalists as Leonid Borodin, Gennadii Shimanov, and Valentina Mashkova-Osipova.[79]

In 1979-1980, the authorities struck at the seminar, again,

[76] *Russkoe vozrozhdenie*, no. 2 (1978), 82-83.
[77] *Russkaia mysl'*, 20 July 1978, p. 5.
[78] *Documents of the Christian Committee*, vol. 4, pp. 485-508.
[79] See the documents in *Vestnik*, no. 119 (1976), and Ellis, *Letters*, pp. 105-108.

and more harshly. Its leaders and most active members—
Ogorodnikov, Vladimir Poresh, Tat'iana Shchipkova, and
others—were given stiff prison sentences. Whether such
repression will halt the emergence of other youth organizations which combine religious and nationalist interests is
something to be watched for during the 1980s.

CONCLUSIONS

Like preservation, the fate of the Russian Church has become a central Russian nationalist concern. Nationalist
spokesmen see the Church as a natural ally in their struggle
against forces and tendencies viewed as threatening the well-
being of the Russian people itself. The Church is perceived
as able to help in reversing the demographic, social, and economic trends which spell eventual ruin for ethnic Russians,
and it is seen as a potentially powerful mobilizational instru-
ment. An attack on the Church, therefore, is interpreted by
nationalists as an attack on Russia herself.

This championing of the cause of Russian Orthodoxy is the
nationalist activity which most serves to strain relations with
the regime. The problem facing the Soviet leadership is this:
Fidelity to Marxism-Leninism requires that religion be suppressed as a particularly insidious enemy, but mobilizational
considerations—connected, for example, with the specter of
a conflict with China—as well as the sheer size of the believing populace, require that it proceed carefully toward that
end. One suspects that the leadership has been skeptical of
claims made by Fr. Dudko and other Orthodox publicists that
the Church could help the state in coming to grips with the
Soviet Union's serious demographic and social problems. The
post-Brezhnev leadership, however, may prove more recep-
tive to such arguments.

Faced with a deep-seated conflict between ideological and
mobilizational imperatives—and with the risk of seriously alienating the believing masses, thereby driving some of them
"underground" beyond the control of the authorities—the
Brezhnev regime chose to temporize. The wide-ranging

Khruschev assault on religion was curtailed but not halted, while leading figures in the persecution, such as Vladimir Kuroedev, remained at their posts. It is noteworthy that when, in 1975, the government undertook the first significant revision of the laws governing religious associations since 1929, the resulting text indicated no major changes in policy toward religion.[80] To sum up, general indecisiveness and selective repression characterized the Brezhnev leadership's attitude toward the Russian Church in the waning days of its power.

[80] For an exact copy of this legislation, see *O religioznykh ob"edineniiakh,* New York, Khronika Press, 1975. An English translation appeared in *Hearings Before the Subcommittees on International Political and Military Affairs and on International Organizations of the Committee on International Relations,* House of Representatives, Ninety-fourth Congress, 2nd Session, June 24 and 30, 1976, Washington, 1976, pp. 69-75. For the text of the 1929 legislation, see Richard H. Marshall et al., eds., *Aspects of Religion in the Soviet Union, 1917-1967,* Chicago, 1971, pp. 438-445.

8

Mentors from the Past

> A class approach is as necessary to the past as it is to the present.
>
> S. Pokrovskii in *Voprosy literatury*[1]

> It has long been time to restore historical justice to the Slavophiles, it has long been time to disperse the curtain covering everything to the right of the revolutionary democrats with a dense shroud. . .
>
> A. Ivanov in *Voprosy literatury*[2]

Present-day Russian nationalists are listening intently to voices from the past which, in their time, contested currents of thought and political movements—the Decembrists, Westernizers, populists, Marxists—which led, directly or circuitously, to the October Revolution. No single voice is being taken as infallible; rather, today's nationalists are casting about for concepts and structures which can serve to extricate Russia from her perceived catastrophic predicament.

In April 1969, at a seminar of literary critics held in Moscow, Feliks Kuznetsov, an influential Marxist purist, remarked upon a new "pole" which he had observed emerging in recent Soviet literature and thought. After stating his belief that this pole was attempting to fill a spiritual vacuum which had been formed in Soviet life, Kuznetsov continued:

> Questings for a spiritual principle are occurring, and this is one of the directions which the quest is taking. This direction enjoys support among the students and intelligentsia. . . . In the nineteenth century, two basic tendencies, two conceptions of spirituality clashed on the field of battle: (1) . . . the Westernizers, revolutionary democrats, populists,

---

[1] S. Pokrovskii, "Mnimaia zagadka," *Voprosy literatury*, no. 5 (1969), 127.
[2] A. Ivanov, "Otritsatel'noe dostoinstvo," *Voprosy literatury*, no. 7 (1969), 132.

and Marxists; (2) a second tradition, stemming from the *liubomudry* [Lovers of Wisdom] and Chaadaev, proceeding through our young Slavophiles, through Dostoevskii, Vladimir Solov'ev, and Konstantin Leont'ev . . . through *Vekhi*, which, I remind you, had the subtitle "Articles on the Russian Intelligentsia," through Berdiaev and Fedotov . . . It is not so easy to ignore this second tradition, as I became convinced when I recently reread the authors I have enumerated. This second tradition used to inflict blows on our Marxist intelligentsia line, which passed through the Westernizers and democrats.[3]

Then, turning to adherents of the "second" tradition present in the room, Kuznetsov warned: "*Today* there is nowhere for you to escape from the October Revolution . . ."[4]

As Kuznetsov's comments, taken from the pages of the "unofficial" neo-Marxist journal *Politicheskii dnevnik* (Political Diary), demonstrate, a current of thought seemingly banished forever by the October Revolution had made a dramatic reappearance in the late 1960s. The aim of this chapter will be to study the effects of this "pole" of thought upon various present-day spokesmen of the Russian nationalist tendency. To simplify the task, I shall limit coverage to five thinkers, or schools of thought, whose influence upon contemporary Russian nationalism probably exceeds that of all others: (1) the so-called Early Slavophiles, particularly Aleksei Khomiakov (1804-1860) and Ivan Kireevskii (1806-1856); (2) Fedor Dostoevskii (1821-1881); (3) Nikolai Danilevskii (1822-1885); (4) Konstantin Leont'ev (1831-1891); and (5) the contributors to the 1909 *Vekhi* collection, especially Nikolai Berdiaev (1874-1948).[5] My intention is not to summarize the views of these thinkers—about whom an ample secondary literature is

[3] "Iz literaturnoi zhizni: Na seminare literaturnykh kritikov," *Politicheskii dnevnik*, 1 (1972), 502-503. See also Kuznetsov's essay on the same topic in *Moskva*, no. 1 (1981), esp. 195-203. I would not join Kuznetsov in including Chaadaev and Solov'ev in the ranks of this "second" tradition.

[4] Ibid., p. 504 (italics in original).

[5] It is noteworthy that the editor of *Veche*, Vladimir Osipov, singled out precisely these thinkers in a 1972 interview. See *Vestnik*, no. 106 (1972), 298.

available[6]—but to examine those areas of their thought which have proved attractive to modern-day Russian nationalists.

THE EARLY SLAVOPHILES

The first three issues of the samizdat journal Veche carried a serialized essay by Mikhail Antonov (b. 1935?), "The Teachings of the Slavophiles: The Acme of Russia's National Consciousness in the Pre-Lenin Period," which is largely devoted to the thought of Khomiakov and Kireevskii.[7] Though the Veche editors make explicit their differences with Antonov's National Bolshevik approach (this term will be discussed in chapter 10), they apparently feel that the virtues of his detailed elaboration of Slavophile ideology outweigh any drawbacks stemming from certain peculiarities and mistaken emphases in his presentation.

In Antonov's opinion, perhaps the Slavophiles' principal achievement was their spirited defense of the peasant commune (obshchina)—which he called the "key to Russian history"[8]—against the encroachments of Western individualism. The communal principle, Antonov wrote, is the pledge of Russia's uniqueness and of her healthy future development. Another important deed of the Slavophiles, as Antonov

[6] See, for example, the following: Nicolas Berdyaev, Leontiev, Orono, Maine, 1968; Peter K. Christoff, An Introduction to Nineteenth Century Slavophilism, 2 vols., The Hague, 1961, 1972; Joseph Frank, F. M. Dostoevsky: The Seeds of Revolt, Princeton, 1976 (the first volume of an important four-volume study); Abbott Gleason, European and Muscovite: Ivan Kireevsky and the Origins of Slavophilism, Cambridge, Mass., 1972; Albert Gratieux, A. S. Khomiakov et le Mouvement Slavophile, 2 vols., Paris, 1939; Stephen Lukashevich, Konstantin Leontev, 1831-1891, New York, 1967; Robert E. MacMaster, Danilevsky: A Russian Totalitarian Philosopher, Cambridge, Mass., 1967; Konstantin Mochulsky, Dostoevsky, Princeton, 1967; Nikolai Poltoratskii, Berdiaev i Rossiia, New York, 1967; Nicholas Riasanovsky, Russia and the West in the Teaching of the Slavophiles, Cambridge, Mass., 1952; Edward C. Thaden, Conservative Nationalism in Nineteenth-Century Russia, Seattle, 1964; and Andrzej Walicki, The Slavophile Controversy, Oxford, 1975.

[7] M. Antonov, "Uchenie slavianofilov—Vysshii vzlet narodnogo samosoznaniia v Rossii v doleninskii period," in Veche, no. 1 (AS 1013), 13-44; no. 2 (AS 1020), 4-27; and no. 3 (AS 1108), 5-49.

[8] Antonov, "Uchenie slavianofilov," Veche, no. 2, p. 11.

saw it, was to champion the concept of *narod* (people) against that of class. Peoples, not classes, are the "chief motive force in history."[9] The clashes of the Slavophiles with their Westernizer opponents on this issue anticipated similar disputes between Russian patriots and doctrinaire Marxists in the Soviet period.

Antonov also credited the Slavophiles with defending traditional Russian mores and customs and with ascribing, like Lenin (the reference is presumably to Lenin's New Economic Policy), great importance to preserving the integrity of the village. Moreover, they opposed the destruction of ancient Russian monuments, thereby thwarting the efforts of the precursors of the present-day nihilists, who threaten ancient churches and landscapes. In Antonov's view, the Slavophiles correctly stressed the essential role of Russian Orthodoxy. Religion is the "embodiment of the essence of a people" and not an "opiate" as Marxists foolishly proclaim.[10]

Aleksei Khomiakov, the intrepid Russian "warrior,"[11] and "the great thinker Ivan Vasil'evich Kireevskii"[12] are, Antonov contended, of greater relevance for contemporary Russia than Hegel, Feuerbach, or Marx. Their prodigious efforts to define Russia's distinctiveness, to delineate the ways in which she differed from the West, and to work out a "world view" for the Russian people can be compared only with the immense achievements of Lenin, the founder of the Bolshevik state. (Antonov's anti-Marxist Leninism eventually proved too much for the authorities and resulted in his being detained for three years in a mental hospital.[13])

The first issue of *Veche* contained a response to Antonov's initial essay by "A. Skuratov" (the pen name of Anatolii Ivanov).[14] Skuratov credited the Slavophiles with working out a

---

[9] Ibid., p. 23.
[10] No. 3, p. 28.
[11] No. 2, p. 27.
[12] No. 3, p. 49.
[13] See Sidney Bloch and Peter Reddaway, *Psychiatric Terror: How Soviet Psychiatry Is Used to Suppress Dissent*, New York, 1977, p. 350.
[14] "Mnenie opponenta," and A. Skuratov, "U istokov russkogo samosoznaniia," *Veche*, no. 1 (AS 1013), 45-47 and 4-12, respectively.

much-needed "countertheory" to the Western-oriented ideas of Chaadaev and the Decembrists and stated his agreement with their stress on the essential role of Russian Orthodoxy and of the communal principle. Unlike Antonov, Skuratov also expressed admiration for the Slavophiles' championing of "freedom of public opinion" and their desire to "remove the yoke from the oral and written word."[15] Allow life to develop freely, he urged, echoing the Slavophiles; and, he added, there was no need for juridical guarantees of such freedom. Skuratov's criticism of the Slavophiles focused upon what he termed their "messianism," i.e., their view that Russia has a unique and universal mission, and upon what he perceived as their quasi-anarchistic tendency to ignore the problem of the state.

The debate over the Slavophiles percolated during 1969 in the official press as well, on the pages of the journal *Voprosy literatury* (Problems of Literature). The discussion began with an article by the journalist and historian Aleksandr Ianov, who is now in the emigration; it called for a reexamination of the Slavophiles and their writings. There were other contributions in subsequent issues. According to one Western commentator, Vladimir Pavlov, the author of a useful summary of the episode, five of the contributions advocated a rehabilitation and thorough study of Slavophilism, five voiced "orthodox Marxist" objections to such a revisionist endeavor, and two occupied a middle ground in the dispute.[16]

The position of the Marxist purists was well represented by S. Pokrovskii's "An Imaginary Riddle." The entire question, Pokrovskii maintained, came down to the "class position" of the Slavophiles, something not overly difficult to determine. Slavophilism was "one of the variants of landowner, nobleman ideology during the period of the crisis of serfdom," and that is about all that needs to be said.[17] Khomiakov, Kireevskii, and their ilk were landlords who sought to ensure the continuance of their wealth and privileges and to fend off the

[15] Skuratov, "U istokov," p. 9.
[16] Vl. N. Pavlov, "Spory o slavianofil'stve i russkom patriotizme v sovetskoi nauchnoi literature, 1967-1970," *Grani*, no. 82 (1971), 196-197.
[17] Pokrovskii, "Mnimaia zagadka," p. 121.

mounting wrath of an oppressed *narod*. As for the Slavophiles' championing of Orthodox Christianity, Pokrovskii confided that he cannot read their blather about "Orthodox grace" or the spirit of humility supposedly characteristic of the Russian people without revulsion.[18] In addition, he pointed out, the Slavophiles were nationalistic, a factor which contributed to the growth of enmity among the peoples of Russia. As if this were not enough, they also supported an unlimited, absolute monarchy, despite their criticisms of various of its policies, and they were harsh accusers of Western revolutionary ideology. In short, Pokrovskii wondered, what was there to discuss about the Slavophiles?

In his contribution to the discussion, critic A. Dement'ev essentially agreed: "In general, S. Pokrovskii has more or less successfully . . . formulated the point of view on Slavophilism prevalent in our scholarship."[19] Let us, he exhorted, stick to the Marxist truth about Slovophilism, especially since "an idealization of the Slavophiles, of their philosophy and 'theory of [national] originality,' of their 'patriotism' and attitude toward the West, and of their 'populism' and 'love for the people' has never brought, and can never bring, anything but harm."[20]

A. Ivanov emphatically dissented from the position taken by Pokrovskii and Dement'ev. The view that the Slavophiles were "reactionaries and nothing more," he recalled, went back to Plekhanov, was encountered again in the 1930s, and characterized those who attacked S. Dmitriev's attempts to draw attention to the "positive moments of Slavophilism" in 1941.[21] The Slavophiles, Ivanov wrote, were particularly relevant because they stressed the Russian "communal" or, as communists would say, collectivist spirit, which is opposed to the individualism and egocentrism of the bourgeois West.[22]

In a later essay, V. Kozhinov emphasized that what was

[18] Ibid., p. 119.
[19] A. Dement'ev, " 'Kontseptsiia,' 'konstruktsiia' i 'model',' " *Voprosy literatury*, no. 7 (1969), 117.
[20] Ibid., p. 129.
[21] Ivanov, "Otritsatel'noe dostoinstvo," p. 129.
[22] Ibid., p. 131.

most important in the Slavophiles was "their affirmation of the *originality* in principle of the historic fate and culture of the Russian people, both in comparison with the West and with the East."[23] In the thirty-odd volumes containing the collected works of the major Slavophiles, he continued, any unprejudiced reader would be able to discover "a wealth and depth of ideas," notwithstanding numerous outdated and one-sided conclusions.[24]

The *Voprosy literatury* debate over Slavophilism appears to have ended in roughly a draw. Pokrovskii, Dement'ev, and their colleagues had little difficulty in showing the unbridge-able ideological gap separating the Slavophiles from the classic teachings of Marxism-Leninism, while Ivanov, Kozhinov, and their associates were able to point to the partiotic and mobilizational use to which the Slavophiles could be put. Those who attack the Slavophiles, the Ivanovs and Kozhinovs intimated, may well be anti-patriots. Both sides were permitted to have an extensive say before the debate was allowed to simmer down in the journal's final issue for 1969.

In 1978, a noteworthy compendium entitled *Literaturnye vzgliady i tvorchestvo slavianofilov, 1830-1850 gody* (Literary Views and Works of the Slavophiles, 1830-1850), was issued by the Nauka publishing house in Moscow, in a rather min-iscule printing of 3,650 copies (a number of which were promptly exported abroad for sale to Western specialists). This volume, the first in a projected series on the Slavophiles— other topics to be treated are "The Decembrists and the Slavophiles," "Gogol' and the Slavophiles," "The revolutionary democrats and the Slavophiles," and "The Slavophiles and F. M. Dostoevskii"—approached its subject with marked circumspection, as this selection from K. N. Lomunov's introductory essay demonstrates:

It is well known that the leaders of contemporary bourgeois ideology, who are carrying out a struggle against Marxist-

---

[23] V. Kozhinov, "O glavnom v nasledii slavianofilov," *Voprosy literatury*, no. 10 (1969), 113 (Kozhinov's italics).
[24] Ibid., p. 129.

Leninist doctrine, place their wagers on two opposite "horses": extreme cosmopolitanism and extreme nationalism. They oppose the first to proletarian internationalism and the second to that lawful feeling of patriotism which belongs to any people that loves its homeland. The attempt of these gentlemen to utilize several mistaken "slogans" of the Slavophiles at the present time for the kindling of national chauvinism and national discord does not and will not have any success if discovered and unmasked in time.[25]

In addition to such external foes, there were, Lomunov suspected, perhaps more insidious enemies within:

One should not think that the weaknesses, inconsistencies, contradictions and mistakes in the views of the Slavophiles are of interest only to our direct ideological opponents in the camp of contemporary foreign "sovietologists." By a strange filiation of ideas, individual points of the Slavophile doctrine elicit sympathy on the part of some (true, very few!) representatives of the Soviet intelligentsia. History does not turn backward. A group of literary critics and publicists from the journal *Molodaia gvardiia* seems to have forgotten this immutable truth when they strive in their own way to resurrect the Slavophile contrast of the patriarchal village to the industrial city and, following that, declare the peasantry to be the sole preserver and mouthpiece of "popular" expectations and convictions for all times—and therefore for today.[26]

Despite such cavils and occasional lurchings toward "orthodoxy," it seems likely that the study of the Slavophiles and the exposition of their views will continue in the official Soviet press. The indisputable decline of attachment to Marxism-Leninism among the populace and the consequent need

[25] K. N. Lomunov, "Slavianofil'stvo kak nauchnaia problema," in *Literaturnye vzgliady i tvorchestvo slavianofilov, 1830-1850 gody*, Moscow, 1978, p. 65. For another recent Soviet study on the Slavophiles, see V. I. Kuleshov, *Slavianofily i russkaia literatura*, Moscow, 1976.

[26] Lomunov, "Slavianofil'stvo," pp. 65-66.

to unearth substitute props for patriotic sentiment render such a process more or less inevitable.

DOSTOEVSKII

If there is a single thinker who serves as a beacon for contemporary Russian nationalists, it is undoubtedly the protean novelist Fedor Dostoevskii. Virtually without exception, they are able to quote chapter and verse from his major writings, as well as from such esoterica as the notebooks to his novels. Dostoevskii's significance for the nationalists is, in fact, so immense that one is tempted to compare it to that of Lenin for Marxist purists in the Soviet Union. This temptation should, however, probably be resisted. While it is true that a quotation from Dostoevskii is often taken by nationalists ipso facto as proof of the verity of a proposition, the novelist is not usually perceived as standing head and shoulders above all other nationalist ideologues—for example, Khomiakov and Berdiaev—as Lenin is by Soviet Marxists. Moreover, Russian nationalism does not represent as "closed" a system of thought as does Marxism-Leninism in the present-day USSR.

Evidence of Dostoevskii's importance may be seen in the collection *From under the Rubble*, which seems to cite the novelist at every turn. Together with the authors of the 1909 *Vekhi* volume, Dostoevskii was the central authority for the compendium's contributors and was often seen as having been a prophet. Shafarevich, for example, wrote that Dostoevskii "felt in his bones" what the twentieth century had in store for mankind.[27] The novelist's religiously based critique of various modern"isms"—socialism, materialism, atheism, determinism—is repeatedly cited by the collection's authors, as is his low opinion of revolution as a solution to social problems and his spirited exposé of the vapidness of the Western-oriented intelligentsia of his time.[28] Dostoevskii's pronounce-

[27] Igor' Shafarevich, "Separation or Reconciliation?," in *From under the Rubble*, Boston, 1975, p. 90.

[28] For examples of Dostoevskii's influence on the thought of the authors of *From under the Rubble*, see pp. 22, 53, 147, 148, 160, 202, 222-223, 233-234, 269.

ments on the "national personality" and on the distinctiveness of nations are likewise enthusiastically embraced by the
collection's contributors.

One issue of *Veche* contained a piece commemorating the
150th anniversary of the writer's birth which attempted to
examine the "ruling idea" in Dostoevskii's writing, an idea
said to be "the appearance in the world of Jesus Christ."[29]
The essay, which is suffused with religious and patriotic sentiment, drew attention to the world significance of Dostoevskii—a poll was cited in which 429 out of 500 Parisian students named him as their favorite author—and portrayed the
novelist's funeral in 1881, which was attended by 25,000-30,000
of his countrymen, as a major national event. The words of a
contemporary, the Slavophile spokesman Ivan Aksakov, were
quoted: "The death of Dostoevskii is a true divine punishment."[30]

"In Dostoevskii," Nikolai Berdiaev declared in a statement
reprinted in *Veche*, "one cannot but see a prophet of the
Russian revolution."[31] According to Berdiaev, Dostoevskii
succeeded in piercing through the "religious" mask of Russian socialism and in seeing that the coming revolution would
be akin to an act of parricide—i.e., the murder of the fatherland, justified by the latter's general sinfulness and un-
prepossessing appearance.

In his *samizdat* autobiography, *Pered smert'iu* (Before
Death), nationalist activist Gennadii Shimanov recounted his
spiritual journey from militant Marxism to religious faith and
Russian patriotism.[32] The son of devout communists of peasant background (his mother had even belonged to the League
of Militant Atheists), Shimanov in his youth had served as a
Pioneer leader and had been a fervent Komsomol member.
While stationed in the armed forces above the Arctic Circle,
however, he chanced to come across a small volume of Dos-

---

[29] "Fedoru Mikhailovichu Dostoevskomu—150 let: Vladychestvuiushchaia
ideia," *Veche*, no. 4 (AS 1140), 8.

[30] Ibid., p. 13.

[31] Cited from "Iz glubiny," *Veche*, no. 9, AS 2040, p. 39.

[32] G. M. Shimanov, *Pered smert'iu*, 1974 (see chapter 7, note 52).

toevskii's writings which completely altered his life. "Dostoevskii," he wrote, "was for me that man who formulated those thoughts and feelings which had already matured in me. Like Dante's Virgil, he took me by the hand and descended with me into the hell of my own soul . . ."[33] Shimanov's experience may be taken as emblematic of numerous volte-faces effected by Dostoevskii's writings. ". . . Dostoevskii loved Russia," former Social-Christian revolutionary Leonid Borodin wrote in *Veche*, "and loved her in a way in which only a Russian can love."[34]

DANILEVSKII AND LEONT'EV

The writers Nikolai Danilevskii and Konstantin Leont'ev are correctly considered by many Russian and Western historians to mark a "decline" in the evolution of nineteenth-century Russian conservative ideology. Though both were gifted thinkers—Danilevskii in certain ways anticipated Spengler and Toynbee, while Leont'ev foreshadowed Nietzsche—their ideas in certain spheres can be seen as potentially harmful for Russia's future development.

"The Role of N. Ia. Danilevskii in World Historiosophy" is the title of an ambitious anonymous essay in *Veche* which attempted to treat such central concerns of Danilevskii as his theory of "cultural-historical types" and his advocacy of a pan-Slav federation. Through a detailed analysis of history, wrote the author of the article, Danilevskii came to the conclusion that the struggle between peoples is more important than that between classes. Proceeding much as a natural scientist would, he then sought to distinguish the characteristic features of various peoples, including Great Russians, and to isolate these features from foreign accretions and intrusions. One result of this research was his conviction that the Russian people were completely alien to the idea of political parties. Like the Slavophiles, Danilevskii believed that the *obshchina*

---

[33] Shimanov, *Pered smert'iu*, p. 9.
[34] Leonid Borodin, "Vestnik R.S.Kh.D. i russkaia intelligentsiia," *Veche*, no. 8 (AS 1665), 132.

was an indigenous institution which sharply distinguished Russia from her Western neighbors. Also like the Slavophiles, he felt that the Russian people should be given "freedom of the word"—a moral, not a juridical, freedom—to make its views and sentiments known.[35]

Danilevskii's ideas concerning the formation of a federation of Slavs, an entity which would also include such non-Slavic peoples as the Greeks, Rumanians, and Hungarians, were summarized in the essay. Such a project was needed, Danilevskii believed, because of the virtual inevitability of Western European aggression against the Slavs (the *Veche* author interpreted this as prophecy of the two world wars). The Slavs must form an "original civilization" as a defensive, isolationist move against the West. Danilevskii insisted that the federation he had in mind would respect the national peculiarities of the smaller Slavic peoples and would not lead to their being merged in a "Russian sea."

In foreign affairs, Danilevskii recommended a pragmatic "eye for an eye" policy in which there would be no place for "the law of love and self-sacrifice."[36] The *Veche* author, who appeared to agree with Danilevskii on this point, noted that Dostoevskii and the Slavophiles held a contrary view, while Leont'ev lined up with Danilevskii on the issue. Danilevskii's lack of "messianism," an unfortunate tendency said to be found in both Dostoevskii and the Slavophiles, was also mentioned approvingly.

One of the *Veche* commentator's few criticisms of Danilevskii concerned the latter's advocacy of the Russification of certain minority peoples in Russia, a position which was not shared by Leont'ev. "Unfortunately," the author wrote, "Danilevskii sympathized with far from every originality [*samobytnost'*]."[37]

It seems clear that Danilevskii's detached, quasizoological view of historical processes could lead disciples of his thought into a callous cynicism in their attitude toward relations be-

[35] "Rol' N. Ia. Danilevskogo v mirovoi istoriosofii," *Veche*, no. 5 (AS 1230), 21.
[36] Ibid., p. 28.
[37] Ibid., p. 24.

tween states, while his strong anti-Western sentiments might serve to reinforce ingrained prejudices. (Citing Danilevskii, Mikhail Antonov has written of the "deep hostility of the peoples of Western Europe toward Russia and the Russian people."[38]) Likewise, his contention that the Ukrainian and Belorussian languages are only "dialects" of Russian, and in general his lack of sympathy for the minority nationalities in Russia, could serve to exacerbate national tensions. Finally, his pan-Slavism could tempt some followers into attempting to retain the Soviet empire by force, though Danilevskii himself would presumably eschew such an approach to the peoples of Eastern Europe.

A summary of the views of the "great Russian thinker" Konstantin Leont'ev was presented in another issue of *Veche*.[39] This account, which was favorably disposed toward its subject, demonstrated that Leont'ev had a tendency to elevate aesthetic criteria of judgement over all others. Thus he contemptuously rejected nineteenth-century Western Europe because, unlike the Middle Ages, it was dull, gray, colorless, dragged down by arid, tedious rhetoric concerning equality and freedom and by "revolutionary cosmopolitanism."[40] Democracy, Leont'ev believed, leads to a depersonalization and leveling of man, whereas what should be sought is maximal variety and differentiation, to be achieved in part through "strong [social] corporations" (here, as in other areas, his thought, I might add, anticipated fascism). He was a passionate defender of distinctive national dress and of popular customs. A fierce opponent of pan-Slavism, Leont'ev felt that the Slavs, who, he believed, manifested innate "democratic" tendencies, were not to be trusted; in Russia, such tendencies had been fortunately counteracted by helpful infusions of Mongol and Teutonic authoritarianism.

The pitfalls inherent in Leont'ev's thought should be fairly self-evident. His neo-pagan aestheticism can, like certain elements in Danilevskii, lead to the application of amoral criteria

[38] Antonov, "Uchenie slavianofilov," *Veche*, no. 1 (AS 1013), p. 24.
[39] "Vzgliady Konstantina Leont'eva," *Veche*, no. 4 (AS 1140), p. 22.
[40] Ibid., p. 31.

on the part of disciples, while his strictness against social "blending" (*smeshenie*) could contribute to an exacerbation of ethnic or racial hostilities. His paeans on the advantages of despotism contain obvious dangers, as does his preaching of maximal social differentiation (one can picture present-day followers of his thought, most of them the sons or grandsons of peasants, lining up for titles in a new Leont'evian aristocracy which would separate them from the "rabble"). Finally, Leont'ev's militant anti-Western sentiments could serve to intensify enmity toward the West.[41]

THE *Vekhi* AUTHORS

The *Vekhi* collection created a remarkable stir when it first appeared in 1909, and it continues to resonate in Russian nationalist circles today. The volume *From under the Rubble*, to take one example, is thoroughly permeated by the views and conclusions of the earlier compendium. "The journal *Vekhi*," writes one contributor, F. Korsakov, "exhausted the subject of the decay of the intelligentsia . . ."[42] And Solzhenitsyn begins his seminal essay, "The Smatterers," which is devoted to the fate of the contemporary Soviet intelligentsia, thus:

> The fateful peculiarities of the educated stratum of Russians before the revolution were thoroughly analyzed in *Vekhi* . . . [E]ven after sixty years its testimony has not lost its brightness: *Vekhi* today still seems to us to have been a vision of the future. And our only cause for rejoicing is that now, after sixty years, the stratum of educated Russian society able to lend support appears to be deepening.[43]

[41] P. Gaidenko, "Naperekor istoricheskomu protsessu," *Voprosy literatury*, no. 5 (1974), 159-199, contains a discussion of Leont'ev's views, knowledgeably contrasting his ideas with those of Dostoevskii, the Slavophiles, and other nineteenth-century thinkers.

[42] F. Korsakov, "Russian Destinies," in *From under the Rubble*, p. 155. The name Korsakov is a pseudonym.

[43] Aleksandr Solzhenitsyn, "The Smatterers," in *From under the Rubble*, pp. 229-230.

Issue no. 7 of *Veche* contained a lengthy exposition of the central theses of the *Vekhi* compilation, while issue no. 9 summarized the contents of the collection *Iz glubiny* (Out of the Depths), a successor volume prepared by many of the same authors during the revolutionary turmoil of 1918 and issued illegally in 1921.[44] The editors of *Veche* introduced the latter by saying, "The opinions of major Russian thinkers and eyewitnesses of perhaps the most decisive hour in our homeland's history are of enormous interest . . ."[45]

The relevance of *Vekhi* and *Iz glubiny* for contemporary Russian nationalists is manifold. First, they contain a wide-ranging critique of the tenets and assumptions of Marxist-Leninist theory. ". . . if the world is chaos and determined by blind material forces," Simeon Frank wrote in *Vekhi*, "then how is it possible to hope that historical development will inevitably lead to the kingdom of reason and the establishment of terrestrial paradise?"[46] Second, the two collections assert and defend the primacy of the spiritual life; and, third, they prophesy apocalyptic horrors which did in fact soon befall Russia. Lastly, some of the contributors speculated in suggestive ways about how the communist yoke might be removed from the country. "The anti-Christian spirits of the revolution," Berdiaev wrote in *Iz glubiny*, "will give birth to their dark kingdom, but the Christian spirit of Russia must manifest its power."[47]

The *Vekhi* contributors thus serve the function of assisting contemporary Russian nationalists to understand what went wrong in 1917, and why, and they help to point the way out of the morass. The fact that certain of the volume's authors— Frank, Gershenzon, Izgoev—are of Jewish origin serves, in-

[44] On the history of the publication of *Iz glubiny*, see the letter by Gleb Struve in the *New York Review of Books*, 22 January 1976, pp. 51-52. On the influence of *Iz glubiny* contributor Nikolai Berdiaev in contemporary Soviet Russia, see Boris Paramonov, "Mal'chik protiv muzha," *Kontinent*, no. 16 (1978), 137-149.

[45] *Veche*, no. 9, p. 36.

[46] Cited in "Chto takoe 'Entsiklopediia liberal'nogo renegatovtsa'?," *Veche*, no. 7 (AS 1775), 70.

[47] "Iz glubiny," *Veche*, no. 9 (AS 2040), 44.

cidentally, to militate against anti-Semitism and to build ideational and conceptual bridges between the two peoples.

To conclude, the concerns of nineteenth- and early twentieth-century Russian thinkers—such as the *obshchina*, Russian Orthodoxy, and the plan for a pan-Slav federation—are being scutinized anew by contemporary nationalists, whose aim is to discover uniquely Russian institutions, to undo the errors of October 1917, and to give shape to a post-Marxist Russia. For mobilizational reasons, the regime is having difficulty in thwarting this quest. Dostoevskii's works are in considerably greater demand today than Lenin's, while the writings of Berdiaev filter into the country in *tamizdat* editions from abroad. Cautious investigations into the thought of the Slavophiles, Danilevskii, and Leont'ev periodically appear in the official press, and bolder essays circulate in *samizdat*. While often at least tacitly anti-Marxist, such writings serve to promote patriotism, and patriotism is a sentiment very much on the mind of the Soviet authorities. As Marxist purist Feliks Kuznetsov warned his colleagues in 1969, a powerful, if disparate, pole of thought is at the door, competing with growing success for the allegiance of the contemporary Soviet intelligentsia.

9

Ideological Struggle

> Must we once again explain that Soviet patriotism cannot
> be reduced to a love for 'primal sources,' for monuments
> and shrines of antiquity, that it includes not only love for
> the past but also love for the present and future of our
> homeland, and that it is inseparable from the friendship of
> peoples and proletarian internationalism?
>
> <div align="right">A. Dement'ev in <i>Novyi mir</i>[1]</div>

> Is the 'Russian idea' the 'main content' of an international
> doctrine which came to us from the West? When Marat
> called for 'a million heads' and asserted that the hungry
> have the right to <i>eat</i> the well-fed (how well we know such
> situations!)—was this also the 'Russian messianic conscious-
> ness' at work?
>
> <div align="right">Aleksandr Solzhenitsyn in <i>From under the Rubble</i>[2]</div>

The emergence of Russian nationalism as a powerful ideational current and inspirer of patriotic sentiment has not, of
course, gone unchallenged in the Soviet Union. Marxist-Leninist purists, neo-Marxist reformers, Western-oriented liberals, and "Catholicizing" Christians have all done battle with
the nationalists—the first-named group in the official press,
the others in *samizdat*. In this chapter, I shall focus upon
three politically significant disputes which occurred during
the Brezhnev period: (1) the so-called "Chalmaev affair," which
was sparked by two articles published by critic Viktor Chalmaev (b. 1932) in the Komsomol journal *Molodaia gvardiia*
during 1968; (2) a searing attack on the nationalists launched
by a high-ranking Party official, A. N. Iakovlev, in the pages

[1] A. Dement'ev, "O traditsiiakh i narodnosti," *Novyi mir*, no. 4 (1969), 229.

[2] Alexander Solzhenitsyn, "Repentance and Self-Limitation in the Life of Nations," in *From under the Rubble*, Boston, 1975, p. 125 (Solzhenitsyn's italics).

of *Literaturnaia gazeta* in 1972; and (3) a *samizdat* controversy touched off by four "anti-Russian" articles appearing in
a 1970 issue of the Paris-based émigré journal *Vestnik
R.S.Kh.D.* (Messenger of the Russian Student Christian
Movement). These disputes offer a useful picture of the ideological weaponry and the political vulnerabilities of both "official" and dissenting Russian nationalists in the contemporary
USSR.

THE CHALMAEV AFFAIR

Viktor Chalmaev's controversial essays "Velikie iskaniia" (The
Great Search) and "Neizbezhnost' " (Inevitability) were the
most sensational salvos in a patriotic barrage that burst forth
from *Molodaia gvardiia* in the late 1960s. The essays were
noteworthy in three respects. First, there was Chalmaev's
conviction that Western "bourgeois" attitudes had been making deep inroads into Soviet society. Though he lashed out at
the contemporary West—a land of "checkbooks and parliamentary twaddle," of "individualistic philistinism," and of "the
chase after the dollar which kills man's conscience, sense of
beauty, and affinity with the soil"[3]—it was the importation of
such plagues into Russia which particularly alarmed him. His
opponent was not so much the West as it was Western-oriented elements in the Soviet intelligentsia and in the ruling
elite. Moral and aesthetic revulsion were evident in Chalmaev's recoil, as he scored a national vice observed by a
Croatian visitor to Russia in the seventeenth century—*chuzhebesie*, a mad passion for things foreign.

The Western-oriented intelligentsia, according to Chalmaev, had little interest in the fate of historic Russia or in
the Russian environment. Its members reminded him of those
in the 1920s and 1930s who called upon their countrymen to
do "simple things," such as to raze the cathedral of St. Basil
in Moscow or to level the city of Novgorod, which they con-

[3] V. Chalmaev, "Velikie iskaniia," *Molodaia gvardiia*, no. 3 (1968), 274,
282, 290.

temptuously referred to as "a funeral parlor of archaeology."[4] "Let us have our way for another twenty years," such activists proclaimed, "and we will dig you a new and better [Lake] Baikal, wherever you want!"[5]

A second feature of Chalmaev's essays was his open preaching of what Soviet historians call the heresy of the "single stream" (edinyi potok) interpretation of Russian history, i.e., a failure to see the revolution as a leap into a higher reality and a tendency to inflate the worth and significance of pre-revolutionary figures and events. The following selection from "Inevitability" conveys well Chalmaev's historical sentiments:

It was not from many golgothas that the diffident Russian soul made known its existence over the centuries . . . Constant labor on the land, the monastery, the king's tavern, and once or twice every century—the ice of Lake Chud, the wild grass in the fields of Kulikovo, Poltava, or Borodino . . . Once every century, the coarse-grained, oft-flogged Russian peasant, weighed down with many burdens, would set out for the Kulikovo Field at hand, and, projecting one hundred years into the night before the battle, he would think about his homeland, about good and evil, and about the world in which he lived . . . And who can tell what complex thoughts may have lived in the hearts and bold heads of those Cossacks—fugitives and runaways—who accompanied Ermak, Khabarov, and Dezhnev through the wilds of the Siberian taiga so that Russia, which was harsh toward them, which threatened them with prison, might freely breathe the open spaces of the Great [Pacific] Ocean with which her soul has such a close affinity? And what of the monastic cells of desert-dwelling patriots such as Sergii of Radonezh, who inspired Dimitrii Donskoi to fight a decisive battle, or the patriot Partriarch Germogen, who during the Time of Troubles sent appeals to every part of the country urging unity? No, our sacred history is not a wil-

[4] Ibid., p. 295.
[5] V. Chalmaev, "Neizbezhnost'," Molodaia gvardiia, no. 9 (1968), 275.

derness; perhaps it has simply not been "explored" as thoroughly as it should be.[6]

A visceral love for Russia's past and a veneration for Russian cultural achievements of the nineteenth and early twentieth centuries made themselves felt in Chalmaev's essays. He went so far as to celebrate the achievements of émigrés, such as the 1933 Nobel prizewinner for literature, Ivan Bunin, who rejected the October Revolution. For Chalmaev, the revolution seemed to be merely a stage in the larger and more important continuum called Russia. In "The Great Search," which traced the literary development of Maksim Gor'kii, Chalmaev suggested that the novelist's quest may have taken him down some unfortunate paths. He expressed a particularly low opinion of the "new men" whom Gor'kii attempted to substitute for the Andrei Bolkonskiis and Starets Zossimas of the nineteenth-century literary canon. A cultural and moral degeneration was seen as having taken place.

The third notable characteristic of Chalmaev's essays—one linked to his "single stream" historical views—was his fervent populism. "Unlike Gor'kii," Chalmaev noted, "Tolstoi and Dostoevskii saw in the people an integral support (due to their religiosity), an innerly monolithic support, which always acted as the 'salvation' of the nobility and of Russia from physical and spiritual degeneracy. And what a support it was!"[7] This idea is of course blatant heresy from a Marxist-Leninist point of view: it was the working class and not the patriarchal peasantry (particularly not the *religious* peasantry!) that served as the vanguard of society. Chalmaev seemed to manifest a genuine affection for the prerevolutionary gentry and nobility, who, he stressed, were physically and spiritually nourished by the Russian peasantry. "For Gor'kii," he wrote, "the people are not a 'support,' not a caryatid, but the chief, the only hero of the historical process. It is this thought that Gor'kii seeks to affirm. But are the people capable of playing this

[6] Ibid., pp. 264-265.
[7] Chalmaev, "Velikie iskaniia," p. 280.

role without the Bolkonskiis and Karamazovs?"[8] The nobility and the peasantry had been mutually interdependent, and both had contributed to the flourishing of a great culture.

An important political and mobilizational argument was concealed behind Chalmaev's emotional and often exalted rhetoric. "One's relationship to the homeland," he warned, "cannot be taken lightly, for a soul devastated by lack of faith cannot become a Donskoi, a Bagration, a Matrosov overnight. Even the religious energy of the Russian was . . . often in the past transformed into military exploits . . ."[9] If his "philistine" opponents won out, the country, Chalmaev contended, would be virtually defenseless before her external enemies.

The impact of Chalmaev's bold essays was considerable. Of the numerous attacks which rained down on him and on *Molodaia gvardiia* from Marxist-Leninist purists, the most significant was probably the one by Aleksandr Dement'ev in *Novyi mir* in 1969. By jumping into the fray at this point, *Novyi mir*, a beacon of liberalism during the sixties, apparently sought to prove its bona fides to the regime, as well as to assail a tendency which its editorial board found particularly dangerous and repugnant.

Dement'ev began by mocking the (in truth) slipshod character of Chalmaev's scholarship. Chalmaev thought that Goethe's Faust was a youth, ascribed well-known lines of the poet Blok to the émigré Bunin, and formed a comical montage—"Nil Sarovskii"—out of the names of two Orthodox saints, Nil Sorskii and Seraphim Sarovskii. But certain tendencies in Chalmaev, Dement'ev said, were far from laughable, especially since he was seeking to give "a certain direction to the interest observable in our days among broad segments of Soviet society, and especially the youth, in ancient architecture, painting, the applied arts, and events of the Fatherland's history."[10]

Chalmaev, Dement'ev claimed, "knows only eternal, thou-

[8] Ibid., p. 281.
[9] Chalmaev, "Neizbezhnost'," p. 268.
[10] Dement'ev, "O traditsiiakh," p. 216.

sand-year-old, indivisible [*edinaia*] Russia . . . ,"[11] i.e., he advocated a "single stream" view of Russian history. His ideas approached those of the Slavophiles, as well as those of nine-teenth- and early twentieth-century "official nationalism,"[12] "ecclesiastical and secular obscurantism," "liberal renegad-ism,"[13] and "Black Hundredism."[14] Chalmaev's praise of pre-revolutionary religious activists—including the reactionary Archpriest John of Kronstadt (d. 1908)—was noisome, as were his approving comments concerning such conservative ideo-logues as Konstantin Leont'ev. One could also discern an an-noying "peasant-loving" (*muzhikovstvuiushchii*) element in his essays. Even worse were the aspersions which Chalmaev cast on the revolutionary democrats. ". . . why," Dement'ev asked, "are the ideals of N. Chernyshevskii and D. Pisarev placed next to 'petty rationalism,' and how is it that their 'halo has grown dim'? In whose eyes? . . . V. I. Lenin's?"[15]

The Russian soul, Dement'ev emphasized, had made itself known not only in monasteries but "in the uprisings of Razin, Bolotnikov, and Pugachev, in the movement of the Decem-brists and *narodniki*, on the barricades of the Russian revo-lution [i.e., of 1905] and in the storming of the Winter Pal-ace."[16] Chalmaev should not have ignored this. Dement'ev was also piqued at Chalmaev's one-sided and extreme view of the contemporary West. Social and class distinctions, not national ones, were what separated the Soviet Union and the West. Chalmaev's perspective alarmingly recalled that of "Slavophile messianism."[17] As for supposed "bourgeois" in-cursions into Soviet society, they were grossly overstated, since

[11] Ibid., p. 221.
[12] On this ideology, see Nicholas V. Riasanovsky, *Nicholas I and Official Nationality in Russia, 1825-1855*, Berkeley, 1959.
[13] This was Lenin's well-known term for the tendency represented by the 1909 *Vekhi* collection.
[14] On the so-called "Black Hundreds," see Hans Rogger, "Was There a Russian Fascism? The Union of the Russian People," *Journal of Modern History*, 36, no. 4 (1964), 398-415.
[15] Dement'ev, "O traditsiiakh," p. 218.
[16] Ibid.
[17] Ibid., p. 221.

by its very nature the USSR was not "predisposed to bourgeois influences."[18]

In a few areas, Dement'ev felt required to press his argument with a certain degree of caution. Thus, he stressed that he did not advocate "destroying our monasteries and churches" and that he was well aware "of the significance of the preservation and restoration of monuments of antiquity."[19] Likewise, he assured his readers that he was opposed to the "vulgar-sociological approach to problems of culture" which at one time led to Dostoevskii's novels falling into disfavor.[20]

Dement'ev thus rolled out his heavy artillery against Chalmaev and his *Molodaia gvardiia* associates, directing his fire especially at the "single stream" interpretation of Russian history, with its implicit downplaying of the role of revolutionary movements, and at perceived religious sentiments in their writings. One would have thought that a Marxist-Leninist regime would have proved sympathetic to Dement'ev's approach. Yet, shortly after the appearance of this article, the editorial board of *Novyi mir* was purged. Aleksandr Ianov has reported that well-informed sources on the staff of the Party Central Committee told him that Dement'ev's article was the chief reason behind the purge. And he commented: "It [*Novyi mir*] fell (what irony!) not for Solzhenitsyn, not for Siniavskii (Tertz), but for an Orthodox Marxist article defending the purity of the ideological vestments of the Party."[21]

A comparison of the purge of *Novyi mir* carried out in early 1970 with that conducted against *Molodaia gvardiia* a year later is instructive. In the former case, both the editor-in-chief, Aleksandr Tvardovskii, and the associate editor, A. I. Kondratovich, were removed, as well as those board members—I. I. Vinogradov, V. Ia. Lakshin, and I. A. Sats—who had given the journal its specific "flavor." *Novyi mir* was dead in the form that both its friends and foes had known it.

In the case of *Molodaia gvardiia*, only the journal's editor-

[18] Ibid., p. 226.
[19] Ibid., p. 234.
[20] Ibid., p. 220.
[21] Alexander Yanov, *The Russian New Right*, Berkeley, 1978, p. 50.

in-chief, Anatolii Nikonov, was removed, while the rest of the board—including such controversial figures as Mikhail Lobanov and Vladimir Soloukhin—remained intact. An obscure person named Feliks Ovcharenko appeared out of the blue as editor-in-chief of the no. 3 issue of 1971, but when this presumably loyal regime man died later that year, he was replaced, beginning with issue no. 4 of 1972, by Anatolii Ivanov, an associate editor of *Molodaia gvardiia* during its heyday. Can one, it might be asked, even speak of a purge having occurred? A warning or "signal" would seem to be a more accurate term for what took place. The noisy excesses of the late sixties were not to be repeated (and they have not been), but the nationalists received reassurance that they remained in essentially good standing.

An open letter which had appeared in a 1969 issue of the mass circulation magazine *Ogonek* (once known as "the Soviet *Life*") perhaps gives us a clue as to why *Novyi mir* fell while *Molodaia gvardiia* escaped with what amounted to a reprimand. Entitled "What Is *Novyi mir* Against?," the letter, which was signed by eleven influential nationalists—including Anatolii Ivanov, the future editor of *Molodaia gvardiia*, and Sergei Vikulov, editor-in-chief of *Nash sovremennik*—took deadly aim at both Dement'ev and the journal. The authors began by dissociating themselves from Chalmaev's errors: "There can be no argument that the above-mentioned articles of Chalmaev [i.e., "Inevitability" and "The Great Search"] suffer from serious defects; they contain coarse factual and methodological mistakes, inaccuracies in a number of formulations, and errors in their system of proof."[22] Furthermore, Chalmaev was "reckless" in quoting from such ideologues of the past as Konstantin Leont'ev and Vasilii Rozanov. But Dement'ev's aim was to exploit such blunders in order to eradicate the whole "tendency" represented by *Molodaia gvardiia*, and therein lay his error:

The journal's primary goal is to develop in the youthful member of the Komsomol feelings of Soviet patriotism, a

22 "Protiv chego vystupaet 'Novyi mir'?," *Ogonek*, no. 30 (1969), 27.

selfless love for his socialist Fatherland, internationalism, and the desire to struggle relentlessly against all kinds of hostile ideological influences . . . In today's world, which is divided into two opposing camps, bourgeois propaganda, by using the provocational tactics of "building bridges" and "ideological coexistence," is carrying on a tireless, increasingly refined, and insidious cultivation of minds, preaching nihilism in all its aspects among the youth, and encouraging a yearning for an easy "refined" way of life, modelled on the Western pattern, and a superficial intellectualism devoid of moral norms.[23]

Adopting Stalin-era tactics, the authors then proceeded to remind their readers of what occurred in Czechoslovakia in the late sixties, when certain trends were allowed to get out of hand, and they pointedly recalled that *Novyi mir* distinguished itself at one time by printing the criticism of Andrei Siniavskii (who was sentenced in 1966 to seven years in the camps for publishing certain of his works abroad under a pseudonym). The real impulse behind Chalmaev's "Inevitability" was a "cry of the soul" against "the penetration or 'infiltration' of our society by unhealthy manifestations of Western (bourgeois) culture."[24] Soviet patriotism cannot, it is true, be reduced to "primal sources" (*istoki*) and historical shrines and monuments, but it also "cannot exist without them." As for Dement'ev's haughty denunciations of "peasant-lovers," the authors pointed out that the term was first put into circulation by Trotskii in the twenties.

Whatever were Chalmaev's *faux pas*, the *Ogonek* correspondents argued that they paled before the infectious, perhaps lethal, bourgeois philistinism that was eating away at Soviet society. Such tendencies threatened the very life of the Soviet state and seriously weakened the country's patriotic and mobilizational supports. It may well be that such arguments helped to carry the day in the Central Committee

[23] Ibid., p. 26.
[24] Ibid., p. 27.

and to pave the way for a decimating purge of the *Novyi mir* editorial board.

The "Chalmaev episode" created such resonance that it attracted the attention of even Solzhenitsyn, a dissident writer not normally interested in the squabbles of the Soviet press. A member of the *Novyi mir* "team" since 1962, Solzhenitsyn, as he has reported in his literary memoirs, was bitterly disappointed by Dement'ev's diatribe, which he called "journalistic swill" and "cold, heartless squalor."[25] The firm support offered for Dement'ev's piece by Tvardovskii and the *Novyi mir* editorial board vexed him still further. Solzhenitsyn noted with aversion *Novyi mir*'s demonstrative embracing of Marxist-Leninist orthodoxy and of militant hostility toward religion. *Molodaia gvardiia*, he observed, "at least indirectly defended religion."[26]

In his comments on Chalmaev, Solzhenitsyn made it clear that he was aware of the *Molodaia gvardiia* critic's limitations. He described Chalmaev as a "mediocre, rather benighted publicist," a fairly typical descendant of Russian peasants yearning "for a vaguely remembered national idea."[27] Solzhenitsyn scored Chalmaev for "kowtowing before ideology" and, in general, for ignoring the self-evident fact that "it is impossible to be both a communist *and* a Russian."[28] He also accused Chalmaev of indulging in unfair attacks on the West and of having an excessively exalted view of Russia.

Despite such differences, Solzhenitsyn clearly sympathized with Chalmaev and his endeavor. He underlined Chalmaev's appreciation of such religious figures of the past as Sergii of Radonezh, Patriarch Germogen, and John of Kronstadt, and pointed to one place where the critic spoke directly of Christ. Solzhenitsyn also noted Chalmaev's high opinion of Dostoevskii and a covert reference to the collection *Iz glubiny* which he managed to get by the censors. Chalmaev was congratulated for opposing the revolutionary democrats "from Cher-

---

[25] Aleksandr Solzhenitsyn, *Bodalsia telenok s dubom*, Paris, 1975, p. 274.
[26] Ibid., p. 272.
[27] Ibid., pp. 266-267.
[28] Ibid., p. 267 (Solzhenitsyn's italics).

nyshevskii to Kerenskii," the *peredvizhniki* movement in art, and Maksim Gor'kii, and Solzhenitsyn concurred with Chalmaev's negative assessment of "enlightened philistinism," adding that the "whole *partapparat*" (Party apparatus) belonged to this current. Like Chalmaev, Solzhenitsyn believed that "in alienation from the land there can be no life" and that "the village is the bulwark of national traditions."[29]

Solzhenitsyn's comments on the Chalmaev affair show the numerous links existing between dissenting and "official" nationalists in the Soviet Union. The chief bone of contention between the two camps would seem to be the degree to which one should be willing to compromise with Marxist-Leninist ideology, i.e., whether a "National Bolshevik" line of development is possible and advisable. Solzhenitsyn obviously felt himself to be much closer to Chalmaev and his *Molodaia gvardiia* colleagues than to the "liberal Marxists" formerly at the helm of *Novyi mir*. Such sympathy did not, however, extend to the authors of the "letter of the eleven," whom he dismissed as nonentities and whose tactics reminded him of the Stalin era.

THE IAKOVLEV EPISODE

A. N. Iakovlev's "Protiv antiistorizma" (Against Anti-Historicism), a lengthy article spanning sixteen full columns in an issue of *Literaturnaia gazeta* late in 1972, represented a far more serious threat to the nationalists than did Dement'ev's assault in *Novyi mir*.[30] In Aleksandr Ianov's words, Iakovlev was the "Party ideologist," since he was at the time the acting head of the Central Committee's Agitation and Propaganda Department.[31] Though Iakovlev made a half-hearted attempt to provide a certain "balance" in his piece— thus, he attacked writers who sought to overemphasize the role of the intelligentsia in Soviet society and criticized the

[29] Ibid., pp. 268, 269.
[30] A. Iakovlev, "Protiv antiistorizma," *Literaturnaia gazeta*, 15 November 1972, pp. 4-5.
[31] Yanov, *Russian New Right*, p. 59.

nationalism of certain non-Russian authors, for example Georgians—it is abundantly clear that the chief purpose of his article was to deliver a knockout blow to the Russian nationalists. As befitted his elevated position in the Party, he was
more militant and self-confident than Dement'ev in carrying
the attack.

In his article, Iakovlev lambasted the "single stream" interpretation of Russian history, which he saw as a totally unac-
ceptable "extra-class and extra-social approach." Lenin, he
reminded his readers, always used to insist that there were
two Russian cultures, not one. The nationalists' positive opinions of such prerevolutionary reactionaries as Leont'ev and
Rozanov showed the degree of their ideological impoverish-
ment. And how could they praise the tsarist general Skobelev, who "suppressed popular uprisings in Central Asia"?
As for the past, Iakovlev stressed that "the authentically democratic and revolutionary elements in the history of our nation
are above all dear to us." In other words: "We see a moral
example not in the 'lives of saints,' and not in embellished
biographies of tsars and khans, but in the revolutionary spirit
of those who struggled for the people's happiness."

Throughout his essay, Iakovlev was consistently and sharply
antireligious. He reminded the "newly-appeared God-bear-
ers (bogonostsy)" among his opponents that it is the Soviet
government which was actively restoring historical monuments. But one should not forget that churches, mosques,
and synagogues have always served as "ideological centers"
for the ruling classes, that "under the arches of churches were
blessed the bayonets of those who smothered the first revolution [of 1905], that Lev Tolstoi was anathematized from the
church pulpit, and that the executioner Kutepov, the hang-
man Denikin, and the bands of Petliura were met with the
ringing of church bells."

As for the nationalists' cult of the patriarchal peasantry, Iakovlev emphasized that attention should be focused on today's collective farmer, not the peasant of the past, particularly not the rapacious miroed. Indicating in what way an
interest in the peasantry may be considered legitimate, Ia-

kovlev wrote: "The love of freedom of the laboring peasantry and its burning hatred of exploiters are dear to us." Such feelings attracted the peasantry into the forces of Razin and Pugachev, "called it to battle with the tsar and the landlords, and, in the final, historical analysis, brought it to the regiments of the Red Army." Nevertheless, it should not be forgotten that it is the working class, not the peasantry, which comes first. In his interpretations, Iakovlev aligned himself with the revolutionary democrats, behind whom, he noted, stood Lenin himself.

The Party ideologist had spoken with authoritative weight on the pages of an important "all-union" newspaper. What was the result of this no-holds-barred attack? Iakovlev was removed from his post in April 1973 and exiled to Canada as ambassador, where he remains to the present day. As Ianov has correctly pointed out, since Iakovlev was the Party spokesman on ideological matters, he could not be answered in the official press, and no "letter of the eleven" appeared to rebut his arguments. A lengthy rejoinder did, however, appear in *Veche*, entitled "The Struggle Against So-Called Russophilism, or the Path to National Suicide." Though writing in a *samizdat* publication, the anonymous author utilized arguments geared to appeal to elements in the Soviet leadership, and in general his article may be seen as almost a *summa* of the concerns of the increasingly important tendency called National Bolshevism (which will be discussed in chapter 10). It is at least possible that certain of the points he raised may have contributed to Iakovlev's loss of his position as head of the Party's *agitprop* department.

Iakovlev's essay, the *Veche* author began, recalled the atmosphere of the twenties and early thirties, "the witches' sabbath of social cosmopolitans."[32] It emitted a doctrinaire "sepulchral chill" and was utterly devoid of life. Iakovlev's views on Russian history were summarized thus:

[32] "Bor'ba s tak nazyvaemym rusofil'stvom, ili put' gosudarstvennogo samoubiistva," reprinted in *Vol'noe slovo*, no. 17-18 (1975), 33.

Before 1917, all is darkness and gloom. The people are seen as slaves and savages (savages because of their patriarchal way of life). Monarchs and landlords are without exception scoundrels. There is absolutely nothing positive in one thousand years of history . . . It would appear that the national spirit is expressed, for example, in an attitude toward serfdom or in granting Russia a constitution, while the essence of class enmity is made manifest precisely during Fatherland wars. (It is interesting to imagine how the "class spirit" of Comrade Iakovlev would manifest itself, for example, during a war with present-day China!)[33]

Iakovlev's historical views, therefore, were not only inaccurate but also ran directly counter to Russia's mobilizational interests. Similarly, Iakovlev's harsh criticism of General Skobelev, "the Russian national hero and liberator of Bulgaria," made one wonder about his ultimate intentions. Skobelev freed the Uzbek, Tadzhik, and Persian populations from the slave trade and plunder of the Turkmen-Iomuds, as well as liberating many Russians from enslavement. Is Iakovlev, the "persecutor of the Russophiles," advocating the dissolution of the Union of Soviet Socialist Republics? Does he want the country's borders to shrink back to what they were in 1918, i.e., the same as those of Muscovy under Ivan III?

Iakovlev, "himself the son of a peasant woman, and a first-generation member of the intelligentsia,"[34] sought to put the working class first and to elevate the intelligentsia above the peasantry in significance. He "despises with all the fiber of his soul" the patriarchal, allegedly backward peasantry and brings "political accusations" against those who dare to see the peasant not as a slave but as the cradle of the national culture.[35] Aleksandr Herzen, the *Veche* author observed, thought differently.

The lamentable state of Soviet agriculture provided the author with a useful club with which to pursue Iakovlev and

[33] Ibid., pp. 35-36.
[34] Ibid., p. 34.
[35] Ibid., p. 41.

like-minded doctrinaire Marxists. "In vain," he wrote, "does Iakovlev complain about the danger of the resurrection of the 'industrious peasant'; the regular failure of the wheat crop bears witness to the absence of a zealous and careful tiller of the land. Calm yourself, Comrade Iakovlev . . . We will buy grain from abroad and hence will have no need for the hardworking peasant."[36] Earlier in his essay, the author had discussed the devastating consequences of the decline of the Russian village, which lost between 25% and 30% of its population in the eleven years between the censuses of 1959 and 1970. The Russian village could obviously no longer serve as the population donor of the nation, and soon there would be a serious manpower shortage in Russian industry. "One can assert with complete assurance," the author concluded, "that the destruction of the Russian village and the migration of Great Russians into the cities is a decorous but certain way of destroying the Russian nation."[37]

Iakovlev was also charged with aggravating the volatile nationalities problem. For example, his attack on Georgians for venerating the memory of Queen Tamara represented a foolish and ill-advised attempt to disparage a talented and humane ruler. "An ideological worker with a Russian name," the Veche author warned, "should not seek to erase whole decades from the history of a brother nation."[38] Elsewhere in the same essay, he fulminated against a nationalities policy which led to Russification, mixed marriages, and the creation of cosmopolitan architecture, a uniform environment, and a non-national literature and art. He continued:

We advise Comrade Iakovlev to experience for himself the low, barbaric chauvinism, the zoological hatred of Russians which has emerged precisely on a *non-national* basis. Present-day chauvinism in the borderlands is a reaction against the falsely internationalist propaganda which calls for unity among renegades, for a union of all who have renounced

[36] Ibid., p. 43.
[37] Ibid., p. 31.
[38] Ibid., p. 48.

their nation. Internationalism, as Lenin understood it, is based on a careful and sensitive relationship to one's culture, mores, and traditions. Trotskiite internationalism, on the other hand, is based on the elimination of national distinctions and the total liquidation of nations in general.[39]

The author criticized Iakovlev's "continual references to the authority of Party leaders" such as Lenin and Brezhnev, while also demonstrating (as we have already seen) that two could play at that game. He had little difficulty in unearthing patriotic utterances made at various times by Lenin, Chernyshevskii, and Herzen. Lenin, he insisted, was above all flexible and pragmatic; if one attempted to canonize his every word as holy writ, ignoring the concrete situation in which it was written or spoken, one could find, for example, a Lenin advocating the secession of the Ukraine! "It would seem," the author concluded, "that Lenin would have created other slogans in 1941, and that in 1973 he would say something quite different from the words which Iakovlev now quotes."[40]

Iakovlev "and those who stand behind him"[41] (the reference may have been to Politburo member Mikhail Suslov[42]) wanted a return to the national nihilism and militant denigration of the past which characterized the twenties and early thirties. But, as the Second World War demonstrated, that path was suicidal. Stalin felt himself unable to trust his own generals, for the first time in history Russian soldiers elected to fight on the side of the enemy during a "patriotic war" (an allusion to the so-called "Vlasovite" movement), and the cult of the heroes of the civil war and class struggle had to be quickly discarded. "On whom," the author asked, "does the 'anti-Russophile' Iakovlev place his hopes in the coming war?"[43] In addition, there was another war which Russia could not afford to lose, that of "saving the Russian people from degeneracy" as a result of the epidemic of alcoholism, wife-beating,

[39] Ibid., (italics in original).
[40] Ibid., p. 39.
[41] Ibid., p. 49.
[42] See Dina Rome Spechler, "Russia and the Russians," in Zev Katz, ed., *Handbook of Major Soviet Nationalities*, New York, 1975, p. 18.
[43] "Bor'ba," p. 50.

cursing, child neglect, and the breakup of the family. Iakovlev's path, in short, was one of "national and state suicide" on both the domestic and foreign fronts. It was one, moreover, which was being intently observed by Russia's external enemies.

Such were the arguments which the *Veche* publicist marshaled against the Party's ideologist. A *de facto* National Bolshevik, he interlarded his article with quotations from Dostoevskii and Berdiaev and did not conceal his high opinion of the patriotic services rendered by the Slavophiles, but he also quoted approvingly from *The Communist Manifesto*, Marx, Lenin, Plekhanov, and the revolutionary democrats. To the Lenin of immutable, frozen "proof texts," he opposed a flexible, pragmatic Lenin who always did what was in the country's best interest. A doctrinaire adherence to ideology, he suggested, is the path to national destruction. Under the National Bolshevik "compromise" which the author proposed, one could have both Lenin *and* Dostoevskii as mentors. A retreat from ideological rigidity would, furthermore, permit the country to reverse the desperate state of its agriculture, help to avert demographic ruination, serve to lessen national tensions, and assist in repairing damages done to mobilizational and patriotic morale. Were not, one wonders, at least some of these arguments used by those who brought about Iakovlev's precipitous fall, thwarting the efforts of those "standing behind him"?

THE *Vestnik* NO. 97 CONTROVERSY

A major *samizdat* debate over Russian nationalism was sparked by four pseudonymous articles which appeared in 1970 in issue no. 97 of the émigré journal *Vestnik*.[44] On this occasion, nationalists were being attacked not by Marxist purists

---

[44] The articles were: N.N., "Metanoia," pp. 4-7; O. Altaev, "Dvoinoe soznanie intelligentsii i psevdokul'tura," pp. 8-32; V. Gorskii, "Russkii messianizm i novoe natsional'noe soznanie," pp. 33-68; and M. Chelnov, "Kak byt'?," pp. 69-80. All of the authors' names are pseudonyms. Translations of the Altaev and Gorskii pieces appear in Michael Meerson-Aksenov and Boris Shragin, eds., *The Political and Religious Thought of Russian "Samizdat"—An Anthology*, Belmont, Mass., 1977, pp. 116-147, 353-393.

but by "Catholicizing" Christians who accused their opponents of an "Old Testament naturalist" attitude toward the national question. In a sense, the articles were reminiscent of Petr Chaadaev's famous "Philosophical Letter," published in the journal *Teleskop* in 1836, which galvanized the renowned Slavophile-Westernizer controversy. The *Vestnik* authors, like Chaadaev, represented a "Catholicizing" tendency and voiced a low opinion of Russian Orthodoxy and of the achievements of Russia's past.

Of the four pieces, V. Gorskii's "Russian Messianism and the New National Consciousness" was unquestionably the most controversial. In his essay, Gorskii set out a twofold "basic problem" which he saw underlying Russia's historical development: (1) a tendency toward messianism; and (2) a tendency toward populism. Both trends were viewed as being exceedingly harmful and deeply anti-Christian, grave spiritual temptations for the Russian nation.

"Messianism," Gorskii wrote, "appeared in medieval Russia in the form of the Russian kingdom's confession of being the sole Orthodox kingdom of the world. . . . [R]ight up to the 20th century, the nation's lower classes thought of Russia's destiny in terms of the Muscovite Kingdom. The Slavophiles and Dostoevskii combined Russia's messianic purpose with the particular designation of the Russian people. . . In Soviet Russia, messianism is linked to a belief in the universal triumph of communism, which Russia must bring to the rest of humanity."[45] Gorskii laid heavy stress on the continuities between old Russia and the USSR, between the monk Filofei's sixteenth-century doctrine of "Moscow the Third Rome" and communist imperial ambitions.

Russia's second endemic sin, populism, said Gorskii, was a false sentiment that had led to the idealization of the Russian people and to a utopian belief in the patriarchal peasant commune. Under the communists, the Russian people had become a grotesque *homo sovieticus*. Bolshevism had produced a "maximum concentration of that traditional Russian god-

---

[45] V. Gorskii "Russian Messianism and the New National Consciousness," in Meerson-Aksenov and Shragin, *Political and Religious Thought*, pp. 356-357.

lessness and nihilism which always existed in the Russian soul."[46] After the revolution the peasants made use of icons to construct barns and erect pigsties. It was the "dunderheaded and deprived" Soviet masses who now constituted a major obstruction to the creative work of the intelligentsia, the Soviet Union's only real hope of salvation.

Gorskii contended that traditional "national-messianic" and populist temptations had to be manfully overcome, largely through the efforts of the intelligentsia. Not national self-glorification but "deep and sincere repentance" for monstrous crimes was needed, as well as a sober realization that "Russified Orthodoxy and culture" had largely failed.[47] One necessary step on the road to national repentance was the dissolution of the Russian Empire: the Baltic countries, the Ukraine, the Caucasus, and the peoples of Central Asia must be permitted to leave "the notorious 'indissoluble union.'"[48] Gorskii concluded:

> For many Russian patriots, such a perspective might bring on a feeling of bitter disappointment and indignation: must all Russian history—the Christening of a primitive people by Prince Vladimir, Kievan Rus', the Tatar yoke, the laborious rise of Moscow, Peter's work, the flowering of culture in the 19th and beginning of the 20th centuries, the prophecies of Khomiakov and Dostoevskii, the nightmare of the revolution, the blood and incredible sufferings of the people—end in an outburst of separatist passions or a "Western type democracy" with a parliament and the struggle of labor unions . . . ? Such bitterness and indignation are fully understandable. But these are not the feelings that should rule us. The sin of our forefathers which cries to heaven has not been expiated.[49]

The other significant essay in the collection, O. Altaev's "The Dual Consciousness of the Intelligentsia and Pseudo-Culture," concentrated on the plight of the intelligentsia. The

---

[46] Ibid., p. 382.
[47] Ibid., p. 392.
[48] Ibid.
[49] Ibid., p. 393.

author asserted that the people and the intelligentsia were "finally quits" in the fifty-second year of Soviet power, and he added: "It would not be so bad if the people now realize their guilt before the intelligentsia."[50] Less optimistic than Gorskii about the chances for renewal in Russia, Altaev saw "chauvinist national-socialist totalitarianism" or a steely technocracy as the most likely paths of development. Either way, he feared, "the ruin will be horrible."[51]

The short introductory piece by "N.N.," entitled "Metanoia," was perhaps the most extreme of the four contributions. The essay exhibited an almost racial repugnance for the petty clerks, uprooted peasants, workers, lower ranks of officers, and "other categories of half-educated or little-educated philistines" who made up the Soviet masses. The Russian people, the author pontificated, "has completely lost the habit of good,"[52] while communist power represented "an organic outgrowth of Russian life."[53] "Russia," he declared meaningfully, "has brought more Evil into the world than any other country . . ."[54] The fourth piece, M. Chelnov's "How Shall We Live?," was primarily an attack on Russian Orthodoxy. The Russian Church was indicted for its general weakness and for failing to be a "mother and preceptress" (the title of a 1963 papal encyclical) to contemporary man.[55]

That these articles elicited polemical responses from contemporary nationalist spokesmen is not surprising. Like Chaadaev's 1836 letter, the *Vestnik* essays viewed Russia's past as delusion and desolation and her religious faith, Orthodox Christianity, as feeble and inadequate. The most intelligent and forceful reply was Solzhenitsyn's "Repentance and Self-Limitation in the Life of Nations," one of his contributions to the collection *From under the Rubble*. Solzhenitsyn

[50] O. Altaev, "The Dual Consciousness of the Intelligentsia and Pseudo-Culture," in Meerson-Aksenov and Shragin, *Political and Religious Thought*, p. 121.

[51] Ibid., p. 147.

[52] N. N., "Metanoia," p. 5.

[53] Ibid., p. 6.

[54] Ibid.

[55] Chelnov, "Kak byt'?," p. 78.

began by drawing attention to a feature of the *Vestnik* essays which impressed other nationalist commentators as well—the authors' seeming lack of identity with the Russian people, whom they claimed to represent. "There is not the slightest hint," he wrote, "that the authors share any complicity with their countrymen, with the rest of us; there is nothing but denunciation of the irredeemably vicious Russian people and a tone of contempt for those who have been led astray."[56] Solzhenitsyn also questioned a number of the assumptions of the *Vestnik* contributors—for example, the presupposition that Russia has brought more evil into the world than any other people. "But the so-called Great French Revolution," he interjects, "did France, that is, bring less? Is there any way of calculating? What of the Third Reich? Or Marxism as such?"[57] It may be, he suggested, that Russia's bloodbath has served as a useful lesson to other nations, that it has, for example, taught a few "obtuse ruling classes" to make needed concessions.

Solzhenitsyn hotly contested the view of the *Vestnik* authors that the Russian people had naturally evolved into a repellent *homo sovieticus*. Following the revolution, he noted, peasant risings against the Bolsheviks inundated Tambov province and Siberia, and in 1918 alone several hundred peasant rebellions in defense of the Church had to be put down by force of arms. It was only after brutal and bloody repression that the degeneration and demoralization began to set in.

Gorskii's tendency to overstress the continuities between old Russia and Soviet Russia exasperated Solzhenitsyn. The main content of old Russia, he pointed out, was the Orthodox faith, while that of Bolshevism was militant atheism and class hatred. If Bolshevism is in fact an embodiment of the Russian idea, how could one explain its fierce assault on the Russian people during the years from 1918 to 1933, when "proletarian messianism" destroyed "the flower of the old classes—gentry, merchants, clergy—then the flower of the intelligentsia, then

[56] Solzhenitsyn, "Repentance," p. 122.
[57] Ibid.

the flower of the peasantry"?[58] To be sure, once Bolshevism was ensconced in Russia, it began to acquire indigenous features, but these should not be exaggerated at the expense of internationalist characteristics. Did Cuban and Vietnamese communism also come from "the unwashed monk Filofei" and his theory of the Third Rome? The guilt of the Russian people should not be downplayed or minimized, but it must be kept in perspective, something the *Vestnik* authors had failed to do.

Other nationalist responses were less restrained. In an essay in *Veche*, Leonid Borodin discerned no "pain" (*bol'*) in the *Vestnik* contributions and marveled that their authors could be Russian (he clearly suspected that they are not). A major aim of his article was to demonstrate the groundlessness of the *Vestnik* authors' contention that they were following in the footsteps of the 1909 *Vekhi* collection, a task he attempted to perform with a barrage of quotations from Berdiaev and others. (Actually, as Leonard Schapiro has observed, the *Vekhi* participants were "midway between the Slavophiles and Westerners,"[59] a factor which can lead both contemporary neo-Westernizers, such as the *Vestnik* authors, and neo-Slavophiles, such as Borodin, to claim them as their own.)

Like Solzhenitsyn, Borodin criticized his opponents for overly stressing the continuities between old Russia and the Bolshevik state. To understand the revolution, he maintained, one need only read *The Communist Manifesto*. On the other hand, there was massive non-Russian participation in the revolution: ". . . were they fighting for the Russian Idea, too?"[60] In point of fact, the Russian revolution was a rejection not only of the social and economic structure of old Russia but, more importantly, of the "whole complex of positive ideas" informing that society.[61] Denationalized Russians in tandem with

[58] Ibid., p. 125.

[59] Leonard Schapiro, "The *Vekhi* Group and the Mystique of Revolution," in Sidney Harcave, ed., *Readings in Russian History*, vol. 2, New York, 1962, p. 125.

[60] Leonid Borodin, " '*Vestnik R.S.Kh.D.*' i russkaia intelligentsiia," *Veche*, no. 8 (AS 1665), 140.

[61] Ibid., p. 142.

denationalized Jews made the revolution and initiated a fateful "break with national conservatism."[62] Borodin did not shy
from admitting that he continued to believe in Russia and her
mission.

In a letter to the editor of *Vestnik R.S.Kh.D.*, nationalist
samizdat writer Gennadii Shimanov protested vehemently
against the publication of "anti-Orthodox and anti-Russian"
articles in a journal supposedly concerned with the fate of
Russia.[63] The authors, who "at least want to appear" to be
Russian, felt no "pain" for the country they excoriated. Shimanov did not deny that Russia had committed many historical sins, but he chose to leave the question of whether she
had committed more sins than other peoples up to "omnis-
cient God." He was particularly incensed by the aspersions
cast by the *Vestnik* authors on the Russian Church and their
confident belief that it was incapable of resurrection. Perhaps, like Christ, the Russian Church would rise when all
hope had been adandoned. In any case, he refused to accept
the contrast of a "flourishing Catholic Church" with a de-
graded Russian one.

Another *samizdat* author, L. Ibragimov, underlined in a
somewhat mystical response that the *Vestnik* articles went too
far in denigrating the Russian people. Had not the Russian
people halted the advance of the Tatar-Mongols between the
thirteenth and fifteenth centuries and the invasion of Napoleon in 1812? Had they not played a "decisive role" in stop-
ping the expansion of the Porte and, directly or indirectly,
saving the peoples of Georgia, Armenia, Moldavia, Serbia,
Bulgaria, and Greece from Turkish oppression? And had they
not arrested the march of German Fascism, "which threatened the whole human race"? Were such services to mankind
to be discounted? Moreover, while it was true that there had
been many atheists in Russia, it was likewise true that there
had been "a great number of Russian martyrs who remained

---

[62] Ibid., p. 146.
[63] Gennadii Shimanov, "Otkrytoe pis'mo N. A. Struve, redaktoru zhurnala
'Vestnik R.S.Kh.D.'" (see chapter 7, note 51).

faithful to Christ."[64] As for the *Vestnik* authors, it was clear that they had no love for Russia and that they were exclusively interested in the intelligentsia, ignoring the rest of the populace.

Such is a sample of the nationalist responses elicited by the *Vestnik* articles. As a footnote, one might add that these reactions—particularly those in the collection *From under the Rubble*, which was, at least to some extent, intended as a rebuttal to the *Vestnik* essays—generated a number of counter-responses from neo-Westernizer circles in the Soviet Union and in the so-called "third emigration." Especially noteworthy were two compilations published in the West in 1976, *Samosoznanie* (Self-Awareness)[65] and *Demokraticheskie al'ternativy* (Democratic Alternatives).[66] These compendia, as well as other neo-Westernizer publicistic writings, in turn generated yet another nationalist refutation in the form of a set of articles written by Shafarevich, Borisov, and others, published in *Vestnik* in 1978.[67]

To sum up, during the late 1960s and early 1970s, Russian nationalism found itself under growing attack from Marxist-Leninist purists, who sought to eliminate it as a tendency, and from neo-Westernizer elements writing in *samizdat*. The response of "official nationalists" to their opponents was to show the bankruptcy of doctrinaire Marxism as a mobilizational device and to demonstrate its ruinous social and demographic consequences, as well as its aggravating effect on

[64] L. Ibragimov, "Po povodu sbornika statei, posviashchennykh sud'bam Rossii, opublikovannogo v No. 97 zhurnala 'Vestnik russkogo studencheskogo khristianskogo dvizheniia,' " *Vestnik*, no. 106 (1972), 312.

[65] P. Litvinov, M. Meerson-Aksenov, and B. Shragin, comp., *Samosoznanie: Sbornik statei*, New York, 1976. Contributors to the volume were: Evgenii Barabanov, Lev Kopelev, Pavel Litvinov, Mikhail Meerson-Aksenov, Dmitrii Nelidov, Richard Pipes, Grigorii Pomerants, Boris Shragin, Iurii Orlov, and Valentin Turchin.

[66] Vadim Belotserkovskii, comp., *Demokraticheskie al'ternativy: Sbornik statei i dokumentov*, Achberg, West Germany, 1976. Contributors to the volume were: Leonid Pliushch, Mikhailo Mikhailov, Vadim Belotserkovskii, Ian Elberfel'd, German Andreev, Iuliia Vishnevskaia, Aleksandr Ianov, Anatolii Levitin-Krasnov, Efim Etkind, and Evgenii Kushev.

[67] See the introduction by Nikita Struve, "Spor o Rossii," *Vestnik*, no. 125 (1978), 3-4.

the nationalities problem. National Bolshevism, a tendency in which national elements and arguments are combined with a diluted and flexible "Leninism," was at times offered to the regime as a decorous escape hatch. Dissenting nationalists, who generally eschew National Bolshevik "compromises" because of their perceived inherent "lie" and insufficient attention to religious thematics, came under concerted attack from neo-Westernizer *samizdat* authors, who called the entire historical development of Russia into question, including its religious traditions. Responding to this neo-Chaadaevist onslaught, the dissenting nationalists focused on the discontinuities between old Russia and the Soviet Union and pointed to the uniquely destructive role of Marxist ideology.

What has been the combined effect of this war on two fronts? The "official nationalists," who, like their Marxist purist opponents, may be likened to attorneys putting their case to a jury—i.e., the Politburo and the Party Central Committee— came out at least even in a deadly struggle with foes seeking their political demise. *Novyi mir* was purged following Dement'ev's assault, while A. N. Iakovlev was removed from his post as acting head of the Central Committee's Agitation and Propaganda Department after his attack in *Literaturnaia gazeta*. The nationalists also suffered losses—Anatolii Nikonov was replaced as editor of *Molodaia gvardiia* and a cautious campaign was launched against excesses of "Russophilism"— but they were certainly no more bloodied than their adversaries. As for the dissenting nationalists, the evidence suggests that their views have considerably greater appeal for the ethnic Russian intelligentsia than do those of their neo-Westernizer opponents. The struggle will no doubt continue.

10

The Contemporary Russian
Nationalist Spectrum

> We need to heal our wounds, cure our national body and
> natural spirit. Let us find the strength, sense and courage
> to put our house in order before we busy ourselves with
> the cares of the entire planet. And once again, by a happy
> coincidence, the whole world can only gain from it.
> Aleksandr Solzhenitsyn, *Letter to the Soviet Leaders*[1]

> At the top of the panel were the dates 1242-1942. And
> beneath was an inscription in red and white Slavic letter-
> ing: "Whoever comes to us with the sword shall perish by
> the sword. On this the Russian land has stood and will
> stand!" (Aleksandr Nevskii) Thus did the Soviet people mark
> the 700th anniversary of the Battle on the Frozen Lake in
> the harsh year of 1942.
> Sergei Semanov, *Heart of the Homeland*[2]

No task is more urgent and necessary for Western analysts
of the Soviet Union than to distinguish between the various
tendencies of contemporary Russian nationalism. A failure to
do so will inevitably lead to misreadings of ideological align-
ments in the USSR and to flawed and potentially misleading
policy recommendations. Unquestionably, the two most significant tendencies in present-day Russian nationalism are (1)
what Solzhenitsyn has named the "Russian national and religious renaissance" whose adherents I shall call *vozrozhdentsy*
(from the Russian word for "renaissance");[3] and (2) the tend-

---

[1] Aleksandr Solzhenitsyn, *Letter to the Soviet Leaders*, New York, 1974,
p. 31.
[2] S. Semanov, *Serdtse rodiny*, Moscow, 1977, p. 46.
[3] Through an intermediary, I have asked Solzhenitsyn what terms he would
use to describe the contemporary Russian nationalist upsurge and its adherents. He replied that he favored the term *russkoe natsional'no-religioznoe
vozrozhdenie* (Russian national and religious renaissance) for the phenome-

ency usually termed National Bolshevism. The *vozrozhdentsy* will be treated first.

THE *vozrozhdentsy*

Virtually all dissenting nationalists should be counted among the ranks of the *vozrozhdentsy*, and many "official nationalists," who attempt to air their views in the Soviet media— e.g., some or even most of the so-called "ruralist" school of writers—could be considered partisans or at least "fellow travelers" of this tendency. Influential cultural activists such as Glazunov could impressionistically be seen as straddling the fence separating the *vozrozhdentsy* from the National Bolsheviks. The *vozrozhdentsy* should not be viewed as uniform in their views; there are important differences between those on the "left wing," such as Solzhenitsyn and Shafarevich, and those on the "right wing," such as Shimanov.

What kind of state and society do the *vozrozhdentsy* want to see established, and what type of foreign policy might they be expected to pursue? As a generalization, one could say that "liberal" *vozrozhdentsy* favor broad and sweeping changes in the present system, while more conservative elements advocate proceeding with greater caution. Aleksandr Udodov (b. 1946), a concentration camp graduate and "right-wing" *vozrozhdenets* now in the emigration, has contended that ". . . one or two conditions are absolutely necessary: first of all, freedom for the Church and then freedom for all the peoples of Russia to live and to realize their indigenous traditions and cultures."[4] This could be taken as the tendency's minimum program. Similarly, in two *samizdat* articles appearing in the nationalist journals *Veche* and *Zemlia*, G. Balashov argued cautiously for the introduction of a private sector into the Soviet economy, with free cooperatives taking over the man-

---

non and *pochvenniki* (from the Russian word *pochva*, soil) or *zemtsy* (from *zemlia*, land) to describe its participants. Solzhenitsyn added that it was possible that in the future the renaissance itself would generate other terms, particularly among those members of a predominantly religious orientation.

[4] "Novo-slavianofil Aleksandr Udodov svidetel'stvuet" (interview), *Russkoe vozrozhdenie*, no. 2 (1978), 160-161.

agement of cafes, hotels, workshops, and small shops and private firms allowed to compete with state enterprises in certain areas of light industry.[5] In their programmatic writings, more "liberal" *vozrozhdentsy* propose a thorough overhaul of the state and social structure of the Soviet Union. Without doubt, the two most important documents of this kind have been Solzhenitsyn's *Letter to the Soviet Leaders* and the collection which he helped to compile, *From under the Rubble*. Though Solzhenitsyn and his colleagues have been at pains to emphasize that the thrust of their program is "in no sense political" but rather moral,[6] these two books have nevertheless sparked political as well as moral reflection.

In his *Letter to the Soviet Leaders*, Solzhenitsyn urged the jettisoning of Marxism-Leninism as the state ideology, a move deemed particularly imperative in light of the danger of war with China and of Russia's suffocation by pollution and industrial blight.[7] Give up external expansion, Solzhenitsyn counseled the Soviet rulers, and concentrate on untapped native resources, especially the underdeveloped Northeast. He also urged that they foster administrative and economic decentralization by, for example, giving the soviets real power; pursue de-urbanization by encouraging an "economy of *nongigantism* with small-scale, though highly developed technology . . .";[8] disband the collective farms; combat the degeneration of the Russian people, manifested in the plague of alcoholism and the collapse of the family; strengthen the traditional props of a healthy Russia, such as church and school; cut down on military spending (only China constitutes an actual threat) and on the space race; and let border nationalities who wish to secede from the Russian federation do so.[9] In sum, Solzhe-

[5] G. Balashov, "Problema chastnogo predprinimatel'stva v SSSR," *Veche*, no. 6 (AS 1599), 104-108; and "O pliusakh i minusakh gosudarstvennoi sobstvennosti," *Zemlia*, no. 2 (AS 2060), 35-41. I have been told that the name Balashov is a pseudonym.

[6] Statement by Solzhenitsyn in *Dve press-konferentsii (k sborniku "Iz-pod glyb")*, Paris, 1975, p. 59.

[7] Solzhenitsyn, *Letter*, pp. 13-26.

[8] Ibid., pp. 37-38 (Solzhenitsyn's italics).

[9] Aleksandr Solzhenitsyn, "Sakharov i kritika 'Pis'ma vozhdiam,' " *Kontinent*, no. 2 (1975), 351.

nitsyn's program is inward-looking and resuscitative, designed to rescue a country perceived as being on the brink of catastrophe.

What political structure ought Russia to have? The lamentable aftermath of the February Revolution convinced Solzhenitsyn that a sudden and unprepared introduction of Western-style democracy would lead to chaos and ruin. He expressed opposition to the "democracy run riot" of the West, in which "once every four years the politicians, and indeed the entire country, nearly kill themselves over an electoral campaign, trying to gratify the masses."[10] Freedom is moral, he wrote, "only if it keeps within certain bounds," while order is not immoral "if it means a calm and stable system," though order always runs the risk of degenerating into "arbitrariness and tyranny."[11] Solzhenitsyn desired neither the system of the totalitarian East nor that of the democratic West. One senses in his writings that he was groping about for a structure rooted in Russian historical tradition. "Should we," he asked, "record as our democratic tradition the Land Assemblies of Muscovite Russia, Novgorod, the early Cossacks, the village commune? Or should we console ourselves with the thought that for a thousand years Russia lived with an authoritarian order . . . ?"[12] An authoritarian system which would gradually pave the way for the emergence of a disciplined and self-controlled democracy might be a possible solution to Solzhenitsyn's dilemma.

In *From under the Rubble*, the task of sketching in the contours of the future society fell to Mikhail Agurskii (b. 1933), a Zionist and a close associate of the liberal Russian nationalists.[13] Like Solzhenitsyn, Agurskii favored a "third way" that would avoid the pitfalls of both Western capitalism and Eastern communism. He urged a halt to the ceaseless expansion of industry through artificial stimulation of demand. Manufac-

[10] Solzhenitsyn, *Letter*, p. 50.
[11] Ibid., p. 51.
[12] Ibid., p. 52.
[13] Mikhail Agursky, "Contemporary Socioeconomic Systems and Their Future Prospects," in *From under the Rubble*, Boston, 1975, pp. 67-87.

turing should be broken down into small, technologically advanced enterprises employing the latest developments in computer science (Agurskii is a cyberneticist by training); the gulf between intellectual and physical labor should gradually disappear; economic and administrative decentralization should be effected, with the result that the central government would play a less important role (only such spheres as defense and mining would remain in the hands of the state). Agurskii did not speculate concerning the future structure of the Russian state, but he warned that the emergence of Western-style political parties would be most unfortunate.

After *Letter to the Soviet Leaders* and *From under the Rubble*, the most important catalyst for thought among the *vozrozhdentsy* has probably been the program of the All-Russian Social-Christian Union for the Liberation of the People (VSKhSON). Though adopted by the underground organization's leadership in 1964, this document became widely known in the Soviet Union only in 1975, after its publication by YMCA-Press in Paris.[14] It therefore entered the intellectual life of modern Russia at approximately the same time as the programmatic writings of Solzhenitsyn and his associates.

Like Solzhenitsyn and Agurskii, Igor' Ogurtsov (b. 1937), the program's principal author,[15] gave his support to a "third way" for Russia's future development, one featuring economic and administrative decentralization, a mixed economy, and the operation of industrial enterprises and service industries by free collectives and associations of the skilled professions. (VSKhSON's interest in corporatism has prompted one recent émigré, Aleksandr Ianov, to interpret the organization's program as being similar to Italian fascism,[16] but the differences between VSKhSON and Mussolini-type fascism are considerably greater than the similarities.) Only such activities as mining, transportation, and defense would be con-

---

[14] *VSKhSON: Sbornik materialov*, Paris, 1975. For an English translation of the program, see John B. Dunlop, *The New Russian Revolutionaries*, Belmont, Mass., 1976, pp. 243-293.

[15] See "VSKhSON: Materialy suda i programma," *Vol'noe slovo*, no. 22 (1976), 5.

[16] Alexander Yanov, *The Russian New Right*, Berkeley, 1978, pp. 29-30.

trolled by the state. Like Solzhenitsyn, the VSKhSON program also advocated a strengthening of the essential pillars of a healthy Russian society—family, church, and school.

The VSKhSON program went a great deal further than Solzhenitsyn and his colleagues in seeking to envision what the future Russian state would be like. The legislative branch, called the Popular Assembly, would be elected on the basis of proportional representation from village and urban communes, industrial and commercial corporations, and associations of the free professions. There would be a Supreme Court and a supervisory or "watchdog" body, called the Supreme Council, with the right of vetoing actions not in accord with the basic principles of Social Christianity. The Supreme Council, of which one-third would be members of the Church's upper hierarchy and two-thirds would be outstanding representatives of the people elected for life, would elect a head of state, who would then have to be confirmed by a popular referendum. The relationship of the head of state—a constitutional monarch seems to be indicated—to the Popular Assembly is left vague, perhaps deliberately so.

"The Social-Christian view of the state," the VSKhSON program proclaimed, "does not confuse it with society."[17] Religious, cultural, educational, and scientific institutions, and the press would all be free of arbitrary control by the state. The government would concentrate upon internal development rather than on foreign affairs, a shift which would lead, among other consequences, to the complete withdrawal of Soviet troops from Eastern Europe. The question of the minority nationalities in the USSR received strikingly little treatment in the program, though this is less strange in a document issued in 1964 than it would be in one appearing a decade later.[18] It is possible that the authors had in mind some kind of federal solution to the nationalities problem.[19]

[17] Dunlop, *New Russian Revolutionaries*, p. 277.

[18] See the comments on this point by former VSKhSON leader Evgenii Vagin in his review article, "Russkie sotsial-khristiane glazami amerikantsev," *Ruskoe vozrozhdenie*, no. 3 (1978), 210.

[19] See Bernard Karavatskii, "Vospominaniia uchastnika," in *VSKhSON: Sbornik materialov*, pp. 206-207.

Vladimir Maksimov (b. 1925), editor of the important émigré journal *Kontinent* and a liberal *vozrozhdenets*, published an interesting programmatic essay, entitled "Reflections on Democracy," in 1979.[20] He began his argument by acknowledging a particular debt to Solzhenitsyn: "I think that for many of my compatriots Aleksandr Solzhenitsyn's *Letter to the Soviet Leaders* served as a stimulus for reflection about the possible future of our country, about its social and political structure, and about its role and fate among other peoples." Like Solzhenitsyn and the VSKhSON program, Maksimov called for a "third way." "Is there no way," he asked, "out of the dead-end dilemma: Western democracy or Eastern totalitarianism?" Revive the commune, he urged, as the fundamental unit of Russian life, and cleanse it of the "poisonous undergrowth" of ideology. This, he believed, could be easily accomplished if the existing administrative and territorial divisions of the USSR—to be renamed the "Russian Federated Land"—were kept and municipal and rural communes were formed throughout the country. Local communes would elect representatives to district communes which, in turn, would elect delegates to provincial colleges of representatives. These last-named bodies would, in turn, elect representatives to the lower house of an Assembly analogous to the British House of Commons. The upper house of the Assembly, analogous to the House of Lords, would be called the Chamber of Nationalities, and each nationality, no matter how large, would elect the same number of representatives to it. The House of Nationalities would have the right to veto any law dealing with nationality questions.

Under Maksimov's scheme, the first session of the Constituent Assembly would make a decision concerning what form of government the Russian Federated Land should have—a republic, an "authoritarian federation," or a constitutional monarchy. The president and the government would be responsible to the Assembly, and there would be a Supreme Court to resolve legal issues. Finally, questions on which "the

[20] Vladimir Maksimov, "Razmyshleniia o demokratii," *Russkaia mysl'*, 23 August 1979, p. 6.

fate of the state system or social structure" would depend would be decided by popular referendum.

Also like the VSKhSON program and Solzhenitsyn, Maksimov sought to free society from the vise-like grip of the state. The church, he argued, should be fully separate from the state, though its role in regenerating society ought to be immense. There should be freedom of the press, except for the propagation of racial, class, and religious discord and the dissemination of pornography. Political parties should be permitted, but only at the local communal level. Economic and administrative decentralization should be realized, with the state remaining in charge only of defense, the general budget, and the conduct of foreign affairs. Maksimov, like Solzhenitsyn, wanted a limitation on foreign investment in the country, fearing a loss of economic independence.

Maksimov, who has lived in the West since 1974, voiced many of the same criticisms of contemporary Western democracy as his Nobel laureate colleague has done. Party politics appall Maksimov; he cited the case of present-day Italy, where no single party is able to rule effectively. Under the Western system, he said, at best "party mediocrities" and at worst "political opportunists or unprincipled hucksters" come to power. Moreover, Western industrial and financial oligarchies frequently enjoy excessive influence. The Western political system, Maksimov declared, had largely run its course.

"Twelve Principles of the Russian Task: A Letter to Russian Patriots" was the title of a programmatic work written in prison during 1978 by Sergei Soldatov (b. 1933), a Soviet dissident sentenced in 1975 to six years in the camps.[21] Raised in Estonia by a Russian father and an Estonian stepmother, Soldatov represents a curious and somewhat eccentric hybrid of a Russian nationalist and "demokrat."[22] Though less gifted than Solzhenitsyn, Maksimov, or Ogurtsov, Soldatov provides useful insights into the conceptual gropings of present-day Russian nationalists.

[21] Sergei Soldatov, "12 printsipov russkogo dela, pis'mo k russkim patriotam" (AS 3256).
[22] See Soldatov's open letter in *Russkaia mysl'*, 27 September 1979, p. 4.

In "Twelve Principles," he advocated broad economic and administrative decentralization and foresaw the possibility of a zero-growth economy in Russia. The document also called for a democratization of the USSR's political structure, but it did not spell out how this was to be accomplished. Acutely concerned over the degeneration of the Russian populace, Soldatov too cried out for strengthening the traditional supports of Russian society, and for an all-out campaign against alcoholism and drug use. His program urged a policy of internal development and suggested that, for example, the areas of Arkhangel'sk, Ukhta, Perm', and Iaroslavl' should receive concerted attention. Soldatov also asked for the recall of all Russians from the other union republics (he estimated their number to be twenty-two million) and the summoning of all Russians home from the emigration.

In certain areas, Soldatov diverged markedly from the "mainline" views of contemporary *vozrozhdentsy*. Thus, while his position that all fourteen union republics should be offered a chance to secede from the Russian federation is held by some liberal nationalists, his view of Siberia as only a "condominium of the Russian state" certainly is not. Likewise, his extreme pro-Westernism finds little echo among present-day *vozrozhdentsy*. Soldatov called for Russia's "political integration" into Europe, her entrance into the European Common Market, and a broad incorporation of Western economic firms into Russian economic life. He also said that ten percent of all Russian teachers and students should study in Europe and that "Each Russian must spend two to four months of his life traveling in Europe . . ."

While there are important differences among the programmatic efforts of various *vozrozhdentsy*, the similarities are more significant: an insistence on the necessity of jettisoning Marxism; the promotion of economic and administrative decentralization; corporatism; decollectivization of agriculture; an absence of political parties; the building up of church, family, and school; emphasis on internal development; and withdrawal from involvement in the affairs of other nations. Issues on which there appears to be less agreement are the degree of "authority" which the state or head of state should enjoy, the manner in which accommodation should be reached with the minority nationalities, and the degree to which Russia should have economic ties with the West.

As should already be clear, many *vozrozhdentsy* favor a return to a monarchistic system of government, some supporting a resurrection of autocracy but more, it would seem, advocating a form of limited or "constitutional" monarchy. Monarchists may be further divided into those who desire a restoration of the Romanov dynasty (the claimant to the throne, Grand Duke Vladimir Kirillovich, presently lives in Spain) and those who want a summoning of a new Land Assembly (*Zemskii sobor*) to elect a new tsar and perhaps a new dynasty. For Americans, who broke their ties with a king two hundred years ago, the fact that modern Russians could seriously contemplate a return to monarchy seems akin to lunacy, but of course the two situations are not comparable. After sixty years of communist rule, the prerevolutionary monarchy does not appear so objectionable to many contemporary Russians.

Here are several examples of the strength of present-day monarchist sentiments in the Soviet Union. In 1972-1973, a study entitled *"Dvadtsat' tri stupeni vniz"* (Twenty-three Steps Down) was serialized in *Zvezda*.[23] It concerned the slaying of Tsar Nicholas II and his family; the title referred to the number of steps leading to the cellar of the Ipat'ev house in Ekaterinburg (now Sverdlovsk), where the murders took place. The serial caused a sensation, and the issues in which it appeared were in such demand that it was virtually impossible to find them in either kiosks or libraries. In 1977, the edifice—which had become an object of pilgrimage—was torn down, even though it was structurally sound and had, until shortly before, been used to house an institute.[24] In January 1977, the editor and assistant editor of the journal *Avrora*

[23] M. Kasvinov, "Dvadtsat' tri stupeni vniz," *Zvezda*, nos. 8 and 9 (1972), 140-176 and 117-172, and nos. 7, 8, 9, and 10 (1973), pp. 110-152, 113-153, 124-152, and 170-193. The work was later published in book form by "Mysl'," Moscow, 1979.

[24] See the account in *Russkaia mysl'*, 5 October 1978, p. 8. See also the *samizdat* article by Boris Turbin, "K 60-letiiu ubiistva tsarskoi sem'i," *Russkoe vozrozhdenie*, no. 3 (1978), 52-64.

were dismissed from their posts for having published a poem lamenting the fate of the Empress Alexandra and her family.[25]

Evgenii Vagin (b. 1938), himself a convinced monarchist, has correctly pointed out that on the whole what we have here are monarchistic moods, rather than adherence to monarchist doctrine.[26] It should be noted, however, that a weighty synthesis of monarchist teaching, Lev Tikhomirov's multivolume prerevolutionary study, *Monarkhicheskaia gosudarstvennost'* (The Monarchic State), does circulate in *samizdat.*[27] The grief which many contemporary Russians feel over the violent death suffered by Russia's last tsar and his family serves to feed monarchist sentiment and links up with the traditional Russian veneration for victims of violent death, particularly when they happen to be princes.[28] The achievements of Russian culture under the tsars are often contrasted to the spare accomplishments of the Soviet period. It is noteworthy that the VSKhSON program, authored by Ogurtsov, a young man in his late twenties, implicitly provided for a monarch as head of state.

Another topic which deserves a brief excursus is that of China. The *vozrozhdentsy* are not particularly obsessed with China, though of course they cannot ignore it. One encounters little talk of a "yellow peril" in their writings, and it is significant that the journal *Veche* carried only one, relatively unimportant article on China in its ten bulky issues. As recent émigré Vladimir Rybakov has shown in his novel *Tiazhest'* (Oppressiveness), which is about the life of Soviet troops on the Chinese border, contemporary Russians have a realistic and sober appreciation for their opponent, an admiration for his strengths, and a conviction that the Chinese soldier is

[25] *New York Times*, 28 April 1977, p. A12.

[26] Evgenii Vagin, "K budushchei svobodnoi Rossii" (interview), *Russkaia mysl'*, 18 January 1979, p. 7.

[27] Lev Tikhomirov, *Monarkhicheskaia gosudarstvennost'*, 3 vols., Munich, 1923 (originally published in 1904). On Tikhomirov and his thought, see the unpublished doctoral dissertation by Von Duane Hardesty, "Lev A. Tikhomirov and the Autocratic Principle," Ohio State University, 1974.

[28] G. P. Fedotov, *The Russian Religious Mind*, vol. 1, Cambridge, Mass., 1946, chapter 4.

superior in motivation to the pampered American one.[29] Solzhenitsyn's view, expressed in his *Letter to the Soviet Leaders*, that a discarding of Marxist-Leninist ideology would automatically serve to reduce tensions with China—because the two countries would cease competing for the role of true interpreter of the "faith"—does not appear to be accepted by all *vozrozhdentsy*, though at least some would agree that a nationalist Russia and a nationalist China might enjoy more of a common ground than is presently the case.

In sum, the distinctive marks of the *vozrozhdentsy* are these: (1) Russian Orthodoxy occupies a central position in their thought and serves to insulate them from any accommodation with the "communist experiment" or with the intensely antireligious founder of the Soviet state, Vladimir Lenin. (2) While cognizant of Russia's historical, cultural, and religious achievements, present-day *vozrozhdentsy* are alarmed over the moral and demographic disintegration currently taking place in the country. (3) To a certain extent, they are concerned with institutional checks on the abuse of government power, such as an independent judiciary, and with the safeguarding of basic freedoms, particularly freedom of religion and freedom of expression; but they also feel that *moral* checks are equally, if not more, important (a conviction perhaps generated by their unhappy experience with the "Stalin Constitution"). (4) In economics, they generally favor a "third way," avoiding the perceived excesses of the capitalist West and of the communist East. (5) Without exception, they seek to accommodate the legitimate ethnic strivings of the minority nationalities in the USSR, advocating full freedom of cultural and religious expression and, in certain cases, leaving open the possibility of secession from a future Russian federation. (6) *Vozrozhdentsy* tend to be anti-urban—though some would admit the possibility of smaller, "man-centered" cities in the future—and to see peasant traditions and mores as the rock upon which national morality and culture should be based. (7) In foreign policy, they lean toward isolationism, arguing

[29] V. Rybakov, *Tiazhest': Byl'*, Frankfurt/Main, 1977. See also Naum Korzhavin, "Only Fifty Years from Now," *Russia*, 1, no. 1 (1981), 50-58.

that Russia must heal her many wounds and withdraw from
debilitating involvement in the affairs of other states. Only
China is deemed a real military threat. (8) *Vozrozhdentsy* tend
to dislike the contemporary West on moral and aesthetic
grounds, but their antipathy is generally a restrained one, not
characterized by beliefs in "Jewish-Masonic" conspiracies or
bourgeois-capitalist hydras.

THE NATIONAL BOLSHEVIKS

Adherents of the second major Russian nationalist tendency, National Bolshevism, are frequently attacked by
vozrozhdentsy for their perceived attempt to foster Russian
patriotism without a Christian foundation. In *From under the
Rubble*, Solzhenitsyn offered this summary of the tendency's
views:

[T]he Russian people is the noblest in the world; its ancient
and its modern history are alike unblemished; tsarism and
Bolshevism are equally irreproachable; the nation neither
erred nor sinned either before 1917 or after . . . [T]here
are no nationality problems in relations with the border
republics . . . Communism is in fact unthinkable without
patriotism; the prospects of Russia-USSR are brilliant; blood
alone determines whether one is Russian or non-Russian.
As for things spiritual, all trends are admissible. Orthodoxy
is not the least more Russian than Marxism, atheism, the
scientific outlook, or, shall we say, Hinduism.[30]

In a 1976 interview, Evgenii Vagin made these comments
concerning National Bolshevism: "For a time, its representatives were grouped around the journal *Molodaia gvardiia*
and the publishing house 'Sovremennik.' Echoes of this tendency could be heard in the first not very successful issues of
the journal *Veche* . . . [T]he representatives of National
Bolshevism have drawn, it seems to me, an incorrect conclusion from Berdiaev's mistaken thesis concerning communism

[30] Aleksandr Solzhenitsyn, "Repentance and Self-Limitation in the Life of
Nations," in *From under the Rubble*, pp. 119-120.

as a manifestation of the Russian spirit. The National Bolsheviks are original revisionists. One could say that they want not socialism with a human face but communism with a national face."[31] Because of its "absolute atheism," National Bolshevism cannot, Vagin feels, extract Russia from the crisis in which she now finds herself.

Solzhenitsyn's and Vagin's remarks, while necessarily schematic, help us to conceptualize a rather elusive tendency of thought and sentiment which currently enjoys significant popularity among certain segments of the Soviet intelligentsia and the ruling *apparat*. (Vagin contends that National Bolshevism lacks a mass base.[32]) Solzhenitsyn and Vagin can be faulted only for failing to discern that there have also been a number of "closet" *vozrozhdentsy* among the contributors to such nationalist journals as *Molodaia gvardiia* and the authors whose works are published by patriotic publishing houses such as "Sovremennik."

Mikhail Agurskii, presently a professor at the Hebrew University in Jerusalem, has done valuable research into the genesis and development of National Bolshevism.[33] The term itself, he has noted, was coined in 1921 by Nikolai Ustrialov, an émigré professor living in Harbin, China, and the most influential contributor to the *Smena vekh* collection. The *smenovekhovtsy*, as was seen in an earlier chapter, advocated a rapprochement between the Bolshevik Revolution and the Russian state, to be achieved through a squeezing out of the "internationalist" elements of the revolution. The original Na-

---

[31] "Litsom k Rossii: Interv'iu E. A. Vagina 'Posevu,' " *Posev*, no. 10 (1976), 58.

[32] Ibid.

[33] Mikhail Agursky, "The Soviet Legitimacy Crisis and Its International Implications," paper prepared for a conference on "What Is Communism?" held at the Center for Strategic and Foreign Policy Studies, University of Chicago, 7-9 April 1977; and "Dmitrievsky and the Origins of National Bolshevism," *Soviet Jewish Affairs*, 7, no. 2 (1977), 53-61. Professor Agurskii informs me that the first-named article has been published in Morton Kaplan, ed., *The Many Faces of Communism*, New York, 1978. See also Agurskii's book, *Ideologiia Natsional-Bol'shevizma*, Paris, 1980. For an important review which contests Agurskii's interpretation of Stalin as a National Bolshevik, see Mikhail Geller, "Iskushenie Natsional-Bol'shevizmom," *Russkaia mysl'*, 23 October 1980, p. 4.

tional Bolsheviks were not religious, but they were not hostile to religion either; and, while opposed to a restoration of monarchy, they wanted a strong dictatorship to rule the country. As Agurskii pointed out, ideas similar to those of the *smenovekhovtsy* continued to crop up in the emigration, most notably among members of the important *mladorossy* (Young Russia) organization. In 1930, a former high-ranking Soviet official, Sergei Dmitrievskii, defected to the West and, in a series of publications appearing during the thirties, developed a fairly coherent policy of National Bolshevism, emphasizing the "sinister dominance" of Russia by a Jewish internationalist clique supposedly headed by Trotskii, Kaganovich, Iaroslavskii, Litvinov, and others.[34] Dmitrievskii lauded Stalin, and portrayed Lenin as having been a dedicated Russian patriot, but sharply criticized the communist attack on the Russian Orthodox Church. Agurskii and other scholars believe that Dmitrievskii was probably a Soviet *agent provocateur*, though there is no proof of this.

Agurskii's analysis of National Bolshevism deserves serious attention. I do not think, as he does, that Stalin was a National Bolshevik, though, as has been seen, the despot carefully balanced patriotic and Marxist elements in the post-1934 period of his rule. A second criticism of Agurskii's argument would be that there is no evidence that the writings of Ustrialov or Dmitrievskii, to take two examples, circulate widely in contemporary Russian nationalist *samizdat*. What is happening, rather, is that present-day Soviet intellectuals are rediscovering on their own the ideas of a previous generation of thinkers.

An important theoretical question concerns the relationship between National Bolshevism and fascism (an ideology which should, of course, be clearly distinguished from the related, but much more extreme, ideology of National Socialism). To anyone familiar with recent Western scholarship on fascism, the similarities between National Bolshevism and fascism are striking: a strong impulse toward deification of the

[34] Agursky, "Dmitrievsky," *passim.*

nation; the desire for a strong totalitarian state; a powerful leadership impulse (contemporary National Bolshevisks speak of a yearning for a *krepkii chelovek*, or strong man); a belief in the necessity of the existence of an elite; a cult of discipline, particularly discipline of the youth; heroic vitalism; an advocacy of industrial and military might, combined at times with ecological concerns; a celebration of the glories of the past; and a militant, expansionist dynamic. As modern scholars of fascism point out in their writings, the borderline between national communism and fascism is often a very thin one.

Professor Juan Linz has argued that fascism can best be understood as an "anti" movement:

> . . . it is anti-Marxist, anti-communist, anti-proletarian, but also anti-liberal, anti-parliamentarian, and, in a very special sense, anti-conservative and anti-bourgeois. Anti-clericalism . . . is a more or less central component . . . Anti-individualism and anti-democratic authoritarianism and elitism are combined with a strong populist appeal. Anti-semitism is not originally characteristic of all fascist movements but central to many of them. Anti-urbanism, or at least, anti-metropolitanism . . . is often an important element. A distinctive type of anti-capitalism is originally present in many fascist movements. Sometimes anti-feminism appears. . . . A number of these anti positions can best be understood by considering them anti-international and anti-cosmopolitan positions.[35]

If Linz's description is accepted, it becomes clear that in National Bolshevism we have an essentially fascist phenomenon, a radical right movement in a state still adhering nominally to a radical left ideology. Of the numerous characteristics which Linz lists, only anti-clericalism does not stand out among contemporary National Bolsheviks, perhaps due to the all-out assault launched by the communists on the Church.

[35] Juan J. Linz, "Some Notes Toward a Comparative Study of Fascism in Sociological Historical Perspective," in Walter Laqueur, ed., *Fascism*, Berkeley and Los Angeles, 1976, p. 16.

Antecedents of present-day Russian fascism include not only the *smenovekhovtsy* and the *mladorossy* but also the writings of Nikolai Danilevskii and Konstantin Leont'ev—both of whom, incidentally, influenced Ustrialov[36]—and the prerevolutionary "Black Hundreds" and the White Army movement. As scholars such as Hans Rogger and Walter Laqueur have demonstrated, two traditionalist elements blocked or retarded the emergence of a full-fledged fascism in these earlier movements: Russian Orthodoxy and monarchism.[37] The Union of the Russian People and the "white" movement, for example, were both religious and monarchist in orientation, factors preventing their evolution into more modern forms of fascism. With the denial or downgrading of Orthodoxy and monarchism, fascism is unleashed.

Sergei Semanov's *Serdtse rodiny* (Heart of the Homeland), which appeared in 1977 in an edition of 35,000, represents a useful compendium of National Bolshevik positions. Unlike the ill-fated Fetisov group of National Bolsheviks, Semanov (b. 1934) sought to play down discrepancies between Marxist ideology and Russian nationalism and to focus instead on the need for and the benefits accruing from a Soviet Russian patriotism. In *Heart of the Homeland*, he celebrated Russian military victories of the prerevolutionary and Soviet periods—seeing no fateful break as having occurred in 1917— and singled out tsarist generals, such as Suvorov and Kutuzov, and Soviet heroes, such as Frunze and Zhukov, for equally effusive praise. Semanov lauds Prince Bagration, "a noble warrior and staunch Russian patriot" mortally wounded during the "First Fatherland War" (against Napoleon), but he also lionizes the communist leader Chapaev. While he expresses concern for the future of Russian historical monuments, Semanov generally comes across as confident and aggressively combative. He drew inspiration from such conservative literary luminaries as Mikhail Sholokhov and

[36] Agursky, "Soviet Legitimacy Crisis," p. 13.
[37] Hans Rogger, "Was There a Russian Fascism?," *Journal of Modern History*, 36, no. 4 (1964), 415, and Walter Laqueur, *Russia and Germany*, London, 1965, p. 84.

Aleksei Tolstoi and voiced approval of the theories of ethnographer Lev Gumilev.

The following selection from *Heart of the Homeland* conveys the flavor of Semanov's "single stream" view of Russian history:

> Toward the end of the Great Fatherland War, a young officer, a native of the Donbas working-class who had been raised and educated in the Soviet period, was serving in the ranks of our troops who had come to save Bulgaria from Hitlerism. Today the name of the poet Aleksei Nedogonov is known to all. At the Shipka crossing, he saw a church which had been constructed over the graves of Russian soldiers who fell in the last century while liberating a fraternal country from the yoke of the Janissaries. And he, a soldier of the Great Fatherland War, felt a link between the old and the new:
>
> > The great temple stood
> > Clutched in the red
> > Of September dawns and stars
> > —Take off your cap, Stalingrader,
> > Our forefathers lie here!
> > Through the sounds of years
> > We hear, grandchildren,
> > The battle
> > And the flight of the Janissaries
> > And the sound of Russian trumpets
> > And the rejoicing of the Bulgarians.[38]

Like one of his avowed mentors, Aleksei Tolstoi, Semanov attempted to combine nationalist and communist motifs in his writing. But in Semanov Marxist ideological elements were downplayed more than in Tolstoi, while nationalist (and even Russian Orthodox) elements received more emphasis. The difference may appear to be slight, but it is, I believe, a critical one, the difference between a National Bolshevik of the 1970s and a patriotic Stalinist of the late thirties and forties.

[38] Semanov, *Serdtse rodiny*, p. 35.

In addition to being an encomium to Russia, Semanov's collection sounded a dread warning against dangerous "cosmopolitan" elements which supposedly threatened the Soviet Union both from within and from without. His articles manifested a strong hatred for Jews, who were seen as viciously Russophobic, dedicated to destroying traditional Russia and to throttling the Russian people into submission. Trotskiism, Semanov maintained, was "a gigantic danger for the peoples of our country," an ideology whose true face was "cold and merciless," while Trotskii himself displayed a "blood hatred toward the Cossacks" and a "fierce hatred for leaders coming from the ranks of the people." An associate of Trotskii, Gol'tsman, was described as having demanded "merciless cane discipline toward the working masses."[39] Until the mid-thirties, Russia was ravaged by "leftist perverts" ("all those Averbakhs and Beskins, Zonins and Leleviches, Briks and other Rodovs . . ."[40]) who demanded the annihilation of the culture of old Russia. Fortunately, Semanov wrote, all these Jewish "pseudorevolutionaries" were put in their proper place by Stalin.

Semanov broadly hinted that the danger of Trotskiism was not over. Western-oriented elements in the Soviet intelligentsia were trying to carry out Trotskii's thwarted intentions. In pursuing this aim, they were abetted by what Semanov called the "dark forces of world capital."[41] Semanov, it turns out, believed (though he expressed the conviction somewhat cautiously) in the "Jewish-Masonic conspiracy" and saw the Russophobic West as essentially controlled by "international Masonic and Zionist financial circles."[42] Such circles supported Miliukov, a leader of the February Revolution, after he went into exile, and they remained active.[43] Not China but this deceitful hydra appeared to be Russia's greatest danger, one deserving the concerted attention of steely Russian "warriors."

[39] Ibid., pp. 102, 103, 104.
[40] Ibid., p. 178.
[41] Ibid., p. 37.
[42] Ibid., p. 163.
[43] Ibid., pp. 162-163.

A second major work of National Bolshevik inspiration, Nikolai Iakovlev's *1 avgusta 1914* (August 1, 1914), was published by the "Molodaia gvardiia" printing house in 1974, in an edition of 100,000.[44] The son of a Soviet general repressed under Stalin and himself a concentration camp alumnus, Iakovlev demonstrated his bona fides to the regime shortly before the appearance of his book by attacking Solzhenitsyn in print.[45] *August 1, 1914*, which concerns Russia's participation in the First World War, celebrated the exploits of the Russian people during the conflict and assailed the Provisional Government for, among other things, being thoroughly penetrated by a "secret Masonic organization." (As British scholar Geoffrey Hosking has pointed out, an interest in the role of the Russian Masons during this period is legitimate,[46] but Iakovlev seems obsessed with their significance.) ". . . the sword of revolution," Iakovlev exulted in one place, "struck the reptile [i.e., the bourgeoisie] at the very moment when it was getting to its feet."[47] He also expressed contempt for the degenerate, pro-Western ruling class, which he said was paralyzed by a do-nothing "Orthodox paganism." A good deal of Iakovlev's information, and at least some of his interpretations, came, interestingly enough, from Vasilii Shul'gin, a well-known former Duma delegate and monarchist activist whom Iakovlev interviewed shortly before Shul'gin's death at an advanced age.

It becomes apparent that Iakovlev has pronounced sympathy—such at least is my reading of certain Aesopian allusions in his book—for the tsarist military, especially for certain generals who soon afterward turned up as leaders of the white movement. (Despite myriad quotations from Lenin, Iakovlev

[44] N. Iakovlev, *1 avgusta 1914*, 2nd ed., Moscow, 1974. This second edition appeared in a printing of 100,000; presumably, the first edition was at least as large.

[45] See Michael Nicholson, "*The Gulag Archipelago*: a Survey of Soviet Responses," in John B. Dunlop, Richard Haugh, and Alexis Klimoff, eds., *Aleksandr Solzhenitsyn: Critical Essays and Documentary Materials*, 2nd ed., New York, 1975, pp. 490-491.

[46] Geoffrey A. Hosking, *The Russian Constitutional Experiment*, Cambridge, 1973, p. 196.

[47] Iakovlev, *1 avgusta 1914*, p. 226.

comes across as somewhat less reconciled to the communist experiment than his colleague Semanov.) One notes with interest Iakovlev's discussion of a memorandum sent by General Alekseev to Nicholas II, urging the tsar to name a military dictator to administer the empire. "Alekseev," Iakovlev commented, "always considered . . . that the army should command by the will of the people, and that it should head both the government and all its undertakings . . ."[48] The patriotism of the future white generals, and their willingness to take decisive action, impressed Iakovlev, who also seemed to approve the "steadfastness" of such "Black Hundred" leaders as A. I. Dubrovin and V. M. Purishkevich.

The lessons drawn by Iakovlev from Russia's calamitous experience in the First World War were: Do not trust the Western powers; do not rely on the bourgeois, pro-Western intelligentsia; patriotism and strong leadership are what is needed. Like Semanov, Iakovlev strikes one as authoritarian, militaristic, intolerant, and more than ready to take harsh measures against domestic and foreign opponents. Religious inclinations are not discernible in his book, though at one point he does praise the courage of Orthodox military chaplains during the war. While seemingly less enthusiastic about the communist experiment than Semanov, Iakovlev had frequent recourse to the "Lenin theme" and carefully covered his flanks against attack by Marxist purists.

Much less is known about the programmatic desires of the National Bolsheviks than about those of the *vozrozhdentsy*, since National Bolsheviks do not generally make use of *samizdat* and must therefore express their ideas elliptically in the official press. An implementation of their ideas would probably lead to what French sovietologist Alain Besançon has called a "pan-Russian police and military empire."[49] A military dictatorship directed by a junta or a party dictatorship (with the CPSU becoming a fascist-style "Russian Party") are both possibilities. Under such a government, there would probably

---

[48] Ibid., p. 182.

[49] "La Technique du Pouvoir en URSS," (interview with Alain Besançon), *L'Express*, 2-9 December 1978, p. 92.

be some leeway for citizens to practice religion and to develop their national cultures, but relations with the minority nationalities might be exacerbated due to the National Bolsheviks' unwavering adherence to a "one and indivisible Russia." Steps would almost certainly be taken to alleviate the country's economic and demographic problems, and the decollectivization of agriculture would probably be initiated. Jews would most likely be encouraged to emigrate; if they refused, they might be thrown out.

In foreign affairs, National Bolsheviks might be expansionist—the fascist nature of the movement renders this likely—though attention would probably be focused more on contiguous areas, such as Iran, Afghanistan, Pakistan, Manchuria, and Japan, than on geographically remote areas, such as Southern Africa or Central America. The specter of a "Jewish-Masonic conspiracy" could be used to justify aggressive policies vis-à-vis Western Europe and the United States, though such a development is not inevitable.

To summarize, the distinguishing marks of the National Bolshevik variant of contemporary Russian nationalism may be described as: (1) a neo-pagan, militaristic cult of the strength and invincibility of the Russian people; (2) a militant and aggressive stance toward Russia's perceived internal and external enemies; (3) a strong anti-Western orientation, at times linked to a belief in a "Jewish-Masonic conspiracy"; (4) an awareness of the country's serious demographic and social problems but a lack of *angst* concerning the future, a "can-do" mentality; (5) a tendency to advocate racial purity and to disapprove of marriages between Russians and representatives of other nationalities; (6) adherence to a "single stream" view of Russian history; (7) a nonreligious but not antireligious posture; and (8) a cult of discipline and of heroic vitalism.

As should be evident, National Bolsheviks and *vozrozhdentsy* share a number of concerns and attitudes, and it is this large area of common interest that allows one to view both tendencies as being "Russian nationalist." Both tendencies are preservationist, seeking to safeguard Russian historical monuments and the environment from defilement and destruction; both deplore present demographic and social trends that are seen as unfavorable to the well-being of the Russian people; both are "polycentric" nationalists, desiring, at least explicitly, the cultural flourishing of all nationalities. In addition, both tendencies exhibit a keen interest in Russian conservative and patriotic thought of the past, though, as a rule, *vozrozhdentsy* are likely to align themselves with the Early Slavophiles, Dostoevskii, and the *Vekhi* authors, while National Bolsheviks are drawn to such "realistic" thinkers as Danilevskii and Leont'ev. The principal differences between the two tendencies lie in their attitude toward Russian Orthodoxy and in their willingness to achieve at least a temporary *modus vivendi* with Marxism-Leninism. Orthodoxy represents the pivot of the thought of most *vozrozhdentsy*, while National Bolsheviks lean toward a quasi-deification of the Russian *narod*. In the eyes of the *vozrozhdentsy*, there can be no accommodation with atheistic, "internationalist," Russophobic, anti-village Marxism-Leninism; National Bolsheviks, on the other hand, are willing to make tactical compromises with it. Other differences center on the question of military-industrial and urban growth—which National Bolsheviks would not oppose, though many of them have strong ecological views—and on the wisdom of conducting an expansionist foreign policy. At times, *vozrozhdentsy* and National Bolsheviks come into conflict—such a difference of opinion seems to have been at least partly behind the 1973-1974 split of *Veche* editors and authors into two opposing camps—but the two tendencies are often able to recognize a communality of interest, as in Solzhenitsyn's generally approving comments, contained in his literary memoirs, on Viktor Chalmaev and the *Molodaia gvardiia* orientation of the late sixties. Il'ia Glazunov's 1978 Manezh exhibit drew praise both from the official nationalist journal *Nash sovremennik* and from such *vozrozhdentsy* as Fr. Dimitrii Dudko and Leonid Borodin.[50]

[50] Oleg Volkov, "Ia uvidel Rossiiu," *Nash sovremennik*, no. 3 (1979), 174-183; Fr. Dimitrii Dudko, "O vystavke khudozhnika Il'i Glazunova," *Russkaia*

As far as the strength of the two tendencies is concerned, the *vozrozhdentsy*, with their close ties to the fifty-million-member Russian Orthodox Church, would appear to have the advantage of numbers, while the National Bolsheviks would seem to be better positioned actually to assume power. National Bolshevik arguments would presumably prove more acceptable to the present members of the Politburo, the Soviet Military Command, and the KGB than would the more radical proposals of the *vozrozhdentsy*, such as those contained in Solzhenitsyn's *Letter to the Soviet Leaders* and the VSKhSON program. According to Alain Besançon, Brezhnev was "accomplishing the goals of National Bolshevism without admitting it."[51] While this statement is too strong—Brezhnev attempted throughout his reign to balance National Bolshevism and Marxist-Leninist purism—Besançon is probably correct in seeing the political tide as running toward the National Bolsheviks. However, if the National Bolsheviks were to come to power, they would be much more vulnerable to the arguments of the intellectually more sophisticated *vozrozhdentsy*, with whom they have numerous ideational and emotional links, than are present-day Marxist-Leninists. (This was also the belief of the late Andrei Amal'rik.)[52] A possible scenario, therefore, would be a brief National Bolshevik interregnum followed by a *vozrozhdenets* period of rule.

SEVERAL MARGINAL TENDENCIES

Several other tendencies which are frequently termed Russian nationalist ought to be discussed at this juncture. What

---

mysl', 24 August 1978, p. 5; and Leonid Borodin, "Po povodu vystavki I. Glazunova," *Russkoe vozrozhdenie*, no. 5 (1979), 61-74. Mikhail Kheifets's article "Russkii patriot Vladimir Osipov," *Kontinent*, no. 27 (1981), 159-214, and no. 28 (1981), 134-179, offers useful, if at times subjective, information on the relations between "official" and dissenting nationalists.

[51] "La Technique du Pouvoir," p. 94. On this trend within the Brezhnev regime, see also Carl A. Linden, "Marxism-Leninism: Systemic Legitimacy and Political Culture," in Teresa Rakowska-Harmstone, ed., *Perspectives for Change in Communist Societies*, Boulder, Colorado, 1979, pp. 42-49.

[52] Andrei Amal'rik, "Ideologii v sovetskom obshchestve," *Russkaia mysl'*, 9 September 1976, p. 5, and 16 September 1976, p. 5.

Evgenii Vagin calls "semi-official Russophilism" (*ofitsioznyi rusofilizm*) is defined by him as a cynical and manipulative attitude toward Russian nationalism exhibited by those close to the center of power.[53] This tendency uses the words "Russian" and "Soviet" interchangeably and refuses to renounce the "internationalist essence" of the politics of the present Soviet leadership. It maintains a purely "souvenir" attitude toward Russia's past. Since the "semi-official Russophiles" have few, if any, ideas, and since they are essentially temporizers, their future is probably limited.

Another tendency is that of neo-Stalinism, a surprisingly weak current considering the authoritarian proclivities of many present-day Soviet intellectuals. Ivan Shevtsov's novel *Vo imia otsa i syna* (In the Name of the Father and the Son) was published in 1970 in an edition of 65,000 copies.[54] The title refers to the conflict of generations in contemporary Soviet society and of course echoes the title of the classic nineteenth-century novel by Turgenev; the work even has pretensions—quite unjustified—to being a *Fathers and Sons* for the present day. Shevtsov is more of an admirer of Stalin than the majority of National Bolsheviks and—what is the crucial test—favors the Stalinist policies of forced industrialization and forced collectivization; he is also virulently anti-*kulak*. No National Bolshevik would subscribe to such sentiments; the furthest one might go would be to hold, like Semanov, that the Soviet working class deserves attention no less than the peasantry. In Shevtsov's novel, on the other hand, the proletariat was elevated to a position of clear-cut superiority over the peasantry. The work calls to mind the received views of the years 1946-1953, the period of high Stalinism. "Homeland, Soviet regime, communist, working class"—these were Shevtsov's slogans. While he is vehemently anti-Semitic, he followed the lead of Stalin's ideologues in treating this question. "Trotskii was a Zionist, and his so-called 'party' a direct branch of Zionism," declares a "good Jew" in the novel, the

[53] "Litsom k Rossii," pp. 57-58.
[54] Ivan Shevtsov, *Vo imia otsa i syna: Roman*, Moscow, 1970. I have used a 1972 reprint of the book, issued by Prideaux Press (Letchworth, England).

Old Bolshevik Aron Gertsovich.[55] Like many National Bolsheviks, Shevtsov saw Trotskiite-Zionists at work, assisted by apostate Russians, seeking to corrode and bring down the mighty Soviet state. As was suggested above, Shevtsov's neo-Stalinist views are not widely held in the Soviet society of today.

There is, lastly, a tendency which may be accurately termed neo-Naziism. An example of this tendency is an anonymous letter sent in 1974 to the editors of *Veche*, which attempted to push the journal toward an overtly neo-Nazi position. Russian Orthodoxy was assailed by the letter's author as a "cosmopolitan" religion seeking to abolish all distinctions between nations, a form of "Judaism for *goyim*," while a renewal of the cult of pagan Slavic gods is seriously suggested as an outlet for religious impulses. The author, who clearly moved in official circles, insisted that only the Bolsheviks could preserve Russia from the world Zionist conspiracy. "The international Zionist concern," he warned, "has currently concentrated 80% of the capital of the nonsocialist world into its hands. This is more frightening than the fascist plague. If they win, that will mean death to all, and first of all to Russians, whom they have labeled zoological anti-Semites . . ."[56]

A second example: While serving a sentence in a concentration camp in the late sixties, the dissident attorney Iurii Handler, now in the emigration, encountered a supporter of neo-Naziism, Viktor Vandakurov. Vandakurov incessantly preached the danger of the "Jewish-Masonic conspiracy" and was an open admirer of Hitler, whose birthday he marked, apparently with the connivance of the prison authorities, by having printed pamphlets distributed with the inscription: "There is no god but Thor, and Adolf Hitler is his prophet." Vandakurov made no secret of his militantly anti-Christian sentiments, proclaiming that "the Jewish incense of Christ

---

[55] Ibid., p. 383.
[56] "Critical Comments of a Russian Regarding the Patriotic Journal *Veche*," in Michael Meerson-Aksenov and Boris Shragin, eds., *The Political, Social and Religious Thought of Russian "Samizdat"—An Anthology*, Belmont, Mass., 1977, p. 442.

has stunk up the whole world."[57] Though prepared to cooperate with the KGB for tactical reasons, Vandakurov did not conceal his loathing of the present communist regime.

Lurid and unsettling as they may be, such manifestations of neo-Naziism seem to be fringe phenomena, and the tendency is extremely unlikely to become dominant. Walter Laqueur has noted the interesting fact that in the Russian emigration, which might seem to have been a good breeding ground for extremist ideologies, "German racialist theories did not in fact find many supporters among the Russians, whatever their political persuasion . . ."[58] One would have to distort the facts grossly to see the neo-Nazis as being even close to preponderant in the present alignment of ideologies in the USSR. Their virulent hostility to Russian Orthodoxy renders them particularly loathsome to many Russian nationalists.

Such, then, are the "faces" of contemporary Russian nationalism. As should be clear from this analysis, it is my belief that the West should do what it can—in the sense of both undertaking new initiatives and ceasing counterproductive practices—to strengthen the *vozrozhdenets* tendency. In chapter 11, I shall make some suggestions concerning how this might be accomplished.

RUSSIAN NATIONALISM AND THE BREZHNEV SUCCESSION

The death of General Secretary Brezhnev in November 1982, combined with the earlier death of Suslov and the removal of Kirilenko from the Politburo—that is, the departure of the first, second, and third Party secretaries—signaled the end of an era in Soviet politics. At the time of this writing (late December 1982), it is too early to gauge the full impact of these

---

[57] From a presentation by Handler at the ninth annual convention of the American Association for the Advancement of Slavic Studies, Washington, 1977. I have also spoken with Handler privately concerning his views on this tendency.

[58] Laqueur, *Russia and Germany*, pp. 113-114.

events on the fortunes of contemporary Russian nationalism. While a new general secretary, Iurii Andropov, has been appointed, it would certainly be premature to claim that the Brezhnev succession is over; Soviet successions can take as long as five years to work through their various stages.

There appear to be at least several Russian nationalist sympathizers in the post-Brezhnev leadership. Two of them, according to previous assertions by Agurskii, are Mikhail Solomentsev (b. 1913), a candidate member of the Politburo and chairman of the RSFSR Council of Ministers, and Ivan Kapitonov (b. 1915), a member of the Central Committee Secretariat and head of the Party Work Committee.[59] There seems to be independent confirmation for Agurskii's belief. For example, on 8 September 1980, only Solomentsev and Kapitonov among the top leadership chose to attend a solemn Kremlin reception marking the 600th anniversary of the Russian victory at Kulikovo Field, an event replete with mobilizational and patriotic significance.[60] According to Agurskii, Solomentsev and Kapitonov appear, at times, to receive cautious support in their activities from Viktor Grishin (b. 1914), first secretary of the Moscow City Committee and a long-time full member of the Politburo.[61]

Such evidence as is presently available suggests that Russian nationalist sympathizers did not support Andropov in his drive for power, particularly in the critical period between May and November 1982, when he gave up the directorship of the KGB to become a member of the Party secretariat. It appears noteworthy that Kapitonov, who had exercised considerable power,[62] suffered what Jerry Hough has termed a

[59] Mikhail Agurskii, "Klokochushchii vulkan," *Russkaia mysl'*, 18 September 1980, p. 13; 25 September 1980, p. 12; 2 October 1980, p. 10; and 9 October 1980, p. 11.

[60] O. Krasovskii, "Pole Kulikovo," *Veche: Nezavisimyi russkii al'manakh*, no. 1 (1981), 64. On the significance of Kulikovo Field for Russian nationalists, see *Moskva*, nos. 7-9 (1980).

[61] Agurskii, "Klokochushchii vulkan," *passim.*

[62] Writing in 1973, Zbigniew Brzezinski saw Kapitonov as a strong candidate to be the next Party first secretary: "Twenty Years after Stalin Who Will Succeed Brezhnev?," *New Leader*, 19 March 1973, pp. 6-9. In a book published in 1980, Seweryn Bialer placed Kapitonov second to Grishin as the

"significant reduction in status" in early June, immediately after Andropov moved over to the secretariat.[63] According to Hough, this "was also a sign that one of Grishin's main hopes was not going to be of any help . . ."[64] The "Andropov group" in the Politburo is said to consist of Defense Minister Ustinov, Foreign Minister Gromyko, Kazakh Party chief Kunaev, and Ukrainian First Secretary Shcherbitskii (they would presumably be joined by the new full member of the Politburo, Geidar Aliev).[65] Several sources maintain that Ustinov and Gromyko, in particular, offered critical support to Andropov in the struggle with his rivals, Konstantin Chernenko and Grishin.[66]

From a Russian nationalist perspective, an Andropov general secretaryship must be worrisome for several reasons. First, Andropov seems to have relied to a significant extent on the support of non-Russians such as Kunaev and Shcherbitskii. Second, Andropov has evidently drawn support "from technocrats eager for a powerful leadership."[67] The technocrats are, of course, declared enemies of the nationalists, who are seen as thwarting the technical and industrial progress of the USSR. In the person of Defense Minister Ustinov, the heavy

---

most likely successor to Brezhnev: *Stalin's Successors*, Cambridge, 1980, p. 77.

[63] Jerry F. Hough, "Soviet Succession: Issues and Personalities," *Problems of Communism*, September-October 1982, p. 39. In supporting this contention, Hough writes: "In recent years, Kapitonov always signed obituaries out of alphabetical order as the first of the CC secretaries not on the Politburo. That is, he signed in front of Dolgikh and Mikhail Zimyanin ('Z' comes before 'K' in the Russian alphabet). . . . beginning with an obituary printed in *Pravda*, June 9, 1982, p. 3, Kapitonov's name was listed in alphabetical order after Zimyanin" (ibid., no. 100). Kapitonov may, however, be attempting a comeback. In an obituary for Mikhail Georgadze appearing in the 25 November 1982 issue of *Pravda* (p. 5), his name once again appears before that of Zimianin.

[64] Hough, "Soviet Succession," p. 39.

[65] "A Top Cop Takes the Helm," *Time*, 22 November 1982, p. 19, footnote. The placement of the Politburo leaders on the Lenin Mausoleum when Andropov delivered the eulogy for Brezhnev would seem to confirm such an interpretation. See the photograph in the *New York Times*, 16 November 1982, p. 7.

[66] E.g., *Newsweek*, 22 November 1982, p. 34.

[67] Ibid., p. 32.

industry-defense complex appears to have tendered powerful, perhaps decisive support to Andropov. Finally, Andropov's reliance on a "KGB mafia" to achieve his aims at least in the initial period of his leadership must be of concern to the nationalists, for obvious reasons.

Assuming that we have witnessed only the initial stages of a protracted succession process, what nationalist constituencies could play a role in the ongoing struggle? The provincial (*obkom* and *kraikom*) first Party secretaries represent one such constituency. In his recent study of ethnic Russian provincial first secretaries, Seweryn Bialer discovered that "almost 70 percent of this group, an astonishing proportion, have been employed throughout their careers in only one province . . ."[68] This factor, which is in sharp contrast to the pronounced mobility of the Brezhnev generation of Party leaders, serves to reinforce localist tendencies. Agurskii has noted that RSFSR *obkom* secretaries are natural allies of Russian nationalists, since they see their political base—Russians themselves—being seriously eroded by unfavorable social, demographic, and economic trends and developments.[69] Petr Proskurin's artistically weak but politically bold novel, *Imia tvoe* (Thy Name), published in 1976, which features an *obkom* first secretary as one of its central characters, offers an inkling of how such an alliance could operate in practice.[70] The *obkom* first secretaries are, of course, well represented on the Party Central Committee, a body which could be called upon to play a role in the succession.

Along with provincial Party first secretaries, the Soviet military is the constituency most likely to add a Russian nationalist dimension to the succession struggle. The intervention

[68] Bialer, *Stalin's Successors*, p. 121. "The core of my sample," Bialer explained, "consists of twenty-two Russian first *obkom* secretaries in the RSFSR. For comparative purposes this group is augmented by first secretaries in the Ukraine and Belorussia and Russian secretaries in the non-Slav republics, altogether a group of thirty-seven individuals" (p. 115, note 26).

[69] Agurskii, "Klokochushchii vulkan," p. 13, and Mikhail Agursky, "The New Russian Literature," Research Paper 40 (1980), Soviet and East European Research Center, Hebrew University of Jerusalem, pp. 15-17.

[70] Petr Proskurin, *Imia tvoe*, Moscow, 1978.

of army leaders was an important factor in the Stalin succession and could figure in the Brezhnev succession as well. As Myron Rush has observed, the most likely role of military chiefs in the Brezhnev succession is "as an ally of a faction in the Party leadership."[71] For mobilizational reasons, the military would appear to have a natural affinity for Russian nationalism. This is probably also true of the important paramilitary organization, DOSAAF, which numbers some 40 to 65 million members.[72]

One wonders how the military will react to Andropov's reliance on the aforementioned "KGB mafia" to achieve his ends and to the pronounced presence of non-Slavs on his "team." Andropov's evident hostility to Russian nationalism and apparent indifference to all ideologies can hardly sit well among those concerned with mobilizational matters. It should be noted that some Western specialists believe that the influence of the Soviet military will inevitably increase in the coming years. Michel Tatu, for example, believes that the USSR "may be a military dictatorship by the end of the century—possibly by the end of the decade."[73] And Jerry Hough reports that there are "major American specialists" who privately predict a military dictatorship in the Soviet Union.[74] A military dictatorship, as distinct from a KGB-dominated dictatorship, would be likely to have a Russian nationalist coloration.

As has been pointed out, Russian nationalists are also influential in such "transmission belt" bodies as the Komsomol and the Union of Soviet Writers, and they have numerous sympathizers in such mass voluntary organizations as the All-Russian Society for the Preservation of Historical and Cultural Monuments. While not likely to be directly involved in the succession, such bodies, through the perceived sentiments of their members, could affect the "climate" in which the succession takes place.

[71] Myron Rush, *Political Succession in the USSR*, 2nd ed., New York, 1968, p. 156.
[72] William E. Odom, "The 'Militarization' of Soviet Society," *Problems of Communism*, September-October 1976, p. 45.
[73] Cited in *Newsweek*, 22 November 1982, p. 42.
[74] Hough, "Soviet Succession," p. 27.

They may at present be "down" (though they are certainly not "out") in the succession struggle, but the nationalists should continue to be a potent force in Soviet society in the foreseeable future. In a sharp attack on the nationalists published in 1980 as part of the mass-edition *Roman-gazeta* series, Anatolii Anan'ev, editor of the journal *Oktiabr'*, paid a backhand compliment to the influence of the nationalists. Nationalism, he warned, is a "seductive worm" which has succeeded in penetrating into Soviet literature, into art, and into "many other offices," but "the most dangerous thing" of all, he cautions, would be if the Russian people itself should bite at this terrible "bait."[75] Whether this "bait" will be taken is of interest not merely to the editor of *Oktiabr'*.

[75] Anatolii Anan'ev, *Gody bez voiny*, vol. 2, Moscow, 1979, p. 111.

11

Theoretical Considerations and
Policy Recommendations

> L'identification du communisme à la Russie est, pour moi, extrêmement dangereuse. Le communisme n'est pas d'essence proprement russe. Il n'est que la mutation, en milieu russe, d'un agent qui était né ailleurs.
>
> Alain Besançon[1]

> Not only are the terms 'Russian' and 'Soviet,' 'Russia' and 'USSR' not interchangeable, not equivalent, and not unilinear—they are irreconcilable polar opposites and completely exclude each other.
>
> Aleksandr Solzhenitsyn[2]

This concluding chapter will deal with several theoretical questions connected with the study of Russian nationalism and then essay some recommendations concerning the policy which the West, and more particularly the United States, ought to develop toward the phenomenon examined in this book. It will be shown that present attitudes toward Russian nationalism in the West are often ill-informed and counterproductive and may even be potentially threatening to world peace.

IS RUSSIAN NATIONALISM IN FACT
A NATIONALISM?

I have frequently employed the word "nationalism" in this study without, however, addressing the theoretical issue of

---

[1] "La Technique du Pouvoir en URSS" (interview with Alain Besançon), *L'Express*, 2-9 December 1978, p. 95. On this question, see also Alain Besançon, *Présent soviétique et passé russe*, Paris, 1980.

[2] Aleksandr Solzhenitsyn, "Remarks at the Hoover Institution," *Russian Review*, 36, no. 2 (1977), 188.

whether or not the phenomenon being discussed does in fact constitute a nationalism. Modern theorists generally hold that nationalism represents a reaction to a perceived foreign rule. "The grievance," K. R. Minogue writes in his seminal study *Nationalism*, "must be caused by foreigners. . . . The point is that nationalism cannot be *purely* a struggle of internal factions within a country."[3] As has been shown, to Russian nationalists of all persuasions, Marxism is a foreign, un-Russian ideology, while the Marxist experiment in Russia has been antinational in essence. ". . . the murky whirlwind of *Progressive Ideology*," Solzhenitsyn wrote in *Letter to the Soviet Leaders*, "swept in on us from the West at the end of the last century, and has tormented and ravaged our soul quite enough . . ."[4] The Russian people, the nationalists believe, have been particularly victimized under Soviet rule—their religion, culture, history, and language have all been subjected to barbaric and nihilistic assault. During the period from 1917 to 1934, Russian national consciousness was almost obliterated, and even today it remains in shackles, at a time when the country faces grave social, demographic, and military threats.

As in the case of other countries, industrialization, modernization, and the spread of popular education have served as catalysts for the rise of nationalism in the USSR. This has in fact been especially true in the Soviet Union, where modernization has been carried out with breathtaking rapidity and almost unmatched ruthlessness. The drastic decline of the village and the accompanying failure of Russian agriculture, the drop in the Russian birthrate, a marked increase in alcoholism and juvenile delinquency, the brutal persecution of the national culture and religion—all have resulted from a frenetic modernization which has been justified and promoted in the name of Marxist-Leninist ideology. The sons and grandsons of Russian peasants who have received an education in Soviet institutes and universities begin to suspect that something is fundamentally wrong in the USSR's crowded

[3] K. R. Minogue, *Nationalism*, London, 1967, p. 26 (italics in the original).
[4] Aleksandr Solzhenitsyn, *Letter to the Soviet Leaders*, New York, 1974, p. 18 (italics in the original).

and polluted cities. Vladimir Soloukhin, a scion of the peasantry, becomes an exemplar of the contemporary nationalist as he returns to his native village and attempts to save the icons, centuries-old books, and utensils of the local church from destruction. Even today, as has been noted, Russia remains remarkably close to her peasant roots, to the spontaneity and traditionalism of agricultural man.

Referring to the phenomenon of the awakening of national consciousness, Minogue writes: "The first stage may be loosely labeled *stirrings*. This is the period in which the nation becomes aware of itself as a nation suffering oppression. Frequently it is a period of revulsion against foreign ideas and foreign ways of doing things. It is the time of casting around for a cultural identity. It is likely, for example, that a religion which was abandoned in the first flush of enthusiasm for foreign ideas will be revived."[5] Clearly the Soviet Union has been going through the stage of national stirrings; they were stimulated by the concessions made by Stalin to patriotic and religious sentiment in the post-1934 period, and they have been increasing in strength since the late 1950s. The process was accelerated by Khrushchev's "secret speech," which dealt a serious, if unintended, blow to Marxist orthodoxy, and it began to speed up even more in the late sixties. At present, Minogue's second stage, "the struggle for independence," may well be in process of emerging.[6] Traditionally, the "fixed terminus" of this stage, according to Minogue, has been the attainment of sovereign independence, i.e., in the case of the Soviet Union, the assumption of power by Russian nationalists. Minogue's third and last stage, "the process of consolidation," would begin to occur once the nationalists were in power and had begun implementing policy.

An "Interrupted" Nationalism

Is, however, Minogue's schema appropriate to contemporary Soviet Russia? Did not, after all, a strong current of Rus-

<hr/>

[5] Minogue, *Nationalism*, p. 26 (italics in original).
[6] Ibid., p. 27.

sian nationalism manifest itself in the nineteenth and early twentieth centuries? Patently, what we have is an "interrupted" or delayed nationalism. The process begun by Khomiakov and Kireevskii—or perhaps by Karamzin, Fonvizin, and Prince Shcherbatov of the previous generation[7]—lost out to its Westernizer opponents, among whom the Marxist-Leninists eventually emerged supreme. During the period from 1917 to 1934, Russian national consciousness was subjected to fierce attack, and the assault, in lesser form, continues up to the present day. Since 1934, however, Russian nationalism has been rebounding. To take one example, Fedor Dostoevskii, roundly defeated by his nineteenth-century arch-rival Chernyshevskii, has been making a dramatic comeback, particularly in the post-Stalin era. The Russian populace is now incomparably better educated than it was before the revolution and hence better able to grasp the views of nationalist spokesmen and theoreticians. It also has a great culture and a religious civilization of a thousand years' duration to look back upon and compare with the USSR's sparse achievements. Finally, contemporary Russians have been taught a stern and indelible lesson by the Stalin holocaust.

A "MODERN" FORM OF NATIONALISM?

A related question concerns whether present-day Russian nationalism can be considered a "modern" form of nationalism. When Count Uvarov proclaimed his famous triad of "Orthodoxy, Autocracy, and Nationality (*Narodnost*')" in 1833, he was citing two traditional legitimizing props of the Russian state and adding a third—*narodnost'*. What Uvarov did not realize was that there is inevitably a degree of tension between nationalism and other, older forms of legitimization. "Nationalism," Hugh Seton-Watson notes, "in fact provides a new principle of *legitimacy* for government, an alternative to

---

[7] See Hans Rogger, *National Consciousness in Eighteenth-Century Russia*, Cambridge, Mass., 1960, and Richard Pipes, *Karamzin's Memoir on Ancient and Modern Russia*, Cambridge, Mass., 1959.

the traditional legitimacy of monarch and religion."[8] Rousseau, the founder of modern nationalism, identified "nation" with "people," and nationalism as a whole has a tendency to substitute the nation for God. This religious dimension of modern nationalism explains the fanaticism of many of its adherents, their willingness to die for their cause.

If the National Bolshevik tendency moves in the direction of fascism, a modern form of nationalism, and generally denies or downplays the importance of religion and monarchy, the *vozrozhdentsy*, by contrast, hold that God and the Orthodox faith are higher than the nation, and many of them construct a second breakwater against fascism—a belief in the necessity of a divinely anointed monarch, a hypostasis of the nation. Like the early Slavophiles and Dostoevskii, many *vozrozhdentsy* seem unclear on what emphasis to give to the *narod*. Vadim Borisov, writing in the collection *From under the Rubble*, seeks to free the idea of nation from its pagan accretions by going back to the Bible. Thus, among contemporary Russian nationalists, modern and traditional legitimizations live side by side and, to some extent, engage in struggle. It is not, incidentally, at all inevitable that the more "modern" version of nationalism, i.e., fascism, should triumph, especially given the strong support for Orthodoxy and, to a lesser degree, monarchy among the populace. Another possibility would be the emergence of a hybrid, perhaps transitional, form of nationalism combining modern and traditional elements, such as occurred, for example, in Franco's Spain.

"Movement" or "Renaissance"?

It will have been noted that I have consistently eschewed use of the word "movement" in describing the activities of contemporary Russian nationalists. In the dictionary sense of the word—"a series of organized activities by people working concertedly toward some goal"—the term is obviously an inaccurate one for this phenomenon. Many nationalist spokes-

---

[8] Hugh Seton-Watson, *Nationalism and Communism*, New York, 1964, p. 4 (italics in original).

men, like Solzhenitsyn, opt for the word "renaissance" (*vozrozhdenie*) to describe the recent religious and national upsurge.[9] Shafarevich's statement, "I do not belong to any group . . . But I think that many hold views close to mine,"[10] appears to be typical of the perception many nationalists have of their ties to like-minded Soviet citizens. At times, however, Russian nationalist sympathizers are brought together in quasi-organizational fashion, the *Molodaia gvardiia* and *Veche* episodes being cases in point. Perhaps "a renaissance in process of becoming a movement" or "in search of a movement" is the most appropriate way of describing the present condition of Russian nationalism.

COUNTERPRODUCTIVE APPROACHES IN THE WEST

What should be the policy of the United States, and of the West in general, toward the critically important and little-understood phenomenon that has been the subject of this study? Obviously, the answer depends to a large extent on one's analysis and assessment—both political and moral—of the phenomenon. Recently several approaches to the question of Russian nationalism—*counterproductive* approaches in my opinion—have received considerable attention and publicity in the United States.

In his books *Détente after Brezhnev* and *The Russian New Right*, recent émigré Aleksandr Ianov has urged the West to exert all of its powers, on the scale of a new Marshall Plan, to ensure that the nationalists, whom he sees as ineluctably evolving in a neo-Nazi direction, fail in their bid for power.[11] If adopted even in part (and I am told that Ianov has his admirers in the U.S. State Department), Ianov's recommendations would send an unmistakable signal to Russian nationalists in the USSR. Solzhenitsyn, who may be regarded as a

---

[9] See chapter 9, note 3.

[10] "Interv'iu korrespondentu gazety *Frankfurter Allgemeine Zeitung*," *Vestnik*, no. 126 (1978), 224-225.

[11] Alexander Yanov, *Détente after Brezhnev*, Berkeley, 1977, and *The Russian New Right*, Berkeley, 1978.

kind of roving nationalist ambassador, recently complained in a BBC interview which was beamed back to his countrymen:

> He [Ianov] has already published two books analyzing the USSR and is extremely hostile to everything Russian . . . In his books, for instance, you will find no hint that the Russian people might have some sort of religion or that this might have some significance in its history and aspirations. . . . Yet intellectual America lionises [such thinkers] because people here expect and want it to be like that: they want to make friends with communism and believe that Russia is bad. One after the other, American professors repeat: "At last, erudite scholars have come and explained to us what we must fear—not communism at all, but the national existence of the Russian people."[12]

Another nationalist spokesman in the emigration, Boris Paramonov, until recently a member of the Department of Philosophy of Leningrad State University, has published a lengthy rebuttal to Ianov's views in the émigré journal *Kontinent*. After demonstrating that Ianov's ideas are not original but stem primarily from Miliukov's well-known essay "The Decomposition of Slavophilism" and Vladimir Solov'ev's antinationalist polemics, Paramonov proceeds to contest Ianov's assertion that "the law of Russian nationalism is evolution in the direction of ideological justification of the worst forms of tyranny."[13] Ianov, Paramonov notes, "ironically admits his lack of competence" in judging the religious and moral problematics underlying Russian history, but this lack of competence is no laughing matter.[14] Similarly, Ianov, who sees Russia's present difficulties as entirely endemic to her historical de-

---

[12] *The Listener*, 22 February 1979, p. 271. Solzhenitsyn's statement also appeared in Aleksandr I. Solzhenitsyn, *East and West*, New York, 1980, pp. 169-170. For Ianov's reply to Solzhenitsyn's charges, see *The Listener*, 24 May 1979, p. 713. Solzhenitsyn elaborated on his views in his essay, "Misconceptions about Russia Are a Threat to America," *Foreign Affairs*, 58 (Spring 1980), pp. 797-834.

[13] Boris Paramonov, "Paradoksy i kompleksy Aleksandra Ianova," *Kontinent*, no. 20 (1979), 234. Ianov replied to Paramonov and other critics in *Sintaksis*, no. 8 (1980), 110-115.

[14] Paramonov, "Paradoksy," p. 239.

velopment, does not, as it were, "notice the date 1917, nor Marxism, nor the Bolshevik dictatorship, nor those Himalayas of evil which the followers of Marx raised up in Russia . . ."[15] The Soviet Marxists attempted to destroy everything positive which had sprouted from Russian soil over a period of a thousand years, "from Orthodox churches to wheat."[16] Paramonov also criticizes Ianov's favorable attitude toward Brezhnev and his belief that the only real choice is between "Brezhnev or a new Stalin."[17] The West's enemy is not Russian nationalism but Marxist ideology; it is Marxism, not nationalism, which demands the suppression of Western civilization.

An example of what happens when Ianov's ideas percolate downward is provided by Olga Carlisle's diatribe, "Reviving Myths of Holy Russia," which appeared in the *New York Times Magazine*.[18] (In her article, Carlisle admits an indebtedness to Ianov's *The Russian New Right*.) Since being rebuked in print by Solzhenitsyn for her role in the publication of two of his works, Carlisle, the daughter of a Russian émigré, has on several occasions made use of the press to attack the novelist and the religious and national tendency which he represents. Her essay in the *Times* is poorly researched and replete with factual errors and uninformed assertions. In her opinion, Vladimir Osipov is an "extremist" and a "Great Russian chauvinist," while Il'ia Glazunov is "an execrable painter." As for Solzhenitsyn, he is said to propose a "restoration of the Orthodox Church" (although in fact he believes that the Church should be separate from the state) and "a voluntary abandonment of modern technology" (when actually he advocates the use of the most advanced modern technology in a context of economic decentralization). Carlisle's view of Russian nationalism is, in short, a caricatured one, in which its most "lib-

---

[15] Ibid., p. 245.
[16] Ibid., p. 246.
[17] Ibid., p. 264.
[18] Olga Carlisle, "Reviving Myths of Holy Russia," *New York Times Magazine*, 16 September 1979.

eral" representatives, such as Solzhenitsyn and Osipov, are depicted as virtual Nazis.

An equally dismal, though far more scholarly, opinion of contemporary Russian nationalism is provided in the writings of Harvard historian Richard Pipes. In his important, albeit one-sided, study, *Russia under the Old Regime*,[19] and in subsequent essays, Pipes expresses the belief that the continuities between Old Russia and the Soviet Union far outweigh any discontinuities and that, consequently, the discarding of Marxist-Leninist ideology would be likely to have little practical effect on the political or social life of the country. No matter what her political form of government, Russia will continue her oppressive and repressive way. In an essay on Solzhenitsyn, Pipes points to "the remarkable continuity of Russian intellectual history, especially its conservative strain . . . Each generation of Russians seems to discover afresh the same answers, partly because the problems which they confront, decade after decade, remain so strikingly similar."[20] Whatever the justness of Pipes' historical interpretations— and they have been criticized on some points by such specialists as Donald Treadgold, Nicholas Riasanovsky, and Dorothy Atkinson[21]—the wisdom of their applicability to the West's dealings with the Soviet Union is another matter.

In a talk given to the Hoover Institution in 1976, Solzhenitsyn fulminated against Western historical studies of Russia which distort the nation's past and proclaim "a persistent and tendentious generalization about 'the perennial Russian slave mentality,' seen almost as an inherited characteristic . . ."[22] Singling out Pipes' *Russia under the Old Regime* for harsh and at times unfair criticism (whatever else it is, Pipes' study is surely not "pseudoacademic"), Solzhenitsyn warned of the

[19] Richard Pipes, *Russia under the Old Regime*, New York, 1974.
[20] Richard Pipes, "Solzhenitsyn and the Russian Intellectual Tradition," *Encounter*, June 1979, p. 53.
[21] Treadgold's review of *Russia under the Old Regime* appeared in *Slavic Review*, 34, no. 4 (1975), 812-814; Riasanovsky's in *Russian Review*, 35, no. 1 (1976), 103-104; and Atkinson's in *American Historical Review*, 81, no. 2 (1976), 423-424.
[22] Solzhenitsyn, "Remarks at the Hoover Institution," p. 187.

dangers of overstressing the continuities between Old Russia and the Soviet Union and of thereby downplaying the ruinous significance of Marxist ideology.

In an essay published two years later, Solzhenitsyn's former associate, Irina Ilovaiskaia, currently editor of the prestigious émigré weekly *Russkaia mysl'*, elaborates upon the novelist's criticism of Pipes' book.[23] Ilovaiskaia sharply contests Pipes' thesis concerning Russia's "mystically determined striving toward a police regime" and accuses her opponent of failing to see that communism is a "pan-human disease" and "a terrible suppression and distortion of Russian history . . ."[24] Pipes' book and similar modern studies of Russia, she says, betray a striking, if unintentional, form of racism: Russians are seen as inherent and immutable barbarians. Moreover, Ilovaiskaia continues, Pipes' chapter on religion shows his helplessness in dealing with spiritual phenomena:

> Richard Pipes completely ignores the whole rich flower of Russian spirituality, naturally ignoring its deep influence on popular life as well. He needs only the testimony of Belinskii to enlist the whole Russian people in a heap as atheists. He does not vouchsafe one word concerning the innumerable Russian saints and ascetics; even St. Sergii of Radonezh is simply not mentioned in the book. . . . And concerning the role of the Church in the Time of Troubles there is not one word.[25]

Pipes' interpretation of Russian history, Ilovaiskaia concludes, is "extraordinarily dangerous for the whole world," since it serves to conceal the international essence of communism.[26]

Wladislaw Krasnow, a Soviet defector who has been living in the United States since the early sixties, has also criticized Pipes' views. Krasnow is particularly exercised by Pipes' bleak opinion of the Russian peasantry: "Apparently sharing Marx's

---

[23] Irina Ilovaiskaia, "Rossiia v otritsatel'no-misticheskom osveshchenii," *Vestnik*, no. 126 (1978), 193-206.
[24] Ibid., pp. 194, 195.
[25] Ibid., p. 200.
[26] Ibid., p. 206.

bias against the 'idiocy of rural life,' Pipes also seems to share his low opinion of the Russian nation as a whole. Since the majority of Russians have descended from peasants . . . all Russians except [the] intelligentsia, Pipes argues, cannot be trusted because they are bound to be guided by no higher moral standard than Social Darwinism of the 'pike-and-carps' syndrome."[27] Pipes' *Russia Under the Old Regime*, Krasnow believes, is especially dangerous for the effect that it could have on United States foreign policy—i.e., it could foster a conviction that "the Soviet leaders are expressing nothing but the collective psychology and historic aspirations of the Russian people."[28]

It seems abundantly clear that the view of Russian history held by Pipes at least until early 1980,[29] a view which in its essential contours is shared by many American scholars and at least some diplomats, serves strongly to exacerbate anti-Western sentiment among even the most moderate Russian nationalists. Professor Pipes and his colleagues are, of course, entitled to express their beliefs concerning Russian historical development and to make predictions about the country's future evolution. If, however, their interpretations were to become the view of the United States government, or were to be perceived as such, then we should not be surprised at a marked growth of hostility on the part of Russian nationalists. My own view on the issue in dispute between Pipes and the nationalists is that, while there are indeed important continuities between Old Russia and the Soviet Union, there are even more significant discontinuities—the most crucial being the USSR's adherence to Marxist-Leninist ideology. Not only

[27] Wladislaw G. Krasnow, "Richard Pipes's Foreign Strategy: Anti-Soviet or Anti-Russian?," *Russian Review*, 38, no. 2 (1979), 188. See also Richard Pipes, "Response to Wladislaw G. Krasnow," *Russian Review*, 38, no. 2 (1979), 192-197.

[28] Krasnow, "Richard Pipes's Foreign Strategy," p. 189.

[29] In an article entitled "Soviet Global Strategy," which appeared in *Commentary* (April 1980, pp. 31-39) shortly before he entered the government, Pipes effected an unexpected *volte-face*, placing the emphasis on Marxist-Leninist ideology rather than on Russian historical continuities as a key to understanding Soviet expansionist behavior. If Pipes has indeed changed his mind, he has offered no explanation.

Solzhenitsyn, but major contemporary thinkers who could not by any stretch of the imagination be termed Russian nationalists—for example, Nadezhda Mandelstam and Aleksandr Zinov'ev[30]—have shown the importance of Marxist-Leninist doctrine for correctly understanding the Soviet Union. Were the USSR to rid itself of Marxist ideology, the consequences, as Alain Besançon has said, would amount to a revolution, and major changes would necessarily ensue.[31] Like Ianov, a thinker with whom he is in disagreement on a number of points, Pipes fails to see the significance of Marxist ideology in today's Soviet Union or the dangers which a perpetuation of Marxist-Leninist legitimacy in the USSR portend, for example in the Middle East, Southern Africa, or Central America.

There are, to be sure, unattractive and potentially threatening currents within the ranks of contemporary Russian nationalists. Could it be otherwise in a country which has suffered numbing losses of life in the past sixty years—both Solzhenitsyn and the late Andrei Amal'rik have contended that some 60 million Soviet citizens perished during the various phases of the terror[32]—as well as nearly unprecedented social, demographic, and moral dislocation and perhaps the most intense persecution of a Christian religion in 2,000 years?[33] But there exist positive and even edifying currents within the same movement. It is my belief that the West should encourage and support, in word and in action, that influential and perhaps dominant tendency which, following Solzhenitsyn, I have called the "Russian national and religious renais-

[30] Nadezhda Mandelstam, *Hope against Hope*, New York, 1970, and *Hope Abandoned*, New York, 1974; and Alexander Zinoviev, *The Yawning Heights*, New York, 1979.

[31] "La Technique du Pouvoir," p. 92.

[32] Solzhenitsyn, *Letter*, p. 30, and Andrei Amalrik, "Victims of Yalta," *Harper's*, May 1979, p. 91.

[33] Alain Besançon writes: "Except during World War II and during the moral NEP . . . the Orthodox Church [in the Soviet Union] has been subjected to the longest and most intense persecution in recorded history, exclusive of the persecution of the Catholic Church in Japan during the seventeenth century. Unlike Japan, Russia had been Christian for a thousand years." (*The Soviet Syndrome*, New York, 1978, p. 26.)

sance," and that it should seek to strengthen this tendency's hand against rival, less promising strands, such as National Bolshevism. The religious proclivities of the *vozrozhdentsy* should strike a responsive chord in the United States, which has traditionally harbored fugitives from religious oppression, while their ecological and preservationist concerns, as well as their desire to come to mutual understanding with the minority nationalities of the USSR, should elicit sympathy rather than opprobrium. Moreover, the tendency's isolationist leanings should be of interest to even the most parochial of American policy makers. Among other results, an inward-looking, nonmilitaristic Russia could save American taxpayers millions of dollars in armament outlays. National Bolshevism, on the other hand, like the Brezhnev synthesis of communism, militarism, and patriotism, could constitute an expansionist threat and place considerable strain on Western military and economic resources.

POLICY RECOMMENDATIONS

The first concrete recommendation to grow out of this study is a semantic one. It is long past time for Western governments, diplomats, and media representatives to cease using interchangeably the words "Russia" and "USSR," "Russians" and "Soviets." This practice understandably irritates many Russian nationalists, who consider it akin to blasphemy to identify Russia and the Soviet Union, and it demoralizes minority nationalists, who prefer not to be called "Russians" at all. If the U.S. government and media were to begin employing these terms properly—as they generally do, for example, with the terms "British" and "English"—this problem, which, it should be stressed, is a major one, would soon disappear.

A second recommendation concerns the list of "captive nations" which, since 1959, Congress has commemorated each year in the third week of July. The present list includes such nations as Poland, Hungary, Lithuania, the Ukraine, Czechoslovakia, Latvia, and Estonia, but, strangely, does not mention Russia herself.[34] As Congressman McClorey of Illinois recently noted, this is an anomaly: ". . . many of the subjugated peoples who make up the Soviet empire are included in this list, but not the Great Russians themselves. . . . it is communism imposed by force which is the cause of there being so many captive nations in the Soviet orbit. The Russian people are not the perpetrators of this tyranny, but one of its chief victims."[35] If Russia were added to the list of "captive nations," it would not only correct an obvious error but would also, one suspects, send a helpful message—via the foreign radio—to ethnic Russians in the USSR: namely, that the United States deems its antagonist to be Marxist-Leninist ideology and not Russia herself.

A third recommendation is that the West begin to exert itself to understand "Slavophile" currents of the past and present. Such understanding will not come easily, especially in America where there are no readily identifiable political equivalents (the Tory tendency in Britain might be a Western analogue, but even there the similarities should not be exaggerated). Though a considerable Western academic literature exists on Russian Slavophiles and conservatives of the nineteenth and early twentieth centuries, knowledge of this literature is generally limited to specialists, and the literature itself is, in certain cases, biased against its subject matter. As should be obvious, a knowledge of Russian Orthodoxy is essential for comprehending the thought of a major wing of contemporary Russian nationalism, yet, as Robert Nichols and Theofanis Stavrou write in their introduction to a collection of essays devoted to the Russian Church in the two centuries preceding the revolution, "American scholarship in this area is in its infancy . . ."[36] Indeed, one could compile an embar-

[34] Public Law 86-90, *Laws of the 86th Congress-First Session*, 17 July 1959. The "captive nations" mentioned are: Poland, Hungary, Lithuania, Ukraine, Czechoslovakia, Latvia, Estonia, White Ruthenia, Rumania, East Germany, Bulgaria, mainland China, Armenia, Azerbaijan, Georgia, North Korea, Albania, Idel-Ural, Tibet, Cossackia, Turkestan, North Vietnam, "and others."

[35] *Congressional Record—House*, 15 July 1981, p. H4397.

[36] Robert L. Nichols and Theofanis George Stavrou, eds., *Russian Orthodoxy Under the Old Regime*, Minneapolis, 1978, p. vii.

rassing list of noted American universities and colleges in which not one course in Russian Orthodoxy is taught or has ever been taught.

Another goal of Western scholarship must be to disentangle the various strands of contemporary Russian nationalism. The tendency among at least some scholars is, as has been seen, to see the movement as an extremist monolith. Those who would tar all Russian nationalists with the brush of anti-Semitism would do well to heed the voice of Leonard Schapiro of the London School of Economics, chairman of the editorial board of *Soviet Jewish Affairs*, who has written:

> . . . it is not correct to identify [Russian] nationalism with antisemitism. Russian thought has traditionally been characterized by a combination of nationalist and Russian Orthodox attitudes in which suspicion of parliamentary democracy and respect for individual liberty are combined. Antisemitism forms no part of this tradition. The accusation of antisemitism occasionally made against Solzhenitsyn is false . . . The church in general is also free from antisemitism . . . The violent Black Hundred type of antisemitism which appears in *samizdat* literature is found among those who reject the church as part of the Judaic corruption of Russia. It may be presumed that this is the *samizdat* element which lies closest to the heart of the KGB . . .[37]

If one wished to send a favorable signal to the moderate nationalists, how would one go about doing it? The most obvious answer would be to make more astute use of foreign radio broadcasting, i.e., in the case of the United States, the Voice of America and Radio Liberty. As specialists are aware, an extraordinary situation presently obtains in the Soviet Union in which virtually everyone, from neo-Stalinist to *demokrat*, listens to the foreign radio, many of them regularly. That the regime is keenly aware of this is evident from a flow of books and articles decrying Western attempts at "ideological subversion" through broadcasting. None of this, however, ap-

[37] Leonard Schapiro, "Communist Antisemitism," *Soviet Jewish Affairs*, 1 (1979), 51-52.

pears to work, and the regime seems effectively to have lost control in this area.

Both Solzhenitsyn and Viktor Sokolov, a former editor of *Molodaia gvardiia* now in the emigration, believe that not enough is being done by the foreign radio in the critical spheres of "the Russian theme" and Russian Orthodoxy.[38] Specifically, they point out that Russian-language broadcasts are not generally aimed at ethnic Russians, whereas broadcasts in the languages of the minority peoples usually address the concerns of those peoples. In addition to being the administrative language of the Soviet Union, Russian happens to be the native tongue of over 137 million ethnic Russians. Indeed, through the foreign radio, the West has an excellent opportunity to influence the Russian national movement in a direction compatible with its own self-interest. Lending support to moderate and Christian elements in the movement might, furthermore, help to retard the emergence of a malignant and militarily expansionist right.

Another fruitful area deserving attention would be that of exchanges. Invitations could be extended, for example, to leaders of the Society for the Preservation of Historical and Cultural Monuments or to *derevenshchik* writers to visit the West, while Western preservationist organizations could be encouraged to send members to the Soviet Union. Similarly, exhibitions could be held in the USSR on the work of Western cultural figures, such as novelist William Faulkner, who are held in high regard by the nationalists.

Lastly, Western books and monographs on Russian nationalist currents and on Russian history should be systematically translated into Russian. Albert Gratieux's classic two-volume study on the Slavophiles might be an appropriate place to begin.[39] Theoretical studies on nationalism, monarchism, fascism, democracy, and law would all be useful. Once trans-

---

[38] Aleksandr Solzhenitsyn, "O rabote russkoi sektsii 'Bi-Bi-Si,' " *Kontinent*, no. 9 (1976), 210-223, and Viktor Sokolov, "Zapiski radioslushatelia," *Kontinent*, no. 12 (1977), 268-286.

[39] Albert Gratieux, *A. S. Khomiakov et le Mouvement Slavophile*, 2 vols., Paris, 1939.

lated and published, such works would eventually find their way into the Soviet Union, where they would be circulated in *samizdat*.

In advocating the adoption of such measures, I am not, it should be underlined, urging that the interests of minority nationalities in the USSR be passed over—to the contrary. But for the West to continue to ignore the concerns of ethnic Russians and the not-so-few Eastern Slavs who identify with them strikes one as folly.

To conclude, I would suggest that the problems facing contemporary Russian nationalists are truly immense and deserving of a response other than contempt. Near-catastrophic social and demographic dislocations, enormous population losses, the threat of a military conflict with China—a tendency that is wrestling with difficulties of such magnitude deserves sympathy rather than reflex condemnation. It is time for us to end our parochialism and begin to acquire the wisdom, will, and courage to see the Soviet Union for what it is and what it could shortly become.

Postscript

The following recent developments and events, which were not covered in the text of this book, seemed worthy of mention.

During 1981-1982, there occurred what might be called the "*Nash sovremennik* affair," an episode perhaps approaching in political significance the *Molodaia gvardiia* affair of the late sixties. Early in 1982, *Kommunist*, chief ideological organ of the Party Central Committee, published two sharp attacks on Vladimir Soloukhin for his "flirtation with goddie" (*zaigryvanie s bozhen'koi*) and his "religio-mystical ideas and sentiments" contained in aphoristic meditations, which had appeared in an article entitled "Pebbles in the Palm [of a Hand]," in an issue of *Nash sovremennik* a year earlier.[1] (Also in 1981, a lengthy article spread over three issues of the antireligious monthly *Nauka i religiia* had assailed Soloukhin for his defense of Orthodox Christian *startsy*. The journal awarded its principal prize for 1981 to the authors of this polemic.)

Soviet journalists are not ordinarily expected to question the views of *Kommunist* in ideological matters, but the editors of *Nash sovremennik* did just that. In issue no. 3 for 1982, the journal published another segment of "Pebbles in the Palm." *Kommunist* and its supporters then resolved to flex their muscles. Soloukhin was reportedly summoned before various organizations for prophylactic chats, and in May 1982, the chief editor and secretary of the Party organization

---

[1] In the discussion of this episode, I have relied heavily on two detailed accounts: "Napadki na Vl. Soloukhina," *Posev*, no. 4 (1982), 3-4, and M. Nazarov, "Dostignet li tseli 'literaturnoe' postanovlenie TsK?," *Posev*, no. 12 (1982), 50-55. It seems noteworthy that the *Kommunist* attack occurred immediately after the death of Suslov; this would appear to confirm reports that, at least in the last years of his life, Suslov served as a powerful protector of Russian nationalists in cultural matters. Recent émigré Semen Reznik reports that the 1978 and 1979 exhibits of Glazunov's paintings enjoyed the "personal support" of Suslov (Semen Reznik, "Kto takoi Sergei Semanov?," *Novaia gazeta*, 11-17 December 1982, p. 10). An American who was a frequent visitor to Glazunov's workshop in the late seventies provided me with the same information.

of *Nash sovremennik* were forced to write a letter of self-criticism, in which they acknowledged the criticism of Soloukhin contained in *Kommunist* to be "just" and promised to do better in the future. (This letter was eventually published in issue no. 8 of *Kommunist* for 1982.) Defiantly, the editors of *Nash sovremennik* then proceeded to publish powerful and polemical works by Valentin Rasputin and Georgii Semenov in issue no. 7 of the journal. This proved too much for *Nash sovremennik*'s opponents, and in late July, a Central Committee directive was issued, entitled "Concerning the Creative Links of Literary-Artistic Journals with the Task of Communist Construction," and published in both *Pravda* and *Literaturnaia gazeta*. Whether this directive would do the trick remained to be seen.

In the same period, other Russian nationalist activists suffered repression and persecution. Former *Veche* contributor Anatolii Ivanov (Skuratov), who enjoyed the protection of such powerful establishment figures as A. Sofronov, the editor of *Ogonek*, was arrested by the KGB, and a number of his acquaintances were called in for questioning.[2] Similarly, National Bolshevik tribune Sergei Semanov was fired from his position as editor of the mass-edition monthly *Chelovek i zakon* and, after a period of unemployment, was able to find work only with the humble almanac *Bibliofil*. When, in August 1982, he was summoned to the KGB in connection with Ivanov's arrest, rumors spread to the West that he had been arrested, but such reports turned out to be untrue.[3]

In May 1982, former VSKhSON participant Leonid Borodin was arrested and a number of his acquaintances were summoned to the KGB for questioning.[4] In September 1982, former VSKhSON members Mikhail Sado, Viacheslav Platonov, and Iurii Buzin were called in to the Leningrad KGB.[5]

In March 1982, Natal'ia Lazareva of the Orthodox women's

<hr/>

[2] Reznik, "Kto takoi Sergei Semanov?"

[3] Ibid. On Semanov, see also Mikhail Agursky, "Soviet Crackdown on Anti-Semite," *Jerusalem Post*, 9 December 1982, p. 8.

[4] "Khronika," *Posev*, no. 11 (1982), 3.

[5] Ibid.

club "Maria" was arrested (for the second time) and was apparently broken in captivity; she is reported to have named more than fifty persons in Leningrad, Moscow, and Riga who were connected in some way with the organization or its work.[6] Five months later, Zoia Krakhmal'nikova, editor of the Orthodox *samizdat* journal *Nadezhda*, was likewise arrested.[7] Other individuals—for example, Nikolai Blokhin, Sergei Budarev, Viktor Burdiug, and Aleksandr Sidorov, all arrested in April 1982—were seized for reproducing Orthodox religious materials.[8]

In both 1980 and 1981, conservative nationalist Gennadii Shimanov succeeded in issuing a bulky *samizdat* almanac entitled *Mnogaia leta* (Church Slavonic for "Many Years").[9] Each of the almanac's two issues contained about 200 pages of text. *Mnogaia leta* represented the first nationalist "fat journal" to emerge unhindered since the suppression of *Veche* in 1974. Shimanov and his coauthors adopt a position close to that of the National Bolsheviks and argue for a concordat between the Russian Orthodox Church and the Soviet state. In the summer of 1982, however, Shimanov and another contributor to the almanac were summoned to the KGB, apparently in connection with the case against Leonid Borodin.[10] It is not known if *Mnogaia leta* will be able to continue publication.

A final area deserving comment is that of the film. I have recently had the opportunity to view several important Russian nationalist films issued during 1979 and 1980: Andrei Mikhalkov-Konchalovskii's brilliant "Siberiade," winner of a special prize at the Cannes film festival in 1979; Nikita Mikhalkov's fine "Oblomov" (1980); and Vladimir Menshov's "Moscow Does Not Believe in Tears," which won an Academy Award in 1980. These films contest Soviet promethean-

---

[6] Iuliia Voznesenskaia, "Soobshchenie iz kluba 'Maria'," *Russkaia mysl'*, 10 June 1982, p. 6.

[7] "Arestovana Zoia Krakhmal'nikova," *Posev*, no. 9 (1982), 2-4.

[8] "Delo o religioznom samizdate," *Posev*, no. 6 (1982), 6-7.

[9] Available from Keston College (see chapter 7, note 51). A review article which I have written, focusing upon *Mnogaia leta*, is scheduled to appear in *Religion in Communist Lands*, 11, no. 2 (1983).

[10] "Vesti iz SSSR," *Novaia gazeta*, 18-24 December 1982, p. 9.

ism and headlong modernization ("Siberiade"), investigate the social, demographic, and moral effects of urbanization and Westernization ("Moscow"), and affirm that "Soviet society, in its harsh driving, has lost something gentle, generous, humane" ("Oblomov").[11] In the cultural sphere, as opposed, perhaps, to the political sphere, Russian nationalism seems very much in the ascendant.

To conclude, it seems clear that the period of Andropov's thrust toward power has witnessed wide-ranging efforts to suppress Russian nationalists of both the *vozrozhdenets* and National Bolshevik varieties. This oppression has understandably served to bring the two strands closer together. As one Western commentator put it: ". . . today both the Russian nationalists and the so-called 'National Bolsheviks' have common opponents."[12]

[11] Richard Grenier, "A Soviet 'New Wave'?," *Commentary*, July 1981, p. 65. During a recent visit to Oberlin College, Mikhalkov-Konchalovskii told me that "Moscow" (100 million viewers) and "Siberiade" (80 million) were the all-time domestic box office hits of the Soviet film industry.

[12] Nazarov, "Dostignet li tseli," p. 53.

Appendices

PREFACE

The appendices which follow are intended to provide the reader with a direct link to the "mind" of the contemporary Russian nationalist. I have chosen not to include materials, no matter how important, which have already appeared in English translation (e.g., the essays in the collection *From under the Rubble*).

Appendix 1. Three statements of purpose, taken from the first issue of *Veche*, edited by Vladimir Osipov; the first issue of *Zemlia*, edited by Osipov and Viacheslav Rodionov; and the tenth issue of *Veche*, edited by an anti-Osipov faction headed by Ivan Ovchinnikov.

Appendix 2. Two interviews with the influential nationalist activists Vladimir Osipov and Il'ia Glazunov.

Appendix 3. Three documents casting light on the *Molodaia gvardiia* affair: the two essays in that journal by Viktor Chalmaev and a letter in defense of *Molodaia gvardiia*, published by "official nationalists" in *Ogonek*.

Appendix 4. A National Bolshevik programmatic essay appearing in the seventh issue of *Veche*. The author attempts to refute various charges made by A. N. Iakovlev, acting director of the CPSU Central Committee's Agitation and Propaganda Department, in an article published in *Literaturnaia gazeta*.

Appendix 5. A *samizdat* rebuttal, written by Leonid Borodin, former Social Christian revolutionary and editor of the short-lived nationalist journal *Moskovskii sbornik*, to counter essays appearing in *Vestnik*, no. 97 (1970). (Several nonessential footnotes have been omitted.)

Appendix 1

To the Veche!

The twentieth century is a time of progress in science and technology, but it is also a time which has witnessed an unprecedented growth of self-interest and crime. In the pursuit of individual material well-being, men have become indifferent to the spiritual treasures of past centuries. This state of affairs can be observed both here and in the West, but we are naturally concerned above all with Russia, our mother, our agony, and our hope.

Our moral state leaves much to be desired. We are witness to the following: an epidemic of alcoholism; the breakup of the family; a striking growth of rudeness and vulgarity; the loss of an even elementary concept of beauty; uninhibited cursing, the symbol of the brotherhood and equality of the pigsty; envy and denunciation; a devil-may-care attitude toward work; stealing; the cult of bribery; double-dealing in social interaction. Is this really us? Is this really the great nation which produced such a multitude of saints, ascetics, and heroes? Do we have the right to call ourselves *Russians*? As if infected by madness, we have renounced our forefathers, our great culture, our heroic history and glorious name. We have renounced our nationality, and, by calling the emptiness and squalor of the present day by that sacred, thousand-year-old name, we demean it.

And yet there are still Russians. It is not too late to turn to the Homeland, to the mother-earth, to the heritage of our forefathers. Morality is always national morality; only amoralism has no national roots. We must revive and preserve our national culture, the moral and intellectual capital of our ancestors. We must continue along the path laid down by the Slavophiles and Dostoevskii.

A weighty and difficult task stands before us. We are isolated from one another. We have evolved our individual ideas without mutual exchange, without debate. Let us now present them to the Russian *veche*. Let our opinions contradict and refute each other, but all our disputes must have one aim—the good of Russia. With this purpose in mind, after a prolonged silence, we begin the publication of a *Russian patriotic journal*. We invite all Russian patriots to participate in our journal. Let the pure, unfading image of Russia bless us! To the *veche*!

The editors
January, 1971

[*Veche*, no. 1 (AS 1013), 2-3]

Back to the Land!

Despite the ill will of its persecutors, it has not been possible wholly to eradicate the national consciousness of the Russian people. Today it makes itself felt fully and openly, and the appearance of a legal, independent press is proof of this. A platform has been won which must be retained without compromise and duplicity by devoted and self-sacrificing people dedicated to the revival of the Fatherland. It is better to remain small in number but strong in spirit than to compromise the truth in word or deed. It is with these convictions that we now initiate the publication of a new patriotic journal. Past experience prompts us to place special emphasis on the following points:

1. Nationalism is inconceivable outside of Christianity. All forms of pagan or atheistic nationalism are demonic. For Russians, such a "nationalism" represents a new abyss and final destruction. Those without mercy, generosity, and the love of God cannot be called Russians;

2. The principal task of Russian nationalism today is to regenerate popular morality and to revive the national culture;

3. The absence of public discussion and of constitutional guarantees of human rights is a hindrance to the realization of national tasks.

As before, we will follow the course charted by the Slavophiles and Dostoevskii. Our efforts are directed first of all to the development of a Russian national ideology. Having strong reservations with regard to modern civilization, we are struggling for a return not only to our *native soil* but also to the *land which nourishes us* [*zemlia-kormilitsa*]. The Russian nation cannot be saved without the social and moral regeneration of the peasantry. While stipulating our loyalty to the existing order and while supporting the state in the face of external threats, we reserve a right to call our countrymen *back to the land*. The times are uncertain and governments are transient, but the people and its truth are eternal. Not a single good seed planted in this soil will perish.

The editors of the journal *Zemlia*:

V. N. Osipov

V. S. Rodionov

[1 August 1974]

[*Vol'noe slovo*, no. 20 (1975), 5-6]

An Announcement from the Editorial Board of the Journal *Veche* (excerpts)

The replacement of the editor has not been followed by any change in the make-up of the editorial board: all members and contributing authors remain at their posts and continue their work as previously.

The goals and direction of our journal also remain unchanged, i.e.:

—to develop in our readers a respect for our national traditions, our national dignity, our history and culture;

—to assist to the best of our ability in the revival of Orthodox self-awareness;

—to save our historical monuments from ruin and wanton destruction;

—to assist to the best of our ability in the reestablishment of cultural continuity;

—to discover and to discuss outstanding problems of contemporary national life and Russian culture.

We are certain that the conscious core of the nation can safeguard the people, and especially the youth, from cosmopolitan degeneration. As before, *Veche*'s bell will awaken the national consciousness of our people. We are absolutely certain that national consciousness, linked to a religious revival, is the only force capable of wresting people from that state of moral weakness, apathy, amorphousness, and anti-aestheticism characteristic of a nonnational existence. We will expose the falseness and groundlessness of the presumptuous (and often hypocritical) supporters of the nonnational.

We were victorious in a deadly struggle with an external foe [i.e., Nazi Germany].

We have ensured to some extent, though not yet adequately, the material well-being of our people.

But if we now lose the battle against the degeneration of the Russian people, the struggle for the preservation of its culture and morality, we will bring to nought all our former accomplishments.

Since all culture is national, the importance of our journal as a mouthpiece for all healthy Russian national forces becomes clear.

Samizdat does not always mean rebellion. In our case, it is an inevitable and necessary expression of the spiritual life of society. At present, when everyone can read and write, and when the printed word in its million-volume editions has become worthless and spiritually impoverished, we are beginning to see a natural return to manuscript literature. True, such literature cannot be available to the masses. However, we can say with certainty that we have a wide and sufficiently varied circle of contributors and supporters. We are all united by *a painful concern [bol'] for the fate of Russia and by a thirst for the truthful Russian word.*

They can persecute and blackmail us, forbid our existence and close our journal—all this will be in vain, as long as there are thinking individuals who have no access to the official press. We shall willingly cease publication as soon as it will be possible to discuss the themes with which we deal in the newspapers and magazines published in our country. It is no secret that a peculiar situation has arisen on the editorial boards of our official journals which does not permit national-patriotic (and specifically Russian) sentiments to appear in print on their pages. The concepts "Russia" and "Russian" are either completely suppressed or doled out in microscopic doses; such are the demands of internal journalistic policy today. Furthermore, the publication of much useful material is blocked by bureaucratic red tape: sometimes articles lie for many years on the editors' desks. Unlike official publications, *samizdat* is characterized by a lively and dynamic spirit.

There is also a real need for a national *samizdat* because of systematic misinformation about the Russian national movement coming from the West. There is clearly expressed support for everything anti-Russian, including anti-Russian *samizdat*, on Western radio broadcasts, which have become more accessible since jamming became less severe. The materials of the nationalist Russian *samizdat* are systematically ignored or distorted, and our movement as a whole is misinterpreted.
. . .

The journal *Veche*, while defending Russian national culture, which has been dealt a very serious blow in the last half-century, expresses its sympathy for and offers moral support to any expression of national culture among the other peoples of our country. Precisely because of our national point of view, we are able to understand better than anyone else the national aspirations of all peoples. Naturally, we do not share the centrifugal tendencies of some nationalistic movements directed at alienating peoples and territories from Russia. We are certain that a considerate attitude toward the national cultures of other peoples on the one hand and the wealth of Russian culture on the other can serve as strong sources of unity for our multinational state.

The journal *Veche* expresses the hope that through a free exchange of the highest values of each national culture we will come to a full mutual understanding with all the peoples that comprise Russia.

We call upon all, Russians and non-Russians alike, to undertake the great task of serving the eternal values of our Homeland.

The editorial board of the journal *Veche*
25 March 1974
[*Veche*, no. 10 (AS 2452), 1-3]

Appendix 2

An Interview of V. N. Osipov, the Editor of the
Journal *Veche*, with Associated Press Correspondent
Stephens Broening and Dean Mills,
Correspondent of the
Baltimore Sun
(25 April 1972)

Question: Do you consider *Veche* to be the center of a social movement or the reflection of a general tendency in Soviet society?

Answer: *Veche* is not the center of a social movement, but
it does reflect an intellectual mood existing in Russian society. The tendency expressed in *Veche* is considered important by those who maintain (and not only in words) that every
nation has a right to its own particular cultural development,
who understand the necessity and admit the possibility of such
development, and in particular all those who are deeply concerned with the fate of the Russian people and who believe
that Russians are strong enough to be culturally independent.
Circumstances have permitted *Veche* to become the *first* periodical of a Russian nationalist orientation in the USSR. Perhaps tomorrow more talented and energetic people will appear, and we will give way to them with pleasure, but for the
present we must accept the responsibility of being a mouthpiece for the national aspirations of our people.

Question: What are the historical roots of the *Veche* group,
and what does the name itself signify?

Answer: Russian national consciousness can be traced back
to ancient Russia. The historian Shcherbatov, in the reign of
Catherine the Great, and Karamzin at the beginning of the
nineteenth century were the first to formulate the idea of the
distinctness of the foundations underlying Russian life. This
national world view was fully developed by the classic Slavophiles, Aleksei Stepanovich Khomiakov, Ivan Kireevskii, the
Aksakov brothers, Leont'ev, and Danilevskii. Of special significance to *Veche* is that genius of world literature and deeply
national thinker, Fedor Mikhailovich Dostoevskii. Right-wing

patriots, such as Gogol', Pobedonostsev, and Tiutchev, are also of interest in relation to specific questions. In considering the prerevolutionary period, we are deeply saddened by the widespread rootlessness and nihilism which were so prevalent among the Russian intelligentsia at the beginning of the twentieth century. We regret that there exists an abyss of several decades between the present supporters of national ideology and our closest predecessors.

The name *Veche* we associate with the spirit of catholicity [*sobornost'*], diversity, and tolerance which has characterized the Russian people from ancient times. The *veche* was the Russian parliament of pre-Mongol Rus', which remained unchanged in the unconquered cities of Novgorod and Pskov and, in the Muscovite period, evolved into a form of *sobornost'*.

Question: What philosophers and writers serve as important sources for discussion? With which Western philosophers are you familiar? What do you think of their ideas?

Answer: We have always maintained a respect for the classical authors of Russian and world literature, since they were among the few who understood and exalted their native tongues. Whom do we consider to be companions or perhaps even guides? In the period following Dostoevskii, we have the writer and philosopher Vasilii Rozanov, who was able to look at the past, the present, and the future with the eyes of a Russian. There is, of course, Nikolai Gumilev. Andrei Platonov was able to express the cosmic and ontological side of the Russian spirit. V. A. Kliuev deciphered the mysterious and forgotten beauty of the sources of the Russian soul.

As for Russian philosophers, we are attracted first of all by Pavel Florenskii, who was able to an astonishing degree to blend an active understanding of the scientific and technical mission of the twentieth century with fervent Orthodoxy. The works of Nikolai Berdiaev are of enormous importance for contemporary Russian thought. Sergei Bulgakov, Frank, Losev, and others are of course of interest to us. There are at present also interesting writers and true thinkers in our country.

We shall not risk condemning or approving contemporary

Western philosophy, which it does not need in any case, but we should admit a deep sympathy for the activity of Martin Heidegger, a great philosopher of our times and perhaps of all time.

We appreciate the spiritual tension and pathos of his search for true existence, his realization that human nature is without end, the uncompromising quality of his quest, his elevated aesthetics, and his tendency toward the patriarchal. We actively reject such philosophers as Sartre and Marcuse and regret that they have produced such a storm in the vacillating minds of Western youth. We leave acceptance of Carnap and Bertrand Russell up to the individual as a matter of taste.

Question: What is the role of Solzhenitsyn in Soviet society? Does he cope adequately with this role?

Answer: In the sixties, Solzhenitsyn emerged as a moral force opposing certain aspects of the present government. In our opinion, Solzhenitsyn has recently made mistakes [the reference is to his book *August 1914*] which could seriously impair his ability to maintain this role in the future. The loss of Solzhenitsyn as a moral force would be very strongly felt by Russian society.

Question: Have the authorities interfered with the publication of *Veche*? If so, in what way? How do the authorities feel about the publication?

Answer: It seems that at the instigation of certain elements in the KGB, the editor of *Veche* has been threatened with arrest and the house in which he lives has been searched.

As to the authorities' attitude toward the journal, you had better consult them. I think that if the Soviet leadership is really concerned with the fate of the Russian people and of all the peoples of Russia, then it will not be antagonistic toward us.

However, we must remember that as long as there exist forces of world cosmopolitanism, no representatives of national and cultural movements can be certain of their safety. But we know that if we are destroyed, *Veche* will have succeeded in its task even more effectively.

Question: Why has *Veche* and the group affiliated with it appeared precisely at this moment in Russian history?

Answer: The white heat of nihilism, which, by the way, produced such a furious Russophobe and slanderer as Pokrovskii, reached such unprecedented levels in prerevolutionary times that it began to threaten the very existence of the state. In the mid-thirties, the authorities permitted the use of the words "Fatherland" and "Russia," and during the war with Germany they slackened the struggle against Orthodoxy. After the war, Stalin decided to use Russian nationalism to strengthen the state. Despite the clear hypocrisy of the Stalin administration, and despite the extreme debasing and speculative exploitation of national sentiment, we still look positively on the fact that the existence of Russian history and culture had at least been remembered and spoken of.

Since the death of Stalin to the present day, our administration has apparently taken a neutral stand on the question of nationalism.

All nations which have not been physically annihilated sooner or later reveal a striving to live a natural, i.e., national life. A turning of contemporary Russian society to its national origins and traditions has been observable since the mid-sixties. This process is an outgrowth of a desire for spiritual cleansing and enrichment, as well as the result of a raising of the cultural level of the country. The journal *Molodaia gvardiia* for a while somewhat weakly reflected this tendency. However, no sooner had Russian patriots raised their voice in an official publication than the bureaucracy protested: "It is time to get rid of this Russophilism!" A change of the editorial board followed shortly (Fall, 1970).

There is one other cause for the turning to nationalist ideology: Russian society does not want to find itself in an ideologically weak position in the face of an increasing threat from Communist China and of unceasing animosity on the part of world capital [literally: cosmopolitan capital].

Question: What are the journal's goals?

Answer: The goals of the journal are these:

a) to save our material and spiritual monuments from destruction;

b) to cultivate respect for our national heritage (culture, history) and our national sense of worth;

c) to promote the restoration of traditional Russian culture, which, in our opinion, is a pledge of future cultural development. We would like to witness the rebirth in our country of that cultural atmosphere which produced the pleiad of Russian geniuses of the nineteenth and beginning of the twentieth centuries;

d) to encourage love of the Fatherland and of the Orthodox Church;

e) to elucidate and discuss vital issues affecting contemporary national life;

f) to elucidate and discuss problems of contemporary Russian culture.

Let us compare contemporary cultured Russian society to a chemical solution saturated with a variety of opinions, trends, sympathies, and antipathies. We would like the ideas presented in *Veche* to act as a crystal, to attract related particles and become a nucleus for the growth of a group of like-minded men who have resolved the question of what is good and what is bad in our culture. This conscious nucleus of the nation will be able to save the people and especially the youth from cosmopolitan decomposition. Let us emphasize that differences of cultural sympathy should not be identified with differences of political outlook, since the latter are impermanent, embrace only the present, and are in many ways dependent on the geographic situation of the individual. (Thus Karl Marx was fully able to admire the art of slave-owning Greece.)

We would like the bell of *Veche* to sound with a tone that would be echoed by the strings of national consciousness. In attuning oneself to this sound, one would be able to determine how he relates to the idea that human existence is national existence; anyone could come to realize that a consciously professed nationalism is the only force that can free

people from a condition of moral decrepitude, apathy, amorphousness, and anti-aestheticism, and of the inferiority and
unworthiness of a nonnational existence. *Veche* would like to
trace all that is great and significant back to its national source,
even when this source appears in masked form. We would
like to expose the falsity and groundlessness of self-reliant
defenders of the nonnational. *Veche* does not have any ready
formulas for achieving these goals and finds its direction by
tuning in to everyday Russian life. This is not easy to do amid
the noisy winds of contemporaneity, but we are convinced
that we will succeed in our task. We believe that men, and
not the times, direct the national spirit to celestial heights
and that it is not too late to change its course.

Question: How many activists do you have on the journal?
How many readers?

Answer: We do not have any "activists." The number of
contributors is perhaps two or three times greater than the
number of articles published. We sought out readers when
the first issue was ready and could have counted their number then. At present, readers themselves seek out the journal, and we no longer have any control over their numbers.

Question: What is your relationship to the "Democratic
Movement"?

Answer: We strongly sympathize with the Democratic
Movement. There can be no doubt that cultural revival is
impossible without a guarantee of human rights and of constitutional freedoms.

Veche and the "democrats" simultaneously embody the
Slavophile principles of internal politics—the national and the
liberal.

Question: Some have maintained that *Veche* and the "democrats" are analogous to the "Slavophiles" and "Westernizers"
of the nineteenth century. Is this analogy correct?

Answer: Superficially, yes. We would like to note, however, that were a more active cultural exchange with the West
possible, we are sure that we would find many like-minded
people there. We became once again convinced of this after

reading the works of the great American writers William Faulkner and Thomas Wolfe.

Question: How much support have you found for the journal?

Answer: We have total support from the Russian people. We know of no instance where a Russian even slightly acquainted with the journal has condemned *Veche*. Many other nationalities also sympathize with our direction (we do not differentiate Ukrainians and Belorussians from Russians).

Question: Are your hopes for a religious revival in the present era realistic?

Answer: God's Providence could not will otherwise.

Question: Are there signs of a revival? What indications do you see?

Answer: As far as we are aware, the signs of such a revival are apparent in many countries.

In our own country, special circumstances make it most difficult. There is freedom in the press only for antireligious propaganda; there are not enough churches and clergy; people have been taught that religion is the "opium of the people."

Nevertheless, the sharp increase of atheistic propaganda which began in August 1971 tells us a great deal about the increase of religious sentiment.

Question: Some Westernizers feel that much of the material found in *Veche* is directed against the Jews. Are you not afraid of a possible dangerous resurgence of anti-Semitism, which always makes its appearance in Russian nationalistic movements?

Answer: *All* the materials published in *Veche* are directed against opposing *views*. If there are Jews among those who hold opposing views, we condemn their *ideas* but under no circumstances the nationality of those who express them.

I would like to address myself specifically to the problem of the "anti-Semitism which always makes its appearance in Russian nationalistic movements." In regard to the word "always," we should like to mention the fact that Jews appeared in Russia only at the end of the eighteenth century, after the partition of Poland. Russian sentiments which would now be considered nationalistic had existed long before then. Those ancient "nationalistic" sentiments marked the origin of the historical life of Great Russia [*Velikaia Rus'*]. As far as "anti-Semitism . . . in the Russian nationalistic movement" is concerned, similar accusations have, as far as we know, been made by the Jewish diaspora against national cultural movements everywhere. Only at one moment within living memory did "Russian nationalistic" sentiments not elicit such accusations, and that was during the Great Fatherland War against German Naziism.

Question: What is your attitude toward Catholics? Toward Protestants?

Answer: We consider Catholics to be our brothers in Christ. Our attitude toward Protestants coincides in the religious sphere with that of the Orthodox Church.

Question: What political system would best serve the objectives of your group?

Answer: We think that the problems of national life should and could be solved under any political system. The Soviet social and political system, based on national principles and the de facto observance of the Constitution of the USSR, suits us quite well.

In conclusion, I would like to express the hope that our fellow Russians abroad will understand and sympathize with *Veche*.

[*Vestnik*, no. 106 (1972), 296-303]

An Interview of Artist Il'ia Glazunov with
Followers of Fr. Dimitrii Dudko (Winter 1979)

Question: Il'ia Sergeevich, are you acquainted with the priest Dimitrii Dudko?

Answer: I made his acquaintance at my exhibit [at the Manezh in 1978].

Question: Have you read his article [in the émigré weekly *Russkaia mysl'*] about your creative work?

Answer: Yes, I was shown it when I was in Paris at the

invitation of UNESCO. Fr. Dimitrii's article struck me by its agitation and by its deep meditation on the fate of Russian culture.

Question: How did you manage to stage your exhibit at the Manezh?

Answer: Since the Union of Artists, as always, refused to show my works, and since the Ministry of Culture has only one hall, the exhibit was held at the Manezh, the same Manezh at which an exhibit of artists was once subjected to criticism by N. S. Khrushchev. I am very grateful to the Ministry of Culture which, at last, deemed it possible, in spite of the opinion of the Union of Artists, to organize my exhibit. Up to that time, my exhibits had always been closed several days after their opening.

Question: Are the reactions of friends and foes to your exhibit known to you?

Answer: My exhibit was visited every day by 35,000 people. The book of comments consists 90% of positive responses, while the negative opinions belong mainly to official and *avant-garde* artists.

Question: Who is hostile to your work?

Answer: Those who are alien to the concepts of a Russian national renaissance and to the development of the traditions of a great Russian culture. Here official critics of the Union of Artists (Nedoshivin, Kamenskii, and others) close ranks with representatives of the "third wave" [i.e., third emigration] well-known for their hatred toward Russia and expressing the ideas of the Comintern of the twenties and of the so-called "*avant-garde*." At home I am subjected to severe criticism for my adherence to ecclesiastical and mystical topics, for my pseudo-Russianness, and for my perceived lack of desire to participate in the building of communism, while in the West they attempt to discredit me as a mouthpiece of Soviet ideology, as a favorite of the Kremlin, and as an agent of the KGB. Against the last-named charge I won a lawsuit in West Germany in 1976.

Question: What is your attitude toward Christianity?

Answer: Our civilization is justly called a Christian one.

The many-centuries-old Russian culture is permeated by the spirit of Orthodoxy. Dostoevskii said: "He who is not Orthodox cannot be a Russian." The role of Orthodoxy in the history of Russia is well-known, while the role of the Church during the years of the war is common knowledge. Orthodoxy and the historic existence of the Russian people were indivisible and organically connected over the course of many centuries. It is sufficient to state that in the twenties a struggle with Russian culture was often substituted for a struggle with religion. This was done by the so-called *avant-garde*, the supporters of a "new art" and the *Proletkul't*.

Question: You are accused of chauvinism and anti-Semitism. What do you have to say to that?

Answer: I am not a chauvinist and not an anti-Semite. A chauvinist considers that his people is the best and that all other peoples are worse. I am a patriot. I love my people, I serve it as I am able; therefore I respect all other peoples. One who loves his own mother will understand how a German, a Frenchman, a Jew, or an Englishman can love his own mother . . . But to love one's own mother does not mean that one considers her the best woman in the world. To be a son of one's people does not mean that one is a chauvinist or anti-Semite. In all of my work, there is not and has never been any national enmity toward any other people. He who accuses me of chauvinism and anti-Semitism betrays his own anti-Russianness. I have always wanted to understand and to express the soul not only of the Russian people but of other peoples as well. And therefore, for example, when the directors of the Jewish National Theater turned to me, I, after listening to the music of composer Iurii Sherling and finding it to be national and contemporary, agreed to be the artist-arranger of the first production of that theater. I believe that world culture has nothing in common with Esperanto but is a bouquet of different national cultures.

Question: You are accused of speculating on the Russian theme. What can you answer to that?

Answer: It is precisely my adherence to the Russian theme that has elicited and continues to elicit frenzied attacks against me. Indeed, many consider that I rehabilitated the theme of Russian history in our art and that I expressed, as best I could, historical Russian national self-awareness. How can a son speculate on his love for his mother?

(Transcribed by V. Sedov)

[*Vol'noe slovo*, no. 33 (1979), 93-96]

Appendix 3

Viktor Chalmaev, "The Great Search" (excerpts)

"That everlasting Russian need of holiday! How sensuous we are, how we crave to be intoxicated with life—not merely delighted, but intoxicated—how we are allured by constant intoxication, by fits of drunkenness, how bored we are with everyday life and with regular work! . . . Aren't the foolery, and the tramping, the ritual orgies, the self-burnings, and all sorts of revolt akin to the 'joy'—or even that amazing picturesqueness, that verbal sensuality for which Russian literature is so famous?"[1] Thus did Ivan Bunin remember the end of the nineteenth and beginning of the twentieth centuries in his *Life of Arsen'ev.*

The atmosphere at that time was tempestuous; Russia was seething with a universal thirst for freedom, renewal, and creative work after the failure of the *narodnik* "going-to-the-village" and the futile and naive attempts of all sorts of petty reformers to bail out with a spoon—according to the theory of "small deeds"—the flood of the people's primordial dissatisfaction. Petty rationalism and formulas of social welfare appropriate for orderly Denmark were exhausted; even the vision of "aluminum palaces" from the dreams of Chernyshevskii's heroine and the Pisarev-like ideals of the "realist" Bazarov had faded into oblivion.

The Russian people could not so easily and painlessly exchange its ancient way of life for checkbooks, parliamentary twaddle, and the ideas of a cozy "iron Mirgorod," as the West had done. The process of bourgeois transformation was not easy for Russia, and the reflection of this transitional period in art was even more complex. "The amputation of conscience" and the degradation of the Russian character as a prerequisite for the establishment of capitalism in the country were accompanied by unprecedented pain and difficulty.

The best, most progressive elements in Russian art suddenly began to thirst for festivity, for unattainable freedom

[1 Taken from Ivan Bunin, *The Well of Days*, New York, 1934, pp. 131-132, 134.]

and unheard-of expansiveness of feeling. The *peredvizhniki*, whose canvases had played their part in exposing a multitude of abuses in Russia after the Great Reform, could no longer express with sufficient emotional and philosophical power the people's yearning for beauty and moral strength in the same way as the paintings of Nesterov, Vrubel', Serov, Levitan, Maliavin, and Korovin—men who had revived the passion of Rublev, a concern for Russia and its people, and the spirit of eternal millenial Russia—had done.

This tremendous uplifting of national consciousness represented a peculiar reaction to the monster of bourgeois materialism, which, in the form of "a bag of gold," had been described by Dostoevskii as early as 1877. Today many of the artistic works of this brief period of Russian history—N. A. Rimskii-Korsakov's last operas *The Golden Cockerel* and *Tale of the Invisible City of Kitezh*; I. Stravinskii's ballets *Petrushka* and *The Rite of Spring*; the art work of *Mir iskusstva* (Rerikh, Benois, Maliavin, Petrov-Vodkin, Somov, and others); the works of the great Russian impresario M. Fokin—are returning to Russia as part of its inalienable spiritual essence, as are the compositions of S. Rakhmaninov, the works of I. Bunin, the voice of F. Shaliapin, the creative work of the brilliant actor M. Chekhov, and the art of A. Alekhin.

Although this culture is as a rule extremely refined, aristocratic in spirit, and complex in thought, there can be no doubt as to its popular roots. . . .

According to Gor'kii's memoirs, L. Tolstoi once, after recounting some wonderful tales about the morals of the aristocracy, pointed, while walking in Iusupov Park, to a peasant woman working in a flower bed "baring her elephant-like legs" and commented: "It is precisely these caryatids who supported all this magnificence and folly . . ."

Gor'kii has probably somewhat "modified" this phrase to fit his own style. Unlike Gor'kii, Tolstoi and Dostoevskii saw in the people an integral support (due to its religiosity), an inner monolithic support which always acted as the "salvation" of the nobility and of Russia from physical and spiritual degeneracy. And what a great support it was! In his *Diary of a*

Writer, Dostoevskii recalls a day in prison when his fellow convicts were drinking and brawling . . .

". . . All of that . . . painfully tormented me. I could never bear without repugnance the people's drunken revelry, in this place especially," writes Dostoevskii. And at that moment, as he lay in the barracks, pretending to be asleep, memories from his childhood began to emerge. He recalled a day in the forest, fear of a wolf, and flight from the woods into a field, to the peasant Marei, who was on his way to fetch a plow and who accompanied his little master home with a kindly smile. "I remembered that tender, motherly smile of a poor peasant serf, his crosses, the shaking of his head: 'See how you are frightened, little child!' I remembered particularly that thick finger of his, soiled with earth, with which he so calmly, with such timid tenderness, touched my trembling lips . . . The meeting was a solitary one, in a vacant field, and only God, perhaps, perceived from above what a profound and enlightened human sentiment, what delicate, almost womanly, tenderness, may fill the heart of some coarse, bestially ignorant Russian serf, who, in those days, had even had no forebodings about his freedom."[2] The writer continues that he afterward looked at prison life with different eyes, that he understood that the shaven, defamed peasant, with branded face, intoxicated and shouting a drunken, hoarse song was perhaps that very same Marei.

Gor'kii boldly attempted to destroy this hated hierarchy of Savel'ich-Grinev, Marei and his little master, Tushin, Timokhin-Andrei Bolkonskii, Karataev-Pierre Bezukhov, in his plays *The Bourgeois* and *Enemies*, in the novel *Mother*, and in the cycle *Around Russia*. He considered as deeply aristocratic and antipopular that division of labor in the creation of culture in which the peasantry for centuries produced songs, epics [*byliny*], and the Russian language itself, while the Karamazovs and Chaadaevs, fed by the peasants' bread, produced a refined, spiritual culture. . . . For Gor'kii, the people are not a "support," not a caryatid, but the chief, the only

[2 Taken from F. M. Dostoievsky, *The Diary of a Writer*, New York, 1954, pp. 209-210. I have made some minor changes in the translation.]

hero of the historical process. It is this thought that Gor'kii seeks to affirm.

But are the people capable of playing this role without the Bolkonskiis and the Karamazovs? . . .

Thus, Gor'kii sees two essentially contradictory elements in the character of the Russian people: a "Konovalov" dreaminess and being ruled by conscience, a yearning for freedom, a desire for song; and "Maiakinskii" realistic severity, firmness, the mocking of any pity, reflection, or idealization. "Gor'kii's common people" become at times anti-intellectual, totally unlike "Dostoevskii's common people," although both writers in their own way historically correctly and accurately express the complex popular psyche. With time, this distinction grows even more important in Gor'kii; the period itself seems to "thrust" new characters at the writer who sometimes embody what is "coarse" and impudent in the people and at other times their statesmanlike rationality. By "mixing" together the Bezukhovs and Karamazovs, aristocracy and patriarchy, Gor'kii created his own peculiar character, his own distinctive common man.

Was this reappraisal of the Russian national character inevitable? After all, Tolstoi, Dostoevskii, and Gor'kii have so much in common! They are united by a common "circulatory system" of language and tradition; by faith in the future of Russia; by great pride in her glorious history; by the spiritual wealth and the health of the people. And, on the other hand, there is a fierce denial of Western, individualistic philistinism, Gor'kii's "City of the Yellow Devil" and Dostoevskii's orderly "ant hill," where the soul is synonymous with the belly and where man becomes nothing but a means and a tool. These are all common, hereditary traits of Russian literature! . . .

Nevertheless, there was much which forced Gor'kii to see the weakness and imperfection in former legends concerning the "God-bearing Russian people" and the "Scythian" principle of the Russian soul. Gor'kii denied the underlying principle of these conceptions. Russia must be understood and discovered and strong bonds must be created with the people not through Christ but through the revolution, which, Gor'kii believed, was uncovering new, deeply rooted aspects of the national consciousness. The Russian people must shield itself from the "virus" of the new barbarism advancing from the West in the form of the laws of ready money and prostituted "cheap" culture, not with icons, prayer, and humility but through the creation of a new social order, of a new man. Gor'kii believed that Russia will be saved by the Vlasovs and Nakhodkas, and not by Starets Zosima and the aristocrat Bolkonskii. . . .

Gor'kii's attempt to free himself from philosophers who saw the common people only as a support and "caryatid" was basically unsuccessful. Having expelled the Bolkonskii's, Bezukhovs, Karamazovs, and Rudins, he was constantly forced to introduce a Maiakin, Luka, Tiunov, or Kozhemiakin, in other words inside-out *"raisonneurs."* The level of their spiritual quest was, of course, much lower; their milieu could never produce a Tiutchev or a Dostoevskii, and Luka's aphorisms seem wretched and primitive when compared to Pechorin's dialogue with Maksim Maksimovich. This period was a pause on the road in quest of a hero who would combine a concern for the times and for the homeland with action. . . .

Gor'kii shows concern for even the most minor expressions of religious idealism in art, for any attempts to "galvanize" meekness, humility, or religious fanaticism as the sole foundations of the Russian national character. "The evil genius Dostoevskii," "the Asiatic and nihilist Ivan Karamazov," "two hundred bruises will not paint Russia a brighter color, for that we need blood and a lot of it, since only blood can paint events a gay, crimson color"—all of these ideas which sound so harsh and inexact to the contemporary ear should be explained historically as excesses in the struggle against individuals who had substituted religion for revolution and idealistic fantasies for a sober vision of Russia's future. For almost an entire decade, Gor'kii was in "opposition" to L. Andreev, M. V. Nesterov, and other figures of Russian culture who, in one way or another, supported the idea of Russian messianism, the Slavophile tradition of idealizing a Russia where "Christ had walked, blessing the people."

Later on, Gor'kii realized that not all "idealism" is religious and that not all modesty, natural gaiety, and boundless spiritual questing are sanctified by the name of Christ, that not all aristocracy and complexity of soul are limited to the upper classes. A nation becomes impoverished when it loses this aristocracy. . . .

Gor'kii, like Blok, saw in the revolution a long-desired solution to many of the problems facing Russia; in its music, he heard a hymn of Russia's greatness. The potential talents of its people had been awakened to life, to historical creativity, and Gor'kii saw in the revolution the resolution of a multitude of Russia's dramas in reality and not in poetic imagination.

In those postrevolutionary days, the question of the fate of Russia's great cultural heritage arose sharply both for Gor'kii and for the revolution as a whole. V. I. Lenin himself was concerned with this question. It was precisely at this moment that V. I. Lenin was forced to struggle against distortions consisting in a pitiless, nihilistic rejection of national forms, of the traditions of Russian culture, of a classical wealth of ideas and of realistic means of expression. . . .

In those days doubts arose about the Russian classics themselves, about their connection with the Russian soil, and with the people, their creator! How, it was asked, could such geniuses of creative thought, from whose light Europe "wanders blinded to this day," have been produced by "unwashed," "backward" Russia? Some Futurist, Constructivist, and Imaginist theoreticians could not understand this in their philistine narrow-mindedness.

Such theoreticians could not grasp what S. Esenin understood when he compared cosmopolitan, soulless American civilization with the spirituality of Russia: "America is that stench in which not only art but the best human tendencies fade into nothingness. . . ."

Here Esenin rejects not the machines themselves but the exaltation of a soulless, mechanical existence into an ideal, and the chase after the dollar which kills man's conscience, sense of beauty, and affinity to the soil. A Tolstoi could never be born here. . . .

Some members of the artistic world did not agree. In 1923, one of the theoreticians of *Lef*, M. Levidov, attacked Russian patriotism with particular fury as an unnecessary luxury and a waste of spiritual energy; he assailed the people's love for their native corner, for their native dialect, as something mystical and ephemeral. In his eyes, the celebration of the peasant hut and of the peasant represents an absurd romantic fog, an idealization, and he compares Russian poetry to a silk top hat on the head of a disgusting peasant beggar. . . .

In his best articles of the twenties and thirties, Gor'kii came out against forcibly lowering the spiritual level of literature, a process often identified with innovation or "popularization." The call "to do simple things," the call to demolish [the Cathedral of] Basil the Blessed and the city of Novgorod as "a funeral parlor of archaeology" and, on the other hand, the attempts to justify militant ignorance as democracy—all of this was deeply inimical to Gor'kii. . . .

The figure of Gor'kii is a symbol of a transitional time, with its peculiarities, historical conflicts, and spiritual dramas. Created by the revolution, he became one of those "flaming souls," one of those heroic individuals, in whose questings, ideas, and world-sense this universal and historical event was reflected.

[V. Chalmaev, "Velikie iskaniia," *Molodaia gvardiia*, no. 3 (1968), 270-295]

Viktor Chalmaev, "Inevitability" (excerpts)

In the seventeenth century, a most intelligent and inquisitive man, Iurii Krizhanich, a Croat by nationality, was brought into our country by one of the many winds blowing into Russia from East and from West. He settled in Moscow and later in Tobol'sk, where he lived for fifteen years. Observing Russia and its people during the tumultuous reign of Aleksei Mikhailovich, he produced a monumental work entitled *Thoughts on Politics* or *Conversations about Sovereignty* (i.e., politics).

The dramatic and sagacious thought of this wandering defender of the Slavic tribe is astonishing! Having arrived in Muscovy with a firm conviction that the Slavs, and Russia in particular, "stand closest in succession to be creators of the world's wisdom, a task carried out in turn by successor nations" (the same idea was later affirmed by all *"pochvenniki"* and Slavophiles), he suddenly discovered that this mighty land suffered from a serious defect: *"chuzhebesie"*—an insane passion for everything foreign, as the author himself explains it. He was also troubled by a tendency which the historian Kliuchevskii describes in the following way: "We do not know how to be moderate, how to keep on a middle course, but instead constantly fall into extremes and wander close to the abyss." . . .

And yet neither "madness for everything foreign" nor that disastrous evil, vodka, which, by Ivan the Terrible's order, replaced beer, the ancient Russian beverage (vodka was first adopted for the *oprichniki!*), could extinguish his faith in Russia. Yes, cruel is the fountain of raw brandy which flows in a stream of pure gold into the hands of parasitic merchants. A Russian philosopher would later say: "Drunkenness is a national vice which takes history away from a people. The good merchant who drinks might have produced a Kutuzov in the fifth generation; instead he gives birth only to a brave captain . . ." But there are also mighty principles in the Russian national character: the sense of national justice, patriotism, courage, a yearning for truth, and a strong sense of conscience—all of these have overcome both "madness for things foreign" and "foreign domination" [*chuzhevladstvo*]. . . .

It was not from many golgothas that the diffident Russian soul made known its existence over the course of centuries . . . Constant labor on the land; the monastery; the crown tavern, and once or twice in every century—the ice of Lake Chud, the wild grass of the fields of Kulikovo, Poltava, or Borodino . . . That is why our history seems so destitute when compared to colorful European chronicles overflowing with a multitude of entertaining events. [In Russia] we find no wealth of debates, no early parliamentarianism, no flowery oratory on eternal values . . . "An eternal silence reigns in the heart of Russia," said Nekrasov. Once in every century, the coarse-grained, oft-flogged Russian peasant, weighed down by many burdens, would set out for the Kulikovo Field at hand and, projecting one hundred years into the one night before the battle, he would think about his homeland, about good and evil, and about the world in which he lived . . . And in this wordless, silent brooding, fused with great deeds, he was able to attain spiritual heights which no mechanical orator could ever hope to reach . . . And who can tell what complex thoughts may have lived in the hearts and bold heads of those Cossacks—fugitives and runaways—who accompanied Ermak, Khabarov, and Dezhnev through the wilds of the Siberian *taiga* so that Russia, which was harsh toward them, which threatened them with prison, might freely breathe the open spaces of the Great [Pacific] Ocean to which her soul has such a close affinity? And what of the monastic cells of desert-dwelling patriots such as Sergii Radonezhskii, who inspired Dmitrii Donskoi to fight a decisive battle, or the patriot Patriarch Germogen, who during the Time of Troubles sent appeals to every part of the country urging unity? No, our sacred history is not a wilderness; perhaps it has simply not been "explored" as thoroughly as it should be. . . .

Although the Russian people took part in a Battle of Poltava or a Stalingrad only once every hundred years, they were being prepared for this throughout the centuries. One's relationship to the homeland cannot be taken lightly, for a soul devastated by lack of faith cannot become a Donskoi, a Bagration, or a Matrosov overnight. Even the religious energy of the Russian was not always, but often, in the past transformed into military exploits, into creative inspiration, i.e., it was directed toward goals which were not all religious. . . .

Money, which as everyone knows has neither odor nor country, will not tolerate a sense of the homeland in those who fall under its sphere of influence. Such a feeling is a kind of "redundancy" which complicates financial transactions. Capital mercilessly transforms a people from a spiritual organism into a mathematical sum consisting of standardized individuals, into a mass of separate units concerned only with common, everyday needs. The bourgiois crowd is always coarsely and vulgarly materialistic; its goals are easily "measured," calculated, and satisfied; it has no spiritual yearning straining far beyond the horizon of antlike humdrum concerns. A man's worth is measured according to his ability as a "businessman." In real life this has led to the one-sided development in bourgeois man of an exclusively voracious system, similar to that of termites. . . .

Debates in the press about national self-consciousness, patriotism, and the place of village prose in our criticism—all of this, unquestionably, is an indirect reflection of the worldwide struggle around the concepts "crowd," "public," and "people," around the problem of how to achieve a reasonable balance between "needs" and "ideals." Unable or unwilling to find a truthful answer to these questions, certain critics turn to a tried "method" of approach.

"Why sigh over the village! " they exclaim. "Over our debt to it for the past! Let's build the peasants new houses with slate roofs, with city furniture, plumbing, and fashionable wallpaper! That's all we owe for the 'feats' of the past! " Such are more or less the sentiments of those who in the name of "progress" protest against the "idealization" of the peasant, against celebrating springs and primal sources. They regard the fate of Lake Baikal and of the Russian forests in precisely the same way: "Let us have our way for another twenty years, and we'll dig you a new and better Baikal, wherever you want! And our debt will be paid!" . . .

At times these "bookkeepers," citing the arguments of scholarship, warn that the village will cease to exist altogether by the year 2000. At other times they suddenly reproach all admirers of nature, rivers, and the earth for being out of touch with the "people"—"Here you are," they say, "sighing over all this, while the people are longing for television and plumbing, for Cognac, a popular 'touristy' ditty, and the 'casual manner' of contemporary culture . . ." And if a poet should have thoughts of "stars in the field," then he is accused of "wearing bast shoes" and of being an "antinational" idealist to boot . . . Maybe they are right, to hell with the Baikal. Can't they dig up as many as they want and build concrete banks all around them . . .

In the modern world, there is no neutral ground on moral and social questions. "Hearts that we do not possess will be immediately conquered by the enemy," Vasilii Fedorov once said. Each new generation entering into the world with a thirst for creativity and a desire to increase beauty must inevitably face a choice of ideational and aesthetic orientation and of development of ideals which can become the spiritual axis of one's whole life. Art is simultaneously a festival of ideas and a battlefield of ideas. For this reason, one cannot in our time afford to be a dilettante in this struggle. . . .

The most sacred concept from which all sorts of "demons" are trying to distract us . . . is the people [narod], with its primordial sense of beauty, its innate feeling of historic stability and balance. Happy is the man whose spiritual outlook allows him to understand the movement of the people, to adopt its points of reference and very structure of soul! . . .

[V. Chalmaev, "Neizbezhnost'," *Molodaia gvardiia*, no. 9 (1968), 259-289]

What Is *Novyi Mir* Against? (excerpts)

A Letter to the Editors of *Ogonek*

We are prompted to address the editorial board of *Ogonek* because articles have recently appeared in the press which give a distorted and at times deliberately perverted interpretation of the position of the journal *Molodaia gvardiia*. Some critics are attempting to eliminate a tendency represented by the journal and to blacken its program as a whole, by making use of certain blunders committed by individual authors. The ideological and at times openly political character of these accusations directed at the journal cannot and should not be allowed to go unanswered.

Of what position of *Molodaia gvardiia* are we speaking? The journal's primary goal is to develop in the youthful member of the Komsomol feelings of Soviet patriotism, a selfless

love for his socialist Fatherland, internationalism, and the desire to struggle relentlessly against all kinds of hostile ideological influences, the danger of which has risen sharply in
the past few years. (Let us recall the well-known events in
Czechoslovakia.) In today's world, which is divided into two
opposing camps, bourgeois propaganda, by using the provocative tactics of "building bridges" and "ideological coexistence," is carrying on a tireless, increasingly refined and insidious cultivation of minds, preaching nihilism in all its aspects
among the youth, and encouraging a yearning for an easy
"refined" way of life, modeled on the Western pattern, and a
superficial intellectualism devoid of moral norms. Any inten-
tional or unintentional attempt at minimizing the importance
of this danger only plays into the hands of our ideological
enemies.

The best and most important pieces which have recently
appeared on the pages of *Molodaia gvardiia* serve the noble
cause of defending communist ideals and of educating the
youth in heroic, patriotic traditions. It was precisely in *Molodaia gvardiia* that the writer L. M. Leonov, the artist P. D.
Korin, and the sculptor S. T. Konenkov published a letter
addressed to the youth urging them to preserve the shrines
of our nation and to love their native land.

The journal has gladly opened its pages for the publication
of articles by illustrious marshals, war veterans, and people
of difficult and heroic professions. . . .

For instance, anyone who has read M. Lobanov's article
"Enlightened Philistinism" (*Molodaia gvardiia*, 1968, no. 4)
without prejudice will feel that it is written sincerely and pas-
sionately and that the author is deeply concerned about the
very real danger of foreign ideological influences, the activization of "enlightened philistinism," and cosmopolitan integration. The critic accurately describes the traits of the contemporary petit bourgeois, who, in the author's eyes, becomes
a synonym for the absence of ideas, for petty backbiting and
trivial vulgarity: "The petit bourgeois has a 'mini'-language,
'mini'-thoughts, 'mini'-emotions—everything is 'mini.' The
homeland and the friendship of peoples are also 'mini' for

them. Only those who want to corrupt the national spirit of peoples would oppose such a friendship."

Such is the position of the journal *Molodaia gvardiia*. It would seem impossible even to doubt the civic and Party-minded spirit of this position. Nevertheless, we repeat that some critics have attempted to do so, falsifying facts by making countless misrepresentations and garblings and arbitrarily interpreting both individual ideas and the complete works of some authors published in *Molodaia gvardiia*. The critic A. Dement'ev has probably carried this furthest in his article "Concerning Traditions and National Consciousness," which the journal *Novyi mir* (no. 4, 1969) was naturally very happy to print.

Why naturally?

It is probably unnecessary to give the reader a detailed explanation of the ideas which *Novyi mir* has long preached, especially in the area of literary criticism. All this is quite widely known. It was on the pages of *Novyi mir* that A. Siniavskii's "critical" articles were printed, while, at the same time, his anti-Soviet, libelous works were being published abroad. It was in *Novyi mir* that blasphemous materials casting doubts on the heroic past of our people and the Soviet army appeared. . . .

In his article "Concerning Traditions and National Consciousness," A. Dement'ev attempts to present in a negative light the ideas of so-called nationalism and pseudopatriotism, which, he claims, have taken over not only the critical section but also other departments of the journal *Molodaia gvardiia*. The most convenient firing ground for a barrage of criticism and for tendentious generalizations concerning the journal's work in general are V. Chalmaev's articles "The Great Search" and, especially, "Inevitability" (*Molodaia gvardiia*, nos. 3 & 9, 1968). In his judgments on other materials found in *Molodaia gvardiia*, be it criticism, poetry, or prose, Dement'ev tries to "cut everyone by Chalmaev's measure," including the author of the tale "Ask the Sunrise," S. Vysotskii, the poet V. Sidorov, and the critics M. Lobanov, P. Glinkin, etc.

We do not deny that the above-mentioned articles of

V. Chalmaev suffer from serious defects; they contain coarse factual and metholological mistakes, inaccuracies in a number of formulations, and errors in their system of proof. We consider that the editorial board of *Molodaia gvardiia* was not sufficiently demanding when it allowed these articles to be published.

Nevertheless, it seems to us that these articles of Chalmaev, and especially "Inevitability," have one major purpose which was accurately understood, sensed, and given its due by Professor A. Metchenko (*Moskva*, 1969, no. 1), who at the same time sharply criticized the author's faulty ideas. He called "Inevitability" a "cry of the soul" protesting against the penetration or "infiltration" of our society by unhealthy manifestations of Western (bourgeois) culture. In fact, a great deal in Chalmaev's article is directed precisely to this purpose of counterpropaganda, to tearing down the "successful" erection of bridges between alien class ideologies. "The measure of authentic intellectualism and progress in art today must inevitably be a real and not illusory participation in the struggle of the Communist Party and the people against the ideological foes of our Homeland," Chalmaev writes. Further on, in explaining the meaning of the article's title, the author states directly: "The consciousness of this uncompromising demarcation of ideologies is the historic inevitability of our time."
. . .

And now we see A. Dement'ev in a new role. In his article "Concerning Traditions and National Consciousness," he speaks dolefully and in passing of his feelings for the Homeland, of the traditions of the Russian people, and of the past glory of Russian arms. But it seems that these half-admissions, half-laments are needed only to attack vehemently the real and not illusory propagation of patriotic ideas found in the journal *Molodaia gvardiia*. And if V. Chalmaev's reckless quotations from K. Leont'ev and V. Rozanov are deserving of criticism, attacks against him for preaching Russian messianism and the chosenness of any one nation are completely without foundation. In the article "Inevitability," he merely speaks of the need for historic truth in examining the "military, labor, and moral exploits of the great Russian people, together with other fraternal peoples." The article affirms Lenin's idea that to the bourgeois slogan of the integration of nations we must oppose the slogan of a rapprochement of socialist nations through a flourishing of the best aspects of all national cultures, that internationalism is not based on a union of cosmopolitan modernistic forms of art and spiritual life. . . .

A. Dement'ev unceasingly stresses that "Soviet patriotism cannot be reduced to a love for 'primal sources' [*istoki*], for historical monuments and shrines . . ." True, it cannot be so reduced. But it also cannot exist without them. . . .

A. Dement'ev contemptuously (and more than once) calls all those who write in *Molodaia gvardiia* concerning the "land" *muzhikovstvuiushchie* [peasant-lovers], although as a historian of Soviet literature he knows perfectly well that this term was put into circulation by Trotskii in the twenties (and regularly appeared on the pages of the RAPP journal *Na literaturnom postu*) to defame Russian writer-patriots (Esenin, Sholokhov, and other well-known writers were called "peasant-lovers"). . . .

We will end where we began. Our time is one of the sharpest ideological struggle. In contrast to A. Dement'ev's diligent appeals that we not exaggerate "the danger of alien ideological influences," we again and again affirm that the penetration into our country of bourgeois ideology has been and remains a most serious danger. If we do not struggle against it, it can lead to the gradual replacement of the concepts of proletarian internationalism, so dear to the hearts of certain critics grouped around *Novyi mir*, by cosmopolitan ideas. . . .

> [Signed by:] Mikhail Alekseev, Sergei Vikulov,
> Sergei Voronin, Vitalii Zakrutkin, Anatolii Ivanov,
> Sergei Malashkin, Aleksandr Prokof'ev,
> Petr Proskurin, Sergei Smirnov, Vladimir Chivilikhin,
> Nikolai Shundik

[*Ogonek*, no. 30 (1969), 26-29]

Appendix 4

The Struggle against So-Called Russophilism, or
the Path to National Suicide (excerpts)

They are once again frightening us with the specter of a growth of centrifugal forces which threaten to destroy that enormous and complex entity, the Union of Soviet Socialist Republics. In the mosaic of events and changing moods, one disturbing question is being asked: Can the growing nationalism of the border republics create chaos within the state or, even worse, bring it to complete disintegration? Many are ready to answer this question in the affirmative and are consequently prepared to adopt a program to root out Russian national self-consciousness, for it is postulated, without any basis either in historical experience or in the experience of the USSR, that zoological nationalism in the borderlands expands in direct proportion to the growth of national sentiment among the Russian people and that, therefore, the destruction of Russian national self-awareness will inevitably lead to the destruction of nationalism among the other peoples of the USSR.

This point of view is not new. Bureaucratic supporters of the USSR, who are actually supporters of the (supposedly) nonnational character of the USSR, proclaimed as early as the twenties and thirties that there is an inseparable link between "chauvinism" in the border republics and "great-power Russian chauvinism." They maintained that "Russian chauvinism" represented "the chief danger" and demanded that "a major blow" be directed against it. However, this was in no way meant to indicate "any lessening in the struggle against local [i.e., borderland] chauvinism." One of the most ardent "proletarian" well-wishers, Leopold Averbakh, wrote the following about "local chauvinists":

These 100% patriots have already been unmasked to a sufficient extent. In the first place, they have been exposed as agents of imperialism, as propagandists advocating secession from the USSR and joining in a conspiracy with foreign capitalists. In the second place, they are seen as people who are always ready to form a bloc with Russian Black Hundreds, Russian great-power-mongers, and Russian chauvinists.

. . . Is it true that we cannot maintain a multinational state without damaging individual national interests, without draining the deepest life forces of individual nations? And, on the other hand, does Russian patriotism really encourage the growth of border "nationalism" and therefore constitute a danger to the unity of the country?

Will the Georgians forget Queen Tamara or the Central Asians, Tamerlane, if we smear our tsars with mud and forget General Skobelev? Will they choose to begin their history with the events which occurred in Petersburg and Moscow in 1917 if we set them such an example? And can we set such an example after losing any feeling of respect for our national history and, consequently, for history in general? Reality requires us to give a negative answer to all these questions. Reality bears witness to the fact that, by destroying the national patriotism of Russians and of other peoples of the USSR, we deprive state patriotism of any content, for it is impossible to speak of an object of love while deliberately excluding that which the heart of a people can love, that which is preserved in historical and cultural national tradition . . . .

"Faith in the strength of the Russian spirit" means faith in the possibility of creating an entity which harmoniously unites diverse parts in itself. It is not by chance that the Russian nation became the unifier of our multinational state. The psychology of the Russian people is suited, as no other, to serve as the center of a voluntary union. "The spirit of Russia is ecumenical. That which is national in Russia is precisely supranational . . . In this Russia is unique and unlike any other country in the world." (N. Berdiaev) Neither the Russian common man nor the Russian philosopher has ever considered nationality to be "the last word and last goal of humanity." "The Russian man is an everyman [vsechelovek]." (F. Dostoevskii) Accepting all peoples into their souls, Russians were able to recognize and respect the good qualities of all peoples, appreciating in others what Russians themselves lacked. Mikhail Prishvin, a most sincere author, wrote about this during the war. Every Russian instinctively feels that "only in a union with humanity can one live a full life."

"But," as F. M. Dostoevskii wrote, "a common humanity [*obshchechelovechnost'*] can be achieved only when every people's nationality is developed to its fullest. The notion of roots and of nationality is a point of support—an Anteus. The idea of nationalities is a new form of democracy."

"The opposition of nationality and humanity is impossible and senseless . . . The establishment of a brotherhood of peoples will result in the consolidation of national particularities rather than in their disappearance." (N. Berdiaev) Contemporary writers seem unaware of the fact that a "higher" unity presupposes the existence of "lower" unities, that a sum cannot exist without its parts . . . There can be no internationalism without nationalism. Internationalism has no meaning without nationalism.

A strong union can be formed only of strong parts. Every element in a multinational state gains strength from its own internal, national bonds. Therefore, the system as a whole, while leaving itself open to the addition of new elements, rejects anything foreign to it because of its organic wholeness; it rejects both the cosmopolitanist impersonalism of purely political entities and the national haughtiness of self-loving nations. . . .

The gravest threat to the cosmopolitan spirit in our country is posed by the spiritual content of the mighty Russian culture and the national self-consciousness of a great people. It is precisely this circumstance which explains the cosmopolitans' extreme hatred of everything Russian (naturally concealed behind a screen of "internationalism"). Overt cosmopolitanism contradicts the Russian political instinct, which strives for an amicable centralized union of peoples, by maintaining the idea of "the inevitable creation of a multinational community of nations" with which Russian consciousness is supposedly incompatible.

But let us see what role Lenin, whom it is difficult to ac-
cuse of chauvinism, anticipated for Russia in the international
community of peoples. We cite his famous article "Concerning the National Pride of Great Russians": "We are not," Lenin
wrote, "unfailing adherents of small nations; we are as-
suredly, all circumstances being equal, for centralization and
against the philistine ideal of federal relations."

Thus, the Great Russian nation is called upon to carry out
"centralization," the same Great Russians whom Averbakh and
Baskin called "great-power-mongers.". . .

It is precisely a struggle against national self-consciousness
which elicits a reaction in the form of zoological nationalism
and does indeed represent a dangerous centrifugal force. Let
the Uzbeks, Tatars, and Georgians concern themselves with
their antiquity, with their history, let them take pride in their
particular culture and their notions of morality, let them
maintain their mores and traditions. Let their nationalism find
a healthy cultural and governmental direction (within the
framework of healthy national cooperation).

Let us recall historical Russia. None of the so-called Russian "colonizers" interfered in the national life of the peoples
[of the Russian Empire]. Neither Muslims, Buddhists, Jews,
nor Catholics experienced any kind of religious persecution
on the part of their Orthodox governors. A huge multinational
state was held together by the moral authority of Great Russian culture and its bearer, the Russian people. The forcible
Russification of some border areas which unfortunately took
place in the second half of the nineteenth century as an inevitable reaction to the appearance of extremist national groups,
especially in Poland, undermined the borderlands' trust in
Russia and became one of many revolutionizing factors in the
years to come. Nevertheless, even in the short period when
the policy of Russification was being carried out, there existed
in Great Russia a mighty opposition movement against it, in
the person of Russian thinkers, writers, and public figures,
who quite soon forced the authorities to reverse their policy
of Russification. At the same time, among the national intelligentsias of the borderlands, influential circles were formed

which constantly and actively spoke out for union with Russia (the "Moscophiles" of the Ukraine, the Belorussian Society of Petersburg University, and similar cultural organizations in Latvia, Georgia, etc.).

The voluntary joining of peoples to Russia is characteristic of Russian history. It is sufficient to recall the cases of the Ukraine, Georgia, Armenia, Kazakhstan, and Buriatia. The claim that the Russian Empire was held together only by bayonets is true only in the sense that Russian bayonets defended the borderlands against cruel neighbors. Russia knew how to inspire love, that was the secret of her strength. Berdiaev warned prophetically: "If Russia loses the ability to inspire love toward herself, she will lose the basis for her great position in the world. Russia's mission is to defend and liberate small peoples. Russia must also act as a defense against the danger of the Mongol East."

It is no secret that the Russians have been and still are the foundation for a multinational power. Let us try to imagine what would happen if the RSFSR were to break away from the USSR, a right granted to her by the Constitution. How long would the remaining Union of the other Soviet Socialist Republics last? The whole multinational immensity of our state turns on a Russian pivot, and if centrifugal forces are now prepared to rip apart that immensity, then one should think in the first place of strengthening the pivot itself.

"Russia is more than a people," wrote V. Solov'ev. "It is a people that has gathered other peoples around itself . . ."

If the borderlands see the embodiment of a higher culture, morality, national tolerance, kindness, and generosity in the center, they will voluntarily be drawn to it. On the other hand, if they see cultural and moral disintegration at the center, if they see that the center embodies the ideals of self-interest and indifference to everything on earth, and even the trampling under foot of human and national self-respect, then the borderlands will try to protect themselves against disintegration by building up a strong barrier of will directed toward separatism.

The cultural and moral forces of the Russian people (and

other peoples of the USSR) can be strengthened in the following ways:

a. Culture is and can only be national. Insistence on "proletarian" or "socialist" culture is senseless and must give way to national cultural tradition.

b. Cultural development is possible only if creative freedom is guaranteed.

c. It must be understood that traditions which have been developed over hundreds of years conform to the psychological makeup of the nation and express it. Therefore, behavior in the spirit of national tradition brings the greatest benefit to the Fatherland.

d. A high level of national morality is attained by the presence of an elevated idea in the soul of every man and in the religious character of its internalization (be it Orthodoxy, humanism, or socialism). However, this dominating idea should never be national pride.

"Ideas are as scarce in the German Empire as in France. In France, there is at least the communist idea; in Germany, there is only 'Long live German pride.' " (F. Dostoevskii) Russia's greatest thinkers have always opposed a primitive understanding of national ideology. It is this fear of obtuse national feeling, which is as destructive of culture as cosmopolitanism, which often frightens the thinker and political activist away from turning national ideology into the ideology of state. We can all remember the time when we tactlessly glorified ourselves as "the first among equals," something of which many Russians were ashamed and which greatly irritated other nationalities. . . .

Patriotism is always linked to love of the soil and to the cultivator and preserver of the land—the peasant. Cosmopolitanism is just as inseparably linked to hatred of the peasant, the creator and preserver of national traditions, morality, and culture. It is the peasant who is most strongly tied to the natural landscape of a given country, and, as a result, "the peasant is the most morally original type." (M. Lobanov) Even the durations in time that each social class has been in existence cannot be compared; tillers of the soil have existed for thousands of years, the workers and intelligentsia for a century or a century and a half. It is natural that all the traditions, the whole world-sense of a people—from popular songs to philosophical constructs—should have their source in the peasantry. This is all the more true in our own society today, where everyone's grandmother, of not mother, was a peasant.

Let us recall that in 1913 only nine percent of Russia's working population was employed in industry and construction, that in 1917 the Russian proletariat consisted of one million people, while the remainder of the laboring masses was made up of peasants. One hundred years ago the working class did not exist as an influential social group; moreover, the workers did not break their connection with the village for a long time afterwards. It is natural that the roots of the Russian working class should go back to the village; the workers' traditions reach back to a centuries-old peasant way of life.

In answer to cosmopolitan claims concerning the reactionary nature of the peasantry, let us emphasize that the socialist revolution—an attempt to realize the ancient dream of justice, a yearning for the establishment of a more moral social order—triumphed in precisely a peasant country. . . .

During the eleven-year span between the censuses of 1959 and 1970, the urban population of our country grew by 36 million, of whom 21 million migrated from the village. The rural population *decreased* by more than 25% in the ten central provinces of Russia and by even more in the northern provinces during these years. At the same time, the rural population in the southern regions of the USSR expanded through a high natural growth. In addition, it must be noted that in the southern regions a farm laborer works only 100-150 days a year, whereas in the central and northern Russian villages each peasant carries the work load of two or three, because shortages of labor are even greater there than in industry. The replacement of traditional villages by settlements made up of agricultural workers has had the opposite effect of what was desired. When the village had its own original mores, its yearly cycle with traditional holidays and seasonal changes of work and mood, with kinship for the soil, interest in life was maintained, and people loved their village. But why live in a settlement for agricultural workers? Very soon and you, the detractors of the village, will be unable to find a workforce of 21 million out of 36 million for a growing Soviet industry. With whom will our descendants replenish the dying urban population?

The Russian village, which has lost 25-30% of its population in the last eleven years, can no longer be the nation's population donor. Not only are there very few workers left in our northern villages, but the age structure of the rural population is becoming increasingly deleterious; here and there, only old men remain, and in some places no one is left at all.

The result of this migration of Russians—a great agricultural nation—into the city (the large cities as a rule have a minimal birth rate) has not long remained without effect. Census data show that, whereas the population of the USSR as a whole is on the average growing twice as slowly as that of the world, the Russian population is growing twice as slowly as that of the rest of the population of the USSR. In the predominantly Great Russian provinces of the center and north of the European part—the cradle of the nation—the death rate has exceeded the birth rate for many years. It is difficult to guess what will happen in the future.

One can assert with complete assurance that the destruction of the Russian village and the migration of Great Russians into the cities is a decorous but certain way of destroying the Russian nation. . . .

We are now witnessing among the Russian people an unprecedented growth of philistinism, self-seeking, egoism, and indifference to the common interest. The honest segment of Russian society is steadily growing smaller, in part by falling prey to the temptation of an easy life originating from "certain representatives" of certain "national minorities." Greed and alcoholism threaten to overwhelm all other interests of the Russian man. An antidote to this degeneration must be found in the upbringing of a new generation, after the example of our spiritual, cultural, and political history. . . .

The forgetting of our history, the denial of our ancient culture, the defamation of historical leaders who selflessly served
Russia and her national glory, inevitably give rise to nihilism
and a state of spiritual emptiness on the part of Russian youth.
This self-defamation elicits feelings of scorn and contemptuous pity from other nationalities who uphold the banner of
national self-respect more firmly than we do. Other peoples
have kings, princes, thinkers, and poets. We can admit the
existence of one or two; the rest are dismissed as fools and
reactionaries. "Russia can only be governed by fools. It has
known nothing else." (A. Solzhenitsyn) Having never learned
how to respect himself and showing no respect for the beliefs
and accomplishments of his ancestors, the Russian boor hacks
at others' beliefs and mangles the life of other nations. Through
our own efforts, the national minorities constantly receive proof
of the worthlessness of everything Russian, and the drunken
Russian boor collapsed under a fence is more and more often
becoming the sole personification of a great nation in their
eyes. . . .

The whole brotherhood of the *Proletkul't* used to shout
mercilessly in the twenties and thirties about the non-Russian
character of the October Revolution. The concept of Russia
itself was provocatively tied to that of "White Army" and "Black
Hundreds." This witches' sabbath of social-cosmopolitans was
broken up in the mid-thirties, but now after four decades it
has been picked up again by an "internationalist" comrade,
Doctor of Historical Sciences A. Iakovlev, in a different historical setting.

A sepulchral chill emanates from Iakovlev's opus. Life?
Creativity? There is not a hint of them. Rather, one senses
grayness, decomposition, and the stench of death . . . This
article appeared on the eve of the anniversary of the USSR
in the November 15, 1972, issue of *Literaturnaia gazeta* and
embodies the official position on this problem.

A man aspiring to the role of Party ideologue unexpectedly
discovers "Russian nationalism" in the official Soviet press.
Distorting quotations and substituting ideas, Professor Iakov-

lev disparages a whole series of Russian writers guilty of the
heresy of "Russophilism."

Iakovlev's schema is extraordinarily simple. Except for the
Soviet Union, every society, including old Russia, is divided
into positive and negative classes: workers, peasants, and the
intelligentsia, who should be loved, and landlords, capitalists,
and monarchs, who should be hated. Soviet society is an exception where workers, peasants, and the intelligentsia co-
exist peacefully, although workers should be considered first-
class people, while peasants and the intelligentsia must, it
seems, share second and third place. However, in view of
space flights and automated assembly lines, the peasant is
increasingly relegated to third place, surrendering second place
to the intelligentsia. Iakovlev himself, the son of a peasant
woman and a first-generation member of the intelligentsia,
looks down somewhat on the peasantry . . . Nevertheless,
Iakovlev the Marxist is unhappy with those who, in his opinion, push forward the intelligentsia, when everywhere and at
all times the working class should occupy first place. . . .

Iakovlev's analysis of Russia's history is just as simplistic.
Before 1917, all is darkness and gloom. The people are seen
as slaves and savages (savages because of their patriarchal way
of life). Monarchs and landlords are all scoundrels without
exception. There is absolutely nothing positive in 1,000 years
of history—obviously, since no dictatorship of the proletariat
was established to overthrow the monarch and divide all of
Russia into "ours" and "theirs." How the great and radiant
Union of Soviet Socialist Republics emerged from this empty—
or more precisely, filthy—spot remains a mystery, and Comrade Iakovlev makes no attempt to explain this historical curiosity. . . . Of course Iakovlev disagrees with the definition
of the War of 1812 as a "period of class peace." It would
appear that the national spirit is expressed, for example, in
an attitude toward serfdom or in granting Russia a Constitution, while the essence of class enmity is made manifest precisely during Fatherland Wars. (It is interesting to imagine
how the "class spirit" of Comrade Iakovlev would manifest
itself, for example, during a war with present-day China!) In

accusing the critic Lobanov of heresy, the Doctor of History, of course, fails to take into consideration facts of history about which Lev Tolstoi knew and wrote [in *War and Peace*]. . . .

But perhaps bourgeois morality is precisely what Comrade Iakovlev wants? It is not by chance that he, like the bourgeois of the time of the October revolution, mocks icons and crosses, i.e., "sacred, religious ecstasy." As for the "progressive ideas" of the age of Pushkin and the Decembrists, let us remember that Pushkin did not share the ecstasies of Robespierre and that he became a convinced monarchist toward the end of his life. By the way, Comrade Iakovlev's reference to the authority of the great poet—a wealthy nobleman and courtier—is rather surprising.

According to an eyewitness, the following conversation took place on a Moscow train seventy years ago:

> "We have no scholarship, no culture, no sense of self-respect. We are slaves from birth."
>
> "True."
>
> "What have we created on our own? Nothing. We have only borrowed. We have always been defeated in battle; only the frost and vast distances saved us."
>
> "True."

Iulian Martynovich Iurskii was speaking and Vershkov was agreeing, as usual. Iurskii discoursed loudly and with spirit . . .

> "Everything is atrocious. And let it be, let it be! The worse, the better. How can we drag ourselves along after Europe? Even the borderlands are miles ahead of us because they are more cultured than we are. The Jews are more cultured, the Finns and Armenians are more cultured. There is no need to mention Poland—Europe has long recognized it. And we? What and whom do we have? Only Lev Tolstoi. And he is well-known only because he denies our right to political existence. The time has finally come for us to understand. Why this infatuation with ourselves? Those times are past. If you are a savage and a slave, you must listen to those who are more intelligent

than you are. You and I, and he, all of us Russians must
understand . . ."

"Are you Russian?" interrupted a young fellow. (From:
K. A. Kalitin, *Third Rome*)

Are not these seventy-year-old revelations surprisingly familiar? Are we not forced to listen to similar opinions in the
most highly educated homes of the capital and the provinces?
Are we not acquainted with that evil, truly serpentine aphorism: "The worse things are, the better"? But a significant
change has also taken place: the most fiery adherents of this
portentous aphorism can now allow themselves the luxury of
not masquerading as Russian patriots . . . We are sincerely
grateful to *Literaturnaia gazeta* and to Comrade Iakovlev for
giving the mass reader an opportunity once again to become
acquainted with an ideology and conception whose stubborn
survivability cannot be explained by chance. To be sure, time
brings about certain changes, and we can easily see this in
Comrade Iakovlev's didactic flow of words.

Iakovlev is very taken with Chernyshevskii's arguments
concerning the slavish nature of the Russian people. Our professor attacks the writer Kochnev for daring to doubt the justice of this devastating characterization of the Russian people.
"Did not our dear Nikolai Gavrilovich [Chernyshevskii] go a
bit too far?" Kochnev wrote. By disagreeing with Chernyshevskii, Kochnev, Iakovlev claims, disagrees with Lenin
himself. But Lenin, while not polemicizing with Chernyshevskii, limits the latter's extremism by parenthetically adding the words "slaves in relation to the monarchy." A significant clarification! But Iakovlev, who tears the quotation from
Lenin out of context and speculates on it, shows no interest
in an honest analysis of the text. Yet such an analysis could
produce very curious results. It is well known that Lenin at
decisive moments did not pronounce words "just like that,"
for the sake of theory: his every word was meant to have a
practical result, to elicit concrete, practical action. . . . It would
seem likely that Lenin would have created other slogans in

1941 and that in 1973 he would say something quite different
from the words which Iakovlev now quotes.

If one were to quote speculatively à la Iakovlev, one could
learn from the same article by Lenin that slaves are those
who call "the strangulation of Poland and the Ukraine, etc.,"
a "defense of the Fatherland." Perhaps we should also em-
ploy this quotation as part of our arsenal? Since we do not
want to be slaves, shall we then build our relationship to the
Ukraine (can you hear? Even the Ukrainian pronunciation is
being used!) on the same principles as our present relationship to Poland? . . .

A. N. Iakovlev, a progressive man of the twentieth century
who lives in an apartment with modern conveniences and
grows roses and apples at his dacha, despises with all the
fiber of his soul the patriarchal, i.e., in his scholarly opinion
backward, peasantry. Enraged, Iakovlev brings *political accusations* against those serious analysts who dare to see in the
peasant not only a "slave," as Iakovlev wants to, but a free
man in the highest sense of the word, a creator, a founder of
life, and who consider the peasant class to be the cradle of
the national spirit and even (!) of the national culture. . . .
The Doctor of Historical Sciences who does not know history
cannot be expected to make an attempt to learn it. Therefore
we will ask him to trust the words—not of those contemporary critics and writers whom he authoritatively refutes—but
of Aleksandr Ivanovich Herzen, the founder of the Russian
revolutionary movement. But before citing Herzen, let us
quote from a passage about Herzen by Plekhanov, an author
whom Comrade Iakovlev also respects: "Herzen warmly defended the interests of the Russian people. He was not lying
when he wrote concerning himself that from early childhood
he possessed a boundless love for our towns and villages. And
he was Russian to his toenails." On March 15, 1861, Herzen
wrote in *The Bell*: "The people's strength is in the land. . . ."

On the basis of his thorough knowledge of Russian peasant
life, which according to Iakovlev is opposed to socialism, Herzen writes: "The rational and free development of Russian
popular mores coincides with the aspirations of Western so-

cialism." Addressing himself to the people of the West (and to Comrade Iakovlev), Herzen wrote: "Has it never occurred to you, while observing the Great Russian peasant and the wide range of his abilities, his loose, confident manner, his manly features and his strong build, that he possesses *another kind of strength* than selfless patience and long-suffering endurance?" By the way, Iakovlev wisely breaks off Lenin's famous quotation about whom and what we should pride ourselves on, a quote which should continue: "We are proud of the fact . . . that the Great Russian peasant is becoming a democrat.". . .

In vain does Iakovlev complain about the danger of the resurrection of the "industrious peasant"; the regular failure of the wheat crop bears witness to the absence of a zealous and careful owner of the land. Calm yourself, Comrade Iakovlev, do not be frightened by an apparition. We will buy grain from abroad and so have no need for a hard-working peasant. Let us remark in passing that the Russian word "*miroed*" means one who controls a whole neighborhood with a tight fist but does not work himself. Usually this was the village storekeeper. Neither the word "*miroed*" nor the word "*kulak*" was ever applied to the peasant, who struggled for existence by the sweat of his brow. . . .

This heir to the masters of political accusations speaks of the "gentry" character of Slavophilism. But not only the Slavophiles were landlords, even the Decembrists and Herzen were! Lenin was the son of a nobleman. The well known commissar of foreign affairs Chicherin came from an ancient aristocratic family. However, if Iakovlev is talking about the views rather than the social origin of the Slavophiles, then, again, did not the Slavophiles struggle for freedom of the press, the abolition of serfdom, and the establishment of conciliar representation?

Iakovlev expresses indignation at any positive evaluation of Skobelev, the Russian national hero and liberator of Bulgaria, which "fails to take into account his reactionary views and role in crushing popular uprisings in Central Asia." It should be made known that by his frame of mind Skobelev was not only a Slavophile and active opponent of pan-Germanism but above all a great Russian patriot. Oleg Mikhailov has drawn attention to the general's prophetic predictions of 1914 and 1941. If this is an example of Skobelev's reactionary character, then Wilhelm II and Hitler should be considered champions of progress. Skobelev crushed popular uprisings? That is not true. General Skobelev freed the Uzbek, Tadzhik, and Persian populations from the Turkmen-Iomuds, whose way of life centered arount the slave trade and robbery. Skobelev's soldiers freed many Russians who had been sold into slavery. If Comrade Iakovlev is uncomfortable with the annexation of Central Asia to Russia, why does he not suggest the dissolution of the Soviet Union in honor of the Jubilee? In 1918, the territory of the Soviet Republic had shrunk back to the frontiers of Muscovy in the reign of Ivan III. The persecutor of the "Russophiles" yearns for this. And what does Iakovlev have in mind when he calls Skobelev a "reactionary"? Is he demonstrating his ignorance of history or is he consciously playing into the hands of Russia's slanderers? Let us listen to General Skobelev himself:

> In the future, I foresee a free union of the Slavic tribes, with complete autonomy for each but the following sectors to be held in common: defense, currency, customs houses. In all else, live as you please and rule yourselves internally as best as you can.

And here is what Iakovlev's hateful "reactionary" has to say about the partition of Poland: "I openly admit that this was fratricide, a historical crime." (V. N. Nemirovich-Danchenko, *Skobelev*, pp. 317-318) . . .

Iakovlev's unfairness is especially apparent in his evaluation of S. Semanov's popular brochure *Memorial to a Thousand Years of Russia in Novgorod*. The author of the brochure very concisely described the history of the monument's creation, listed the names of the Russians represented on the monument, and related the barbarous behavior of the Hitlerites. As is well known, the following figures are represented on the monument: Cyril and Methodius, Ermak, Ivan Susanin, Nestor, the Knights of Kievan Rus', Aleksandr Nevskii, Suvorov, Kutuzov, Bagration, Barclay de Tolly, admirals Kornilov, Pakhomov, and Lazarev, the victor of Kunersdorff Fieldmarshal Saltykov, the Prince of Tver', Mikhail Iaroslavovich, killed by the Tatars, Bogdan Khmel'nitskii, Dmitrii Donskoi, Minin and Pozharskii. Iakovlev scolds S. Semanov for not using class criteria in evaluating the monument and the ideological tendency of its content. In vain he speculates on Herzen's name, forgetting that the editor of *The Bell* was incensed at the omission from the monument of General Ermolov, who also, probably, "crushed popular uprisings" in the Caucasus. To further spite Semanov, Iakovlev also mentions that *six years ago* the historian praised Kerenskii in some connection. It turns out that one can unearth a "Russophile" who is moved by the Mason Kerenskii! This is already the product of diseased fantasy!

The defender of Marxist purity marshals accusation after accusation. Some are accused of idealizing Skobelev, others Queen Tamara, still others are guilty of publishing Iazykov's poems. Iakovlev then comes to a conclusion similar to that of procurators in Iagoda's time: "We are forced to object most strongly to even a simple flirtation with the reactionary-conservative traditions of the past, which lead to *an interest in the ideology of classes which have been overthrown* . . ." (Fortunately, these objections have so far not led to decisive acts!)

And yet the Georgians are certainly justified in their love of Tamara. Neither the death penalty nor corporal punishment was ever used in her reign. The lot of the peasant was improved, governors who misused their power were removed, a council was convoked to deal with disorder. . . . An ideological worker with a Russian name should not seek to erase decades from the history of a brother nation.

The Party ideologue, you see, is worried that the "hyperbolization of historical figures" could become one of the sources for the revival of nationalistic prejudices! We advise Citizen Iakovlev to experience in his own person the low, barbaric chauvinism, the zoological hatred of Russians which has emerged precisely on a *nonnational* basis. Present-day chauvinism in the borderlands is a reaction against the falsely-internationalist propaganda which calls for unity among renegades, for union of all who renounce their nation. Internationalism, as Lenin understood it, is based on a careful and sensitive relationship to one's own national culture, mores, and traditions. Trotskiite internationalism, on the other hand, is based on the elimination of national particularities, the total liquidation of a nation in general. Incidentally, the Comintern was dissolved not only in the interests of the coalition against Hitler. It was also dissolved because the communist parties rejected a nihilistic attitude toward their fatherlands. Nevertheless, the Fourth International, which mummifies the old formula maintaining that the proletariat has no Fatherland, still survives.

On the eve of the fiftieth anniversary of the USSR, this article by a Party ideologue brings us back to the theories of RAPP and the *Proletkul't*. It was these Trotskiite "guardians of the mind" who wrote: "The words 'Russian' and 'national' have lost their significance: no form of humanism can strengthen and unify the working class in its social practice at a time of sharp class conflict." (From the journal *Na literaturnom postu*, nos. 21 & 22, 1930) It seems that Iakovlev and those who stand behind him would like a return to that period of evil memory of national nihilism and of demeaning the past. No wonder that Iakovlev does not condemn cosmopolitanism. . . .

Why, for example, was an army [i.e., the Vlasovites] which fought on the side of the enemy in a patriotic war formed for the first time in Russian history in the forties of the twentieth century? Why could not Stalin, the supreme commander, trust his apparently loyal generals and constantly shuffled military cadres, fearing treachery and conspiracy? Why was it that during the same Fatherland War, when the country was in deadly peril and we needed to arouse extraordinary strength of spirit, "Soviet patriotism" (in the sense proposed by Comrade Iakovlev) proved inadequate, and it was necessary on short notice to recall the Church, Aleksandr Nevskii, Peter I, and Suvorov, i.e., princes, tsars, and reactionary military commanders? Why did the cult of the heroes of the civil war and of the class struggle prove insufficient? And on whom does the "anti-Russophile" Iakovlev place his hopes in the coming war?

The twenty million people who died from 1941 to 1945 in defense of the Great Homeland with its past and present will not forgive a scornful neglect of our national shrines.

As never before, a need is felt by public opinion and, we hope, by the government as well to ensure calm and to maintain lawfulness and order, thus creating conditions favorable to the development of culture and the revival of national morality. We emerged victorious from a deadly struggle with an external foe, we won the battle for the material well-being of our populace, but if we lose the present war to save the Russian people from degeneracy, the struggle for culture and for morality, we will bring to nought all our former achievements.

The bugbear of "Russian nationalism" is needed by those who want to eliminate men and ideas which are ready to stand in the way of the monstrous, all-devouring slogan: "The worse things are, the better!" In light of the obvious and hidden successes of the forces of corruption, a general alarm is being felt for the future of Russia. Under these circumstances, the struggle against so-called Russophilism indicates the shortest road to national and state suicide. The ideological leader Iakovlev should have mused on this before presenting his ideas to an All-Union audience [i.e., in *Literaturnaia gazeta*].

Forces of international cosmopolitanism, together with Chinese chauvinists and other enemies of Russia, will correctly evaluate the position of the newly-emerged Russophobes. Foes as well as friends can see that only a distinctive Russia is able to stand up against the Chinese threat.

It is in the interests of the Homeland and the whole world that we develop and strengthen Russian national sentiment rather than destroying it, that we raise Russian national prestige and Russian national culture, as well as the national cultures of all the peoples of the USSR.

This is the only road to our national and state salvation.

[*Vol'noe slovo*, no. 17-18 (1975), 19-51]

Appendix 5

Leonid Borodin
"*Vestnik R.S.Kh.D.* and the Russian Intelligentsia"
(excerpts)

The age-old stench of neglect "in the holy places," the centuries-long pride of the "Russian idea," . . . the whole abomination of imperialist arrogance by which the Russian intelligentsia has stubbornly lived—all this presses like a heavy stone on the soul of Russia . . . (p. 6) . . .

Notice that the words "Russian idea" are already in quotation marks. They have finished with it. It turns out to have been simply "national messianism"! The respected authors would like to start off precisely with this ill-fated Russian idea, a phenomenon which seems so abominable to them that they have even hammered it into quotation marks. But to appear solid they need a theoretical explanation. One cannot simply seize a Russian who up until now has wallowed in "national messianism" and stun him out of the blue with the following declaration:

. . . it is not "national rebirth" but a struggle for Freedom and spiritual values that must become the central creative idea of our future. (p. 61)

Notice the quotation marks once again! But the authors are cautious. It takes them sixty pages to explain to the Russian [reader] the illegality and sinfulness of his national consciousness. It turns out that the Russian idea is not only "national messianism" but also "Muscovite imperialism," while Christianity, i.e., in this instance Orthodoxy, is only a convenient tool used to implement and embody execrable intentions . . . And therefore:

Russia's primary task must be to overcome the temptation of national messianism. (p. 61)

Russia will be unable to free itself from despotism until it frees itself from the idea of national greatness. (p. 61)

First of all, the traditional interpretation of Russia's destiny as a vehicle for the future universal happiness of mankind must be rejected. (p. 63)

Thus, to overcome our centuries-old sin we are asked to cease being Russian as soon as possible! And it seems that we fell into this ruinous state long ago, four centuries ago to be precise, when the monk Filofei, maddened with pride, proclaimed Moscow to be the Third Rome. Then came the Slavophiles whose basic ideas

we do not need to disprove today . . . The bankruptcy of their religious ideas and historical scholarship is more than apparent. (p. 44)

Because:

In the assertion of Russia's religious and national exclusiveness, one hears the voice not of Christianity but of a still persisting Old Testament naturalism . . . (p. 44)

Mr. Gorskii certainly has an amazing ear! But let us continue: The Slavophiles, and the *narodniki* after them, have further aggravated our sin by worshipping a nonexistent phenomenon—the *narod* [people]. The former considered the people to be God-bearing, and the latter, to be the bearer and preserver of socialist ideals. But

"The people" has turned out to be an imaginary entity, useful today only for concocting mythologies . . . (p. 52)

The notorious "God-bearing people" has shown its bestial face in the revolution . . . (p. 52)

Further on we find veritable miracles! The heir to the Russian chauvinists' national-messianic aspirations turns out to be *Russian Marxism*. Gorskii is not disturbed by the absurdity of the term itself—Russian Marxism—and he briskly goes on to describe the centaur he has created and to sketch in the Russian Fall.

Russian Marxism, which replaced populism . . . and changed the concept of people into that of class, should be seen as one of the forms of populist-messianic consciousness. (p. 47)

Although the revolutionary struggle and the revolution itself were carried out under a banner of internationalism, nevertheless its main content was "the Russian idea," the idea of the "new word" which Russia had to tell the whole world . . .

At one time, many could not forgive Trotskii for maintaining that the revolution would be victorious only when it adopted his theory of permanent revolution as a weapon. Must one prove that so-called revolutionary consciousness presupposed a radical breakup of the whole national-psychological constitution of members of all nationalities and that the concept of international proletarian brotherhood was not simply a slogan for revolutionary action but the basis for the formation of a new, in the words of N. A. Berdiaev, anthropological type of man, who alone would be capable of bringing the revolution to its logical end? Finally, need one demonstrate that all the basic components of revolutionary psychology were already clearly expressed in *The Communist Manifesto*? And indeed, this type of psychology could have no other source. Who nowadays is ignorant of the fact that Lenin based the possibility of victory for revolution and socialism in Russia on historical and economic considerations which not only were in no way connected with any past variant in Russian history but even in principle excluded any subconscious historical continuity? How can we explain the participation of foreigners in the revolution if we disregard its internationalist essence? And the cohorts of Jews, were they also fighting for the Russian idea? It is precisely the active participation of Jews in working out the revolutionary idea and their even more wholehearted participation in revolutionary action which represents the main argument against Gorskii's unusually fantastic ideas. One need only open the first page of Lenin's work "Left-Wing Communism, an Infantile Disorder" and read that as soon as the revolution will occur in another more developed country, Russia will *again* become a backward country in the Soviet and socialist sense of the word. Again! In other words, Russia has always been on the periphery of history. The elemental force of world capitalist development capriciously presented her with an opportunity which she did not disregard. That is all. The approaching world revolution (for the specter of communism has been haunting Europe since 1848) will put everything in its place, and Russia will once again retire to the periphery. "We must not be afraid of this," states Lenin. In other words, we should not be thinking of a position of leadership or of any messianism. We are merely presented with an opportunity which it would be a crime to let pass. But success should not make us dizzy.

Is it not finally clear that the Bolshevik tendency was victorious in the revolution precisely because its ideology represented the most total overcoming of the traditional psychology of the Russian intelligentsia? The Bolsheviks turned out to be more mobile than the SRs (the most powerful revolutionary party in Russia) precisely because they could rid themselves of all the prejudices of the intelligentsia, in both theory and practice. And only in this sense, the manifestation of a negative maximalism, was Bolshevism an indisputably Russian phenomenon (unlike Menshevism, for instance). But it is one thing to carry out a successful revolution, i.e., simply to seize power, outstripping one's rivals, and another to retain that power, i.e., to establish a working government. To do the latter in isolation from or ignorance of traditional national institutions is absolutely impossible. Any revolution prepares the way for the establishment of a new political existence which, despite its novelty, tends to lean toward national conservativism, since any government can exist only as an expression of national existence. There is nothing surprising in the fact that as soon as the new government was established, the internationalist-revolutionary slogans which brought it to power began to acquire a nationalist overtone. This development elicited various shades of opposition both in the Party as a whole and in the ruling elite. Those members who

could not overcome the temptations of internationalism found
themselves in the opposition. The story of the Treaty of Brest-
Litovsk is the last act in the tragedy of that part of the intelligentsia of which N. A. Berdiaev spoke the following:

> The Russian *intelligent* considered himself to be a citizen
> of the planet, of the world, but not Russia. . . .

Gorskii wants to prove unequivocally that the revolution
occurred as a result of the obstinate support given by the
Russian intelligentsia to the "abomination of great-power arrogance," i.e., to "national messianism," i.e., to "the Russian
idea." In actuality, the revolution rejected not only the socioeconomic structure of old Russia but also the whole complex
of positive ideas which formed the spiritual foundation of the
empire and characterized both those in power and in opposition. Failure to understand this means failure to understand
the Russian revolution.

It is true that the revolution was bloody and cruel, and that
the level of violence of the antagonists grew in proportion to
the weakening of what one might conditionally call "national
conservatism." In 1905, the people still approached the tsar
carrying religious banners, and relatively few Bolsheviks or
SRs fought on the barricades at Krasnaia Presnia. But a
procession with religious banners is already a protest, of course,
already a revolution. G. P. Fedotov notes correctly that: "The
revolution of 1905 was already a popular explosion, although
not a very deep one." (G. P. Fedotov, *Novyi grad*, New York,
1952, p. 51)

The bitterness of the revolution grew in proportion to the
denationalization of its participants. . . . In another article by
G. P. Fedotov, we read:

> . . . beginning with the 1880s, there occurred a noticeable
> merging of the Russo-Jewish intelligentsia, not only in their
> common revolutionary task and spiritual enthusiasms but
> more importantly in their fundamental style of life, in their
> ardent rootlessness and eschatological prophecy. In its spir-
> itual depth, this atmosphere was reminiscent of early

Christianity, although it was of course devoid of the pivot of faith and therefore capable of giving birth to a variety of at times fanatically sectarian deviations. Russian reactionaries are correct in connecting the intelligentsia with Jewry. They only distort the historical perspective when they portray the Jews as the seducers of innocent Russian youths. (G. P. Fedotov, *Russkie zapiski*, no. 3, Paris, 1938, pp. 72-73)

We have no intention of considering Jewry to be the seducer of Russia, but it is impossible to disregard the role played by the Jews in the denationalization of a particular part of the Russian intelligentsia if we want to discover more fully the essence of the spiritual processes in Russia which led to the acceptance of Marxism and the revolution.

Denationalized Jewry became a sustaining medium for the Russian engaged in tearing his ties with the nation, with traditions, and with indigenous estates in his search for "truth and justice." This can hardly be explained by a simple coincidence of interests. To a certain degree, ailing Russia herself provided a peculiar kind of sustaining medium for the activization of Jews, who, in F. Stepun's opinion, "while appearing to be concerned with labor and agrarian problems were in the final analysis engaged only in a struggle to gain equal rights for themselves.". . .

Thus the path of the Russian *intelligent* toward the revolution was accomplished through a global overcoming of tradition and Russian national consciousness, through "a break with national conservatism" by means of militant denationalization, for, according to the Marxist scheme, the revolution in Russia was only supposed to be the first act of a worldwide occurrence—world revolution. . . .

There is another aspect of this problem which the authors of the articles in *Vestnik* pass over in silence, not because of ignorance, of course, but again to support a preconceived idea. Certainly the phrase "the Russian people was punished by atheism, which has afflicted the whole world with a satanic hatred of God . . ." sounds passionate and impressive. It [i.e., the people] was punished, of course, for the same "centuries-old pride of the Russian idea." But what about the rest of the world? Does it remain virginally pure, does it fulfill the commandments of Christ in word and deed, does it tremble while contemplating the monster to the East? Is it not surprising that somehow this monster does not pine away for lack of company, this same monster which was born in mysterious manner on the Eurasian continent to the astonishment of the sinless rest of the world? It seems that the gentlemen from *Vestnik* have never heard of the so-called Renaissance, which became the source for the crisis of world Christianity, nor of the guillotines of the French Revolution, nor of the first two Internationals, nor of Fascism. For, according to their scheme, the whole world dwelled in Christian piety, and only Russia, bogged down in national messianism, in contrast to other nations fell away from God in cataclysmic fashion and raves on, as if possessed by Satan, before the astonished eyes of humanity.

Have not Messrs. Chelnov, Gorskii, and Altaev heard of monstrous technocratic utopias, of the socialist movement, of moral crises? Are they not aware of the alarming, at times desperate, pronouncements of the Roman popes, do they not know that skepticism, apathy, and cynicism have long ago become an integral component of Western civilization? And finally, could they be ignorant of the fact that Western Christianity, while maintaining its legal and social position, has long been progressively changing into a tradition of ethnic normatism?

I make so bold as to declare to these gentlemen-detractors, without justifying that which needs no justification, that even if we admit that Russia, being a particular nation, from henceforth bears no responsibilities before the rest of the world, she has already fulfilled her mission, because in her present condition she has told the world that truth about itself and about herself which the West has not been able and may never be courageous enough to admit because of its bourgeois-philistine and cowardly nature.

Like the *whole world*, Russia has slowly and steadily fallen away from God. Not to a greater degree than some countries, and even less than others. But precisely because of the particularities of the Russian national psychology, the Russian nation on the whole could not and did not want to live with half-truth, for Christianity, transformed into ritual tradition, deprived of its life-giving power, results in half-truth and in a sin perhaps more damning than the complete truth: the Pharisee is farther away from God than the pagan! . . .

[B]oth Sholokhov, living on his estate, and Galanskov, dying on a prison cot, lived and died with the certainty that they were sons (sons and not stepsons) of the Russian people. There is a paradox in the fact that each of them had the right to hold this conviction. In his time, G. P. Fedotov noticed this peculiarity among the modern Russian—and I emphasize *Russian*—intelligentsia:

> The new intelligentsia . . . is organically dedicated to the Soviet system, feels a blood tie with the ruling class, and therefore, *even while in opposition or, let us say, even in revolutionary struggle against the regime, it cannot be changed* into that rootless, maximalistic, and eschatological type—or even religious order—which we are wont to call the Russian intelligentsia. (p. 16)

"We may say with certainty," Fedotov wrote, "that the traditional type of Russian *intelligent* has died out in today's Russian culture."

This assertion, of course, is in need of clarification, but G. P. Fedotov's principal idea is correct: today's Russian of the educated class is evolving through a slow, careful, consistent, albeit sometimes incorrect and one-sided, process of nationalization, and this process is accelerating progressively every year. . . .

The government and the people [the *Vestnik* authors believe] are ossifying in Satanism while the intelligentsia must solve the problem of Russia's salvation.

Marx saw the salvation of the world in the proletariat, while the authors of the articles see it in the intelligentsia. This is indeed "Old Testament naturalism." Incidentally, all well-known *Russian* thinkers always connected Russia's fate with processes which embrace or should embrace the nation as a whole, its innermost depths (see N. A. Berdiaev, *The Russian Idea*).

The authors of the articles are also linked to Marx by their making a similar demand which must be fulfilled by the messianic class as a prerequisite for its success: denationalization. . . .

[*Veche*, no. 8 (AS 1665), 131-160]

Index

abortion, 4, 10, 100, 108. *See also* demographic issues, fertility
Abramov, Fedor, 41, 58, 131; speech at Sixth Congress of Soviet Writers, 110-11
Agurskii, Mikhail, 46, 109, 120, 129-30, 269, 271; open letter to *Veche*, 149-54; contribution to *From under the Rubble*, 245-46; on National Bolshevism, 255-56
Aksakov, Ivan, 33, 210, 301
Aksenov, Vasilii, 109, 117
alcoholism, 93, 102, 103-105, 114, 123, 193, 232, 250, 275, 296, 319, 334
Alekseev, Mikhail, 131, 326
All-Russian Society for the Preservation of Historical and Cultural Monuments, *see* VOOPIK
Allworth, Edward, 34-35
Altaev, O., 235-36, 351
Amal'rik, Andrei, 48, 61, 265, 285
Anan'ev, Anatolii, 132, 273
Andropov, Iurii, 269, 270, 272, 294; "Andropov group," 270
anti-Semitism, 25, 41-43, 46, 81, 144, 146-49, 151-52, 153, 159, 216, 257, 260, 266-67, 288, 307-308, 310. *See also* minority nationalities
Antonov, Mikhail, 41-42, 213; "The Teaching of the Slavophiles," 203-204
Arkhiv samizdata (Radio Liberty), 31n, 45
assimilation, 136, 138-39, 150. *See also* Russification, minority nationalities
Astaf'ev, Viktor, 58, 110
Averbakh, Leopold, 78, 327-28, 330

Bagration, General, 12, 18, 33, 159, 221, 258, 320, 342
Baikal, Lake, 89, 219, 321-22. *See also* preservation of the environment

Barghoorn, Frederick, 28, 147
Belinskii, Vissarion, 15, 24, 132, 283
Belorussia, 154-58, 213, 307
Belov, Vasilii, 40, 110, 113-15, 117, 131
Berdiaev, Nikolai, 28, 36, 202, 209, 210, 215, 216, 233, 254, 302, 328, 331, 347, 349, 353. *See also* Vekhi
Besançon, Alain, 262, 265, 274, 285
Bialer, Seweryn, 271
"Black Hundreds," 151, 161, 222, 262, 288, 335
Bociurkiw, Bohdan, 39-40, 170n
Boldyrev, Petr, 158
Borisov, Vadim, 140-41, 278
Borodin, Leonid, 44, 46, 167, 168, 198, 211, 238-39, 264, 293, 295; arrest of, 292
Brezhnev, Leonid, 18, 35, 37, 43, 54, 84, 86, 113, 165, 232, 265, 271, 281; fate of Russian nationalism under, 60-61; death of, 61, 268
Bunin, Ivan, 220, 221, 312

"captive nations" week, 286-87
Carlisle, Olga, 281-82
Carr, E. H., 3, 8
Chaadaev, Petr, 44, 202, 234, 236, 314
Chalmaev, Viktor, 39, 57, 264, 295; controversy surrounding, 217, 218-27; "The Great Search," 312-18; "Inevitability," 318-22
Chernyshevskii, Nikolai, 4, 15, 24, 132, 222, 226-27, 277, 312, 338
China, 23, 65, 72n, 91, 95, 99, 105, 108, 158, 194, 199, 230, 244, 260, 290, 304, 336; views of Russian nationalists on, 252-54
Chivilikhin, Vladimir, 90, 326
Chornovil, Viacheslav, 156
Christian Committee for the De-

Library of Congress Cataloging in Publication Data

Dunlop, John B.
  The faces of contemporary Russian nationalism.
  "Sponsored by the Hoover Institution on War, Revolution and Peace,
Stanford University, Stanford, California."
  Includes index.
  1. Nationalism—Soviet Union. I. Title.
JC311.D86 1983   320.5′4′0947   83-42554
ISBN 0-691-05390-1